From Rome to Byzantium AD 363 to 565

The Edinburgh History of Ancient Rome
General Editor: J. S. Richardson

Early Rome to 290 BC: The Beginnings of the City and the Rise of the Republic
Guy Bradley

Rome and the Mediterranean 290 to 146 BC: The Imperial Republic
Nathan Rosenstein

The End of the Roman Republic 146 to 44 BC: Conquest and Crisis
Catherine Steel

Augustan Rome 44 BC to AD 14: The Restoration of the Republic and the Establishment of the Empire
J. S. Richardson

Imperial Rome AD 14 to 192: The First Two Centuries
Jonathan Edmondson

Imperial Rome AD 193 to 284: The Critical Century
Clifford Ando

Imperial Rome AD 284 to 363: The New Empire
Jill Harries

From Rome to Byzantium AD 363 to 565: The Transformation of Ancient Rome
A. D. Lee

From Rome to Byzantium
AD *363 to 565*

The Transformation of Ancient Rome

A. D. Lee

EDINBURGH
University Press

To the memory of my father
and of my aunt Ruth

© A. D. Lee, 2013

Edinburgh University Press Ltd
22 George Square, Edinburgh EH8 9LF

www.euppublishing.com

Typeset in Sabon
by Norman Tilley Graphics Ltd, Northampton,
and printed and bound in Great Britain
by CPI Group (UK) Ltd, Croydon CR0 4YY

A CIP record for this book is available from the
British Library

ISBN 978 0 7486 2790 5 (hardback)
ISBN 978 0 7486 2791 2 (paperback)
ISBN 978 0 7486 3175 9 (webready PDF)
ISBN 978 0 7486 6835 9 (epub)
ISBN 978 0 7486 6836 6 (Amazon ebook)

The right of A. D. Lee
to be identified as author of this work
has been asserted in accordance with
the Copyright, Designs and Patents Act 1988.

Published with the support of the Edinburgh University
Scholarly Publishing Initiatives Fund.

Contents

Maps   vii
Illustrations   viii
Series editor's preface   x
Author's preface   xi
Acknowledgements   xvi
Abbreviations   xvii

1. The Constantinian inheritance   1

Part I *The later fourth century*
2. Emperors, usurpers and frontiers   19
3. Towards a Christian empire   39
4. Old Rome, new Rome   57

Part II *The long fifth century*
5. Generalissimos and imperial courts   81
6. Barbarians and Romans   110
7. Church and state, piety and power   134
8. Anastasius and the resurrection of imperial power   159
9. Rome's heirs in the west   178

Part III *Longer-term trends*
10. Urban continuity and change   199
11. Economic patterns   223

Part IV *The age of Justinian*
12. Justinian and the Roman past   243
13. Justinian and the Christian present   264
14. Justinian and the end of antiquity   286

Chronology   301
Lists of rulers   304
List of bishops of Rome   307
Guide to further reading   308
Select bibliography of modern works   313
Index   322

Maps

1. The Mediterranean world and the Near East in late antiquity   xix
2. The western provinces and the Balkans in late antiquity   xx
3. The eastern provinces in late antiquity   xxi
4. The Roman empire at the death of Julian (363)   xxii
5. The city of Rome in late antiquity   58
6. The city of Constantinople in late antiquity   71
7. The barbarian kingdoms in the 520s   179
8. The Roman empire at the death of Justinian (565)   287

Illustrations

Figure 1 Relief from the base of the obelisk of Theodosius I
depicting foreign envoys presenting gifts to the emperor
in the hippodrome in Constantinople   28
Figure 2 Ivory leaf depicting a priestess before an altar,
sprinkling incense on a flame, with an attendant   53
Figure 3 The Projecta casket from the Esquiline Treasure
in Rome   70
Figure 4 The aqueduct of Valens in Constantinople   75
Figure 5 Intaglio of sardonyx and gold, depicting the
symbolic investiture of Valentinian III   86
Figures 6–7 Ivory diptych of Flavius Aetius   88–89
Figure 8 Ivory diptych leaf of the Empress Ariadne   105
Figure 9 A section of the Theodosian Walls, Constantinople   119
Figure 10 Wooden carving of a besieged city being relieved   129
Figure 11 Basalt panel from a chancel screen in a church,
depicting St Simeon the Stylite on his column   156
Figure 12 View of the walls of Dara, northern Mesopotamia   170
Figure 13 The granaries at Dara, northern Mesopotamia   171
Figure 14 A marble gambling machine, with reliefs of
chariot racing   212
Figure 15 A contorniate with inlaid decoration depicting
a four-horse chariot   213
Figure 16 Sixth-century houses from the village of Serjilla
in the Limestone Massif east of Antioch   229
Figure 17 A press house for processing olive oil, Serjilla,
in the Limestone Massif east of Antioch   230
Figures 18–19 Cross-sections of Hagia Sophia in
Constantinople   268
Figure 20 Floor plan of Hagia Sophia in Constantinople   269
Figure 21 Interior of Hagia Sophia, Constantinople   270
Figure 22 Part of a peacock arch from the Church of
St Polyeuctus, Constantinople   272

The author and publisher thank the following for providing illustrations: Victoria and Albert Museum London (Fig. 2), The Trustees of the British Museum (Fig. 3), The State Hermitage Museum, St. Petersburg (Fig. 5), Collections musées de la ville de Bourges (Figs 6–7), Kunsthistorisches Museum, Vienna (Fig. 8), Bildarchiv Preussischer Kulturbesitz (Figs 10, 11, 14), Christopher Lillington-Martin (Fig. 12), Rheinisches Landesmuseum, Trier (Fig. 15), Pearson Education Ltd. (Figs 18–20), Cinzia Maggiore and Tony Parry (Fig. 21), and the Institute of Archaeology, Oxford (Fig. 22).

Series editor's preface

Rome, the city and its empire, stands at the centre of the history of Europe, of the Mediterranean, and of lands which we now call the Middle East. Its influence through the ages which followed its transformation into the Byzantine Empire down to modern times can be seen across the world. This series is designed to present for students and all who are interested in the history of western civilisation the changing shape of the entity that was Rome, through its earliest years, the development and extension of the Republic, the shift into the Augustan Empire, the development of the imperial state which grew from that, and the differing patterns of that state which emerged in east and west in the fourth to sixth centuries. It covers not only the political and military history of that shifting and complex society but also the contributions of the economic and social history of the Roman world to that change and growth and the intellectual contexts of these developments. The team of contributors, all scholars at the forefront of research in archaeology and history in the English-speaking world, present in the eight volumes of the series an accessible and challenging account of Rome across a millennium and a half of its expansion and transformation. Each book stands on its own as a picture of the period it covers and together the series aims to answer the fundamental question: what was Rome, and how did a small city in central Italy become one of the most powerful and significant entities in the history of the world?

John Richardson, General Editor

Author's preface

President Bartlet: What are you doing? ...
Charlie Young: I'm making notes for a final in modern American history: the consumer movements in late twentieth century America.
Bartlet: Modern American history sucks.
Charlie: I had a hunch.
Bartlet: You want to study history, study the Crusades, the fall of the Roman Empire from Theodosius to Justinian.
Charlie: The Visigoths.
Bartlet: Damn right, the Visigoths. Modern history's another name for television.

(*The West Wing*, series 3, episode 9 [2001])

Sgt. Jay Landsman: [surveying, with pained expression, an unexpectedly congested 'unsolved cases' board] All that from overnight?
Det. Ed Norris: All that from Freamon. He's out early today, rooting through empties [derelict houses where corpses have been found].
Landsman: You know what he is? He is a vandal. He is vandalizing the board. He is vandalizing this unit. He is a Hun, a Visigoth, a barbarian at the gate, clamoring for noble Roman blood and what's left of our clearance rate.

(*The Wire*, series 4, episode 13 [2006])

It is striking that two acclaimed, but very different, television dramas of recent years – one about the upper echelons of American political life, the other about urban drug crime and gang warfare – should both have included references to the final centuries of Roman history in these exchanges between central characters. To be sure, it is unsurprising that Jed Bartlet – Nobel laureate in economics and former college professor with a penchant for quoting Latin and a bookish interest in a diverse range of obscure subjects – should be familiar with the Emperors Theodosius and Justinian (and indeed, their

inclusion was perhaps intended precisely to reinforce that aspect of
his persona). However, it is rather more surprising to find Charlie
Young and Jay Landsman showing some knowledge of late Roman
history: while both are undoubtedly intelligent men, neither has the
educational background of Jed Bartlet. Yet their knowledge suggests
that the respective writers of the series, Aaron Sorkin and David
Simon, expected the general public to understand these allusions.

What then do these allusions indicate about popular perceptions
of the late Roman empire? The two themes that are emphasised are
the interlinked ones of the fall of the empire and the barbarian threat
to Rome. As this volume will show, barbarians were certainly a
significant feature of late Roman history, the city of Rome was
captured by barbarians on a number of occasions, and the empire in
the west did come to an end. But however gratifying it may be for
the scholar of late antiquity to see Roman history from Theodosius
to Justinian endorsed by the president of the United States (albeit a
fictional one) as an appropriate subject for meaningful historical
study, as a summary of late Roman history the emphasis on the fall
of Rome in the face of barbarians is an oversimplification of what
was a much more complex period. An appreciation of that complexity may begin by noting that the eastern half of the empire did
not fall, or at least not until a millennium later, in the very different
circumstances of the Turkish capture of Constantinople in 1453, and
while there were bloody conflicts between Romans and barbarians,
there was also much peaceful interaction, with many individuals of
barbarian origin faithfully serving the Roman state. Moreover, even
after the end of the empire in the west in the later fifth century, the
various barbarian successor states actively preserved many elements
of their Roman inheritance, while the eastern half of the empire
regained control of Italy and north Africa during the sixth century.

One of the reasons why the eastern half of the empire endured
for so long was the emergence of a new focal point in the city
of Constantinople (founded on the site of the ancient Greek city of
Byzantium) – a development which coincided with the corresponding marginalisation of the city of Rome. This shift in the empire's
geographical and political centre of gravity is one of the most
important changes which distinguishes late antiquity from earlier
periods of Roman history. Even more important was the shift in
the empire's religious centre of gravity, as Christianity became first
the favoured and then the official religion of the empire. While it has
been fashionable since at least Edward Gibbon to see this change as

a major factor in the weakening of imperial power, such a view risks overlooking the fact that it was the more Christianised east which endured, and the ways in which Christianity could sometimes also act as a force for social cohesion in late Roman society. It is changes of these sorts which warrant viewing late antiquity in terms of transformation and change, as much as disruption and decline.

As for the chronological parameters of this volume, 363 may be a less common starting-point, but it is one which has its merits. For one thing, the death of the Emperor Julian (361–3) marked the end of the Constantinian dynasty and was therefore an important caesura in the political history of the empire. It was also a significant time in relation to the theme of the empire's political unity, for the Roman empire in its entirety was never again to be ruled by one man for any significant period of time,[1] thereby effectively signalling the irreversible diverging of the trajectories of west and east. Most important of all, however, the death of Julian – the Christian who had converted to paganism and had sought to undo the consequences of the Emperor Constantine's support for Christianity – signified the end of any state-sponsored attempt to reverse the momentum of Christianity as the dominant religious force in the empire. At the other end of the volume, the terminal date of 565 was the last year in the long and important reign of the Emperor Justinian (527–65) and therefore has a readier justification – which is not to say that it is completely unproblematic. For it is of course a division which privileges political events over other aspects of historical change such as underlying trends in society and the economy, which by their very nature do not usually lend themselves to narratives framed in terms of the language of turning-points. Since this volume has no successor in the series of which it forms a part, it will be necessary, and important, to include some reflections on post-Justinianic developments in the concluding pages of the final chapter.

Between these two points in time lie just over two centuries of history, during which the Roman world underwent profound changes of enduring significance. Writing a general history of this, as of any other, substantial period poses the question of how best to

---

1. The two potential exceptions are disqualified by the brevity of the periods involved: Julian's successor, Jovian (363–4), was sole ruler, but he reigned for only seven months and never had the opportunity to set foot in Constantinople, let alone in the west, while Theodosius I (379–95) was also sole ruler, but only for the final four months of his reign, following his defeat of Eugenius (pp. 20, 27 below).

structure one's treatment. All historical writing necessarily involves selection, but in this particular case, there are additional constraints arising from the parameters of the series in which the volume appears, including title, word limit, and the overall conception of the series. In accordance with the series' emphasis on providing an analytical narrative, three of this volume's four parts are defined chronologically – the later fourth century from the death of Julian (363) to the death of Theodosius I (395), the long fifth century from 395 to the death of Justin I (527), and the age of Justinian (527 to 565). The rationale for this periodisation is that, first, Theodosius I was the last emperor to undertake military campaigns in person for some considerable time, with his successors adopting a palace-centred style of rule, while his reign also marked a more uncompromising stance in various aspects of religious policy; and second, Justinian's long reign was characterised by a proactive approach in so many areas that, whatever one's reservations about focusing on significant individuals, his reign warrants treatment in its own right.

The chapters within each of these three parts provide accounts of the most important political, military and religious events and developments within their social context, alongside portions with a more clearly thematic focus, most obviously an early chapter on the cities of Rome and Constantinople, and thematic sections within subsequent chapters, such as those on the dynamics of political power in the fifth century and the multifaceted character of Roman–barbarian relations in that same period. Some themes, however, are too large to be confined within one of the three chronological parts: hence the inclusion of a separate part devoted to longer-term trends in relation to, on the one hand, cities – that archetypal feature of Roman civilisation – and, on the other, the economy, where the importance of agriculture also allows scope for some consideration of the countryside, to complement that of the city. Although the focus is firmly on the Roman empire, the barbarian successor states of the fifth- and early sixth-century west also receive attention in a chapter of their own, both to provide context for Justinian's western ventures and because these states preserved many elements of Roman institutions and culture, and were therefore also part of the 'changing shape of the entity that was Rome' (to quote the series' preface).

Needless to say, there are other ways in which a treatment of this period could have been structured, but it is hoped that this particular approach will provide a more detailed narrative of pivotal political, military and religious developments than is available in other current histories of late antiquity, alongside clear discussions of major themes and issues, particularly the positive perspective which an examination of long-term trends in urban life and the economy brings to a consideration of these tumultuous centuries – all informed by the most important developments in recent scholarship.[2] The overarching theme is the one signalled in the volume's title – the transition from Rome to Byzantium, encompassing not only the shift in the empire's political centre of gravity from west to east, but also the cultural corollaries of that change, above all the growing influence of Hellenic cultural traditions and of Christianity, which represented a profound transformation of the inheritance of ancient Rome.

2. Constraints of space, however, mean that supporting references can make no claim to be comprehensive, while coverage of publications which appeared after 2010 has had to be selective.

Acknowledgements

Much of the work for this book was undertaken during a period of extended leave granted by the University of Nottingham in 2007–8. Major administrative duties slowed progress significantly during 2008–10, before a further semester's leave in the latter half of 2010 allowed serious resumption, for which I thank the University. I also thank the series editor John Richardson and the editorial staff at Edinburgh University Press for their patience during the delays in completing this project, and John Richardson for his helpful comments on a draft version. Fiona Sewell's careful copy-editing has once again saved me from numerous inconsistencies and errors of detail.

John Drinkwater, Geoffrey Greatrex, Simon Loseby and Andy Merrills kindly read and commented on a number of draft chapters, and I am very grateful for their ready willingness to do so and for their constructive feedback, which has saved me from various errors and oversights. For help with aspects of image acquisition, I thank Christopher Lillington-Martin, Katharina Lorenz, Simon Malloch and Marlia Mango. I also want to thank students past and present at Nottingham who have taken various incarnations of my Special Subject on the fourth century and my Justinian module, whose questions and comments have contributed to my thinking about many of the subjects which feature in the book.

My sons, James and Philip, and my daughter Naomi have assisted the completion of the task by their increasingly regular enquiries as to progress, while my wife Anna has shown her customary forbearance as yet another book has encroached on family life. This book is dedicated to the memory of two members of the wider family who are greatly missed – to my aunt Ruth, who maintained a close interest in my work at all times and was looking forward to the appearance of this book, and to my father, who passed away less recently but whose life of generous self-giving continues to be remembered with deep affection.

Doug Lee

Abbreviations

Abbreviations for ancient sources, epigraphic collections and journals follow those in the *Oxford Classical Dictionary*, 3rd edition (1996). In addition, the following abbreviations are used:

ACO	*Acta Conciliorum Oecumenicorum*, ed. E. Schwartz, Berlin: de Gruyter, 1914–40
AnTard	*Antiquité Tardive*
ByzAus	*Byzantina Australiensia*
CFHB	*Corpus Fontium Historiae Byzantinae*
CMH 1	P. Fouracre (ed.), *The New Cambridge Medieval History* vol. 1: *c. 500–c. 700*, Cambridge: Cambridge University Press, 2005
Coleman-Norton	P. R. Coleman-Norton (tr.), *Roman State and Christian Church: A Collection of Legal Documents to* AD *535*, London: SPCK, 1966
Coll. Avell.	*Collectio Avellana*, ed. O. Günther, Vienna: CSEL 35, 1895
fr.	fragment
Festugière	A. J. Festugière (tr.), *Éphèse et Chalcédoine: Actes des conciles*, Paris: Beauchesne, 1982
IAph2007	J. Reynolds, C. Roueché and G. Bodard, *Inscriptions of Aphrodisias* (2007) (http://insaph.kcl.ac.uk/iaph2007)
JECS	*Journal of Early Christian Studies*
JLA	*Journal of Late Antiquity*
Jones, LRE	A. H. M. Jones, *The Later Roman Empire, 284–602: A Social, Economic and Administrative Survey*, Oxford: Blackwell, 1964
JRA	*Journal of Roman Archaeology*
Price and Gaddis, Chalcedon	R. Price and M. Gaddis (tr.), *The Acts of the Council of Chalcedon*, Liverpool: Liverpool University Press, 2005

Abbreviations

SCH	*Studies in Church History*
T&M	*Travaux et mémoires*
TTH	Translated Texts for Historians (Liverpool)

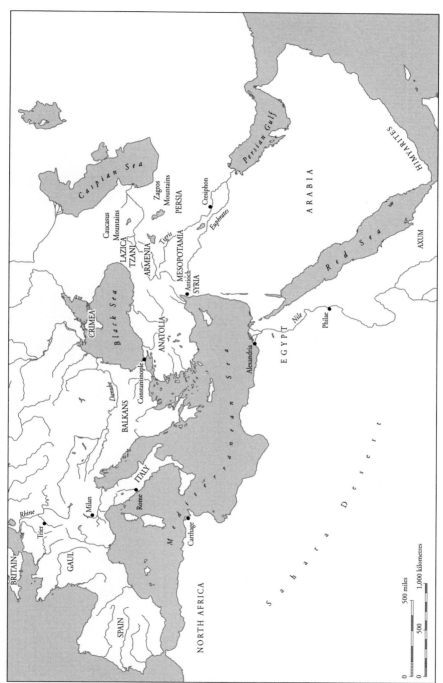

Map 1 The Mediterranean world and the Near East in late antiquity

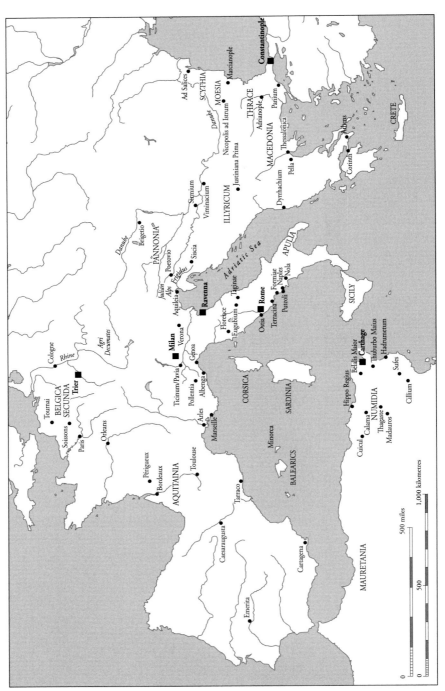

Map 2 The western provinces and the Balkans in late antiquity

Map 3 The eastern provinces in late antiquity

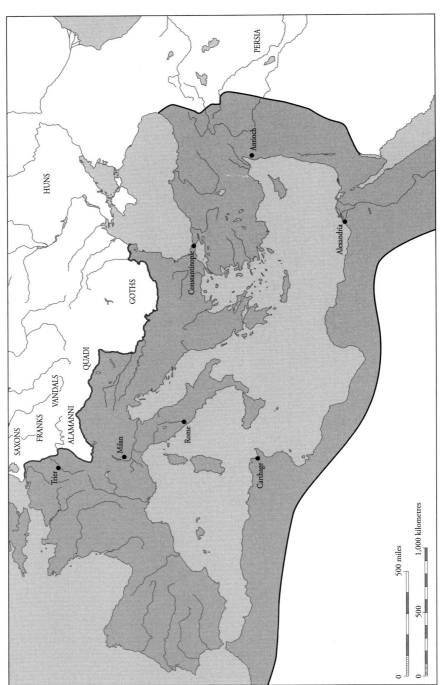

Map 4 The Roman empire at the death of Julian (363)

SAXONS

FRANKS

VANDALS

ALAMANNI

QUADI

GOTHS

HUNS

PERSIA

Trier

Milan

Rome

Carthage

Constantinople

Antioch

Alexandria

0   500 miles

0   500   1,000 kilometres

CHAPTER 1

The Constantinian inheritance

The empire's geopolitical context

In the mid-fourth century the Roman empire encompassed almost as much territory as it had during the second century – the period often regarded as the peak of Roman power.[1] Although the mid-third century had been a turbulent period for the empire, not least on its frontiers, it had survived surprisingly well territorially, with only minimal losses of land: the most substantial of these had been that of the province of Dacia north of the lower Danube (modern Romania), with the other significant area being the region known as the *Agri Decumates*, the wedge of territory between the upper reaches of the Rhine and the Danube (the Black Forest region of modern Germany). The Mediterranean Sea remained a 'Roman lake' in the fourth century, and the empire continued to control virtually the same amount of land mass as it had for a number of centuries, with all that that implied for tax revenues in an age when government income derived overwhelmingly from agricultural production.

Nevertheless, the empire of the fourth century did find itself in significantly changed geopolitical circumstances from the empire of the second century. To the east, the Parthian Arsacid rulers had been replaced by the Sasanian Persians. A leading aristocratic family from Persis in southern Iran (modern Fars), the Sasanians had overthrown the Arsacids in the 220s and quickly proved themselves much more politically adept and militarily aggressive neighbours, so much so that by the fourth century they had staked a strong claim for Persia to be recognised as the Roman empire's political and military

---

1. Cf. Gibbon's famous description of the 'prosperous condition' of the empire between the reigns of Nerva and Marcus Aurelius in the early chapters of his *Decline and Fall of the Roman Empire* (1776–88). For good accounts of the empire's history during the first half of the fourth century, see (in addition to the relevant sections of the general histories noted on p. 312 below) D. Potter, *The Roman Empire at Bay, AD 180–395*, London: Routledge, 2004, chs 8–13, and J. Harries, *Imperial Rome AD 284 to 363: The New Empire*, Edinburgh: Edinburgh University Press, 2012.

equal – a claim which the Romans found themselves reluctantly having to concede.[2] This was certainly a novelty compared with earlier centuries when the Roman empire had effectively been the sole 'superpower' of the Mediterranean and Near East.

Significant changes were also taking place along the empire's northern frontiers. Where emperors of the first and second centuries had, for the most part, faced small, fragmented barbarian tribes rarely able to pose serious problems for the empire, emperors of the fourth century had to confront more significant military threats from this direction – the result, it seems, of the smaller groups of earlier centuries amalgamating into larger groupings, notably Franks on the lower Rhine, Alamanni in the former *Agri Decumates*, and Goths on the lower Danube.[3] None of these tribal groupings constituted a military threat on the same scale as Sasanian Persia in the east, but significant incursions into Roman territory during the third century had created major problems for the empire, particularly if they happened to coincide with Persian aggression. So it was that the fourth-century empire found itself facing the possibility of major conflict on more than one frontier at the same time – an unfamiliar prospect prior to the third century.

Fortunately, the most economically valuable regions of the empire were far removed from these potential trouble spots. Egypt had always been the most productive part of the empire since its acquisition by Augustus in 30 BC. This may seem surprising given that 90 per cent of it comprised desert; however, this apparent handicap was more than offset by the extraordinary fertility of the Nile valley from which, during the first three centuries AD, the Roman authorities were able to extract sufficient surplus to supply about two-thirds of the grain needed by the population of the city of Rome (conven-

2. Cf. the language of diplomacy (emperor and shah as 'brothers' by the 350s: Amm. Marc. 17.5.3, 10), as well as other aspects of diplomatic practice (e.g., the role of hostages and conventions of treaty-making). For a comparison of their economic and military resources, see J. Howard-Johnston, 'The two great powers in late antiquity: a comparison' in Averil Cameron (ed.), *The Byzantine and Early Islamic Near East* III: *States, Resources and Armies*, Princeton: Darwin Press, 1995, 157–222; for mutual cultural influence, M. C. Canepa, *The Two Eyes of the Earth: Art and Ritual of Kingship between Rome and Sasanian Iran*, Berkeley: University of California Press, 2009.
3. For the Franks, see E. James, *The Franks*, Oxford: Blackwell, 1988; for the Goths, P. J. Heather, *The Goths*, Oxford: Blackwell, 1996, and M. Kuliskowski, *Rome's Gothic Wars from the Third Century to Alaric*, Cambridge: Cambridge University Press, 2007; and for the Alamanni, J. F. Drinkwater, *The Alamanni and Rome, 213–496*, Oxford: Oxford University Press, 2007 (who is, however, sceptical about the scale of the threat they posed).

tionally estimated to have been about one million inhabitants in this period) – though one of Constantine's legacies was the redirecting of this surplus to his new foundation at Constantinople (pp. 71, 76 below). To the west, the provinces of north Africa (modern Tunisia and Algeria) were the most important region economically for the western Mediterranean – highly productive in both wheat and olive oil. Neither of these regions was obviously vulnerable to any military threat in the fourth century: their southern perimeters faced desert from which nomadic tribesmen sometimes made raids, but never on anything like a scale to jeopardise their underlying security.[4]

Government and army in the fourth century

The altered geopolitical circumstances of the empire had been of sufficient magnitude during the third century to bring about major changes in the political and military character of the empire. One of the most significant areas of change was the social profile of emperors. During the first two centuries AD, all emperors were of senatorial origin – that is, from the social elite of the empire. Over the course of the third century, however, strategic exigencies had increasingly demanded that men of proven military experience be in charge of the empire, with the result that emperors were increasingly drawn from those who had made a career in the army and therefore came from less elevated social backgrounds. In parallel with this, there developed a greater emphasis on court ceremonial and on the emperor as *dominus* ('master') rather than *princeps* ('leading citizen'), perhaps reflecting increased concern on the part of these individuals to legitimate their position.[5] Just as the empire's strategic difficulties facilitated the emergence of these military emperors, so also there was an increase in the size of the army, even if the scale of that increase is difficult to determine.[6] A larger army required more resources, and hence tighter administrative control over the provinces. This need prompted the reorganisation of the empire into a larger number of smaller provinces, which in turn entailed an increase in the number of administrative officials.

4. R. S. Bagnall, *Egypt in Late Antiquity*, Princeton: Princeton University Press; D. J. Mattingly and R. B. Hitchner, 'Roman Africa: an archaeological review', *JRS* 85 (1995), 165–213.
5. P. Garnsey and C. Humfress, *The Evolution of the Late Antique World*, Cambridge: Orchard Press, 2001, 25–33.
6. For an overview of the evidence and arguments, see A. D. Lee, *War in Late Antiquity: A Social History*, Oxford: Blackwell, 2007, 74–8.

Many of the senior officials had unfamiliar titles, or familiar titles with novel responsibilities. The most obvious example of the latter was the office of praetorian prefect. During the early centuries AD, this post had originated in the command of the emperor's body-guard. Early in the fourth century, however, the office was stripped of its military role, and instead designated the most senior civilian posting, with responsibility for oversight of, on the one hand, justice, and on the other, taxation on agricultural produce (two tasks which many peasants must have felt were mutually incompatible). Taxation on agriculture was the main source of government revenues and was now paid in kind, to facilitate its primary purpose, namely feeding the army – hence the Latin phrase which referred to it, the *annona militaris*. Taxes in gold and silver were also levied on other sectors of the economy, and were overseen by a financial official bearing the new title of *comes sacrarum largitionum* ('count of the sacred largesses'). Another financial official, the *comes rei privatae* ('count of the privy purse') was responsible for income from the very substantial imperial estates. The *quaestor sacri palatii* ('quaestor of the sacred palace') was the emperor's chief legal adviser, while the *magister officiorum* ('master of the offices') was the senior official in charge of the central administration, who also oversaw maintenance of the imperial communications system – that is, the empire-wide network of roads and official way stations, horses and wagons; this official also increasingly came to play an important role in the conduct of diplomacy. The use of the epithet 'sacred' in some of these titles is another reflection of the more distant and overbearing conception of imperial power which had developed by the fourth century.[7]

The Roman army of the mid-fourth century also looked different from the army of the early centuries AD. Its senior commanders no longer combined military and civilian duties, as provincial governors had often done in the past; they now bore the title of *magister* (lit. 'master'), and they were experienced career soldiers, in contrast with the senatorial commanders of earlier centuries whose military experience could be quite variable. The army itself now comprised many more smaller-sized units, divided into two broad categories: those troops assigned to the permanent field armies (*comitatenses*,

---

7. For a magisterial description of late Roman government and bureaucracy, see Jones, *LRE*, chs 11–14, 16, and for a lively interpretative essay, C. Kelly, *Ruling the Later Roman Empire*, Cambridge, MA: Harvard University Press, 2004.

because they had their origin in the troops which accompanied the emperor) commanded by a *magister*, and those troops stationed in frontier provinces (*limitanei*, derived from *limes*, the term for frontier provinces) under the command of a *dux* (lit. 'leader').[8] Responsibility for the evolution of this structure has been much debated, but important elements of it undoubtedly owe much to Constantine.[9] It has sometimes been seen as a response to the strategic problem of dealing with simultaneous threats on different frontiers.

Another important difference in the character of government by the fourth century was the emperor's base of operations. The strategic crises of the third century had required emperors to exchange the comforts and safety of the city of Rome for a peripatetic life on the frontiers, and as emperors increasingly came from the ranks of the army rather than the senatorial elite, this change of focus proved less and less of a hardship. Emperors in the late third and early fourth century spent most of their time in centres near the northern or eastern frontiers – locations such as Trier, Milan, Sirmium and Antioch – and rarely visited Rome, except perhaps for important ceremonial occasions. As a result, what would once have been unthinkable began to come to pass – the city of Rome became largely peripheral to the central issues which emperors faced.

This highly significant development was advanced by the decision of the Emperor Constantine (306–37) to establish a new imperial centre in the eastern Mediterranean on the site of the ancient city of Byzantium, which lay at the communications crossroads between Europe and Asia, and the Black Sea and the Aegean. This new imperial centre, which he named Constantinople ('the city of Constantine'), can be seen as having a number of purposes in Constantine's reckoning. Its name served to memorialise its founder, as many cities had done previously (most famously, Alexandria), but it also fulfilled a strategic need in the sense that it provided a base with easier access than Rome to the two principal strategic concerns of fourth-century emperors – the eastern frontier with Persia, and

8. B. Isaac, 'The meaning of the terms *limes* and *limitanei*', *JRS* 78 (1988), 125–47.
9. For the character and evolution of the army, see Jones, *LRE*, ch. 17, M. J. Nicasie, *Twilight of Empire: The Roman Army from the Reign of Diocletian until the Battle of Adrianople*, Amsterdam: Gieben, 1998, A.D. Lee, 'The army' in *CAH²* 13.211–37, and M. Whitby, 'Emperors and armies, AD 235–395' in S. Swain and M. Edwards (eds), *Approaching Late Antiquity*, Oxford: Oxford University Press, 2004, 156–86.

the lower Danube. In the event, Constantinople did not function as a regular imperial base any more regularly than Rome until towards the end of the fourth century.

Religious trends

Given the increasing importance of Constantinople during late antiquity and its significance in the medieval world, Constantine's decision to establish a new capital there was one of his most important legacies. It was not, however, *the* most important one, for that accolade must go to his decision in 312 to lend his support to the Christian church. Coming so soon after a period in which emperors had actively attacked Christianity, this dramatic *volte face* in official policy was, in the long term, to have consequences of enduring and fundamental significance for world history. Within the more immediate context of the early fourth century, it had the initial effect of creating a 'level playing field' between Christianity and other religious traditions in the Roman empire, particularly when viewed against the background of recent persecution of Christians. The playing field did not, however, remain level for very long. Even if, from a legal point of view, Constantine did not soon discriminate against pagan sacrifice – a question about which the state of the surviving evidence leaves scope for debate – he certainly began very quickly to give practical expression to his support for the church by channelling significant material resources in its direction which facilitated the construction of church buildings and the expansion of its charitable activities. Indeed it could be argued that, even without any practical support of this nature, the very fact of the emperor making it known that he favoured a particular religion automatically gave that religion an important advantage over its rivals and was likely to have an effect on the religious loyalties of inhabitants of the empire.

That Constantine's conversion to Christianity did not necessarily spell the end for traditional pagan cults is demonstrated above all by the life and reign of his nephew Julian, who, having been brought up as a Christian, effectively read his way into understanding of and sympathy with pagan cults, secretly renounced Christianity in favour of paganism in the early 350s, and upon becoming emperor in 361, set about trying to undo the consequences of Constantine's support for the church. More will be said about Julian towards the end of this chapter, but his life makes it clear that although many inhabitants of the empire may well have adopted Christianity in the wake of Constantine's support for it, significant numbers remained dedicated devotees of traditional cults. These encompassed a huge diversity of beliefs and practices, ranging from state-sanctioned cults associated with well-known deities such as Jupiter and Mars, through those of eastern origin which had spread widely around the Mediterranean world such as those of Isis and Mithras, to those which were much more localised and parochial. Another important influence on paganism, at least among intellectuals (including Julian), was Neoplatonism, which viewed the plethora of pagan deities as manifestations of one overarching and all-encompassing being. This elite quasi-monotheism was matched at the popular level by widespread reverence for 'the highest god'. In the midst of all this, the imperial cult continued to be acknowledged, even by the Christian Constantine and his sons, all of whom also continued to hold the ancient pagan office of *pontifex maximus* ('chief priest'). These anomalies may reflect their concern not to alienate the still substantial numbers of non-Christians in the empire and/or their recognition that the imperial cult and the office of *pontifex maximus* were as much to do with politics and political loyalties as with religion.[10]

The contrast between a fissiparous and variegated paganism and a monolithic Christianity should not be drawn too starkly, since Christianity had its own divisions. This is hardly surprising in a religion which set great store on exclusivity and having a monopoly on truth, since disagreements about the details of that truth were bound to arise. In the early fourth century, the focus of much debate within the church, particularly in the eastern Mediterranean, concerned the nature of the Trinity, especially the relationship between God the Father and God the Son. An Alexandrian clergyman, Arius, took the view that God the Father must have created God the Son, implying that the Son was in some sense inferior to the Father. The philosophical rationality of this view met with considerable sympathy and support among many Christian leaders in the eastern Mediterranean, but also generated fierce arguments. Constantine attempted to resolve these by calling the first ecumenical (i.e.,

10. For further details and references, see A. D. Lee, 'Traditional religions' in N. Lenski (ed.), *The Cambridge Companion to the Age of Constantine*, Cambridge: Cambridge University Press, 2006, 159–79, and on pagan monotheism, S. Mitchell and P. van Nuffelen (eds), *One God: Pagan Monotheism in the Roman Empire*, Cambridge: Cambridge University Press, 2010.

empire-wide) church council at Nicaea in 325 but the agreed formula which emerged, with its statement that Christ was 'of the same substance' (*homoousios*) as the Father, used terminology not found in scripture, and proved insufficient to resolve the issue definitively.

Indeed, during the decades after Constantine's death in 337, opponents of the Nicene Homoousian formula found reason to disagree with one another as well, so that Arian opinion separated out into three broad positions. The most extreme were the Anomoians, who argued that Christ was inferior to the Father to the extent that he was unlike (*anomoios*) him. Of the other two positions, the one closest to the Homoousian view was that of the Homoiousians, who accepted that Christ had 'a substance like' – but, crucially, not the same as – the Father's (*homoiousios*), while the third position – the Homoians – baulked at the word 'substance' (*ousia*) and argued that Christ was simply 'like' (*homoios*) the Father. Constantius II (337–61), who inherited the eastern half of the empire from Constantine, was sympathetic to Arian views and eventually aligned himself with the Homoian position, whereas Constans (337–50), who ruled the west from 340 to 350, gave his support to the Nicene Homoousian position.[11]

Although church leaders in the western Mediterranean were also largely supportive of the Nicene position (the Balkan region of Illyricum was the primary exception), they had to contend with their own internal problems, notably in north Africa where a rival church had emerged in the form of the Donatists. At issue was a matter of conduct, rather than theology. During the final persecution of the church in the early years of the fourth century, the imperial authorities had required church leaders to hand over any copies of the Christian scriptures which they possessed to their local authorities, a measure which was enforced with particular vigour in north Africa. Many refused to comply and sometimes suffered martyrdom as a result, but others co-operated. After the persecution ended, the question arose of what to do about these so-called *traditores* ('handers-over'): some took the more generous view that, after due repentance, they could be readmitted to communion, but others, no doubt embittered by the memory of those who had perished as a result of refusing to comply, adopted a hard-line stance that such

11. L. Ayres, *Nicaea and its Legacy: An Approach to Fourth-Century Trinitarian Theology*, Oxford: Oxford University Press, 2004, chs 4–6 and Epilogue.

individuals could only be readmitted to communion if they underwent the more rigorous process of re-baptism. The latter were outraged that some bishops who had complied simply resumed their posts, and so they began selecting alternative, untainted bishops for these posts. One of the earliest was a man named Donatus, from whom this movement took its name. As with the Arian controversy, Constantine also tried to resolve this dispute through church councils, but failed to reach any sort of agreement which could be presented as a resolution, however tenuous. He then resorted to forcible suppression of Donatists, but when this too failed, he effectively gave up, as the Arian dispute increasingly monopolised his attention. By the mid-fourth century, the Donatists had developed a parallel church structure in north Africa, and had also spawned their own armed wing, the *circumcelliones*, who believed that there was nothing wrong about using violence against rival Catholic Christians.[12]

Also lurking on the periphery of the church in this period was an intriguing movement known as Manichaeism. As with Arianism and Donatism, its name also derives from an individual, but in this instance, an individual from outside the empire. Mani had lived in Persia during the mid-third century where he grew up as a member of a Judaising Christian sect which laid strong emphasis on baptism. He developed his own religious views which owed most to Gnostic thinking (a strand of quasi-Christian thought which taught that salvation was gained through special knowledge) and envisaged the world as involved in a dualistic struggle between good and evil, with the cause of good upheld by the 'Elect', supported by 'Hearers'. The Elect sought to release particles of light into the world through adhering to an ascetic, vegetarian regime. Christ held an important place in the Manichaean worldview, but so too did Mani, his 'yoke-fellow'. Mani's teachings achieved considerable success during the later third century, spreading eastwards into China and westwards into the Roman empire; indicative of their continuing appeal was the decade-long adherence of the young and intellectually gifted Augustine (354–430), prior to his conversion to Christianity and subsequent career as an influential bishop.[13]

12. See W. H. C. Frend, *The Donatist Church*, Oxford: Clarendon Press, 1952; B. D. Shaw, *Sacred Violence: African Christians and Sectarian Hatred in the Age of Augustine*, Cambridge: Cambridge University Press, 2011.
13. S. N. C. Lieu, *Manichaeism in the Later Roman Empire and Medieval China*, 2nd

Another important religious group in the empire of the mid-fourth century with a much longer and respected history was the Jews, who, over the course of centuries, had become dispersed around the Mediterranean. After a tradition of toleration by the Roman authorities, even despite various rebellions in the first and second centuries, the advent of emperors supporting Christianity was bound to be a dangerous time for Judaism, given the way in which Christianity had, over the years, come to define itself in contradistinction to the group out of which it had originally emerged. Although Constantine and his sons did not take any significant discriminatory measures against Jews, his interest after his acquisition of the eastern half of the empire in 324 in encouraging the development of the Holy Land as a focus for Christian devotion and pilgrimage, through sponsoring the construction of churches at sites associated with Christ, certainly impinged on Jewish communities still resident in the area, as well as claiming the region symbolically for Christianity.[14]

One of Constantine's most significant policies was his expanding the role and authority of bishops well beyond the ecclesiastical sphere by giving them legal authority in areas previously reserved for government officials, notably the power to manumit slaves and to hear legal cases, even about matters which had no connection with church affairs. Bishops certainly did not always welcome these additional responsibilities, but this was nevertheless one factor among a number which contributed to the increasingly high profile which bishops came to have beyond the parameters of church affairs, and which was to be one of the most important developments in the social history of the empire during late antiquity.[15]

Alongside the emerging importance of bishops in the early fourth century was another important development in Christianity which could be regarded as posing a potential challenge to the authority of bishops – the efflorescence of various modes of ascetic practice as

edn, Tübingen: Mohr, 1992; N. Baker-Brian, *Manichaeism*, London: Continuum, 2011; P. Brown, *Augustine of Hippo*, London: Faber, 1967, ch. 5.
14. F. Millar, 'The Jews of the Graeco-Roman diaspora between paganism and Christianity, AD 312–438', in J. Lieu et al. (eds), *The Jews among Pagans and Christians*, London: Routledge, 1992, 97–123; G. Stemberger, *Jews and Christians in the Holy Land: Palestine in the Fourth Century* (tr. R. Tuschling), Edinburgh: T&T Clark, 2000.
15. P. Brown, *Power and Persuasion in Late Antiquity*, Madison: University of Wisconsin Press, 1992, ch. 3; J. H. W. G. Liebeschuetz, *The Decline and Fall of the Roman City*, Oxford: Oxford University Press, 2001, ch. 4; C. Rapp, *Holy Bishops in Late Antiquity*, Berkeley: University of California Press, 2005.

alternative expressions of spirituality. There were of course well-established precedents for the basic principle of self-denial, not only within early Christianity, but also in pagan and Jewish contexts;[16] what was different in the fourth century, however, was first, the novelty of some of the forms which ascetic practice took, and secondly, the scale of the phenomenon. The most famous individual Christian ascetic in the fourth century was Antony of Egypt, whose eremetic expression of ascetic endeavour – that is, withdrawing alone into the desert to battle demons and achieve union with God – was popularised through a biography written by Athanasius, bishop of Alexandria. Athanasius wrote a life of Antony not only because of admiration for the man, but also as a way of 'domesticating' his influence and harnessing that influence in the interests of Nicene Christianity. A second major figure in the ascetic landscape was another Egyptian, Pachomius, who is credited with pioneering communal asceticism in the Nile valley. By the time of his death in the mid-fourth century there were reported to be seven Pachomian monasteries with about 7,000 inhabitants. Athanasius tried to domesticate Pachomius too, by having him ordained as a clergyman, but Pachomius resisted. Nevertheless, this form of asceticism was to have very wide-ranging and far-reaching influence beyond Egypt, serving as the inspiration for developments which led ultimately to the medieval monastery.[17]

Cultural horizons

'Culture' can refer to a diverse range of phenomena, depending on context. In respect of the Roman world of the mid-fourth century, it might refer to 'high culture', in the sense of literary works in Greek and Latin accessible only to those with the education (*paideia*) to appreciate the skill entailed; it might also refer to 'popular culture' in the sense of forms of popular entertainment which nonetheless drew upon the traditions of classical literature; and it might refer to

16. G. Clark, *Christianity and Roman Society*, Cambridge: Cambridge University Press, 2004, ch. 4; R. Finn, *Asceticism in the Graeco-Roman World*, Cambridge: Cambridge University Press, 2009, chs 1–3.

17. D. Brakke, *Athanasius and Asceticism*, Baltimore: Johns Hopkins University Press, 1998; P. Rousseau, *Pachomius: The Making of a Community in Fourth-Century Egypt*, Berkeley: University of California Press, 1985. For counter-currents to the popularity of asceticism in the later fourth century, see D. G. Hunter, *Marriage, Celibacy and Heresy in Ancient Christianity: The Jovinianist Controversy*, Oxford: Oxford University Press, 2007.

cultural expressions unrelated to classical literature, but drawing instead on different indigenous traditions and languages.

Since access to 'high culture' depended on education, and education in the Roman world depended on wealth, high culture was necessarily the almost exclusive preserve of the elite and the very badge of their superiority. For those with the means to pursue a traditional education, this continued to involve mastering the archetypal exemplars of classical literary achievement, above all epic poetry – Homer in Greek, Virgil in Latin. But of course such education ranged more widely into other forms of poetry, prose writing and philosophical discourse. Some idea of the influence of classical models can be observed in historical writing, the most important instance of which from the fourth century is that of the historian Ammianus Marcellinus. Generally regarded as the last great Roman historian to have written in Latin, intriguingly he came from a Greek background, probably from Antioch. Although the first half of his history has not survived, it seems that he began it at the point where Tacitus concluded his *Histories*, with the start of the reign of the Emperor Nerva in 96, thereby implying a claim to be Tacitus' successor. His style is also regarded as owing a considerable debt to the important Republican historian Sallust, and the surviving second half of Ammianus' history contains innumerable allusions to classical literature.[18]

Ammianus was pagan in his religious sympathies and the structure and focus of his history strongly suggest that it was inspired by his admiration for the Emperor Julian, to whom a disproportionate amount of his history is devoted and with an overwhelmingly approving attitude.[19] However, Christian authors in this period were also often well educated and well versed in classical literature. A good example is provided by the rhetorician Lactantius from north Africa, who became tutor to Constantine's son Crispus in the early fourth century. Although best known for his polemical tract about the fates of the emperors who had been presumptuous enough to persecute the church (*De mortibus persecutorum* ['On the deaths of the persecutors']), he wrote a much more substantial and thoughtful treatise entitled the *Divine Institutes* which presented a reasoned

18. See G. Kelly, *Ammianus Marcellinus, the Allusive Historian*, Cambridge: Cambridge University Press, 2008.
19. J. Matthews, *The Roman Empire of Ammianus*, London: Duckworth, 1989; Kelly, *Ammianus*.

case for the claims of Christianity, but did so by deploying the full panoply of classical learning in a way which has permitted the reconstruction of the library of classical works on which Lactantius drew.[20]

Lactanius' career highlights the continuing importance of oratory in classical *paideia*. Training in rhetoric was viewed as an important avenue of advancement for ambitious young men, whether in the legal field or in the imperial administration. So it was that a skilled rhetorician like Libanius found himself teaching a steady stream of young men from the wealthier families of Antioch and Syria. Although he bemoaned the fact that many of them then went on to work in the imperial bureaucracy, his voluminous correspondence shows that he also liked to maintain contact with them and exploit the influence which they might be able to exercise on his behalf in Constantinople and elsewhere, reflecting the continuing importance of ties of patronage in the late Roman world.[21] Training in Roman law also continued to be an important avenue for success in the wider imperial world, with renowned schools in Rome, Beirut and, in due course, Constantinople.[22]

Access to education was of course limited to a relatively small proportion of the empire's population. However, this did not prevent others, especially urban inhabitants, from enjoying popular entertainments which had their roots in classical culture but which were delivered through oral and visual media, above all in the theatre. The principal forms these took in the fourth century were pantomime, in which a skilled dancer depicted a story based on mythological themes to the accompaniment of music and singing, and mime, in which performers acted out comic scenarios, some of which drew on traditional comedy. Neither medium lent itself to preservation in the form of scripts, not least because the educated elite often adopted a disdainful attitude towards such forms of entertainment. However, a fair idea of their content can be derived from criticism of them by Christian writers concerned about inappropriate subject matter, whether references to pagan deities or dubious sexual morality, as

20. R. Ogilvie, *The Library of Lactantius*, Oxford: Clarendon Press, 1978; A. Bowen and P. Garnsey, *Lactantius: Divine Institutes*, Liverpool: Liverpool University Press, 2003.
21. R. Cribiore, *The School of Libanius in Late Antique Antioch*, Princeton: Princeton University Press, 2007.
22. D. Liebs, 'Roman law', in *CAH*[2] 14.238–59, at 253–5.

well as from the occasional individual who wrote a defence of them as being based on reputable literary traditions.[23]

As for non-classical cultural traditions, although numerous indigenous languages clearly remained in use in the Roman world, the majority have not left any literature from the late Roman period (e.g., Punic in north Africa), which is why the most significant instances of this phenomenon relate to Syria and Egypt. In Syria, the Semitic language of Aramaic developed one of its regional dialects – Syriac – to a state where it became the medium for an increasingly significant literature. The impetus of Christianity in this was important, as was also the case in Egypt where the written version of indigenous Egyptian known as Coptic gradually superseded the previous common script known as Demotic, not least because it employed more easily comprehensible characters, most of them based on Greek letters. It is all too easy to think of the Roman empire as being a two-language world – Latin and Greek – so it is worth remembering that alternative cultural traditions also existed – and thrived.[24]

Julian's legacy

In sketching the state of the Roman world in the mid-fourth century, much of this chapter has inevitably focused on aspects which betray the imprint of the Emperor Constantine. However, for understanding the more specific circumstances of the decades after 363, it is also important to rehearse some of the salient aspects of the life and reign of the Emperor Julian (361–3), who, despite the brevity of his reign, nevertheless left a major mark above all because of the way he went against the prevailing religious trends of his day. Although he took considerable care to avoid creating martyrs among the Christians of the empire, his attempts to undo Constantine's support for the church, and the deaths of Christians which resulted from the over-enthusiasm of some pagan supporters, could not fail to leave a

23. T. D. Barnes, 'Christians and the theater' in W. J. Slater (ed.), *Roman Theater and Society*, Ann Arbor: University of Michigan Press, 1996, 161–80; R. Webb, *Demons and Dancers: Performance in Late Antiquity*, Cambridge, MA: Harvard University Press, 2008.
24. Punic: P. Brown, 'Christianity and local culture in late Roman Africa', *JRS* 58 (1968), 85–95; Syriac: S. Brock, 'Syriac culture, 337–425' in *CAH*[2] 13. ch. 23a; Coptic: M. Smith, 'Coptic literature, 337–425' in *CAH*[2] 13. ch. 23b, S. Emmel, 'Coptic literature in the Byzantine and early Islamic world' in R. S. Bagnall (ed.), *Egypt in the Byzantine World, 300–700*, Cambridge: Cambridge University Press, 2007, 83–102.

legacy of bitterness among Christians towards Julian's memory. His notorious ban on Christians being teachers of classical literature also prompted great resentment among educated Christians. A central question for the post-Julianic period was how strongly emperors and/or church leaders would react against Julian's policies.

Another important aspect of Julian's legacy lay in the field of foreign relations. A range of possible objectives underlying Julian's Persian expedition in 363 has been canvassed: perhaps replacing the Persian king Shapur II with another pro-Roman Persian prince, Hormizd, who had been living as an exile in the Roman empire for some decades and who participated in the expedition; perhaps redressing the balance between the empire and Persia in favour of the empire after a period in which Persia had been more dominant; or perhaps the desire of Julian, like many before him, to emulate Alexander the Great. Whatever the objectives, however, the actual outcome of the expedition – Julian's death in battle and his army left stranded in Persian territory – had rather different consequences. The Persians were able to dictate terms in return for the safe withdrawal of the army. Although territorial losses were not perhaps as substantial as might have been expected, given that a decade or so previously Shapur had proclaimed his intention of recovering the lands once controlled by the Achaemenid Persians in the fifth century BC (i.e., all of Syria and Anatolia), they were nevertheless humiliating enough for the Romans since they entailed the surrender not only of the eastern half of northern Mesopotamia and territory beyond the Tigris (acquired by Diocletian at the end of the third century), but also of the fortress of Nisibis, which had withstood three concerted attempts by the Persians to capture it between 337 and 350. So Julian's expedition resulted in the loss of the linchpin of Roman defences in northern Mesopotamia, and created the prospect of further difficulties on that frontier in the future. Moreover, the death of the emperor on campaign was bound to raise questions about the wisdom of the emperor's leading the army in person and exposing himself to danger in this way. Although personal military leadership allowed the emperor to claim military glory for himself directly and maintain closer relations with his troops, the negative consequences of death on campaign might be thought to outweigh these, particularly when, as in the case of Julian, the lack of an obvious and clearly designated heir meant that his death precipitated a succession crisis – a crisis exacerbated by the fact that it occurred on foreign soil.

But Julian's Persian plans were also linked to affairs on another frontier, the lower Danube. In 362, Julian's advisers had urged him to act against the Gothic tribes which had established themselves in that region during the late third and early fourth century. Julian had ensured that the troops stationed in those parts were well supported and supplied, but he had declined to undertake an expedition against the Goths, reportedly dismissing them as fit prey for slave traders, whereas he sought 'a better enemy', by which he must have meant the Persians (Amm. Marc. 22.7.7–8). In other words, Julian's pre-occupation with Persia resulted in a degree of neglect of the Danube frontier which, in hindsight, could be seen to have unfortunate consequences for the empire. Of course, it is unclear how serious a threat the Goths were at this stage, but they had certainly proved themselves to be a problem in the mid-third century and the early fourth century during Constantine's reign, and so perhaps Julian's advisers were wise to suggest he should give focused attention there rather than Persia.

The Roman world of the mid-fourth century was one, then, which still owed an enormous debt to developments of the more distant past, and where, particularly in the area of cultural horizons, classical traditions continued to exercise a strong influence. However, more recent developments had also effected significant changes, and it was Constantine who was the most important influence in this respect. It was he who had engineered some of the most noteworthy aspects of the reorganisation of the administrative and military infrastructure of the empire; it was he who was responsible for the establishment of Constantinople as the new imperial base in the eastern Mediterranean; and it was he who, through lending his political authority and material support to the Christian church, set in train even more momentous changes to the religious complexion of the Mediterranean world. The Roman world of the mid-fourth century was, then, one in the process of adjusting to some very significant changes. More immediately, the Emperor Julian had tried, ultimately unsuccessfully, to undo some of these changes, most notably the growing power of the church. His efforts left a legacy of religious turmoil and bitterness, while his military aspirations had resulted in a significant defeat for the empire and bequeathed an uncertain future with regard to the imperial succession. In the summer of 363, therefore, the Roman empire was in a state of instability in a variety of respects. How would Julian's successors respond to the challenges which they inherited?

Part I

The later fourth century

CHAPTER 2

Emperors, usurpers and frontiers

Emperors and usurpers from Jovian to Theodosius I

Like his hero Alexander the Great, the Emperor Julian died in Persia at the age of 32, and like Alexander, he left no heir or clearly designated successor.[1] This was a testing transitional situation of a kind which the Roman empire had not encountered for many decades, exacerbated by the fact that, unlike Alexander, Julian had not succeeded in conquering Persia. Decisions about a new emperor had therefore to be made without the aid of any recent precedent and under the highly pressurised circumstances of an increasingly difficult military retreat from deep within enemy territory.

An urgent meeting of senior military officers resulted in stalemate: those generals who had been promoted by Julian were opposed by those of longer standing with ties back to Constantius' regime, and the compromise candidate – an experienced senior civilian official accompanying the expedition, the praetorian prefect Salutius – declined the offer on grounds of ill health and advanced years. At this juncture, further deliberations were pre-empted by the actions of another group, probably members of the imperial guard, who acclaimed as emperor one Jovian, first in rank of the *protectores domestici*, an elite corps of middle-ranking officers attached to the emperor. The historian Ammianus, who was an eye-witness and provides the most detailed account of Jovian's succession, dismissively describes Jovian's supporters as 'a few rabble-rousers' and proceeds to emphasise Jovian's lack of suitable qualifications for the imperial throne (Amm. Marc. 25.5), but it is apparent that Ammianus has slanted his account to exaggerate the contrast

---

1. For Julian's admiration for Alexander (as well as its limits), see R. B. E. Smith, *Julian's Gods*, London: Routledge, 1995, 10–11. Julian had married the Emperor Constantius' sister Helena in 355, but they had no children (there is a report of a postnatal death and miscarriages, attributed to the jealous machinations of Eusebia, the childless wife of the Emperor Constantius: Amm. Marc. 16.10.18–19).

between his beloved Julian and an obscure and unworthy Jovian.

In fact, Jovian had a reasonably distinguished military pedigree – his father and father-in-law had both held military commands of importance in recent years – and he himself had enjoyed some prominence through being required to escort the corpse of the Emperor Constantius from his place of death in Cilicia across Anatolia to Constantinople, which might account for the hint in one source (Them. *Or.* 5.65b) that he was briefly considered as a possible successor to Constantius in 361. At any rate, Jovian actively modelled his daily routine as emperor on that of Constantius (Amm. Marc. 25.10.14), no doubt hoping thereby to reinforce his claims to legitimacy.[2]

In the event, Jovian's reign proved to be short-lived, lasting less than eight months and ending (probably by inadvertent carbon monoxide poisoning from a charcoal brazier[3]) before he had even completed his journey back from the eastern frontier to Constantinople. The brevity of his reign meant that Jovian had little opportunity to make his mark and his reputation became inextricably linked with the ignominy of his first major action as emperor – negotiating a humiliating peace settlement with Persia (pp. 28–9 below). Despite the fact that Jovian was not responsible for the predicament in which the Roman army found itself and that he had little choice but to accept the terms dictated by the Persians, this necessary step towards extracting Roman troops from enemy territory has coloured perceptions of him adversely. Ammianus certainly exploited to the full Jovian's potential as a convenient scapegoat for what were actually Julian's failings, while also omitting to mention the new emperor's important initiative in religious policy (pp. 39–40 below), thereby imparting to this short reign an unduly negative image.

Unlike Julian, Jovian did have an heir, a very young son whom he had made fellow consul with himself at the start of 364, a clear

---

2. For further discussion and detail on the points made in this and the next paragraph, see J. Matthews, *The Roman Empire of Ammianus*, London: Duckworth, 1989, 183–5; P. Heather, 'Ammianus on Jovian: history and literature' in J. W. Drijvers and D. Hunt (eds), *The Late Roman World and its Historian: Interpreting Ammianus Marcellinus*, London: Routledge, 1999, 105–16; N. Lenski, 'The election of Jovian and the role of the late imperial guards', *Klio* 82 (2000), 492–515.

3. Ammianus (25.10.13), however, perhaps insinuates foul play by drawing a comparison with the mysterious death of Scipio Aemilianus in 129 BC (cf. G. Kelly, *Ammianus Marcellinus, the Allusive Historian*, Cambridge: Cambridge University Press, 2008, 245–6).

indication of his dynastic intent. However, that son did not figure in deliberations about a successor, and understandably so: in the aftermath of a military debacle, strong leadership was essential, and so it is unsurprising that when the leading military and civilian figures in Jovian's entourage assembled to consider suitable candidates in Nicaea (the major centre nearest to where Jovian had died), all the individuals discussed were military officers. From among these, there was prompt agreement on a certain Valentinian whose background was very similar to that of Jovian – he came from the Balkans (like so many serving in the fourth-century army), his father had held high military commands, and Valentinian himself was at that time an officer in the imperial guards. Perhaps his most important distinction, however, was that, due to his having been dismissed from the army in 357 as a casualty of the power struggles between Julian and Constantius' generals in Gaul and only being restored to military rank in the early months of Jovian's reign, he was not associated with Julian's reign or tainted by involvement in the failed Persian expedition.

Valentinian was duly presented in the appropriate regalia to the assembled troops in Nicaea on 26 February 364 to allow their symbolic approval of his accession, but the soldiers present, who 'had learnt from recent experience how precarious is the position of those in high places' (Amm. Marc. 26.2.4), seized the opportunity to voice not only their endorsement of Valentinian but also their desire that he appoint a fellow emperor. Although Valentinian had a son, Gratian was not yet five years old and so would not satisfy this demand for insurance against a repetition of the uncertainty and instability engendered by the unexpected deaths of Julian and Jovian in quick succession. Valentinian conceded the wisdom of this request and when he subsequently sought the advice of senior courtiers as to the best course of action, one of the generals present eventually had the nerve to speak plainly: 'Your highness, if you love your relatives you have a brother, but if you love the state look carefully for another man to invest with the purple' (Amm. Marc. 26.4.1). As this remark implies, the new emperor's brother Valens was not an obvious candidate for the imperial office, for he seems to have spent most of his adult life overseeing the family's rural property and was 'schooled in neither military nor liberal disciplines' (Amm. Marc. 31.14.5). Nevertheless, a month later Valentinian proclaimed Valens emperor in Constantinople. No doubt Valentinian's decision was influenced by an understandable desire to have a compliant colleague (perhaps mindful of the problems which had arisen between Constantine's sons), but there must also have been an additional element of astute political calculation involved: 'The trouble with choosing the "best man" ... was that it left too many disappointed candidates; the advantage with brothers is that no one can question that that is what they are.'[4]

The brothers spent the first five months of their joint rule together in Constantinople and then en route through the Balkans to the important centre of Sirmium, in the course of which they finalised plans for the division of responsibilities and personnel. That division was determined along geographical lines, with Valentinian assuming oversight of the western half of the empire and leaving the eastern half to Valens. It is difficult to know whether Valentinian chose the west because he reckoned it posed a greater or less serious challenge than the east. From a military perspective, he may well have regarded himself as shouldering the heavier burden: it was a reasonable assumption that, with Persia's immediate goals having been satisfied by the peace settlement of the previous year, the eastern frontier would be less demanding for the time being and he is unlikely to have anticipated the developing Gothic problem on the lower Danube, whereas there had been no imperial presence in the west for a number of years and so the Rhine frontier would almost certainly require significant attention, as indeed proved to be the case (cf. pp. 30–1 below). On the other hand, there was also the linguistic angle to consider. Although Latin remained the primary language of central administration throughout the empire, Greek was otherwise predominant in the eastern half. Valentinian's Pannonian origin and career in the army will have left him with a minimal grasp of Greek at best, creating a strong incentive for him to head westwards and leave his similarly monolingual brother to cope with the frustrations of living in a linguistic environment which was predominantly alien.[5]

Whatever Valentinian's motivations for his choice, however, the significance of the decision to apportion the empire in this way ought not to be underestimated. The death of Theodosius I in 395, and the

4. Matthews, *Ammianus*, 190. For detailed discussion of the accessions and backgrounds of Valentinian and Valens, see N. Lenski, *Failure of Empire: Valens and the Roman State in the Fourth Century A.D.*, Berkeley: University of California Press, 2002, 14–67.
5. Linguistic considerations will also have made it less easy to install Pannonian supporters in positions of importance in the east than in the west (cf. Lenski, *Valens*, 59).

succession of his sons Arcadius in the east and Honorius in the west, has traditionally been seen as the point at which the two halves of the empire began following divergent paths. However, despite the rhetoric of harmony which the coinage and panegyrics of their reigns promoted, the regimes of Valentinian and Valens effectively operated independently of one another, not least because of the practical limitations on timely communication, so that 364 can with justice be regarded as marking the real beginning of a divided empire.[6]

If the rationale for having two emperors was to provide a greater degree of continuity and stability than the empire had experienced during the early years of the 360s, then overall the arrangement must be considered a success, even if the brothers never saw one another again after they parted in 364. Both men remained in power for more than a decade, albeit not without occasional crises. Valentinian reigned for just over a decade until 375, spending the majority of that time based at Trier on the Moselle and engaged in the strengthening of the Rhine frontier (pp. 30–1 below). Valens out-lived his brother by three years. Despite Jovian's settlement with Persia in northern Mesopotamia, he found himself having to spend a substantial portion of his time dealing with Persian attempts to destabilise the Armenian section of the eastern frontier (p. 30 below), while the Gothic groups living north of the lower Danube became an increasingly important priority with the passage of time (pp. 32–6 below). However, the first major challenge Valens faced was the attempted usurpation of Procopius, an episode which reveals much about the nature of imperial power in this period.[7]

Procopius represented a very serious challenge to Valens because he was a relative of Julian and so was able to claim continuity with the Constantinian dynasty – and it is clear that the name of Constantine still carried enormous weight.[8] The precise nature of his relationship to Julian is not made clear in the ancient sources, but it was enough for him to fear for his life in the aftermath of Julian's death and Jovian's accession, and it was clearly an important factor later in his ability to win over many army units to his cause. After

6. As noted by Matthews, *Ammianus*, 190–1, and argued more fully by R. M. Errington, *Roman Imperial Policy from Julian to Theodosius*, Chapel Hill: University of North Carolina Press, 2006.

7. For detailed discussions, see Matthews, *Ammianus*, 191–203, and Lenski, *Valens*, 68–115.

8. Cf. the way in which the orator Themistius tried to strengthen Jovian's acceptability by hailing him as a (metaphorical) Constantine (*Or.* 5.70d).

lying low initially, Procopius seized the opportunity presented by Valens' absence from Constantinople en route to Syria in the summer of 365 to gain the support of units of soldiers passing through the capital, by appealing to their loyalty to the memory of Julian as well as offering them financial incentives.[9] He was also able to exploit the discontent which had already been generated by Valens' vigorous pursuit of tax debts; imperial finances were undoubtedly in desperate need of additional funds in the aftermath of the failed Persian expedition, but Valens' officials alienated many by 'exacting penalties four-fold from innocent and guilty alike and hunting out debts as far back as the time of the Emperor Aurelian [270–5]' (Amm. Marc. 26.6.7). Procopius soon controlled Constantinople, Thrace and north-western Anatolia, with his skilful propaganda contrasting the legitimacy of his own claim to the throne against the dubious entitlement of the 'beer-swilling, degenerate Pannonian' (Amm. Marc. 26.7.16, 8.2). The growing momentum behind Procopius, and Valentinian's decision to prioritise the needs of the west over coming to his brother's aid, apparently prompted Valens at one point to 'fall into such despair that he thought of casting off the heavy burden of his imperial robes' (Amm. Marc. 26.7.13). In the event, he held his nerve and by the spring of 366 had been able to marshal superior military and financial resources from the eastern provinces to confront and defeat Procopius' forces in central Anatolia, aided by the calculated desertion of Procopius' two leading generals. Procopius himself was quickly captured and executed, and his head despatched to Valentinian in Gaul as proof of Valens' ability to cope unaided with a major crisis.

Both brothers eventually died unexpectedly by the agency of foreigners – Valens through death in battle against the Goths in 378 (p. 35 below), Valentinian (well known for his hot temper) as a result of an apoplectic fit triggered by the insolent behaviour of Quadian envoys during an audience with the emperor at Brigetio on the middle Danube in 375. Since he had already promoted his elder son Gratian (then eight years old) to the rank of Augustus in 367 when Valentinian fell dangerously ill, there should have been no uncertainty about Gratian, now sixteen, assuming effective control

---

9. Despite Procopius' emphasis on his familial connection with Julian, however, there are no good grounds for regarding his rebellion as having a specifically pagan edge: Lenski, *Valens*, 110–11.

in the west.[10] Resident in Trier in northern Gaul at the time, however, Gratian was a long way from Brigetio, and some of Valentinian's generals thought it wise to pre-empt any attempted usurpation by seeking the troops' approval of Gratian's half-brother, the four-year-old Valentinian, who was readily to hand, as Gratian's titular colleague in the west (Amm. Marc. 30.10).[11] Needless to say, it would be some years before Valentinian II exercised any power in his own right.

The younger Valentinian's tender years no doubt explain why, when his uncle Valens perished three years later, Gratian did not simply assign the eastern half of the empire to him.[12] The turmoil arising from the Gothic victory at Adrianople in which Valens died demanded strong and experienced leadership in the east, forcing Gratian and his advisers to consider candidates without family ties to the Valentinianic dynasty. Their eventual choice was one Theodosius, homonymous son of the most prominent and effective of Valentinian I's generals with a proven record in his own right as 'an aggressive and skilful commander' (Zos. 4.24.4).[13] Theodosius' family background lay in Spain, rather than the Balkans, although it is possible to overemphasise the significance of that difference, given that Theodosius is likely to have passed his formative years in a variety of army camps rather than in Spain.[14] Following his elevation in January 379, Theodosius spent the first three and a half

---

10. His position had been further strengthened recently by his marriage to a member of the Constantinian line, Constantia, daughter of Constantius II (Amm. Marc. 21.15.6, 29.6.7).

11. One source (Philostorgius *Hist. eccl.* 9.16) intimates that the young Valentinian's mother, Justina, also played a role in instigating his acclamation, a notion which gains credibility from the fact that she was not Gratian's mother (she was Valentinian I's second wife), as also from her subsequent history of political brinkmanship with Ambrose and Theodosius (p. 48 below).

12. Valens' own son Galates had predeceased his father c. 370 before reaching the age of five.

13. For the circumstances of Theodosius' accession, see J. Matthews, *Western Aristocracies and Imperial Court, AD 364–425*, Oxford: Clarendon Press, 1975, 88–100, modified on certain details by R. M. Errington, 'The accession of Theodosius I', *Klio* 78 (1996), 438–53. For the alternative suggestion that Theodosius' elevation was effectively a usurpation to which Gratian was forced by circumstances to accede, see H. Sivan, 'Was Theodosius I a usurper?', *Klio* 78 (1996), 198–211; N. McLynn, '*Genere Hispanus*: Theodosius, Spain and Nicene orthodoxy' in K. Bowes and M. Kulikowski (eds), *Hispania in Late Antiquity*, Leiden: Brill, 2005, 77–120, at 88–94.

14. McLynn, '*Genere Hispanus*', argues that the significance of Theodosius' Spanish background has been overemphasised, especially for his religious policies.

years of his reign preoccupied with containing the Gothic problem in
Thrace and with church affairs (pp. 36–7 and 44–7 below).

The priority of military experience over heredity was also demonstrated in the west in 383 when Gratian faced a challenge from his
military commander in Britain, Magnus Maximus, who perhaps felt
that he had as good a claim to the throne as Theodosius and that
Gratian's youth and inexperience were a liability. As the two sides
confronted one another near Paris, Gratian's troops deserted him
and the fleeing emperor was soon caught and killed. Maximus made
no immediate move against Valentinian II, then in Milan, seeking
instead to win recognition from Theodosius. The latter was in no
position yet to respond militarily, so prevaricated and even began to
make some formal acknowledgement of Maximus' regime in 386.
The following year, however, Maximus did act against Valentinian,
invading Italy and forcing the latter to flee eastwards, finally bringing a decisive response from Theodosius. In 388 his forces advanced
through the Balkans and, in two hard-fought battles at Siscia
and Poetovio, defeated those of Maximus, who was captured and
killed.[15]

Theodosius charged Valentinian II (now about seventeen years
old) with the task of re-establishing imperial authority in Gaul and
Britain, under the guidance of an experienced general, Arbogast,
while he himself remained in Italy until 391, when he returned to
Constantinople. His thoughts during this period must have dwelt
regularly on future dynastic arrangements, since Theodosius had
two sons of his own – Arcadius (eleven years old in 388) and
Honorius (four years old) – whom he will understandably have
wished to inherit imperial power (Arcadius had already been
proclaimed Augustus in 383). Valentinian was a complicating factor
in such plans, but not for long. Theodosius had been back in
Constantinople for little more than six months when news came
of the death of Valentinian in southern Gaul. Although suicide is
the most likely explanation, his relations with Arbogast had been
strained and suspicion fell on the general.[16] Arbogast pleaded his
innocence and protested his loyalty to Theodosius, but when after a
number of months it became clear that this was to no avail, he opted
for open rebellion.

---

15. For Maximus' usurpation and Theodosius' response, see Matthews, *Western
Aristocracies*, 173–82, 223–7, Errington, *Imperial Policy*, 31–7.
16. B. Croke, 'Arbogast and the death of Valentinian II', *Historia* 25 (1976), 235–44.

Although his Frankish origin need not necessarily have ruled him out as a viable candidate for emperor,[17] Arbogast must have decided that support for his regime would be broadened if he found a figure-head acceptable to the elite in the west – hence his choice of a cultured (and compliant) civilian in the person of the rhetorician and bureaucrat Eugenius.[18] Further attempts to negotiate with Constantinople were unsuccessful, and in 394 Theodosius marched west again, this time facing, but eventually overcoming, more formidable military opposition at the battle of the River Frigidus, just inside the eastern border of northern Italy. Arbogast committed suicide and Eugenius was executed, but Theodosius himself did not long outlive them, succumbing to unexpected illness in Milan in January 395, despite his still being less than fifty years old.[19] He had, however, already put in place arrangements for the succession of his sons which, in contrast to the circumstances surrounding the deaths of every emperor for the preceding half century, ensured a trouble-free transfer of power.

Frontiers: (1) Persia

Close and direct involvement in activities on the empire's frontiers, whether making war or peace, had become a central feature of the emperor's role and responsibilities over the course of the previous century or so, a change reflected in the time spent by emperors at frontier bases at the expense of the city of Rome. The eastern frontier with Persia had become particularly important in this respect because of the significant threat which Persia posed to Roman interests. Although the challenge of Persia diminished in the decades after Julian's death, it nonetheless remained a frontier of importance during the later fourth century, and even when diplomatic negotiation assumed greater importance than military success,

---

17. The general Silvanus who had himself acclaimed emperor during the reign of Constantius II in 355 was also of Frankish origin, although he was a second-generation resident of the empire (as is reflected in his Romanised name).
18. The idea that support for traditional pagan cults was an integral element of Arbogast's rebellion is difficult to substantiate: Matthews, *Western Aristocracies*, 140–3; Errington, *Imperial Policy*, 253–8; Alan Cameron, *The Last Pagans of Rome* (Oxford: Oxford University Press, 2011), 74–131 (who notes [85–6] the tenuous nature of the evidence for Arbogast even being pagan).
19. For Arbogast's revolt and Eugenius' regime, see Matthews, *Western Aristocracies*, 238–52.

Figure 1 Relief from the base of the obelisk of Theodosius I depicting foreign envoys from Persia (lower left) and northern barbarians (lower right) presenting gifts to the emperor in the hippodrome in Constantinople. © Marku1998/ Wikimedia Commons

the emperor could still be portrayed in a positive, dominant manner (cf. Fig. 1).

The gradual reduction in the significance of the eastern frontier in the decades after Julian's death was largely due to the peace settlement which Jovian agreed with the Persians in July 363. By the terms of this settlement the Romans surrendered five regions beyond the Tigris, together with fifteen forts and the major strong points of Nisibis, Singara and Castra Maurorum (Amm. Marc. 25.7.9) – so effectively the eastern half of the northern Mesopotamian plain between the Euphrates and the Tigris. From the Persian perspective, these terms achieved two important objectives: first, they made amends for the humiliation of the peace which Diocletian had imposed on them in 299, for although the five Transtigritane regions in 363 were not identical in every respect with the five regions ceded to the Romans in 299, the recurrence of the figure five presumably satisfied Persian honour; and secondly, the Romans were deprived of control of the fortified centres in the eastern half of northern Mesopotamia which provided advanced bases for Roman thrusts into Persia's heartlands and obstacles to Persian expansion westwards. From the Roman perspective, these losses could be considered relatively light compared with alternative scenarios, but this did not prevent the peace being viewed by many contemporary commentators as a humiliating blight on the memory of Jovian, above all because of the surrender of Nisibis. This important centre, 'the strongest bulwark of the east' (Amm. Marc. 25.8.14), had successfully resisted three Persian attempts to capture it between 337 and 350, which made its handing over without a fight in 363 seem all the more abject. The fact remains, however, that Julian's immediate legacy to Jovian left him in no position to bargain, if he wished to extract his starving troops from Persian territory, and having gained their most important objectives in northern Mesopotamia, the Persians had no incentive to renew warfare in this region for the remainder of the fourth century.

However, while northern Mesopotamia had always been the region of critical importance for Roman–Persian relations, the eastern frontier comprised other sectors, particularly Armenia, to the north, concerning which there was also provision in the settlement of 363. The sources are less clear about the details – Ammianus, for example, talks about the Romans agreeing not to come to the aid of the Armenian king, their one-time ally Arsaces (Arshak) (25.7.12) – but this lack of clarity may reflect deliberate vagueness in the treaty terms regarding Armenia which both sides hoped to exploit to their advantage. Certainly, it was Armenia which now became the focus of tensions between the two powers, albeit in a less resource-consuming manner.[20]

Valens seems to have feared Persian intentions early in his reign since he was travelling eastwards through Anatolia towards Syria when Procopius was proclaimed emperor in Constantinople (September 365). Confronting Procopius occupied Valens for the next eight months, after which he needed to re-establish his authority in Constantinople and adjacent regions. Since Procopius had received support from the Gothic tribes on the lower Danube, Valens

20. For further details and discussion of the 363 settlement, see R. C. Blockley, *East Roman Foreign Policy: Formation and Conduct from Diocletian to Anastasius*, Liverpool: Francis Cairns, 1992, 27–30; Lenski, *Valens*, 160–7.

also embarked on a series of campaigns against them which lasted from 367 to 369 (p. 32 below), so it was only in 370 that he was able to return east. In the meantime Persian forces had invaded Armenia and captured Arshak, whose son Pap escaped to Roman territory. After occupying Armenia in 370 and restoring Pap to the throne, Roman forces defeated Persian military intervention the following year, paving the way for an agreement which effectively acknowledged Roman hegemony over Armenia. This lasted until 377, when the Gothic crisis (p. 37 below) forced Valens to withdraw Roman troops. Persian attempts to regain control of the region were thrown into disarray by the death of the long-reigning Persian king Shapur II in 379, allowing Armenia to enjoy a brief period of independence until negotiations between Theodosius and Shapur III in 387 resulted in its formal partition (the Romans conceding control of four-fifths to Persia).[21]

Frontiers: (2) The Rhine and middle Danube

After parting ways with his brother at Sirmium in August 364, Valentinian spent the next twelve months in northern Italy, mainly at Milan, making administrative arrangements in the west. He then proceeded to northern Gaul where he spent most of the next decade with Trier as his base. Situated about fifty miles up the Moselle valley, this gave him convenient access to the middle Rhine frontier without the risks of direct exposure to possible attack. The imperial presence there for a sustained period of time meant that the city enjoyed a further period of prosperity and development.[22] It is also indicative of Valentinian's priorities, namely ensuring the security of the Rhine frontier against threats from various barbarian groups – Alamanni, Franks and Saxons. Achieving this objective entailed a variety of strategies: strengthening fortifications, making destructive expeditions into enemy territory, constructing strong points on enemy land, trying to eliminate troublesome enemy leaders, and reaching diplomatic accommodations when appropriate. Ammianus' history provides the most detailed account of Valentinian's activities, while archaeological evidence has confirmed his construction

21. G. Greatrex, 'The background and aftermath of the partition of Armenia in AD 387', *Ancient History Bulletin* 14 (2000), 35–48.
22. For details see E. M. Wightman, *Roman Trier and the Treveri*, London: Hart-Davis, 1970.

projects along and beyond the Rhine.[23] By and large Valentinian was successful in his efforts, although it has been suggested that the challenge was not as great as it was made out to be – that the Alamanni in particular were not a major threat, but that imperial propaganda exaggerated the scale of that threat in order to enhance the emperor's reputation.[24] No doubt this was sometimes the case – it was an inherent feature of panegyric to overstate an emperor's achievements – but Valentinian's efforts to eliminate certain Alamannic leaders (e.g., the assassination of Vithicabius: Amm. Marc. 27.10.3–4, 30.7.7) and to harness the aid of the Burgundians against them (Amm. Marc. 28.5) imply that the threat was sometimes genuine.

Some of the strategies which Valentinian employed on the Rhine were used with less success by his subordinates on the middle Danube. The attempt to build strong points north of the frontier in 374 met with protests from the Quadi, and when the local Roman commander then had their leader murdered during a dinner held to discuss the issue, the Quadi and neighbouring Sarmatians launched attacks into Roman territory. It was this which brought Valentinian from northern Gaul to Brigetio for the confrontation with Quadian envoys which resulted in his death (p. 24 above). Despite this, however, the middle Danube frontier appears to have remained relatively untroubled over the following two decades, as also did the Rhine: Gratian campaigned against the Alamanni in 378 (Amm. Marc. 31.10), while Magnus Maximus and Arbogast, both experienced generals, each undertook military action against the Franks in the mid-380s and early 390s (Gregory of Tours *Hist.* 2.9). At the time of Theodosius' death in 395 there was, therefore, no reason to suspect that, a decade later, the Rhine would be the scene of a major invasion with ultimately devastating consequences for the west (pp. 112, 115–16 below).

23. For Ammianus' narrative, see R. Seager, 'Roman policy on the Rhine and Danube in Ammianus', *CQ* 49 (1999), 579–605, at 594–7; for the archaeological evidence, see S. Johnson, *Late Roman Fortifications*, London: Batsford, 1983, with discussion in J. F. Drinkwater, *The Alamanni and Rome, 213–496*, Oxford: Oxford University Press, 2007, 295–302
24. See Drinkwater, *Alamanni*; for reservations, see Errington, *Imperial Policy*, 273 n.6; P. Heather, 'Review of Drinkwater, *Alamanni*', *Nottingham Medieval Studies* 52 (2008), 243–5.

Frontiers: (3) The lower Danube and the Goths

Although there were signs of discontent among the Goths during Julian's reign (p. 16 above), there is no reason to think that they posed a serious danger to the empire in the mid-360s. The reinforcements heading for the lower Danube on Valens' order in the summer of 365 – until they were diverted into supporting Procopius' usurpation in Constantinople (pp. 23–4 above) – were relatively small in number, implying there was no significant cause for concern. When, therefore, after the suppression of Procopius, Valens announced his determination to campaign against the Goths on the grounds that they had responded positively to the usurper's request for military aid, this sounds like a mere pretext. Ammianus reports that he did so at the instigation of his brother (27.4.1), while it has also been plausibly proposed that a primary motivation was the need to strengthen the legitimacy of his position with a successful military campaign in the aftermath of Procopius' revolt.[25]

In the event, the campaigning proved less than glorious. In the first year (367) the Goths fled for safety into the mountains and Valens was unable to bring them to battle; in the second year (368) unseasonal flooding made it impossible to cross the Danube; and in the third year (369), although Valens did inflict a defeat on one group of Goths, their flight prevented him from pressing any advantage. It was only the imposition of an embargo on cross-frontier trade and the resulting famine which finally induced their leader Athanaric to agree to peace negotiations, famously conducted by the two leaders from boats moored midstream in the Danube. This arrangement suggests that both sides had compromised; certainly events in Armenia were demanding Valens' attention. The ancient sources lack the degree of desirable detail about the specific stipulations of the settlement, but it seems that the terms included, on the one hand, permanent restrictions on trade, now limited to two locations on the lower Danube, and an end to Roman subsidies to the Goths, and on the other, the lifting of the Gothic obligation to provide troops when requested by the Romans.[26]

25. Lenski, *Valens*, 126–7.
26. For discussion of the war and the peace terms, see P. Heather, *Goths and Romans 332–489*, Oxford: Clarendon Press, 1991, 115–21, and Lenski, *Valens*, 127–37. For doubts about the interpretation of a crucial phrase in Themistius' allusive rhetoric concerning the peace, see Seager, 'Roman policy', 600 n.97.

Six years elapsed before Valens was forced to give his attention once more to the lower Danube frontier.[27] In the early months of 376 Gothic envoys sought permission from the imperial authorities for their people to cross the Danube and settle on Roman land in Thrace where, they promised, they would live peacefully and supply soldiers for the Roman army when required. This surprising request arose from the impact of the Huns. Despite the fact that they were to play an increasingly important part in the empire's history over the next century, however, surprisingly little is certain about the origins of the Huns or the reasons for their advent on Roman horizons, a situation not aided by the tendency of Roman commentators in the late fourth century to fill out what limited information they had by resort to classical stereotypes. What is clear is that the Huns were originally from the Eurasian steppe, they pursued a nomadic lifestyle based on horsemanship and the herding of livestock, and they lacked political cohesion at this stage. It seems that groups of Huns began raiding around the top of the Black Sea into the northern fringes of Gothic-occupied territory in the early 370s and the more northerly Gothic grouping of the Greuthungi found their prowess as mounted archers difficult to combat. After two successive Greuthungian leaders died in the ensuing encounters, their people began to retreat towards the relative safety of regions further south. Athanaric's Tervingi, who already lived further south, also began to suffer from Hunnic attacks and when his defensive measures proved inadequate, his authority was fatally compromised, and most of the Tervingi then began to move even further south under the new leadership of Alavivus and Fritigern. It was their envoys who eventually requested admission to the empire.[28]

With the benefit of hindsight, it is natural to wonder whether Valens' decision to agree to the Gothic request was sensible, but in the immediate circumstances his decision is understandable.[29] The

27. For Roman–Gothic relations during 376–8 see Heather, *Goths and Romans*, 122–47, Lenski, *Valens*, 320–67, and M. Kulikowski, *Rome's Gothic Wars from the Third Century to Alaric*, Cambridge: Cambridge University Press, 2007, 123–43.
28. For the Huns in the late fourth century, see Matthews, *Ammianus*, 332–42; for the influence of classical stereotypes about nomads, see B. D. Shaw, '"Easters of flesh and drinkers of milk": the ancient Mediterranean ideology of the pastoral nomad', *Anc. Soc.* 13–14 (1982–3), 5–31; and for the importance of not overemphasising the speed or coherence of the Hunnic advance in this period, see P. Heather, 'The Huns and the end of the Roman empire in western Europe', *English Historical Review* 110 (1995), 4–41, at 5–11.
29. As to whether the conditions of admission included Gothic conversion to (Arian)

prospect of substantial numbers of Gothic recruits for the army was a strong incentive for Valens, given that Julian's Persian expedition had incurred significant losses of troops, and Valens and Valentinian seem to have spent their reigns trying to make good those losses (a situation which will not have been helped in the east if indeed Valens' agreement with Athanaric in 369 included an end to the Gothic obligation to provide troops).[30] Moreover, since Valens was on the eastern frontier at the time and negotiations were therefore conducted at a distance, it was less easy for the emperor to appreciate just how large the number of Goths seeking admission was, although he did turn down a parallel request from the Greuthungi; at the same time, it is worth emphasising that there was a long tradition of the empire receiving such settlers in substantial numbers.[31] Nor could he have anticipated the failings of his officials in Thrace who oversaw the movement of the Tervingian Goths onto Roman territory, for it seems to have been their willingness to exploit and abuse the refugees for their own gain, by, for example, bartering dog-meat in return for the enslavement of able-bodied Goths (Amm. Marc. 31.4.11), which contributed significantly to growing discontent among the immigrants.

That discontent spilled over into open rebellion in early 377 after a clumsy attempt by the local Roman commander to engineer the murder of the leadership of the Tervingian Goths.[32] The problem was exacerbated as Gothic numbers were swelled by Greuthungian Goths who had managed to cross the Danube in large numbers, despite being denied official permission to enter the empire, because Roman frontier troops were preoccupied with supervising the Tervingian immigrants. As the year 377 progressed, the seriousness of the problem became increasingly apparent, from Gothic forces defeating local Roman units near Marcianople in the spring, to a major battle at Ad Salices in the late summer in which Roman troops, reinforced by units from both the eastern frontier and the

Christianity, see N. Lenski, 'The Gothic civil war and the date of the Gothic conversion', *GRBS* 36 (1995), 51–87 (for arguments against and references to earlier discussions).

30. Lenski, *Valens*, 307–19; N. Lenski, 'Valens and the monks: cudgeling and conscription as a means of social control', *DOP* 58 (2004), 93–117.

31. The data is conveniently assembled in G. E. M. de Ste. Croix, *The Class Struggle in the Ancient Greek World: From the Archaic Age to the Arab Conquests*, London: Duckworth, 1981, appendix 3.

32. Fritigern escaped, but since Alavivus is not heard of again, it has been plausibly assumed that he was killed or at least imprisoned (Lenski, *Valens*, 328).

west, nonetheless failed to inflict a decisive defeat on the Goths while suffering significant losses themselves.

It took some time for Valens to extract himself from his eastern commitments, but by May 378 he and a substantial number of elite military units from the east had at last reached Constantinople, where, however, he found a hostile populace unnerved by the threat of Gothic attack. He did not remain long in the capital before advancing westwards into Thrace, reaching the vicinity of Adrianople in late July. In principle, a favourable outcome to a decisive confrontation with the Goths ought not to have been in doubt. The Gothic leadership were struggling to control disparate bands of warriors who were regularly going off on uncoordinated raids, and Valens was expecting further reinforcements from the west.

At this point, however, two things happened which helped to direct events towards a different outcome. First, Valens received a message from Gratian advising that he had been delayed by an Alamannic incursion across the Rhine, but that he would join him shortly; and secondly, Valens received a report from his own skirmishers that the Gothic force in the locality numbered only about 10,000. Although some of his generals counselled caution and the wisdom of waiting for Gratian and his forces, others urged Valens to strike immediately, presumably reckoning that they already enjoyed significant numerical superiority over an enemy force of 10,000 (but evidently overlooking the fact that the dispersed character of Gothic forces meant that there were actually many more Goths in the area than this). A history of rivalry and tension between Valens and his nephew encouraged Valens to ignore Gratian's request that he wait and to side with the generals urging immediate action,[33] and on 9 August Valens and his army advanced against the Goths. By the time his troops engaged with the enemy in the afternoon they had been wearied by their lengthy march through the heat of the summer sun and of deliberately lit brushfires, while a series of deputations from Fritigern bought time for a large body of Gothic cavalry to be summoned and supplement his forces to devastating effect against the Roman cavalry. The Roman infantry fought on bravely but found itself increasingly overwhelmed, and by nightfall nearly two-thirds of the Roman troops present had been killed, along with Valens himself and many of his officers, including two

33. Lenski, *Valens*, 356–67.

senior generals: 'No battle in our history except Cannae [against Hannibal in 216 BC] was such a massacre' (Amm. Marc. 31.13.14).[34]

Just as Cannae did not spell the end of the Roman state, neither did Adrianople. As already seen (p. 25 above), a competent new emperor in the east was soon appointed in the person of Theodosius, and although the loss of two-thirds of an army was a serious blow, it was only one among a number of armies at the disposal of the empire. At the same time, it must be acknowledged that recovery from this setback was much less complete than that achieved in the late third century BC. Hannibal was eventually forced to evacuate Italy and was then decisively defeated in north Africa – events which were the prelude to Roman expansion into the eastern Mediterranean. Theodosius, on the other hand, was unable to drive the Goths back north of the Danube and was finally forced to reach an accommodation with them.

In the immediate aftermath of the battle, Gothic attempts to capture and plunder Adrianople, Perinthus and Constantinople were thwarted by Roman fortifications and the Goths' lack of expertise in undertaking sieges (Amm. Marc. 31.15–16), and additionally, in the case of the capital, by the initiative of Valens' widow Domnica in organising an impromptu militia (Socrates *Hist. eccl.* 5.1.3, Sozom. *Hist. eccl.* 7.1.2) – an intriguing glimpse into the exercise of authority by an empress about whom little is otherwise known. Goths remained in control of the Thracian countryside for some time to come, however, and the resulting disruption to east–west communications prompted Theodosius to make Thessalonica, rather than Constantinople, his base of operations for almost the first two years of his reign. His relocation to the capital in November 380 implies that some degree of security had been restored, at least in the southern Balkans, but it is also clear that Gothic forces remained a serious problem further north.[35]

---

34. For debate about the order of magnitude of Roman casualties, see Heather, *Goths and Romans*, 146–7 (minimising) and Lenski, *Valens*, 339 (more substantial). For evaluations of the significance of the battle in the late fourth century, see N. Lenski, '*Initium mali Romano imperio*: contemporary reactions to the battle of Adrianople', *TAPA* 127 (1997), 129–68.

35. In addition to written sources, archaeological survey work in the region in recent decades has revealed extensive abandonment of rural villas in the final quarter of the fourth century, consistent with the turmoil of these years: A. Poulter, 'Cataclysm on the lower Danube: the destruction of a complex Roman landscape' in N. Christie (ed.),

In the absence of a detailed narrative history of Theodosius' reign (Ammianus, understandably cautious about commenting on the reigning emperor, ended his with Adrianople), the speeches of the orator Themistius during the early years of Theodosius' reign have generally been viewed as the next best guide to changes in thinking about the Gothic problem at the imperial court and hence the nature of the problem itself. The hyperbole and circumlocutions of panegyrical language allow scope for debate about interpretation, but there does seem to be a shift from the confident assumption, in the first year or so of Theodosius' reign, that the Goths would be expelled from the empire, to a marshalling of rhetorical arguments designed to make compromise palatable – tacit acknowledgement that Theodosius, still hamstrung by the losses at Adrianople, did not have the military resources to achieve a definitive victory.[36]

That compromise was formalised in a peace settlement in October 382, the precise terms of which are, however, uncertain. As far as can be reconstructed from the unsatisfactory sources, the Goths were allowed to settle on Roman land in Thrace under their own leaders who would provide soldiers for military service when requested by the emperor – troops usually referred to as *foederati* or federates (from the Latin term *foedus*, meaning 'treaty'). As has been noted by many scholars, this implies that the Goths enjoyed a degree of autonomy not previously granted to any barbarian settlers, making this settlement one of momentous significance.[37] 'The Theodosian settlement in Thrace in effect allowed a bridgehead of *barbaricum* [barbarian territory] to be established within a Roman frontier province'[38] – which is why, although the latter half of this chapter is concerned with frontiers, it is appropriate to include comment on Roman relations with these Gothic settlers during the remaining years of Theodosius' reign.

The most important developments in those relations happened in the context of the usurpation of Eugenius in the early 390s, but first

Landscapes of Change: Rural Evolutions in Late Antiquity and the Early Middle Ages, Aldershot: Ashgate, 2004, 223–53, at 242–4.

36. P. Heather and D. Moncur, *Politics, Philosophy and Empire in the Fourth Century: Select Orations of Themistius*, Liverpool: Liverpool University Press, 2001, 199–283 (accepting corrections by Errington on various points of detail to the earlier discussion in Heather, *Goths and Romans*).

37. Jones, *LRE*, 157 (with 1099 n.46 for the sources); Heather and Moncur, *Themistius*, 255–64 (among many others).

38. Errington, *Imperial Policy*, 66.

there occurred in 386 an episode involving a different group of Goths who tried to cross the Danube into Roman territory and were turned back by Roman forces (Zos. 4.35.1, 38–39). This incident serves as a reminder that even after the events of 376–82 there remained significant numbers of Goths living north of the imperial frontiers. It also implies that eight years after Adrianople Roman military resources in the east were much further advanced down the road to recovery. As for developments around the time of Eugenius' usurpation, there is a report of fierce argument within the Gothic leadership about the merits of maintaining loyalty to the empire (Zos. 4.56), and it has been suggested that this might have been sparked by Theodosius calling on the Gothic settlers to provide contingents of federates for his western expedition against Eugenius.[39] Gothic troops certainly did participate in that expedition and, according to one source (Oros. 7.35.19), were in the front line at the decisive and hard-fought battle of the River Frigidus in 394, where they experienced heavy losses. The possibility that this might have been by deliberate design on Theodosius' part with a view to weakening the Goths has interesting potential implications for Roman–Gothic relations after 395 (pp. 110–15 below).

39. Heather, *Goths and Romans*, 181–8.

CHAPTER 3

Towards a Christian empire

Emperors and traditional cults: (1) From Jovian to Valens

Given Julian's attempts to unpick the measures of Constantine and his sons which had helped to give the church pre-eminence in the religious landscape of the mid-fourth century, it would not have been surprising if, with the return of emperors who were Christian in their allegiance (as Jovian and all his successors were), there had been a corresponding reaction by these emperors against the traditional cults whose position Julian had sought to foster and strengthen. Such a reaction, however, did not occur, or at least not for more than a decade after Julian's death. Why there was so substantial a delay is a question to which there is no easy or simple answer, but various matters considered in this chapter can contribute towards an understanding of the reasons.

Despite the brevity of Jovian's reign, there survives from it a substantial text of relevance to this subject. The orator Themistius delivered a speech at Ancyra on New Year's Day 364 in celebration of Jovian and his infant son's assuming the consulships for that year, and the theme which received the greatest attention in that speech was the importance of religious tolerance, most notably in a passage (68d–69a) whose advocacy of religious pluralism uncannily foreshadows the argument in Symmachus' better-known plea of 384 (pp. 50–1 below):

> You do not stand in the way of healthy rivalry in religious devotion and you do not blunt the keenness of enthusiasm for the divine which comes from competition and vying with one another. Everyone competing in the stadium heads for the judge awarding the prize, but they do not all take the same route. Some start in one place, others in another, and those who do not win are not completely without honour; in the same way, you understand that there is one great and truthful judge of the contest, but that there is not just one route to him – there is the route that is very difficult to

travel along and the more direct one, there is the rough route and the
level one; but they all alike converge on the one destination.

This feature of the speech has sometimes been interpreted as an
attempt by the pagan Themistius to persuade the Christian Jovian
not to instigate a backlash against those who had supported Julian's
religious policies. However, it has been persuasively argued that
Themistius was effectively acting as court spokesman, and that his
speech makes clear both that Jovian had already issued legislation
guaranteeing religious tolerance, even if the text of that legislation
has not survived, and that Jovian intended to persist with his policy
and would not be deflected by Christians advocating discrimination
against pagans.[1] As to why Jovian adopted this course of action, it
is only possible to speculate. He is known also to have adopted a
conciliatory policy towards Christian groups in disagreement with
one another (p. 43 below), so perhaps he was genuinely convinced
of the merits of toleration; or his motivation may have been more
pragmatic, arising from the realisation that the insecurity of his
political position required him to build support among as many
constituencies as possible.

Surviving glimpses of what this policy meant in practical terms
suggest that Jovian did indeed try to tread a careful middle course in
his treatment of traditional cults. In unhelpfully allusive language
Themistius (*Or.* 5.70b) reports that he was allowing temples to
remain open, but not 'haunts of imposture' (perhaps shrines associated with particularly distasteful practices such as ritual prostitution), and was permitting 'lawful sacrifices' (presumably those
involving non-blood offerings such as incense; cf. Socrates, *Hist.
eccl.* 3.24.6). The Neoplatonic philosophers Maximus and Priscus,
close associates of Julian and participants in his Persian expedition,
are known to have remained welcome at his court (Eunap. *VS*
7.4.10), but at the same time Julian's policy of restoring to temples
the lands which Constantine and his sons had confiscated was
reversed to the benefit of an imperial treasury struggling to cope

---

1. See R. M. Errington, 'Themistius and his emperors', *Chiron* 30 (2000), 861–904, at
873–8; P. Heather and D. Moncur, *Politics, Philosophy and Empire in the Fourth
Century: Select Orations of Themistius*, Liverpool: Liverpool University Press, 2001,
154–73 (including a translation of Themistius, *Oration 5*). As Errington notes, the
speech, originally delivered in Ancyra in the presence of Jovian, was repeated before the
senate in Constantinople shortly afterwards (Socrates, *Hist. eccl.* 3.26.3), so indicating
the importance Jovian placed upon its subject matter.

with the costs of military failure (*Cod. Theod.* 10.1.8).[2] Jovian is also credited with repealing Julian's notorious prohibition on Christians teaching classical literature.[3]

Jovian's general principles of toleration were for the most part espoused by Valentinian and Valens. A law of Valentinian issued in their joint names in 371 refers back to 'the laws issued by me at the start of my reign, in which everyone was granted the freedom to practise whatever religious observances they have imbibed in their minds' (*Cod. Theod.* 9.16.9), and there is corroboration of Valentinian's position by a variety of commentators, not least by Ammianus (30.9.5; cf. Symmachus, *Relat.* 3.20), who was no doubt conscious of the contrast with the policies of Theodosius I, during whose reign he completed his history:

> [Valentinian's] reign became famous for its toleration, for he took a neutral stance on matters of religious difference. He did not interfere with anyone by ordering this or that cult to be worshipped, and he did not force his subjects by means of threatening decrees to adopt his own religious observances. Rather, he allowed the different cults to remain undisturbed as he found them.

Within this framework, there were some restrictions on rituals, notably maintenance of the ban on blood sacrifice (Lib. *Or.* 30.7), but the construction of temples continued during the brothers' reigns, as did the initiation of pagan priests into mystery cults.[4] As with Jovian, it is only possible to speculate about motivation. Valentinian is known to have regarded church affairs as an area lying for the most part outside his competence (p. 43 below), so it is possible that this informed his view of religious policy more generally. Valens might then be supposed to have been following his brother's lead with regard to traditional cults – except that, as will become apparent (p. 44 below), he did not feel any obligation to do so in his dealings with ecclesiastical matters. Perhaps therefore it was ultimately again a question of pragmatism: the need to win support

2. This may also explain why, in restoring Constantine's grain subsidies to churches which Julian has revoked, Jovian did so only to a third of their former level (Theodoret, *Hist. eccl.* 4.4).
3. *Cod. Theod.* 13.3.6. For plausible arguments attributing this measure to the early months of Valentinian and Valens' reigns, however, see R. M. Errington, *Roman Imperial Policy from Julian to Theodosius*, Chapel Hill: University of North Carolina Press, 2006, 293 n.10.
4. N. Lenski, *Failure of Empire: Valens and the Roman State in the Fourth Century* A.D., Berkeley: University of California Press, 2002, 211–18.

for the new regime in both west and east dictated that neither risk alienating significant interest groups – unless they felt their position was directly threatened.

Such a situation arose in the early 370s, when vigorous action was taken by the brothers to suppress magical practices, notably among the senatorial aristocracy in Rome and members of the bureaucratic elite in the eastern provinces, especially in Antioch. In his detailed accounts of these episodes, Ammianus emphasises the pervasive fear which these investigations engendered, not least because of the wide-spread use of torture (28.1, 29.1–2). What is also apparent, however, is that the emperors acted in this way not out of religious concerns, but because of the long-standing links between magic and treason, illustrated most clearly by the incident which triggered imperial action in Antioch – the use of magical technology (a sort of Ouija board) to reveal the name of Valens' successor. Ironically, the answer, although misinterpreted at the time, in retrospect apparently confirmed the efficacy of the technique, since it indicated someone whose name began with the letters 'Theod-' (Amm. Marc. 29.1.32).[5]

Emperors and church in the later fourth century

It is symptomatic of the extent to which affairs of state and church had become intertwined since the reign of Constantine that bishops were the first individuals to lobby the new Emperor Jovian, when he had scarcely had time to catch his breath after concluding peace with Persia. This is unsurprising in the immediate context of Julian's reign: Constantius had exiled many eastern bishops who were out of sympathy with his semi-Arian, Homoian stance (p. 8 above), and when Julian allowed most of them to return, considerable strife in church affairs was inevitable. As early as September 363, while passing through northern Mesopotamia and Syria from the eastern frontier, Jovian was approached at Edessa by two Anomoian bishops from western Anatolia seeking his support (Philostorgius, *Hist. eccl.* 8.6). The highest-profile advocate of Nicene Homoousian ortho-doxy, Athanasius of Alexandria, had – in a predictable exception to Julian's general policy – been exiled by that emperor, and Athanasius duly intercepted Jovian later that month at Hierapolis seeking

5. Valens' actions against Julian's Neoplatonic supporters, Maximus, Priscus and Oribasius, ought likewise to be viewed as politically, rather than religiously, motivated: cf. Lenski, *Valens*, 107–13, 226–7.

imperial sanction for his return (Athanasius, *Festal Index* 35). At some unspecified point in Jovian's progress towards Antioch, a group of moderate Homoiousian Arian bishops also petitioned him for support against their ecclesiastical opponents (Socrates, *Hist. eccl.* 3.25). In Antioch itself Lucius, Athanasius' Homoian rival in Alexandria, doggedly sought on four occasions to gain the emperor's favour (*PG* 26.820–4 [= Coleman-Norton no. 124]).[6] However, while Jovian did sanction Athanasius' restoration (*PG* 26.813 [= Coleman-Norton no. 125]) and repeatedly rejected Lucius' attempts to reverse that decision, the new emperor's overall guiding principle was epitomised by his response to the Homoiousian bishops: 'For my part, I detest contentiousness, but I love and honour those who are partisans of unanimity' (Socrates, *Hist. eccl.* 3.25) – a sentiment consistent with the policy promoted through Themistius' speech at Ancyra on 1 January 364 (pp. 39–40 above).[7]

Whether Jovian would have been able to sustain an even-handed policy in the long term must remain doubtful, although the relief of church leaders at Julian's unexpected demise may have created a unique opportunity for greater progress than might otherwise have been expected.[8] In the event, the accessions of Valentinian and Valens created a new and more complex scenario. To be sure, as already noted (p. 41 above), Valentinian gained a reputation for neutrality in religious matters, and by and large this extended to church disputes. When he too was accosted in the early days of his reign by bishops seeking imperial support, he responded that 'I am but one of the laity and so have no right to interfere in these matters' (Sozom. *Hist. eccl.* 6.7.2; cf. 6.21.7). However, since the Nicene position had found wider support in the west than east, Valentinian's half of the empire was less prone to ecclesiastical disputes, which made it both easier and more feasible for him to distance himself from involvement in church affairs without risking instability.[9]

6. For doubts about the authenticity of this text, see A. Martin, *Athanase d'Alexandrie et l'église d'Égypte au IVe siècle (328–373)*, Rome: École française de Rome, 1996, 588–9.
7. For further discussion of Jovian's dealings with bishops, see T. D. Barnes, *Athanasius and Constantius*, Cambridge, MA: Harvard University Press, 1993, 159–60, and Lenski, *Valens*, 237–8.
8. Cf. the willingness to shift their theological stance on the part of the semi-Arian, Homoian Meletius and his fellow bishops in response to Jovian's emphasis on unanimity: Socrates, *Hist. eccl.* 3.25.
9. For further discussion of Valentinian's dealings with bishops, see Lenski, *Valens*, 234–42; D. Hunt, 'Valentinian and the bishops' in J. den Boeft et al. (eds), *Ammianus after Julian*, Leiden: Brill, 2009, 71–93.

Valens, on the other hand, faced a much less doctrinally homo-geneous situation in the east which he failed to handle with any great success. His own sympathies lay with the Homoian position and this brought him into conflict at various points with Nicene supporters, whose number included such formidable figures as Athanasius of Alexandria and Basil of Caesarea. Valens did not adopt a consist-ently aggressive line against Nicene churches, notably during Procopius' revolt when pragmatism necessarily prevailed, but he was prepared to resort to force on occasions, particularly in Egypt after Athanasius' death in 373. As Valens set out from Antioch for Thrace in the spring of 378, he again relented and allowed exiled Nicene bishops to return to their sees, a move which, following Valens' death at Adrianople, left them in a stronger position to press their case – reinforced by the belief that Valens' fate was divine judgement on his ecclesiastical policies.[10]

The accession of Theodosius in January 379 has long been seen as marking a fundamental turning-point in the theological orientation of the eastern half of the empire, with the new emperor often portrayed as the uncompromising champion of Nicene orthodoxy from the outset (not least by the church historians writing a gener-ation or two later). This view has been informed by a number of considerations: first, Theodosius' origin in the west has been regarded as significant for the strength of his allegiance to the Nicene cause; and secondly, Theodosius' issuing of two laws early in his reign which gave clear expression to his support for the Nicene cause in the east has contributed to the image of a proactive intervention-ist. The first of these laws (*Cod. Theod.* 16.1.2) was promulgated on 28 February 380 and expressed the desire that all those under his rule should adhere to the theological principles approved by Damasus, the current bishop of Rome, and by Peter, the current bishop of Alexandria, to the effect that all three members of the Trinity were equal, while also promising divine judgement and imperial punishment for any who continued to adhere to heretical dogma. The second law (*Cod. Theod.* 16.1.3), issued on 30 July 381, required all church buildings to be surrendered to bishops who supported the Nicene position.

There can be no doubting that, from a panoramic perspective,

---

10. For Valens' interventions in church affairs, see Lenski, *Valens*, 242–63, with impor-tant discussion of Valens' recall of exiled bishops in 378 in R. M. Errington, 'Church and state in the first years of Theodosius I', *Chiron* 27 (1997), 21–70, at 26–33.

Theodosius' reign proved to be of enormous importance for the evolving theological complexion of the east. However, recent reconsiderations of the finer detail of his background and of events during the early years of his reign have given good grounds for qualifying and nuancing the traditional image of Theodosius in important respects. First, with regard to the significance of his Spanish origins, it has been noted that, in view of his father's military career, Theodosius is likely to have spent his formative years, not in Spain, but in military camps, which is the context in which clues to his theological formation need to be sought.[11] Whether this then warrants downplaying his familiarity with the theological cross-currents of the period is, however, much less certain, since even the uneducated laity showed an interest in such matters in the fourth century,[12] while Theodosius' contemporary, Magnus Maximus, provides an example of another military man from the west who had very definite views on doctrinal controversies (see p. 47 below). While accepting that his Spanish origin had less influence on his doctrinal affiliation than is usually assumed, therefore, there is less reason to think that Theodosius was uncommitted to the Nicene cause at the time of his accession.

This is not to say, however, that his initial residence in Thessalonica during 379 and 380 was unimportant for what followed, above all because it exposed him to the influence of that city's bishop, Acholius, whom recent studies have identified as an important figure at Theodosius' court in this early phase. Despite being bishop of an eastern city, Acholius' allegiances lay with the Nicene west, especially the bishop of Rome, who, significantly, received specific mention in the first of Theodosius' laws.[13] The importance of that law of February 380 has, however, also been de-emphasised in various ways, in particular by underlining that it was addressed specifically to the inhabitants of Constantinople, and by pointing out that Theodosius took no steps to carry out its threat of punishment

11. N. B. McLynn, 'Genere Hispanus: Theodosius, Spain and Nicene orthodoxy' in K. Bowes and M. Kulikowski (eds), Hispania in Late Antiquity, Leiden: Brill, 2005, 77–120, at 100–8.
12. A. D. Lee, War in Late Antiquity: A Social History, Oxford: Blackwell, 2007, 202–3.
13. N. B. McLynn, Ambrose of Milan: Church and Court in a Christian Capital, Berkeley: University of California Press, 1994, 106–9; Errington, 'Church and state', 33, 37; E. D. Hunt, 'Imperial law or councils of the church? Theodosius I and the imposition of doctrinal uniformity' in K. Cooper and J. Gregory (eds), Discipline and Diversity, Woodbridge: Boydell, 2007 (= SCH 43), 57–68, at 58.

against heretics.[14] Indeed, when Theodosius eventually moved to Constantinople in November 380 he very promptly summoned the popular Homoian bishop of the city, Demophilus, and gave him the chance to remain in post if he would adhere to the Nicene position (Socrates, *Hist. eccl.* 5.7.3–11) – which suggests that in the interim he had come to appreciate that there was also a role for tactful diplomacy in church affairs.

Demophilus, however, rejected Theodosius' proposal and withdrew outside the city walls with his supporters, whereupon Theodosius appointed as bishop the (relatively recently arrived) leader of the Nicene community, Gregory of Nazianzus. Theodosius followed this up by calling a general church council in Constantinople from May 381 to approve Gregory's appointment and affirm the Nicene faith – a significant move on his part, given that this was the first imperially sponsored council for more than two decades.[15] Since the 150 bishops who attended were predominantly Nicene, with some moderate Homoiousian Arians, it can hardly be viewed as fully representative of opinion among Christian leadership in the east, but it did show that Theodosius recognised the importance of being seen to consult, rather than simply imposing measures by imperial fiat. Moreover, when the council queried the legitimacy of Gregory's election on the grounds that it contravened one of the canons of the Council of Nicaea (325),[16] Theodosius accepted Gregory's resignation, and subsequent developments showed a continuing willingness on his part to try to facilitate episcopal consensus, even if the overall direction was now inexorably towards Nicene uniformity.[17] At the same time, it is worth noting that one of the council's canons helped to prepare the way for future dissension. In declaring that 'the bishop of Constantinople shall have the primacy of honour after the bishop of Rome, because Constantinople is the new Rome' (Canon 3), the council provoked resentment in Alexandria, which had long been accustomed to being the pre-eminent see in the east,

---

14. McLynn, '*Genere Hispanus*', 79–88; Errington, *Imperial Policy*, 218.
15. An important point highlighted by Hunt, 'Imperial law', 61.
16. Specifically that individuals appointed bishop in one place could not subsequently become bishop somewhere else (Canon 15); Gregory had previously (and, it seems, unwillingly) been consecrated bishop of one of the less important sees in his native Cappadocia.
17. See Hunt, 'Imperial law', for further detail and argument on the theme of consensus, to which might be added Theodosius' appointment of Nectarius to be Gregory's replacement as bishop of Constantinople, since Nectarius proved adept at winning over anti-Nicene parties in the city.

and unhappiness in Rome, since it implied that its primacy derived from the city's secular standing rather than its apostolic heritage.

It is tempting to contrast Theodosius' relatively flexible dealings with Arians with the behaviour of the usurper Magnus Maximus in the west in the mid-380s (p. 26 above) when confronted by the Priscillianist controversy, although the latter was admittedly a novel phenomenon whose possible Manichaean elements were bound to provoke an uncompromising reaction. Priscillian was a well-born Spanish layman who attracted a following in the 370s through his advocacy of extreme ascetic practices. He also had his critics within the church because some of the practices he espoused were vulnerable to the charge of having Manichaean overtones, notably his rejection of marriage and his promotion of vegetarianism (p. 9 above), and because his adherents included a suspiciously high proportion of females. Initially his opponents tried to have him disciplined through regular church channels and then by appeal to officials at the court of the Emperor Gratian, but when that ultimately failed, it looked as though all possibilities had been exhausted. However, when Gratian was unexpectedly overthrown by Maximus in 383, Priscillian's chief opponent appealed to the new emperor to intervene in the case.

The eventual upshot of a complex sequence of events was that Priscillian was tried by a secular court in Trier, condemned for magic, and executed, along with a number of his closest associates. Although the charge of magic suggests that the case might have been viewed by the imperial authorities in a manner analogous to the magic trials instigated by Valentinian and Valens (p. 42 above), it is less easy to see how Priscillian and his associates could have been regarded as a potential political threat in the way that senatorial aristocrats in Rome or imperial officials in Antioch might have been, and in a subsequent letter to Siricius, bishop of Rome, Maximus defended his action as that of a godly ruler concerned to uphold orthodoxy against the insidious threat of heresy (which, interestingly, he refers to as Manichaean) (*Coll. Avell.* 40 [= Coleman-Norton no. 203]).[18]

---

18. There is a substantial literature on the Priscillianist controversy. For his writings see M. Conti, *Priscillian of Avila: The Complete Works*, Oxford: Oxford University Press, 2010. Helpful discussions include J. Matthews, *Western Aristocracies and Imperial Court, AD 364–425*, Oxford: Clarendon Press, 1975, 160–71, H. Chadwick, *Priscillian of Avila: The Occult and the Charismatic in the Early Church*, Oxford: Clarendon Press, 1976, and V. Burrus, *The Making of a Heretic: Gender, Authority, and the Priscillianist*

Although, as already noted, there was much less sympathy for any of the non-Nicene stances among bishops in the west, there were occasional disputes, including a famous episode involving the forceful pro-Nicene bishop of Milan, Ambrose, in 386. Ambrose's predecessor as bishop of Milan had been Auxentius, a Homoian who had been appointed in the final years of Constantius' reign, and so there was an established non-Nicene presence in that city. After Gratian's death in 383, the residence of Valentinian II there assumed much greater significance, with his mother Justina championing the Homoian cause. The culmination of the ensuing confrontation between Justina and Ambrose occurred during Easter 386 when Ambrose resisted the attempt of imperial troops, enforcing a law issued earlier that year (*Cod. Theod.* 16.1.4), to take control of one of the Milanese churches for use by Homoian Christians. Ambrose pre-empted the troops by staging a tense 'sit-in' with some of his congregation, their morale bolstered by the innovation of singing hymns (a long-standing feature of church services in the eastern half of the empire).[19] The sources for this episode and the events leading up to it present many problems of interpretation, and it has been argued that the fundamental issue was not so much control of church buildings as the desire of the Empress Justina to drive Ambrose out of Milan completely.[20] If that was her aim, then she did not succeed, being forced rather to flee Milan herself the following year when Maximus advanced from Gaul into northern Italy.

However, while no subsequent emperor ever showed any sympathy towards any of the doctrinal positions associated with Arian views, Arianism continued to exercise an influence as late as the sixth century, most obviously because various barbarian groups who settled in the empire adopted an Arian form of Christianity, most notably the Goths and the Vandals (p. 33 n.29 above). Arian Christianity enjoyed a significant afterlife as the religion both of the ruling elites of barbarian kingdoms which emerged in the west

Controversy, Berkeley: University of California Press, 1995. T. D. Barnes, 'Religion and society in the age of Theodosius' in H. A. Meynell (ed.), *Grace, Politics and Desire: Essays on Augustine*, Calgary: University of Calgary Press, 1990, 157–75, makes the important suggestion (at 163) that Priscillian's consecration as a bishop was invalid and that he was therefore tried as a layman.
19. Ambrose, *Ep.* 76, August. *Conf.* 9.7.15.
20. This is the argument of W. Liebeschuetz, *Ambrose of Milan: Political Letters and Speeches*, Liverpool: Liverpool University Press, 2005, 124–36. For other discussions, see McLynn, *Ambrose*, 158–208; J. Moorhead, *Ambrose: Church and Society in the Late Roman World*, London: Longman, 1999, 132–50.

during the fifth century and of barbarian soldiers serving, sometimes at very high levels, in the imperial armies of the east (pp. 98 and 187–9 below).

Emperors and traditional cults: (2) From Gratian to Theodosius I

It would have been cause for surprise if, on the death of his father in November 375, the sixteen-year-old Gratian had been quick to initiate any major change from Valentinian's broad policy of toleration towards traditional cults. It was nonetheless during his reign, albeit not for some years yet, that the first significant discriminatory measures against them were taken since before the reign of Julian. The sources are imprecise about their timing, but 382 or 383 are the most likely dates. They comprised two elements:[21] removal of the Altar of Victory from the senate house in Rome, and termination of payments from the imperial treasury for the maintenance of traditional priesthoods and their ceremonies in Rome, including the Vestal Virgins. Both were essentially symbolic gestures, but no less significant for that. The altar dedicated to the divine personification of victory had a long history, having been placed in the senate house by the Emperor Augustus in 29 BC, and the offerings of incense and wine on it at the start of senate sessions were no doubt seen by many as guarantees of the empire's continued military success. Although the effective 'disestablishment' of traditional cults and their personnel in Rome might appear to be a more practical measure, the real issue was not money but the severing of the link between the state and its gods. Certainly, these measures provoked a reaction from pagan senators in Rome, who sent a delegation to protest to Gratian in Milan, but to no avail.

Gratian's willingness to take these actions must relate to the relocation of his court from Trier to northern Italy in the early 380s, although not necessarily because that brought him within the orbit of Ambrose – the latter later denied any role (Ambrose, *Ep.* 10.2).

---

21. A third element has usually been associated with these measures, namely Gratian's renunciation of the ancient office of chief priest (*pontifex maximus*); however, it has long been recognised that the sole source for this (Zos. 4.36) is problematic, while more recently it has been highlighted that a number of fifth-century emperors bore the title *pontifex inclitus*, prompting the attractive argument that what Gratian did was to modify the title and reinterpret the role in a Christian sense, as sanctioning the emperor's authority in church affairs: Alan Cameron, 'The imperial pontifex', *Harv. Stud.* 103 (2007), 341–84.

Rather, it is likely to have been the way in which this move exposed Gratian to more persistent lobbying by prominent Christians from Rome.[22] Since the removal of the altar from the senate house would have to be carried out by the prefect of Rome, it has been plausibly suggested that a Christian incumbent of that office proposed the measure to the emperor – with two credible candidates in post during 382 and 383.[23]

Two developments, however, gave the issue a new lease of life: first, Gratian's death in the summer of 383 left as emperor in Italy Valentinian II, still only twelve years old; and secondly, the office of prefect of Rome passed in the summer of 384 to a respected pagan, Quintus Aurelius Symmachus, who was prepared to use his office and the change of emperor to try to effect a reversal of Gratian's decisions concerning the altar and state subsidies. The instrument through which he attempted to do so was his famous third *Relatio* (an official memorandum from prefect to emperor) in which he made a measured appeal to the emperor for religious tolerance, evoking a personification of Rome requesting respect for her traditions, and arguing for religious pluralism in the following memorable lines:

> We request peace for the gods of our forefathers, for our patron deities. Whatever each person worships, it is reasonable to think of them as one. We see the same stars, the sky is shared by all, the same world surrounds us. What does it matter what wisdom a person uses to seek for the truth? It is not possible to attain to so sublime a mystery by one route alone. (Symmachus, *Relat.* 3.10)

On this occasion there is no doubt about Ambrose's role in the outcome. The son of a praetorian prefect and himself the governor of north-western Italy prior to his unexpected election as bishop of Milan in 374, Ambrose was well equipped to engage in court politics, which Valentinian's residence in Milan in 384 gave him the opportunity to do. When Ambrose's contacts alerted him to the arrival and nature of Symmachus' missive, Ambrose fired off an immediate rebuttal, followed by a second, more detailed response after he had seen a copy of the text (*Epp.* 72–3).[24] His background

---

22. McLynn, *Ambrose*, 151; Alan Cameron, *The Last Pagans of Rome*, Oxford: Oxford University Press, 2011, 35–6.

23. Errington, *Imperial Policy*, 200, suggesting Anicius Auchenius Bassus; but his predecessor Valerius Severus is also possible if Gratian acted in 382.

24. It seems, however, that Valentinian decided to turn down Symmachus' request after receiving the first of Ambrose's rejoinders: McLynn, *Ambrose*, 167.

and education meant that he was more than able to counter Symmachus' arguments with his own fluent rhetoric, but he also had no qualms about pressing the thirteen-year-old emperor with thinly veiled threats, such as the following from his initial response:

> If this were a dispute in the law courts, there would be an opportunity for the other party to respond. It is a dispute about religion, so I as bishop claim that right. Let a copy of the memorandum sent be given to me, so that I too may respond more fully, and when Your Clemency's kinsman [Theodosius] has been consulted on all points, he may see fit to give a response. Certainly, if something different is decided, we bishops cannot endure it with equanimity and disguise our dissatisfaction. You may come to church, but you will not find this bishop there, or you will find him unco-operative. (Ambrose, *Ep.* 72.13)

In the light of this sort of approach, it is unsurprising that Symmachus' request was dismissed by the emperor and his advisers.[25]

Given the importance of Ambrose's intervention in this episode, it is worth considering why he was so determined to block Symmachus' request, which, to those living in modern pluralistic societies, seems perfectly reasonable. Important clues are contained in an early section of Ambrose's initial response (*Ep.* 72.4). First, he refers to past pagan persecution of Christians which resulted in death and in destruction of church buildings – most obviously an allusion to the Diocletianic persecution of the first decade of the fourth century – and effectively brands pagans now advocating the merits of tolerance as hypocrites. Secondly, he makes specific reference to Julian's law against Christians teaching classical literature as a prime example of pagan intolerance; this measure clearly rankled – Ambrose would have been in his early twenties when it was issued – and his reference to it is an important indication of the long-term repercussions of Julian's polarising of the religious landscape. Thirdly, Ambrose refers to significant numbers of Christians having lapsed, a problem corroborated by a series of laws from the early 380s imposing significant penalties on anyone apostatising

25. For further discussion, see Matthews, *Western Aristocracies*, 203–11; Cameron, *Last Pagans*, 39–51. It has been suggested that the most important factor in Ambrose's success was actually the debt Valentinian owed him for his undertaking an embassy to Magnus Maximus in Gaul in the final months of the previous year which effectively forestalled Maximus' invading northern Italy at that time (McLynn, *Ambrose*, 167, with discussion of Ambrose's embassy at 158–64). Errington, *Imperial Policy*, 203–4, argues that the importance of the episode has been exaggerated by Ambrose.

from Christianity (*Cod. Theod.* 16.7.1–3).[26] It would appear, then,
that Ambrose's uncompromising attitude in 384 was motivated by a
determination to minimise any possibility of another pagan revival.

Meanwhile in the east, Theodosius' preoccupation with ecclesiastical controversies seems to have deflected him from any concerns
about traditional cults. Indeed, a law from 382 (*Cod. Theod.*
16.10.8), while reiterating the prohibition on sacrifice, stipulated
that a major temple in the province of Osrhoene was to remain open
so that the public could appreciate the artistic qualities of its cult
statues. The need for such a law, however, hints at growing pressure
from some Christian quarters to take more active steps against focal
points of traditional cults, corroborated by a speech of the pagan
teacher of rhetoric, Libanius, from the mid-380s in which he
criticised groups of Christian monks for taking matters into their
own hands and destroying rural shrines in the hinterland of Antioch
(*Or.* 30). In making his attack, Libanius was careful to emphasise
his presumption that these actions did not have the approval of
emperor, but he did refer to the collusion of an unnamed imperial
official. That official has often been assumed to be the praetorian
prefect Maternus Cynegius, who is named in other sources (e.g.,
Zos. 4.37.3) as responsible for the destruction of pagan shrines in
the eastern provinces during his tenure of office (384–8). Cynegius'
reputation as a religious vandal may, however, have a less secure
basis than has usually been taken for granted.[27]

Nonetheless, in 391 Theodosius did issue more unequivocal pronouncements which not only reiterated the prohibition on sacrifice
but now also banned access to temples (*Cod. Theod.* 16.10.10–11)
– measures which have traditionally been seen as marking a significant step in the discarding of the pagan past and the evolution of a
Christian empire. That view has not always given sufficient weight
to certain limiting features of these two laws – the fact that they were
directed specifically to officials in the cities of Rome and Alexandria,

---

26. See Cameron, *Last Pagans*, 793–7, for a different interpretation of the evidence for
'apostasy' from Christianity (namely, Christians assuming provincial priesthoods which
no longer involved pagan rituals but were tainted with pagan associations).
27. See the ingenious arguments of McLynn, '*Genere Hispanus*', 108–19. Libanius
(*Or.* 30.26–9) warned that violence was likely to be counterproductive and that any
conversions would be 'apparent, not real'. For the progress of Christianisation in regions
of the later fourth-century west, see C. Stancliffe, *St Martin and his Hagiographer*,
Oxford: Clarendon Press, 1983, 328–40; M. Humphries, *Communities of the Blessed:
Social Environment and Religious Change in Northern Italy*, AD 200–400, Oxford:
Oxford University Press, 1999, chs 6–7.

Figure 2 Ivory leaf (29.8 × 12.2 cm) (c. 400) depicting a priestess before an altar, sprinkling incense on a flame, with an attendant. The panel is half of a diptych, whose partner is in Paris. The pair has long been interpreted as celebrating a marriage between two aristocratic families, the Symmachi and the Nicomachi, but on more recent interpretations it may actually be marking a funeral, perhaps that of the famous Symmachus. © Victoria and Albert Museum, London

and the way in which the laws do not specify penalties for anyone other than imperial officials.[28] More significant, in fact, was a third law issued the following year (*Cod. Theod.* 16.10.12 [392]) which introduced a comprehensive ban on all forms of pagan worship – not just animal sacrifice, but also other expressions such as the offering of incense and libations of wine (cf. Fig. 2).[29]

Although any direct link with the second law (to Alexandrian officials) is tenuous, an episode in Alexandria later in 391 or early 392 has certainly encouraged a sense that the tide was turning ever more strongly against pagans during Theodosius' final years. When workmen renovating a basilica for church use uncovered some

28. Since the second of the laws was issued from Milan, where Theodosius resided from 388 to 391 after his suppression of Maximus, there has also been an understandable inclination to assume that it reflects Ambrose's influence, but this possibility has found less favour in recent studies: McLynn, *Ambrose*, 331–3; Cameron, *Last Pagans*, 63–4.
29. See Cameron, *Last Pagans*, 59–74, for arguments minimising the significance even of this measure.

underground chambers containing pagan cult objects which the
bishop of Alexandria then paraded through the streets in a
triumphalist manner, pagan elements in the population reacted
angrily, and major bouts of street-fighting between Christians and
pagans ensued. The latter eventually withdrew to the precinct of
the temple of Serapis, a renowned shrine situated on an elevated
position in the south-western part of the city. When it became clear
to the city authorities that these pagans would only vacate the
precinct under compulsion, advice was sought from Constantinople
as to how to proceed. The eventual imperial response ruled that no
vengeance was to be exacted against those pagans who had killed
Christians during the street-fighting (whom one Christian source
refers to as martyrs), but that the root causes of the disturbance – the
pagan cults themselves – were to be destroyed. On the strength of
this, Roman troops occupied the temple precinct, pulled down
the superstructure of the temple, and broke up the magnificent cult
statue of Serapis, the wooden portions of which were then burned
in public places around the city. Theodosius also instructed that
precious metals from this and other cult objects were to be melted
down for uses which would benefit the poor of the city. Such was the
fame of the Alexandrian Serapeum that this episode was seen as epit-
omising the hardening of imperial policy towards pagans and the
terminal decline of pagan cults, even though pagan practices were to
continue in various forms, albeit less visible, for a long time to come
(see pp. 150–3 below), and even though the violence associated
with this episode owed much more to local conditions than to the
initiative of the emperor.[30]

Emperors and Jews in the later fourth century

One of the most famous episodes involving the Emperor Theodosius
and Ambrose occurred in 388 when a band of Christians, led by
their bishop, plundered and burnt down the synagogue in the
frontier town of Callinicum on the Euphrates. When a local official

---

30. The major ancient accounts are Rufinus, *Hist. eccl.* 11.22–3; Socrates, *Hist. eccl.*
5.16–17 (who includes the detail about the proceeds of the recycled cult objects);
Sozomen, *Hist. eccl.* 7.15; Eunap. *VS* 6.11.1–7. Modern discussions include C. Haas,
Alexandria in Late Antiquity, Baltimore; Johns Hopkins University Press, 1997, 159–69;
Errington, *Imperial Policy*, 249–51, 309 n.109 (on the chronology). For the surviving
material evidence of the temple, see J. S. McKenzie, S. Gibson and A. T. Reyes, 'Recon-
structing the Serapeum in Alexandria from the archaeological evidence', *JRS* 94 (2004),
73–121.

referred the matter to Theodosius, recently arrived in northern Italy after his campaign against Maximus, the emperor responded by ordering that those responsible should be tried and punished, while the bishop was to see to the rebuilding of the synagogue out of his own pocket. When Ambrose learned of this and protested at Jews being shown favour over Christians, Theodosius rescinded the penalty on the bishop, and then when Ambrose continued to complain, the emperor eventually agreed to drop the whole case (Ambrose, *Ep.* 74, *Ep. extra coll.* 1).

This episode has usually received most attention for what it implies (or may not) about the relationship between emperor and bishop.[31] However, it also has important implications for the position of Jews in an increasingly Christian empire. Despite the brutal suppression of two revolts in Judaea in the first and second centuries and of the more widespread one in the eastern provinces during the reign of Trajan (115–17), Jews remained a significant presence in the empire's wider population and otherwise continued to be treated reasonably well by the Roman government into the fourth century.[32] The advent of Christian emperors did see the introduction of some new discriminatory measures during the first half of the fourth century, but these related only to Jewish ownership and treatment of slaves (*Cod. Theod.* 16.9.1–2). Julian's short reign, on the other hand, was disproportionately significant in heightening tensions between Jews and Christians. His emphasis on the common ground between pagan and Jewish ritual, and his attempt to have the temple in Jerusalem rebuilt with a view to winning Jewish support and scoring ideological points against Christianity (cf. Amm. Marc. 22.5.3–4, Sozom. *Hist. eccl.* 5.5.7), gave Christian polemicists plenty of anti-Jewish ammunition in the decades that followed.[33] As the Callinicum episode indicates, that polemic could sometimes inspire physical violence against synagogues which, since the destruction of the temple by Titus, had become the focal point of Jewish communities (Ambrose refers to an almost contemporaneous incident of

31. For readings which shift the emphasis away from episcopal dominance, see McLynn, *Ambrose*, 298–309; Moorhead, *Ambrose*, 185–92.
32. For the difficulties in arriving at even approximate figures for the number of Jews in the Roman world, see B. McGing, 'Population and proselytism: how many Jews were there in the ancient world?' in J. R. Bartlett (ed.), *Jews in the Hellenistic and Roman Cities*, London: Routledge, 2002, 88–106.
33. See, e.g., R. L. Wilken, *John Chrysostom and the Jews: Rhetoric and Reality in the Late 4th Century*, Berkeley: University of California Press, 1983.

the same kind in Rome: *Ep.* 74.23). Matters were not helped by the fact that the behaviour of some Jews towards Christians was not always blameless: Constantine had had to legislate against Jews attacking Jewish converts to Christianity (*Cod. Theod.* 16.8.1, 5), Jews had apparently joined in pagan attacks on church buildings during Julian's reign (Ambrose, *Ep.* 74.15), and the attack on the synagogue in Callinicum may have been triggered by Jews insulting monks (Paulinus, *V. Ambrosii* 22).

Christian–Jewish relations in this period, however, were not characterised solely by animosity. It is apparent from a series of sermons delivered by John Chrysostom in Antioch in the mid-380s that some Christians found elements of Judaism very attractive, particularly festivals and some rituals, prompting grave concerns about the prospect of Christians converting to Judaism.[34] An imperial law of 383 directed at Christians apostatising to Judaism provides corroboration (*Cod. Theod.* 16.7.3).[35] What is striking about the decades after Julian, however, is the way in which imperial policy continued for the most part to protect the interests of Jews. To be sure, Theodosius did penalise intermarriage between Christians and Jews (*Cod. Theod.* 3.8.2 = 9.7.5 [388]), but in another law of 393 (so after the Callinicum episode) he reiterated that 'the sect of the Jews is prohibited by no law', and that they should therefore have the freedom to assemble, without their synagogues being subject to attack by Christians (*Cod. Theod.* 16.8.9). Whether out of respect for the antiquity of Judaism or concern for public order, the Jews were evidently viewed by emperors in the later fourth century as less of a concern than heterodox Christians and pagans.[36]

34. Wilken, *Chrysostom and the Jews*, 66–94.
35. There are also a number of epitaphs for Jewish converts, although they can only be dated broadly to the fourth century and do not necessarily refer to converts from Christianity: D. Noy, *Jewish Inscriptions of Western Europe*, Cambridge: Cambridge University Press, 1993–5, 2.62, 577.
36. For a convenient collection of the texts of the laws, with translation and commentary, see A. Linder, *The Jews in Roman Imperial Legislation*, Detroit: Wayne State University Press, 1987. For good discussions of the position of Jews in the fourth and early fifth century, see the two papers by F. Millar, 'The Jews of the Graeco-Roman diaspora between paganism and Christianity, AD 312–438' in J. Lieu et al. (eds), *The Jews among Pagans and Christians*, London: Routledge, 1992, 97–123, and 'Christian emperors, Christian church, and the Jews of the diaspora in the Greek east, AD 379–450', *Journal of Jewish Studies* 55 (2004), 1–24 (both reprinted in F. Millar, *Rome, the Greek World and the East* vol. 3, Chapel Hill: University of North Carolina Press, 2006, 432–56, 457–86).

CHAPTER 4

Old Rome, new Rome

The city of Rome in the later fourth century

It is one of the paradoxes of the history of the late Roman empire that emperors rarely spent time in the city of Rome.[1] From the mid-third century, military imperatives dictated that they base themselves near the frontiers, with only occasional visits to Rome, and this pattern continued during the fourth century. The only emperor definitely known to have visited the city between 363 and 395 was Theodosius, who spent two and a half months there in 389 celebrating his suppression of Magnus Maximus. It is possible that he made a second visit, in late 394, and Valentinian II may also briefly have come to the city on one occasion, but even if they did, the overall pattern remains clear.[2] The absence of a sustained imperial presence over many decades could not fail to affect the city in a variety of ways (pp. 61–2 below), but the weight of history ensured that it retained enormous symbolic significance in the wider context of the empire. The historian Ammianus regularly referred to it as 'the eternal city',[3] and when Ausonius, a Gallic rhetorician who gained political prominence under the Emperor Gratian, came to write a poetic ranking of the empire's cities, there was no question as

1. In addition to the various studies referred to below, note also the helpful introductory overview by B. Lançon, *Rome in Late Antiquity* (tr. A. Nevill), Edinburgh: Edinburgh University Press, 2000.
2. Valentinian II is reported to have been heading for Rome by sea in 388 in the context of Theodosius' campaign against Maximus (Zos. 4.45.4, with F. Paschoud, *Zosime: Histoire nouvelle*, II.2, Paris: Budé, 1979, 441–2), and Theodosius is said to have visited Rome in late 394 (Zos. 4.59 with Alan Cameron, 'Theodosius the Great and the regency of Stilicho', *Harv. Stud.* 73 (1969), 247–80, at 248–64). For scepticism about Theodosius' second visit, see, e.g., F. Paschoud, *Cinq études sur Zosime*, Paris: Belles lettres, 1975, 100–24. A possible visit by Gratian in 376 has been discounted: for the debate, see T. D. Barnes, 'Ambrose and Gratian', *AnTard* 7 (1999), 165–74, at 168 n.17.
3. J. Matthews, 'Ammianus and the eternity of Rome' in C. Holdsworth and T. P. Wiseman (eds), *The Inheritance of Historiography, 350–900*, Exeter: Exeter University Press, 1986, 17–29. Cf. also the epithets used in imperial laws: e.g., 'the eternal city', 'the renowned city', 'the august city' (*Cod. Theod.* 15.1.11, 19, 27).

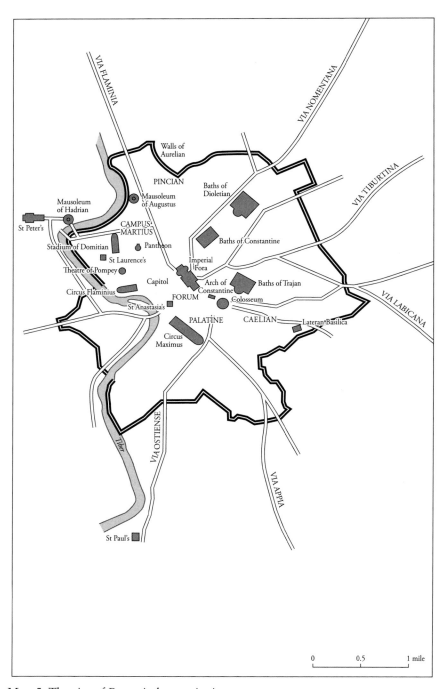

Map 5 The city of Rome in late antiquity

to where he should begin – 'First among cities, home of the gods, is golden Rome' (*Ordo nob. urb.* 1) – while at the poem's conclusion, a panegyric to his city of origin, Bordeaux, he wrote, 'This is my homeland (*patria*), but Rome transcends all homelands; Bordeaux I love, but Rome I revere' (*Ordo nob. urb.* 166–7).[4]

If the evocation of 'golden Rome' suggests above all the architectural wonders of the city's public buildings, then it seems that that image remained largely justified for the duration of the fourth century, albeit not without some emerging causes for concern. When Constantius II visited the city in 357, he is said to have 'looked with amazement at the forum, that sublime monument of pristine power, and wherever he turned he was dazzled by the concentration of wonderful sights' (Amm. Marc. 16.10.13). No doubt there is an element of idealisation here, but the detailed account of the emperor's ensuing tour of the city centre substantiates the impression that, at this point in time, the monumental fabric of the city remained in good condition (cf. *Expositio totius mundi* 55).

Less than a decade later, however, there appears, in an imperial law concerning Rome's public structures, a reference to 'buildings which have fallen into unsightly ruins' (*Cod. Theod.* 15.1.11 [364]), and this, together with two further laws (*Cod. Theod.* 15.1.19 [376], 27 [390]), sought to prevent officials from embarking on new construction projects out of imperial funds without formal approval and to urge instead that energy and resources be directed towards the restoration of existing buildings in need of repair. Clearly there was more prestige to be gained from new structures than from renovations, but emperors in these decades at least tried to set a good example by focusing their efforts on less eye-catching but more useful repairs to public structures which served practical purposes, such as bridges, water towers and porticoes.[5] The local elite were, it

4. For Ausonius' life and career, see H. Sivan, *Ausonius of Bordeaux*, London: Routledge, 1993. Ausonius' sentiments are even more striking when one takes into account that he almost certainly never visited the city. For the ideal of Rome in fourth-century Latin literature more generally, see F. Paschoud, *Roma Aeterna: Études sur le patriotisme romain dans l'occident latin à l'époque des grandes invasions*, Rome: Institut Suisse de Rome, 1967, and for the late fourth and early fifth century, M. Roberts, 'Rome personified, Rome epitomized: representations of Rome in the poetry of the early fifth century', *AJPhil.* 122 (2001), 533–65.
5. N. Lenski, *Failure of Empire: Valens and the Roman State in the Fourth Century* A.D., Berkeley: University of California Press, 2002, 277–8, 398; B. Ward-Perkins, *From Classical Antiquity to the Middle Ages: Urban Public Building in Northern and Central Italy*, AD 300–850, Oxford: Oxford University Press, 1984, 38.

seems, prepared to follow this lead to the extent of contributing to the periodic repair of the structure most likely to win popular favour, namely the Colosseum.[6] The one exception to the general principle of emperors in this period not starting new building work was the commencement of the grand church of St Paul 'outside the walls' in 384, intended to rival St Peter's in scale[7] – a prominent example of the most obvious way in which the cityscape of Rome changed during these decades (p. 63 below).

If emperors had little incentive to travel to the city, however, it seems that it still exercised a strong attraction over other inhabitants of the empire, even without the presence of the emperor and his court. Estimates of the city's population in the fourth century vary considerably, from an optimistic maintenance of earlier levels at about one million inhabitants, to a pessimistic decline to under half a million. The optimists have almost certainly made insufficient allowance for the high mortality rates which are typical of large pre-industrial urban centres, while the pessimists are likely to have underestimated the scale of immigration in the fourth century and its capacity to offset the impact of disease.[8]

Even if the more pessimistic estimates are accepted, however, they still leave Rome as the largest city in the empire, with all that that implies for the continuing challenges of maintaining an adequate supply of the necessities of life. One might have thought that a smaller population in the fourth century would reduce the pressure on food resources and hence the frequency of shortages, but this does not seem to have been the case – and for at least one obvious reason. Grain imports from Egypt, which had contributed a major proportion of Rome's requirements since the reign of Augustus,

6. R. Lim, 'People as power: games, munificence, and contested geography' in W. Harris (ed.), *Transformations of* Vrbs Roma *in Late Antiquity*, Portsmouth, RI: *JRA* Supp. 33, 1999, 265–82, at 267. For the case of one aristocrat from the 360s who restored numerous buildings, but then added inscriptions describing himself as their builder, see Amm. Marc. 27.3.7, with J. Matthews, *Western Aristocracies and Imperial Court, AD 364–425*, Oxford: Clarendon Press, 1975, 21–2.

7. Details in R. Krautheimer, *Rome: Profile of a City, 312–1308*, Princeton: Princeton University Press, 1980, 42–3.

8. For a convenient summary of the range of estimates, see D. Noy, 'Immigrants in late imperial Rome' in S. Mitchell and G. Greatrex (eds), *Ethnicity and Culture in Late Antiquity*, London: Duckworth, 2000, 15–30, at 15. For an eloquent statement of a pessimistic view, see N. Purcell, 'The populace of Rome in late antiquity: problems of classification and historical description' in Harris, *Transformations*, 135–61, at 137–50. Purcell's scepticism about levels of immigration does not, however, give sufficient attention to the epigraphic data assembled by Noy, 'Immigrants'.

had been redirected by Constantine to support the city of Constantinople, leaving Rome once again primarily reliant on the north African provinces. Shortages invariably led to mob violence on the streets of the city, and although such episodes no longer directly threatened the safety of the emperor's person, they were at the very least an embarrassment which could not be ignored.[9] Nor were they confined to grain. The substantial proportion of the city's populace which was still entitled to the free monthly handouts of bread which had been instituted as far back as the first century BC (in the original form of a grain dole) had in the interim also become entitled to free allowances of oil and pork and a subsidised quota of wine, and delays in the provision of these could also result in unrest (the oil also came from the African provinces, while the pork and wine were sourced more locally from within Italy).[10] While the supply of these comestibles was at the mercy of the vagaries of Mediterranean winds and/or the fallibilities of ancient modes of transport, the supply of that other essential – water – was more readily amenable to human control since it depended to a significant degree on the upkeep of the city's complex of aqueducts, and there is indeed evidence for the repair of various structures related to the city's water supply during the later fourth century – activity which reflects the importance of water not just for drinking but also for that archetypal Roman social activity of public bathing.[11]

Responsibility for all these matters rested ultimately with the prefect of the city (*praefectus urbi*), an office whose primary role during the Principate had been to maintain public order in the city (Tac. *Ann.* 6.11). By the fourth century, the withdrawal of emperors from residency in Rome had led to his remit being expanded in a variety of directions. It now included supervision of the officials responsible for the city's food supplies and for maintenance of public

9. For Valentinian I's efforts to improve the infrastructure for provisioning the city, see Lenski, *Valens*, 279.
10. For the various allowances, see Jones, *LRE*, 695–705, with further detail regarding grain, in G. Rickman, *The Corn Supply of Ancient Rome*, Oxford: Clarendon Press, 1980, 198–209. For unrest resulting from actual and feared shortages of grain or other foodstuffs in fourth-century Rome, see the catalogue in H. P. Kohns, *Versorgungskrisen und Hungerrevolten im spätantiken Rom*, Bonn: Habelt, 1961, 110–214, and L. Ruggini, *Economia e società nell 'Italia annonaria'*, Milan: Giuffre, 1961, 152–70.
11. Ward-Perkins, *From Classical Antiquity*, 1984, 42 (repairs), 127–8 (bathing); R. Coates-Stephens, 'The water-supply of Rome from late antiquity to the early Middle Ages', *Acta ad archaeologiam et artium historiam pertinentia* 17 (2003), 165–86, at 165–8.

buildings, and the prefect was still expected to maintain public order without the aid of the Augustan urban cohorts, which disappeared early in the fourth century (perhaps disbanded by Constantine at the same time as he abolished the praetorian guard). The prefect of the city had also become the chief judge for inhabitants of Rome and its hinterland, and president of the senate. As a result, in the bureau- cratic hierarchy of the fourth century, the office ranked just below that of praetorian prefect, the most powerful civilian post, and had come to be seen as the pinnacle of a senatorial career.[12]

But if great honour attended the position, so too could great risks and frustrations. The risk factor arose from popular anger some- times being directed at the person of the prefect and at his property (see Amm. Marc. 27.3 for examples of the residences of incumbents and past prefects being attacked and even burned down in this period); the frustrations stemmed from the fact that the prefect's fulfilment of his responsibilities could, it seems, be made more difficult by the unhelpful actions of officials in the central bureau- cracy in Milan. The best insights into this derive from the dossier of memoranda preserved from the prefecture of Symmachus in 384, such as one in which Symmachus tackled the delicate task of complaining, in the politest and most respectful manner, to Valen- tinian II about the poor quality of individuals appointed to work in various capacities under him – decisions made by imperial officials, but in the emperor's name.[13]

The prefect sometimes also faced problems arising from the existence of another position whose source of authority, however, lay outside governmental structures – the bishop of Rome (see further pp. 141–3 below). Constantine had been particularly generous in endowing the church in Rome with material resources and so it is hardly surprising that, in due course, the Roman episcopate became a prized appointment for ambitious individuals.[14] Among various

---

12. The definitive study remains A. Chastagnol, *La Préfecture urbaine à Rome sous le Bas-Empire*, Paris: Presses Universitaires de France, 1960, with succinct overviews in Jones, *LRE*, 689–92, and Matthews, *Western Aristocracies*, 18–23.
13. *Relat.* 17, with helpful discussion in R. M. Errington, *Roman Imperial Policy from Julian to Theodosius*, Chapel Hill: University of North Carolina Press, 2006, 125–33.
14. For data on the Roman church's material resources in the mid-fourth century, see C. Pietri, *Roma christiana: Recherches sur l'église de Rome, son organisation, sa politique, son idéologie de Miltiade à Sixte III (311–440)*, Rome: École française de Rome, 1976, 77–96, who notes, however, that those resources were still modest compared with many senatorial fortunes (90).

indications of the growing power and privileges associated with the position in the later fourth century is the famous reported jest of a prominent pagan aristocrat to one incumbent, 'Make me bishop of the city of Rome, and I will become a Christian without delay!' (Jer. *Contra Iohann. Hieros.* 8 [*CCSL* 79A, III, 2.15]), while in 366 competition for the vacant see reached such an intensity that it spilled over into notorious violence between the supporters of two rivals, Damasus and Ursinus, leaving well in excess of a hundred individuals dead and creating ongoing problems for the incumbent prefect and his successors.[15]

The growing prominence of the bishop is, of course, one out of a number of ways in which Christianity increasingly impacted on the city of Rome. Another obvious and important way was through the construction of churches and associated structures. As has often been noted, the churches which Constantine had built were situated around the periphery of the city, a pattern which has sometimes been interpreted as reflecting, in part, his unwillingness to offend pagan opinion,[16] but is probably better explained with reference to other, more positive considerations.[17] Certainly, the new church whose construction was initiated by emperors in the later fourth century also conformed to this pattern – St Paul's 'outside the walls' (p. 60 above) – but this period also saw bishops of Rome sponsoring the building of churches near the city centre. In particular, Damasus (bishop from 366 to 384) 'significantly extended the monumental Christian presence in Rome by creating a new church in the Campus Martius [St Laurence (S. Lorenzo)] and by placing a basilica at the south-western corner of the Palatine Hill [St Anastasia], a particularly striking demonstration of the increasing importance of Christianity in the city'.[18]

Yet another important way in which the impact of Christianity was felt was through its adoption by members of the senatorial aristocracy, who, as the most prominent and powerful social group in Rome, warrant separate consideration.

15. Errington, *Imperial Policy*, 191–2.
16. Krautheimer, *Rome*, 30–1.
17. E. D. Hunt, 'Imperial building at Rome: the role of Constantine' in K. Lomas and T. Cornell (eds), *'Bread and Circuses': euergetism and municipal patronage in Roman Italy*, London: Routledge, 2003, 105–24.
18. J. R. Curran, *Pagan City and Christian Capital: Rome in the Fourth Century*, Oxford: Clarendon Press, 2000, 156.

The senatorial aristocracy of Rome

A Roman senatorial aristocracy had existed in one form or another almost as long as Rome itself, and certainly for significantly longer than the office of emperor.[19] Both its composition and fortunes had, however, changed over the centuries. The relatively closed elite which had dominated Republican political life and been drawn initially from Rome, and then the Italian peninsula, had, with the advent of emperors from the late first century BC, stabilised at about double the size (c. 600 men) and gradually absorbed members of the empire's provincial elites, while at the same time having to content itself with steadily diminishing political influence. Meanwhile, as imperial patronage brought infusions of fresh blood into the senate, many older families disappeared from the historical record.[20] By the end of the third century, emperors were no longer drawn from the senatorial aristocracy and were therefore even less concerned about senatorial interests, and senators had been excluded from military responsibilities, but they nonetheless remained a clearly defined, largely hereditary body with elite status, prestige and privileges, and with the city of Rome as their focal point.

By the end of the fourth century, however, the definition of senatorial rank had undergone radical revision, first, through the creation of a second, eastern senate in Constantinople (p. 77 below), and secondly, through emperors allowing senior imperial bureaucrats to acquire the rank. This trend resulted in the number of individuals with formal senatorial rank increasing dramatically, thereby diluting its value as a marker of social status[21] – a development symbolised by the report of a prodigy in the early 370s when the brooms used to sweep the senate house in Rome were said to have 'burst into leaf, an omen that some people of the lowest sort would rise to high offices of state' (Amm. Marc. 28.1.42).

19. And indeed was to continue long after the last western emperor (p. 299 below).
20. For discussion of the reasons for this, see K. Hopkins and G. Burton, 'Ambition and withdrawal: the senatorial aristocracy under the emperors' in K. Hopkins, *Death and Renewal*, Cambridge: Cambridge University Press, 1983, 120–200.
21. For this development, see P. Heather, 'Senators and senates' in *CAH*[2] 13.184–210, and J. Haldon, 'The fate of the late Roman senatorial elite: extinction or transformation?' in J. Haldon and L. I. Conrad (eds), *The Byzantine and Early Islamic Near East* VI: *Elites Old and New in the Byzantine and Early Islamic Near East*, Princeton: Darwin Press, 179–232, at 179–98. For more general discussion of the issues arising from defining the senatorial aristocracy in the fourth century, see M. R. Salzman, *The Making of a Christian Aristocracy: Social and Religious Change in the Western Roman Empire*, Cambridge, MA: Harvard University Press, 2002, 19–24, 28–43.

Throughout all this, however, those select families who could claim senatorial ancestry from before the fourth century, and who usually had the landed wealth to back it up – famously described by one of their number as 'the better part of the human race' (Symmachus, *Ep.* 1.52) – maintained their prominence in the affairs of the city of Rome (a prominence further facilitated, of course, by the absence of emperors).

While acknowledging the importance of ancestry, its limits also need to be noted. In one of his famous digressions on the city of Rome, Ammianus poked fun at the way some senators 'plume themselves on what they consider distinguished forenames, such as Reburrus, Flavonius, Pagonius, and Gereon, or trace their descent from the Dalii or Tarracii or Ferasii, or some other high-sounding family' (28.4.7), implying that their claims to eminent ancestry were specious. Certainly, there were only a small number of families, such as the Acilii, who could trace their pedigree back as far as the Republican period. More recent lineage was the rule for the majority, as in the case of the most illustrious senatorial family of the later fourth century, the Anicii, whose earliest known member to have held the consulship did so during the reign of Septimius Severus, in 198.[22] However, this still interposed a good century between them and those bureaucrats and others who owed their elevation to Constantine and his successors.

The passage of time was also important because it had allowed many of the older senatorial families to acquire substantial landed wealth. In a well-known passage, the historian Olympiodorus is reported to have expressed his amazement at the urban residences of senators in the early fifth century in the following terms: 'Each of the great houses of Rome contained within itself, as he says, everything which a medium-sized city could hold – a hippodrome, fora, temples, fountains and different kinds of baths. At this, the historian emotes: "One house is a town; the city hides ten thousand towns"' (Olympiodorus, *fr.* 41, 1). This is, of course, hyperbole, but it

---

22. For these examples, as part of a very detailed prosopographical discussion of the evolution of the senatorial aristocracy between Principate and late empire (including helpful tables), see F. Jacques, 'L'ordine senatorio attraverso la crisi del III secolo' in A. Giardina (ed.), *Società romana e impero tardoantico* I, Rome: Laterza, 1986, 81–226, at 153 (Acilii), 158 (Anicii). Also valuable, but with a narrower focus, is D. M. Novak, 'The early history of the Anician family' in C. Deroux (ed.), *Studies in Latin Literature and Roman History* I, Brussels: Collection Latomus, 1979, 199–265. A good argument has recently been made for the Symmachi also having aristocratic roots in the Severan period: Alan Cameron, 'The antiquity of the Symmachi', *Historia* 48 (1999), 477–505.

captures something of the impact of the physical expression of senatorial wealth on an outsider. Archaeological investigation has gone some way towards identifying and interpreting late Roman aristocratic mansions in Rome, with one example on the Caelian Hill covering 8,000 m^2 and providing ample evidence of lavish decoration.[23] This can be complemented by the surviving correspondence of Symmachus which reveals 'how much time and money he and his senatorial friends spent on the embellishment and enlargement of their urban properties, giving ... insight into the importance of the appearance of the *domus* for senatorial self-conception'.[24]

Urban residences were, however, only the start of senatorial property-holding. Senators also typically owned villas elsewhere in Italy and estates in other parts of the western Mediterranean. Although Ammianus claimed that fourth-century senators were prone to exaggerate their land-holding – they would 'hold forth unasked on the immense extent of their family property, multiplying in imagination the annual produce of their fertile lands, which extend, they boastfully declare, from farthest east to farthest west' (14.6.10) – Symmachus is known to have had further residences in Ostia and outside Rome on the Appian Way, numerous villas on or near the Bay of Naples (at Lucrina, Baiae, Puteoli, Bauli, Cora, Formiae, Terracina and Capua), and estates in southern Italy (Apulia), Sicily and north Africa (Mauretania), and there is no reason to think that this was atypical, since Symmachus is described in one near-contemporary source as 'a senator of middling wealth' (Olympiodorus, *fr.* 41, 2).[25] Although they would have been incensed by such a description, it is for this reason that they have been referred to by one eminent scholar as 'landgrabbers'.[26]

23. N. Christie, *From Constantine to Charlemagne: An Archaeology of Italy, AD 300–800*, Aldershot: Ashgate, 2006, 238–41, summarising the work of Federico Guidobaldi and other Italian archaeologists. See also the well-illustrated overview in S. Ensoli and E. La Rocca (eds), *Aurea Roma: dalla città pagana alla città Cristiana*, Rome: Bretschneider, 2000, 134–60.
24. J. Hillner, '*Domus*, family, and inheritance: the senatorial family house in late antique Rome', *JRS* 93 (2003), 129–45, at 133.
25. See *PLRE* 1.869–70 for details of Symmachus' holdings, with more general comments on senatorial wealth in C. Wickham, *Framing the Early Middle Ages: Europe and the Mediterranean, 400–800*, Oxford: Oxford University Press, 2005, 162–4. It has recently been argued that Olympiodorus' comment on Symmachus' 'middling wealth' should be interpreted as ironic, and that Symmachus was in fact 'one of the super-rich' (Cameron, 'Symmachi', 499).
26. Alan Cameron, 'The last pagans of Rome' in Harris, *Transformations*, 109–22 at 109, elaborated in Cameron, 'Symmachi', 492–503.

It was, however, landed wealth on this scale which enabled senators to live the life of leisure (*otium*) which was another way in which they maintained their social distinctiveness.[27] Again, Ammianus satirised those senators whose leisure comprised self-indulgence in ostentatious banqueting, elaborate excursions to the baths, and unseemly interest in chariot-racing, and who 'hate learning like poison, but avidly read Juvenal and Marius Maximus [i.e., insufficiently serious authors]' (28.4.8–14). But the targets of his caricature probably comprised a minority at one end of the spectrum, and it is apparent from a variety of sources that there were senators who devoted time to more serious cultural pursuits. While the depth of their knowledge of classical culture ought not to be overstated,[28] neither should it be unduly minimised. Consider, for example, the following excerpt from his wife's tribute on the funerary monument of the eminent pagan senator Vettius Agorius Praetextatus, who died in 384:

> Sprung of proud lineage, you illumine your country, the senate and your wife by your integrity of mind, your character and your scholarship all at once. By these you attained the highest peak of virtue, for by translating whatever is proclaimed in either tongue [i.e., Latin and Greek] by the thought of the wise, to whom the gate of heaven lies open – both the poems which the learned have composed and the prose works recited aloud – you have improved upon what you have found written down. (*CIL* 6.1779 = *ILS* 1259 [tr. B. Croke and J. Harries])

Also relevant is the manuscript evidence for emendations of the texts of classical authors by senators from the late fourth and early fifth century,[29] the circumstantial detail in the correspondence of Symmachus concerning the literary interests which he shared with aristocratic friends (e.g., *Epp.* 7.15, 9.13), and the poetic inclinations of the family of Petronius Probus, another eminent senator from this period, whose sons acted as patrons to the rising poet Claudian when he first arrived in Rome in the mid-390s,[30]

27. For discussion of which, see Matthews, *Western Aristocracies*, 1–12.
28. Cf. Alan Cameron, *The Last Pagans of Rome*, Oxford: Oxford University Press, 2011.
29. J. E. G. Zetzel, *Latin Textual Criticism in Antiquity*, New York: Arno, 1981, 227–31, emphasising, however, that these individuals were not engaging in textual criticism in the modern sense. The wider cultural significance of the phenomenon has been minimised by Cameron, *Last Pagans*, chs 12–13.
30. Alan Cameron, *Claudian: Poetry and Propaganda at the Court of Honorius*, Oxford: Clarendon Press, 1970, 30–6.

as well as dabbling in poetry composition themselves.[31]

Probus' family is also an interesting case because, unlike Prae-textatus and Symmachus, they were Christians, and a further important issue concerning the traditional senatorial aristocracy in the later fourth century is how typical they were, that is, the extent to which members of his order embraced a religion which had largely been spurned by their forebears. This already featured as a point at issue in the debates of the time, with Ambrose disputing Symmachus' claim that the various requests for the restoration of the Altar of Victory in the early 380s represented the desire of a majority of the senate (Ambrose, *Ep.* 72.10–11).[32] Modern analyses have likewise arrived at divergent conclusions. On the one hand, epigraphic evidence attesting the continuing commitment of some senators to traditional cults through the 380s and the pagan sympathies of some of those who supported Eugenius' usurpation in the early 390s have pointed to a strong residual core of senators committed to traditional cults in the final decades of the fourth century,[33] while on the other, statistical analysis of available data for the religious affiliation of senatorial aristocrats has suggested a rapid and early Christianisation during the first half of the fourth century.[34]

Such divergences reflect, in part, the incomplete nature of the evidence, but also, more fundamentally, the inherent problem of defining what constituted conversion, as highlighted by the renowned exchange between the eminent rhetorician Marius Victorinus and the clergyman Simplicianus some time towards the middle of the fourth century:

31. Alan Cameron, 'Petronius Probus, Aemilius Probus and the transmission of Nepos' in J.-M. Carrié and R. Lizzi Testa (eds), *'Humana sapit': Études d'antiquité tardive offertes à Lellia Cracco Ruggini*, Turnhout: Brepols, 2002, 121–30, at 121 (epigrams in the *Epigrammata Bobiensia*), who also notes, however, that the evidence sometimes adduced for Probus himself and his forebears writing poetry (*Anth. Lat.* 1.783) has been misinterpreted.
32. It has been suggested that this apparent disagreement can be explained if 'Ambrose was thinking of the whole senatorial class, whereas Symmachus refers only to the majority at a particular meeting' (T. D. Barnes, 'Religion and society in the age of Theodosius' in H. A. Meynell (ed.), *Grace, Politics and Desire: Essays on Augustine*, Calgary: University of Calgary Press, 1990, 157–75, at 164).
33. H. Bloch, 'A new document of the last pagan revival in the west, AD 393–394', *Harv. Theol. Rev.* 38 (1945), 199–244 (though his interpretation of the inscription which prompted the article has recently been challenged: Cameron, *Last Pagans*, 90–2).
34. T. D. Barnes, 'Statistics and the conversion of the Roman aristocracy', *JRS* 85 (1995), 135–47.

Victorinus was extremely learned and most expert in all the liberal disciplines. He had read and assessed many philosophers' ideas, and was tutor to many noble senators ... Although he had defended pagan cults for many years with a voice terrifying to opponents, he was not ashamed to become a servant of Christ ... Simplicianus said Victorinus read holy scripture, and all the Christian books he investigated with special care. After examining them he said to Simplicianus, not openly but in the privacy of friendship, 'Did you know that I am already a Christian?' Simplicianus replied: 'I shall not believe that or count you among the Christians unless I see you in the church of Christ.' Victorinus laughed and said: 'Then do walls make Christians?' (August. *Conf.* 8.3–4 [tr. H. Chadwick])

Victorinus was, admittedly, an intellectual rather than an aristocrat (albeit one who moved in senatorial circles), but the anecdote nonetheless illustrates nicely the issue of definition, and indeed for many of the Roman elite it will not have involved any clear-cut decision, but rather what has been aptly characterised as a 'drift into a respectable Christianity'.[35] Imperial endorsement of the church was clearly important in facilitating this process, the role of aristocratic women perhaps less so than often assumed.[36] Above all, however, a majority of Christian leaders did not proclaim any irreconcilable differences between Christianity and most, though not all, aspects of classical culture, which made the transfer of religious allegiances more palatable to the many aristocrats for whom classical culture remained so important (see further pp. 219–22 below) (cf. Fig. 3). Within a generation of the death of Theodosius I (395), there will have been few, if any, members of the traditional Roman senatorial aristocracy who had not managed to accommodate themselves, in one way or another, to Christianity.[37]

---

35. P. Brown, 'Aspects of the Christianization of the Roman aristocracy', *JRS* 51 (1961), 1–11, at 10. Although modifying some of Brown's other conclusions, Salzman, *Making of a Christian Aristocracy*, effectively agrees on this aspect with her description of the process as involving 'a moving away by pagans from traditionally pagan religious structures and a breaking down of once significant differences between pagan and Christian aristocrats' (136).

36. Salzman, *Making of a Christian Aristocracy*, 178–99 (imperial influence), 138–77 (aristocratic women).

37. For the Christianisation of those living and working on aristocratic estates, see K. Bowes, *Private Worship, Public Values, and Religious Change in Late Antiquity*, Cambridge: Cambridge University Press, 2008, 125–88. Some aristocrats, especially females, embraced Christian asceticism with an enthusiasm which caused concern in some quarters: see Curran, *Pagan City*, ch. 7.

Figure 3 The Projecta casket from the Esquiline Treasure in Rome (28.6 × 55.9 × 43.2 cm) (c. 380). A silver casket, with partly gilt decoration, whose main panel depicts Venus in a shell, dressing her hair and flanked by sea-creatures and cupids. Along the lower edge and just visible is an inscription reading 'Secundus and Projecta, may you live in Christ', while the top of the casket, above Venus, shows a couple surrounded by a wreath. The casket was probably a wedding gift, for use in Projecta's toilette, and in addition to illustrating the wealth of the Roman aristocracy, it is of interest for its combination of mythological scenes with a Christian epigraph. © The Trustees of the British Museum

Constantinople and its development in the later fourth century

Constantine's decision to develop a new imperial centre for the eastern half of the empire on the site of the ancient Greek colony of Byzantium would surely rank as his most important legacy,[38] were it not for the even more far-reaching impact of his decision to embrace and support Christianity. With the passage of time, it became common to refer to Constantinople as the 'new Rome'. One fifth-century historian went so far as to claim that Constantine had issued a law that it should be so designated (Socrates, *Hist. eccl.* 1.16), while sixth-century writers developed those features of the city's prehistory and topography which lent themselves to clear resonances of Rome, such as the presence of seven hills on the site, and the legendary founder Byzas becoming the enemy of his brother Strombos, like Romulus and Remus.[39] However, the paucity of

38. Because of the title of this volume and the significance of Constantinople for the changing identity of Rome and the empire, space has deliberately been given in this section to the development of the city in the decades prior to 363.
39. G. Dagron, *Naissance d'une capitale: Constantinople et ses institutions de 330 à 451*, Paris: Presses Universitaires de France, 1974, 14–15. For recent discussions of these sixth-century writers, see A. Kaldellis, 'The works and days of Hesychios the Illoustrios of Miletos', *GRBS* 45 (2005), 381–403, and W. Treadgold, *The Early Byzantine Historians*, London: Palgrave Macmillan, 2007, 270–9.

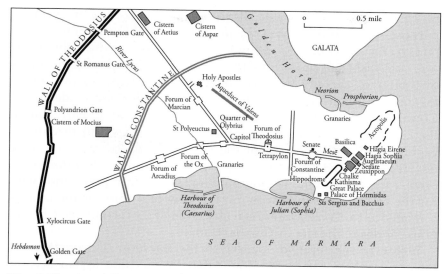

Map 6 The city of Constantinople in late antiquity

relevant sources from Constantine's own day leaves room for debate as to whether this was how Constantine himself envisaged Constantinople from the time of its official foundation in 324. One possibility that has to be entertained is that he originally conceived it simply as another conveniently placed 'tetrarchic capital', none of whose predecessors had ever sought to challenge the pre-eminence of Rome, and that it was only gradually that he came to think of it as twin, rival or successor to Rome. A contemporary poet does, admittedly, refer to it as 'second Rome' (*altera Roma*) in a context which suggests he was writing in the mid-320s (Porfyrius, *Carm.* 4.6), but there are too many uncertainties about his circumstances to know whether he was articulating Constantine's view or merely seeking to flatter.[40]

The earliest official pronouncement which hints at the idea of Constantinople as New Rome is a law in which Constantine refers to his foundation as 'a city on which we have bestowed, by the command of God, the eternal name' (*Cod. Theod.* 13.5.7), but this dates from 334, a full decade after the city's foundation. In due course, the city acquired its own senate and a free handout of bread for citizens, both of which have obvious parallels with Rome, but the

40. For discussion of the issues, see T. D. Barnes, 'Publilius Optatianus Porfyrius', *AJPhil.* 96 (1975), 173–86.

bread distribution was not instituted until 332 and its primary purpose seems to have been the pragmatic one of attracting inhabitants to the city (pp. 76–7 below), while the date at which the senate was established is uncertain (p. 77 below). Moreover, the office of prefect of the city was not instituted until towards the end of the reign of Constantius II, in 359. Perhaps the best evidence for Constantine regarding his city as the New Rome at an early date is the coinage, specifically the parallel series of coins and medallions beginning in 330 (the year of the city's formal dedication), whose obverses refer, respectively, to *Urbs Roma* and *Constantinopolis*, often with appropriate iconography on the reverse (wolf and twins for the former, personification on the bow of a ship for the latter – a reference to Constantine's naval victory over Licinius at Chrysopolis, opposite the site of Constantinople).[41]

Whatever the ultimate answer to the question of Constantine's intentions, there can be no doubt that by the time Jovian became emperor in 363, Constantinople had generally come to be regarded as the second city of the empire and Rome's equivalent in the east. Speaking in 357, the orator and philosopher Themistius referred to Constantinople as sharing Rome's name (*Or.* 3.42ab), while in 363 the rhetorician Libanius ranked his native Antioch as 'next in line to the two capitals' (*duo tas prōtas*) (*Or.* 15.59). This had happened despite the fact that problems on the Persian frontier had prevented Constantius II from spending much time in the city,[42] while Julian had also spent little more than six months there after his accession. Despite military distractions, however, Constantius had taken substantial steps towards consolidating the position of Constantinople, above all through the development of its senate (p. 77 below). The reigns of Jovian and Valens were to see a continuing pattern of imperial absence. Jovian was, to be fair, en route to Constantinople at the time of his premature death, but Valens rarely spent time in the city, partly because of military preoccupations in the east and on the lower Danube, partly out of resentment at the way the city had supported the usurper Procopius, and it was not until the reign of Theodosius that an emperor finally spent substantial stretches of time living there (380–7, 391–4). Significantly, it was early in his

41. J. P. C. Kent, '*Urbs Roma* and *Constantinopolis* medallions at the mint of Rome' in R. A. G. Carson and C. M. Kraay (eds), *Scripta Nummaria Romana: Essays Presented to Humphrey Sutherland*, London: Spink, 1978, 105–13.
42. Details in T. D. Barnes, *Athanasius and Constantius*, Cambridge, MA: Harvard University Press, 1993, 219–24.

reign that, as previously noted (p. 46 above), the general church council held in Constantinople in 381 agreed that the bishop of Constantinople should come second in seniority after the bishop of Rome 'because Constantinople is the new Rome' (Canon 3). Certainly, Theodosius' sustained presence there facilitated the embedding and growth of permanent administrative structures in the city to a degree which the peripatetic behaviour of his predecessors had inhibited, enabling Constantinople to become the governmental focal point of the eastern half of the empire in a way which had not previously been possible.[43]

Even during Valens' reign, there were other telling indications of the city's wider recognition. Living emperors may not have spent very much time there before Theodosius' reign, but dead ones did, and not just those who had reigned over the eastern half of the empire. Constantine, Constantius and Jovian were all entombed there, but so also was Valentinian I, despite his having spent almost all of his reign in the west. It is possible that the mortal remains of Gratian and Valentinian II might also have been removed eastwards, had it not been for the intervention of Ambrose, who took advantage of the unsettled circumstances of Maximus' and Eugenius' usurpations to claim these remains for Milan. Significantly, although Theodosius himself died in Milan while Ambrose was still bishop, his body was transported back to Constantinople for burial.[44]

Over the preceding three decades there had been important developments in the monumental fabric of the city, building on the earlier work of Constantine, Constantius II and Julian. The city was situated on a tongue of land projecting eastwards into the Bosporus, with the original Greek settlement on the elevated eastern tip doubling in size under Roman rule by the end of the second century AD. Constantine had advanced the land wall a further three or so kilometres westwards so that the area of the city more than trebled. This left it still only about half the size of Rome (as defined by the Aurelianic Walls), but did give it a comparable area to the great cities

---

43. Cf. Errington, *Imperial Policy*, 144–6.
44. For this whole subject, see P. Grierson, 'The tombs and obits of the Byzantine emperors, (337–1042)', *DOP* 16 (1962), 1–65, at 23–5. Julian was buried at Tarsus in Cilicia until his remains were relocated to Constantinople in the 390s (although, interestingly, the historian Ammianus, writing soon before the relocation, believed that his ashes should have been laid to rest in 'the eternal city' of Rome amongst earlier emperors: 25.10.5); the cottage in which Valens took refuge during the battle of Adrianople was burned down by the Goths, and so there were no identifiable remains to bury.

of the eastern Mediterranean, Alexandria and Antioch. Within this enlarged compass, Constantine had laid down the broad framework for future developments, establishing a forum, building the church of the Holy Apostles (and perhaps a handful of other Christian shrines), developing the palace–hippodrome complex, and linking all these with a grid of streets based on the central east–west spine of the broad thoroughfare which came to be known as the Mesē ('in the middle').[45] Constantius began construction of a large bath complex, a substantial colonnade and (probably) the church of Hagia Sophia,[46] while Julian initiated the expansion of harbour facilities on the southern side of the peninsula (Zos. 3.11.3).

Despite his distrust of its inhabitants, Valens took important steps to relieve the city's chronic shortage of water by completing the construction of a cistern begun under Julian and an aqueduct commenced by Constantine and Constantius, whose impressive remains still adorn modern-day Istanbul (Fig. 4), as well as constructing two bath complexes; he was also responsible for the addition of further granaries near the harbours on the northern side of the peninsula.[47] Theodosius added another forum on the Mesē to the west of Constantine's, modelled on that of Trajan in Rome (with whom Theodosius shared a Spanish origin), complete with a spiral column celebrating his defeat of the Goths in 386 (p. 38 above), and saw to the erection of an impressive Egyptian obelisk in the hippodrome and a triumphal arch,[48] both commemorating his victory over the usurper Maximus (p. 26 above); in addition to these items with an overt ideological purpose, he undertook further expansion of harbour facilities on the southern side of the peninsula.[49] By 384 the

---

45. C. Mango, *Le Développement urbain de Constantinople (IVe–VIIe siècles)*, Paris: Boccard, 1985, 23–36, with A. Berger, 'Streets and public spaces in Constantinople', *DOP* 54 (2000), 161–72, for the street grid. Fuller details on these, and the following structures, can be found in the invaluable illustrated reference work by W. Müller-Wiener, *Bildlexikon zur Topographie Istanbuls*, Tübingen: Wasmuth, 1977.

46. N. Henck, 'Constantius *ho philoktistes*', *DOP* 55 (2001), 279–304, at 284–203.

47. Lenski, *Valens*, 393–5, 399.

48. J. Bardill, 'The Golden Gate in Constantinople: a triumphal arch of Theodosius I', *AJArch.* 103 (1999), 671–96.

49. Mango, *Développement*, 39–40, 42–4; B. Croke, 'Reinventing Constantinople: Theodosius I's imprint on the imperial city' in S. McGill et al. (eds), *From the Tetrarchs to the Theodosians*, Cambridge: Cambridge University Press, 2010, 241–64. The obelisk and the famous Theodosian reliefs around its base remain in situ in Istanbul (cf. Fig. 1), whereas only fragments of the spiral column survive (further detail on both monuments in B. Kiilerich, *Late Fourth Century Classicism in the Plastic Arts: Studies in the So-Called Theodosian Renaissance*, Odense: Odense University Press, 1993, 31–64, and on

Figure 4 The aqueduct of Valens in Constantinople. © Szoszv/Wikimedia Commons

orator Themistius was able to point to the transformation and growth of Constantinople, where

> the land encompassed by the city, which in earlier times was half empty, is now full of innumerable amenities, where the uninhabited districts are no longer more extensive than the inhabited, where we no longer plough an area within the walls greater than that occupied by dwellings, and where the beauty of the city is no longer scattered and dispersed. On the contrary, the whole area is now fully populated and made complete – like a robe embroidered to its edges with gold and purple – by the palace which bears the imperial name, by baths, and by fora and places where the youth gather. The area which was in former times on the margins of the city has become its centre. O father, o blessed Constantine, do you see how this emperor has made the city splendid instead of undistinguished and ramshackle, so that its beauty is now a reality and no longer a mere sketch? (*Or.* 18.222b–223a)

Another fascinating snapshot of the city's development is provided by a document from the early fifth century known as the 'register of the city of Constantinople' (*Notitia urbis Constantinopolitanae*),

the obelisk base in B. Kiilerich, *The Obelisk Base in Constantinople: Court Art and Imperial Ideology*, Rome: Bretschneider, 1998).

compiled c. 425 and listing the buildings of the city region by region, including the following totals: 5 palaces, 14 churches, 2 basilicas, 4 fora, 2 theatres, 2 amphitheatres, 52 porticoes, 8 public and 153 private bathhouses, 5 meat markets, 322 apartment blocks (*vici*) and 4,388 houses (*domus*).[50]

Even with the aid of such a document, estimating what the city's growth meant in terms of the number of inhabitants is a very difficult exercise, since interpretation of the figures for blocks and houses in the *Notitia* is problematic.[51] However, if the area enclosed by Constantine's wall was fully occupied by the mid-380s, then that might suggest a population in the region of 150,000,[52] although that figure still raises questions about density of habitation. The suggestion of 500,000 by the year 400[53] is surely far too optimistic, particularly given the limitations of water supply, consideration of which has prompted a more cautious estimate of between 300,000 and 400,000 by the middle of the fifth century.[54]

Whatever the precise figure, the need to augment the city's provision of water and harbour facilities is a clear indication of an expanding population in the second half of the fourth century. As for food, Constantine had instituted a regular free handout of bread for 80,000 individuals (with the amount given adequate for the needs of two adults) as part of a strategy to encourage people to migrate to his new city. However, apart from a very modest increase in 392, that number was otherwise never raised, so that as the city's population grew, so did the number of inhabitants who will have had to buy their grain on the open market, imported largely, but by no means solely, from Egypt. That the non-privileged became an increasingly large proportion of the population is no doubt reflected in the *Notitia* recording 120 private bakeries as against 20 state-owned ones. The tighter constraints on imperial generosity in the fourth century are further reflected in the fact that, unlike in Rome,

50. The text can be found in Seeck's edition of the *Notitia Dignitatum*, 227–43. This document postdates the further westward extension of the city perimeter by Theodosius II (p. 118 below).
51. Dagron, *Naissance*, 526–7.
52. Dagron, *Naissance*, 524.
53. J. L. Teall, 'The grain supply of the Byzantine empire', *DOP* 13 (1959), 89–139, at 92, 134–5 (who takes insufficient account of the limited scale of habitation in the large area between the walls of Constantine and Theodosius II).
54. Mango, *Développement*, 40–2, 51. For detailed analysis of the evolution of the city's water-supply infrastructure, see J. Crow, J. Bardill and R. Bayliss, *The Water Supply of Byzantine Constantinople*, London: *JRS* Monographs 11, 2008.

those who qualified for the free handout of bread did not receive any other subsidised foodstuffs.[55]

A particularly important feature of the development of Constantinople during the fourth century was the evolution of the city's senate, which had implications well beyond the life of the city itself. Constantine is credited with having established its senate with 'second rank' (*Origo Constantini* 30) – that is, second after Rome – but evidence for the first practical steps in the development of Constantinople's senate only appears under Constantius II. From early in his reign derives legislation specifying the conditions for entry (namely, holding one of three praetorships and funding the games associated with them) (*Cod. Theod.* 6.4.5–6 [340]), while it was he who was responsible for a concerted effort to expand the size of this body in the late 350s by recruiting appropriate individuals from among the membership of city councils around the eastern Mediterranean – a process which benefited Constantinople at the expense of other cities by siphoning off some of their wealthiest and most politically experienced citizens (at this stage, membership of its senate meant residence in Constantinople). Constantius' policies benefited him politically by building up a base of support among the elite of the eastern half of the empire, but they also had implications for the senate in Rome. For it was he who effectively established the division of the senatorial order on geographical grounds, so that Roman senators resident in the east had to enrol in the senate at Constantinople, thereby restricting the role of the senate in Rome to the western half of the empire and signalling that the senate in Constantinople was to be treated as its eastern equivalent.[56]

During the decades when the senate of Constantinople was emerging as the institutional twin of the senate in Rome, the character of the senatorial order itself was undergoing significant redefinition,

---

55. For the figure of 80,000, see Socrates, *Hist. eccl.* 2.13, with discussion in Jones, *LRE*, 696–701; further discussion and references in J.-M. Carrié, 'L'institution annonaire de la première à la deuxième Rome: continuité et innovation' in B. Marin and C. Virlouvet (eds), *Nourrir les cités de Méditerrané: antiquité–temps modernes*, Paris: Maisonneuve & Larose, 2003, 153–211. That the bread ration was designed to attract inhabitants is the clear implication of the sub-category of *panes aedium*, specifically ear-marked for those who built a house in Constantinople.
56. For discussion, and differing views on the roles of Constantine and Constantius, see Jones, *LRE*, 132–3, P. Heather, 'New men for new Constantines? Creating an imperial elite in the eastern Mediterranean' in P. Magdalino (ed.), *New Constantines: The Rhythm of Imperial Renewal in Byzantium, 4th–13th Centuries*, Aldershot: Ashgate, 1994, 11–30, and Errington, *Imperial Policy*, 148–58.

with major implications for both bodies. That redefinition arose from the expansion of the imperial bureaucracy during the fourth century and the increasing tendency of emperors from Constantine onwards to reward those who held high office with a grant of senatorial status (p. 64 above). This initially *ad hoc* practice was formalised by Valentinian and Valens in 372 in a series of laws which created a unified status system for senators of aristocratic lineage and those who were achieving senatorial status through high-level administrative or military service. It meant that the senatorial aristocracy was increasingly one of service rather than birth, and that the number of senators grew significantly by the end of the fourth century, since by this time there were about 3,000 posts in each half of the empire which qualified their holders for senatorial status. At the same time, an increasingly complicated set of gradations developed under the umbrella of senatorial status in order to maintain distinctions between those of older and more recent standing.[57]

By the end of the fourth century, then, the city of Rome continued to maintain its prestige, although its practical influence on the affairs of the empire had long been curtailed, especially by the absence of the emperor, while Constantinople had developed to the point where its claim to be the second Rome could no longer be dismissed as empty rhetoric, not least because the Emperor Theodosius did reside there for much of his reign, during which he did much to develop the city as an imperial capital. Circumstances following his death in 395 were to ensure further dramatic twists in this tale of two cities, for Constantinople's growing eminence was to be consolidated, even as Rome experienced turbulence and trauma on an unprecedented scale.

57. Heather, 'New men', 18–21.

Part II

The long fifth century

CHAPTER 5

Generalissimos and imperial courts

Court politics: (1) The Theodosian dynasty

Although the half century or so following the death of Theodosius I included the reign of the emperor who occupied the throne longer than any other incumbent in the history of the Roman empire (Theodosius II), the emperors of this period were almost all comparatively minor players on a stage dominated by others (the exception was Constantius III, who was, however, emperor in the west for little more than six months in 421). This can be accounted for in part by the young age at accession and inexperience of nearly all the emperors in this period – individuals who owed their elevated position above all to concern for dynastic continuity. At the time of his unexpected death in January 395, Theodosius was still only in his late forties, and his two sons, Arcadius and Honorius, whom he had already ear-marked to rule the eastern and western halves of the empire respectively, were only seventeen or eighteen and ten years old. At the time of Arcadius' relatively early death in 408 (aged thirty-one), his sole son Theodosius was a mere seven years old, while Honorius, who reigned until 423, but with no male offspring from his marriages, was eventually succeeded in 425 by his six-year-old nephew Valentinian, the son of Theodosius I's daughter Galla Placidia and her husband Constantius III.

Since Theodosius II ruled until 450 and Valentinian III until 455, all four of Theodosius I's male descendants spent substantial proportions of their reigns as adults, but adulthood did not seem to bring with it the propensity to exercise power in the way that their illustrious forebear had. Leaving aside the unanswerable question of genetic predisposition, the most likely explanation is that those responsible for government during their formative years discouraged any inclination towards independence of thought or action. Perhaps the most important consequence of this was that emperors in this period no longer participated in military campaigning, an important

change with ramifications in a variety of directions. While it had
the undoubted benefit of protecting the empire from any repetition
of the temporary political instability which ensued from the deaths
of Julian and Valens on the battlefield, it also had the less happy
effect of distancing the emperor from the army and increasing the
likelihood of military usurpation.[1] It meant too that emperors during
the first half of the fifth century spent most of their time in their
imperial capital (which in the east was, obviously, Constantinople,
but in the west, less obviously, a combination of Rome and Ravenna,
with the latter predominant until 440 for reasons which will become
clearer below [pp. 111–12]). Particularly in the east, this shift away
from a peripatetic imperial lifestyle, already anticipated to some
extent by Theodosius I, facilitated the evolution of centralised
bureaucratic structures and the elaboration of palace-based imperial
ceremonial (p. 104 below).

As already noted, the exception to the general rule about emperors
in this period was Constantius III, a successful career soldier from
the Balkans who became the leading general in the west from 411 to
421. In 417 he established a formal link with the imperial family
when Honorius consented to his marrying his half-sister Galla
Placidia (against the latter's wishes) – a necessary step towards
the ultimate prize which Constantius achieved four years later,
when he induced a reluctant Honorius to make him co-emperor
(Olympiodorus, *fr.* 33). Constantius' attainment of imperial office,
though cut short by a fatal illness, is nonetheless symptomatic of an
important feature of political life in this period – the crucial role
played by generals, especially in the west.[2] Arbogast's dominance
at the court of the young Valentinian II in the early 390s presaged
this development (p. 26 above), which was first fully realised in the
person of Stilicho.

Flavius Stilicho came from a military family, his father – by origin
a Vandal – having served as a cavalry officer under the Emperor
Valens. Stilicho himself held various ranks in the army under the

1. For further discussion, see A. D. Lee, *War in Late Antiquity: A Social History*,
Oxford: Blackwell, 2007, 30–4.
2. On this phenomenon generally, see J. M. O'Flynn, *Generalissimos of the Western
Roman Empire*, Edmonton: University of Alberta Press, 1983, P. MacGeorge, *Late
Roman Warlords*, Oxford: Oxford University Press, 2002, and W. Liebeschuetz,
'Warlords and landlords' in P. Erdkamp (ed.), *A Companion to the Roman Army*,
Oxford: Blackwell, 2007, 479–94. For Constantius, see W. Lütkenhaus, *Constantius III:
Studien zu seiner Tätigkeit und Stellung im Westreich, 411–421*, Bonn: Habelt, 1998.

Emperor Theodosius before eventually achieving a senior command in the early 390s. In the meantime Stilicho had strengthened his position through marriage (in around 384) to Theodosius' niece and adopted daughter, Serena. In 394 Stilicho was one of the two commanders of Theodosius' forces in the western campaign against Arbogast and Eugenius (p. 27 above), and following that victory, Theodosius appointed him senior general in the west and guardian of Honorius, pending Theodosius' return eastwards to deal with problems which had arisen during his absence; Theodosius no doubt calculated that Stilicho's habit of faithful service combined with family loyalty arising from his marriage to Serena would ensure that he acted in Honorius' best interests rather than treating him as Arbogast had Valentinian II.[3] Over the thirteen years during which Stilicho exercised power, he certainly never made any move to eliminate Honorius, but he did also take care to strengthen his own position in various ways. He gave his elder daughter Maria in marriage to Honorius (398), and took steps to ensure the centralisation of military power in the west in his own hands.[4] He also showed an acute appreciation of the importance of influencing elite opinion as an essential ingredient in maintaining power by extending his patronage to the precocious and prolific talent of the poet and panegyrist Claudian.[5]

During his tenure of power Stilicho had two main preoccupations. The first was relations with Constantinople, which were bound to be problematic from the outset after Stilicho announced that it had been Theodosius' dying wish that he also act as guardian for Arcadius in the east;[6] needless to say, there were already other ambitious individuals in Constantinople more than willing to take on that role (pp. 89–91 below). As a result, there arose what has aptly been described as a 'state of cold war' between west and east,[7] as a result of which Stilicho found himself in 397 being formally declared a public enemy by the senate in Constantinople, and facing a rebellion in north Africa instigated by his enemies in the east (Zos.

3. Zos. 4.59.1 with Alan Cameron, 'Theodosius the Great and the regency of Stilicho', *Harv. Stud.* 73 (1969), 247–80, at 274.
4. Zos. 5.4.1–2, with Jones, *LRE*, 174–5.
5. Alan Cameron, *Claudian: Poetry and Propaganda at the Court of Honorius*, Oxford: Clarendon Press, 1970.
6. Cameron, *Claudian*, 38–40.
7. Alan Cameron and J. Long, *Barbarians and Politics at the Court of Arcadius*, Berkeley: University of California Press, 1993, 166.

5.11.1–2). The former may have been a purely symbolic attack of no
practical significance, but the latter had very serious implications
since the city of Rome relied so heavily on north African grain
(p. 61 above). Suppression of the rebellion was potentially a difficult
task, since it was led by a Mauretanian prince, Gildo, who had also
loyally held the command of Roman forces in the region for the past
decade, and must therefore have built up a substantial power base;
fortunately for Stilicho, however, Gildo had alienated his brother
Mascezel, who agreed to lead a force from Italy against him and
achieved surprisingly rapid success.[8]

On the other hand, the problems arising from Stilicho's second
main preoccupation – the Goths – were not so easily solved. The
nature of those problems will be elucidated in the next chapter
(pp. 110–13 below); suffice it to say for the moment that they placed
increasingly serious pressures on the military and financial resources
of the western empire, exacerbated by the advent of significant
groups of barbarian invaders across the middle Danube and Rhine
in 405–6 (p. 112 below); the latter in turn triggered a military rebellion in Britain (407) which then spread to Gaul under the leadership
of a usurper capitalising on the talismanic name of Constantine.
These pressures opened up rifts in Stilicho's relations with Honorius
and the senatorial aristocracy of Rome, which were exploited by his
enemies in the summer of 408 with the claim that Stilicho was plot-
ting to place his own son Eucherius on the throne in Constantinople.
Military units assembling at Ticinum in northern Italy in preparation
for a campaign against the usurper Constantine were provoked into
mutiny during a ceremonial review by Honorius and proceeded
to lynch many of the senior officials accompanying the emperor, so
eliminating Stilicho's most important allies at court. Stilicho himself
was not present, but a no doubt badly shaken Honorius was soon
persuaded to order his arrest and execution.[9]

The elimination of Stilicho inaugurated a number of years of
political instability in the west, during which the Goths besieged and
eventually sacked Rome (pp. 113–14 below), and a degree of order
was only gradually re-established from 411 onwards largely through
the endeavours of the general Constantius (who, among other

8. Although the success was Mascezel's, Stilicho clearly took care to claim the credit in
Rome, where an inscription honoured Stilicho with a statue 'because of his having
replenished Rome with food supplies by subduing Gildo, public enemy' (*AE* 1926.124).
9. Zos. 5.32–4, with discussion in J. Matthews, *Western Aristocracies and Imperial
Court, AD 364–425*, Oxford: Clarendon Press, 1975, 270–83.

things, finally defeated the usurper Constantine), culminating in his brief period as co-emperor in 421 (p. 82 above). Contemporary appre-ciation of his energetic activities during the second decade of the ∞fth century are reflected in the praise he received from the Gallic senator and poet Rutilius Namatianus, who described him as 'the one salvation of the Latin name',[10] as also in an intriguing inscription from the town of Albenga on the Ligurian coast of north-ern Italy which presents him not only as an effective general but also as a city-founder:

> While the courageous, diligent, victorious, aptly-named Constantius was recovering Gaul and putting Liguria in order, he himself appointed a site for the walls and traced the foundations in the freshly-cut sod and gave an established constitution. Constructing buildings, he set up a citizen body, habitations, a forum, harbours, commerce and gates, and, while restoring the world, he promoted me to be a leading city. He did not refuse that my gate should speak in an inscription, and to the furious waves of wicked tribes he opposed the wall of the name of Constantius. (*CIL* 5.7781 = *ILS* 735 [tr. E. Courtney])

Constantius' premature death was soon followed by that of Honorius himself in 423, and since the latter's marriages had been childless, his demise signalled another period of competition for power between generals and court officials until eastern forces brought Honorius' nephew from Constantinople and installed him as Valentinian III in 425 (cf. Fig. 5). However, despite the best efforts of his formidable mother Galla Placidia, Valentinian's youth still left plenty of scope for his generals to exercise real power, with two of them – Aetius and Boniface (the pair famously described by a sixth-century historian as 'the last of the Romans' [Procop. *Wars* 3.3.15]) – competing for ascendancy between 425 and 432. It was Aetius who eventually won that long-running contest, to become the dominant figure in the west for the following two decades until his murder in 454.

Aetius' intriguing background is detailed by a contemporary historian:

> His father was Gaudentius, a man of no mean rank in the province of Scythia, who had begun his military service as a staff officer and who rose to the high position of master of the cavalry. His mother

10. H. S. Sivan, 'Rutilius Namatianus, Constantius III and the return to Gaul in light of new evidence', *Medieval Studies* 48 (1986), 522–32, at 524 (Frag. B, l.10).

Figure 5 Intaglio of sardonyx and gold (8.2 × 11.8 cm), depicting the symbolic investiture of Valentinian III as western emperor in 425 by his predecessors, his (deceased) father Constantius III (r) and uncle Honorius (l), accompanied by angels. It therefore serves as an assertion of dynastic continuity and legitimacy. Above Valentinian is the Christian chi-rho symbol and the Greek letters for alpha and omega, while below, 'Flavius Romulus, *vestiarius* [keeper of the imperial clothing], made this'. Photograph © The State Hermitage Museum, St Petersburg. Photo by Vladimir Terebenin, Leonard Kheifets, Yuri Molodkovets

was an Italian aristocrat of substantial wealth. Their son Aetius, who became a military tribune while still a youth, spent three years as a hostage of Alaric [the Goth], and was then passed on to the Huns. (Renatus Profuturus Frigeridus, in Gregory of Tours, *Hist.* 2.8)

Like Stilicho, therefore, Aetius came from a military family, while his stints as a hostage during his youth gave him invaluable knowledge of and contacts with important barbarian groups which he was able to exploit to his advantage at various points during his career. For example, during the turmoil after Honorius' death in the mid-420s, Aetius intervened with a large force of Huns whose backing enabled him to negotiate a favourable position for himself in the military hierarchy of Valentinian's new regime; likewise, after setbacks in his struggle for power with Boniface, he fled to the Huns, 'with whose friendship and help' he was able to retrieve his situation (Prosper Tiro, *Chron. s.a.* 425, 432).[11]

11. The most detailed study of Aetius is T. Stickler, *Aëtius: Gestaltungsspielräume eines*

Once he had established his position in the early 430s, his energies were primarily directed towards dealing with various barbarian groups in Gaul and Italy – Goths, Franks, Burgundians and Huns (pp. 115, 120 below). Like Stilicho, he also appreciated the value of promoting his image through the literary endeavours of a poet, in this case Flavius Merobaudes.[12] But there also survives independent testimony of the esteem in which he was held by the Roman senate, in the form of a (somewhat damaged) inscription, dating c. 440:[13]

> ... and also master of the soldiers in Gaul – a region which, on account of victories pledged in war and peace, he has recently restored to Roman rule – and master of both branches of the army [i.e., infantry and cavalry], consul ordinary for the second time [cf. Figs 6–7] and patrician, always devoted to the state, adorned with every military honour. On account of the safety of Italy, which he victoriously preserved by conquering distant peoples and destroying the Burgundians and subduing the Goths, the senate and people of Rome set this up for this man, by order of our lord emperors Theodosius and Placidius Valentinianus, ever Augusti, in the Hall of Liberty, which [by his own ability, like a father?] he establishes, extends and preserves, and likewise a [golden? bronze?] statue, for a man who is upright in his conduct, abstemious with regard to wealth, a staunch opponent of informers and public enemies, a defender of freedom, and an avenger of honour.

While Aetius never attempted to oust Valentinian or have himself proclaimed co-emperor on the pattern of Constantius III, he did arrange for the betrothal of his son Gaudentius to Valentinian's daughter Placidia, which would have given Gaudentius a claim to the throne in due course. Soon after this, however, he succumbed to the jealousy of the emperor (encouraged by envious courtiers), with a momentous significance noted by an early sixth-century chronicler: 'Aetius, the main salvation of the western empire and a scourge to king Attila [the Hun], was cut down in the palace together with his friend [the praetorian prefect] Boethius by the Emperor Valentinian, and with him fell the western kingdom and it has not yet been

---

Heermeisters im ausgehenden Weströmischen Reich, Munich: Beck, 2002. For briefer discussions in English, see the relevant pages in the studies referred to in n. 2 above.

12. For his surviving poems and panegyrics (small in number compared with those of Claudian), see F. M. Clover, *Flavius Merobaudes: A Translation and Historical Commentary*, Philadelphia: American Philosophical Society, 1971.

13. *CIL* 6.41389, with discussion in Stickler, *Aëtius*, 255–73. Despite the loss of the opening lines, there is no doubt that Aetius was the honorand.

Figure 6 First leaf of an ivory diptych of Flavius Aetius, presumably issued in honour of one of his three consulships (432, 437, 446), and depicting him presiding over games (involving wild beast hunts in the arena) which he staged in celebration of his holding office. © Collections musées de la ville de Bourges

able to be restored' (*Chron. Marc. s.a.* 454 [tr. B. Croke]). Strictly speaking, Aetius' death did not mark the end of the western empire, but his elimination undoubtedly made its eventual demise much more likely. The following year Valentinian himself was murdered by some of Aetius' resentful retainers, so bringing the Theodosian dynasty to an end, and no subsequent western emperor was able to

Figure 7 Second leaf of an ivory diptych of Flavius Aetius. © Collections musées de la ville de Bourges

retain power for more than five years during the remaining twenty years or so of its existence (pp. 94–6 below).

The eastern empire, on the other hand, proved more resilient, despite having to cope with comparable problems. When he embarked on his campaign against Eugenius and Arbogast in 394, Theodosius set an important precedent by leaving his older son

Arcadius not in the care of a general, but in that of his senior civilian official, the praetorian prefect Rufinus. Since Arcadius had formally been made co-emperor with his father more than a decade earlier, Theodosius' death did not present any procedural problems with regard to the succession in Constantinople, and Rufinus initially remained in place as Stilicho's effective equivalent in the east (Zos. 5.1.1). That he would face a more difficult time maintaining his dominance, however, soon became apparent. Like Stilicho a few years later, Rufinus seems to have had plans to use marriage to strengthen his hold on power by arranging for his daughter to wed the emperor, but those plans were thwarted when, as early as April 395, Arcadius married the beautiful and strong-willed Aelia Eudoxia (Zos. 5.3). Arcadius' choice of bride was immediately significant for two reasons: first, Eudoxia was the daughter of a general, the Frank Bauto, and although Bauto had died some years ago, in the late 380s, she had been raised in the household of the son of another distinguished general (also, incidentally, an enemy of Rufinus), making it plausible to see Arcadius' marriage as a move designed to win favour more generally among the military elite in the east; and secondly, Eudoxia's candidacy is said to have been promoted by a courtier, the eunuch Eutropius, who went on to replace Rufinus as the dominant figure in Constantinopolitan politics following the latter's brutal death in November 395. As Honorius was to do at Ticinum in 408 (p. 84 above), Arcadius found himself witnessing the lynching of a senior civilian official during a military parade outside Constantinople to welcome troops returning from the west. Since the soldiers responsible were from units sent back by Stilicho, suspicion understandably fell on him, but as the prime beneficiary, Eutropius is the more probable candidate.[14]

A eunuch might seem an unlikely person to exercise effective power in the eastern empire for the next four years, particularly given that, like most eunuchs, Eutropius was a freed slave.[15] How-

14. J. H. W. G. Liebeschuetz, *Barbarians and Bishops: Army, Church and State in the Age of Arcadius and Chrysostom*, Oxford: Clarendon Press, 1990, 92.
15. Since castration had long been outlawed within the Roman empire, most eunuchs were also foreigners by birth, although Eutropius is said to have been born near, rather than beyond, the Persian frontier (Claud. *In Eutropium* 1.58). For a lively discussion of the political power of eunuchs in late antiquity, see K. Hopkins, *Conquerors and Slaves*, Cambridge: Cambridge University Press, 1978, 172–96; for a more recent study, H. Scholten, *Der Eunuch in Kaisernähe: zur politischen und sozialen Bedeutung des praepositus sacri cubiculi im 4. und 5. Jahrhundert n. Chr.*, Frankfurt: Lang, 1995 (including a useful prosopography).

ever, their physical handicap meant that eunuchs' loyalties were thought to be much less open to other pressures and as a result, they came to be widely employed in the imperial household during late antiquity. The close proximity to the emperor of those who, like Eutropius, achieved the highest rank open to them, *praepositus sacri cubiculi* (superintendant of the sacred bedchamber), gave them opportunities to wield significant influence, whether through being in a position to offer informal advice for or against a particular course of action, or by controlling the access of others to the imperial presence – the scope for which increased significantly once emperors from Arcadius onwards ceased to lead the army in person and spent most of their time in the imperial palace.

Unsurprisingly, their lowly social origins and anomalous gender status, combined with their opportunity for political manipulation, meant that imperial eunuchs often attracted opprobium from ancient commentators, and Eutropius was no exception, with the two most detailed ancient sources for his tenure of power – the historian Zosimus and the poet Claudian – scathing in their attacks on him (the latter additionally influenced by Eutropius acting against the interests of Claudian's patron Stilicho).[16] This invective makes it difficult to arrive at a balanced assessment of his exercise of power. He was certainly prepared to secure his position by acting against the military, as the trial and exile of the prominent generals Timasius and Abundantius in 396 demonstrated (Zos. 5.8–10), and he had no hesitation in claiming the consulship for himself in 399, albeit at the expense of Claudian's withering sarcasm: 'O, shame of earth and heaven: in consul's robes an old woman is displayed through the cities and makes the title of the year effeminate' (*In Eutropium* 1.10). On the other hand, the independent record of legislation during these years indicates commendably even-handed treatment of the interests of different social groups.[17]

This, however, was not enough to save him when, in the summer of 399, a military mutiny broke out among Gothic federates in central Anatolia, demanding that Eutropius be removed from power. Eutropius sent forces to suppress the rebellion, but when the general in command, a Goth named Gainas, reported that the rebellion could not be suppressed by military means and that it would be

---

16. See Cameron, *Claudian*, 124–55; J. Long, *Claudian's* In Eutropium: *Or, How, When and Why to Slander a Eunuch*, Chapel Hill: University of North Carolina Press, 1996.
17. T. Honoré, *Law in the Crisis of Empire, 379–455 A.D.*, Oxford: Clarendon Press, 1998, 81–90.

best to grant the rebels' demand, Arcadius, fearing for the security of Constantinople, reluctantly dismissed Eutropius and sent him into exile (from where he was soon recalled and executed). By this stage Gainas had won the support of the rebel forces and had moved with them to the vicinity of Constantinople, but his underlying agenda remains difficult to ascertain. If his aim was to establish himself as the Stilicho of the east, then he found that more difficult to achieve than expected.

During the first half of 400, Arcadius continued to concede Gainas' further demands for the dismissal of other officials, but in July tensions within Constantinople reached such a state that elements of the urban populace finally attacked any Goths within the city, going so far as to burn down a church in which many had taken refuge. Gainas and his forces remained as a threatening presence occupying the hinterland of the city until the autumn, when they were finally engaged and defeated by a Roman army commanded, somewhat surprisingly, by another Goth, Fravitta – a victory which brought such relief that it was commemorated in poetry (four books in heroic metre by a student lawyer who was an eye-witness [Socrates, *Hist. eccl.* 6.6.36]) and monumental art (a column bearing a spiral relief, unfortunately preserved only in drawings by a much later visitor to the city).[18] Gainas escaped north with some residual forces and crossed the Danube, no doubt hoping to find sanctuary in his homeland, only to encounter and be killed by a band of Huns.

Much remains puzzling about this whole episode because of the particular difficulties of the surviving sources, not least the fact that the only surviving contemporary one was written in the form of an allegory.[19] What is clear, however, is that the practice of government by civilians survived in the east, and that part of the reason for that is that military power had not been centralised there in the way that Stilicho had orchestrated in the west. There continued to be five separate field armies in the eastern empire – two based near Constantinople (the so-called 'praesental' armies because of their proximity to the emperor's presence), one in the eastern provinces,

18. Images and discussion in Liebeschuetz, *Barbarians and Bishops*, 273–8 and plates 1–7.
19. For discussion of the sources and the Gainas episode more generally, see Liebeschuetz, *Barbarians and Bishops*, 104–25, and Cameron and Long, *Barbarians and Politics*, 199–252, 301–36. The fact that such eminent scholars can disagree on how to reconstruct what happened is symptomatic of the difficulties posed by the sources (the outline above generally adheres to Cameron and Long's version).

one in Thrace and one in Illyricum (*Not. Dign.* [*or.*] 5–9) – so Gainas did not have a monopoly on elite troops, and Fravitta and his field army were eventually able to be deployed against him. Fravitta's role also serves as a useful warning against making blanket assumptions concerning the loyalties of Goths to the empire.

By comparison with the tumultuous events of 395 to 400, political life in the east during the first half of the fifth century could be considered relatively tranquil – which is not to say that the east did not also face significant military challenges during these years (see pp. 118–20 below). The remaining years of Arcadius' reign, and the early decades of Theodosius II's, saw a succession of able civilians holding high office, sometimes for substantial periods of time, most notably Anthemius, praetorian prefect from 405 to 414, and Helion, master of the offices from 414 to 427.[20] Imperial eunuchs continued to feature as influential figures, particularly Antiochus during the first two decades and Chrysaphius in the 440s,[21] while against a background of renewed military crises, senior generals began to impinge on political life again, most notably in the form of the family of the Ardaburi. Ardabur was by origin an Alan, an Asiatic nomadic people who first came in contact with the empire at about the same time as the Huns in the 370s. As a senior general in the Roman army, he oversaw the military campaign which placed Valentinian III on the western throne in 425 and was honoured with the consulship in 427.

His son Aspar also played a role in that campaign, and by the early 430s had been promoted to a post as a senior general, becoming consul in 434 – the occasion for the production of a decorated silver plate which serves as physical testimony of the degree to which this generalissimo of barbarian origin had become integrated into elite culture, with its traditions of giving and receiving valuable gifts.[22] The extent of Aspar's political influence was only to become fully apparent after the death of Theodosius II in 450 (see pp. 98–9

20. For a helpful succinct overview of Theodosius' reign, see J. Harries, '*Pius princeps*: Theodosius II and fifth-century Constantinople' in P. Magdalino (ed.), *New Constantines: The Rhythm of Imperial Renewal in Byzantium, 4th–13th Centuries*, Aldershot: Ashgate, 1994, 35–44, with more detailed thematic analysis in F. Millar, *A Greek Roman Empire: Power and Belief under Theodosius II (408–450)*, Berkeley: University of California Press, 2006.

21. For the former, see G. Greatrex and J. Bardill, 'Antiochus the *praepositus*: a Persian eunuch at the court of Theodosius II', *DOP* 50 (1990), 171–97.

22. R. Leader-Newby, *Silver and Society in Late Antiquity*, Aldershot: Ashgate, 2004, 46–7.

below), but clearly its basis was being laid during these decades. It is worth noting, however, that another general also came to the fore in the 440s – Flavius Zeno from the region of Isauria in south-eastern Anatolia (an important military recruiting ground).[23] This is significant both for the precedent he provided for his better-known namesake in the second half of the fifth century (pp. 99–101 below), and for the way he presents another illustration of the existence of multiple senior military commands in the east helping to counteract the political ambitions of individual generals. Like Aspar, he too showed an appreciation of elite culture, reflected in this instance in a hexameter inscription on the floor of a bath house commissioned by his wife Paulina, replete with Homeric allusions (*SEG* 41 (1991) 1408).

Court politics: (2) Western dissolution, eastern resilience

Neither Theodosius II nor Valentinian III had produced any male offspring, and as both died unexpectedly while still in the prime of life, they had taken no steps to nominate a successor.[24] There was therefore the potential for novel developments on the political front – a potential, however, only partially realised, and sometimes in rather unexpected ways. Turning first to the west: since Valentinian had eliminated Aetius only sixth months prior to his own death, there had been little opportunity for any other ambitious individual to establish a position of influence at the western court, with the result that the succession was wide open but also, for that reason, likely to generate uncertainty and instability. Two prominent senators (Petronius Maximus and Eparchius Avitus) tried in quick succession to secure the throne for themselves, but within eighteen months a new generalissimo had emerged in the form of Flavius Ricimer.[25] A grandson of the Gothic ruler Vallia, he had served under Aetius before gaining prominence in 456 through successful military action against a Vandal fleet. His defeat of Avitus later that year left him as kingmaker in the west, a role he exercised for the next fifteen years until his death in 472.

During this period he promoted to the position of emperor Majorian, an army officer of ability (457–61), Libius Severus, an obscure individual about whose social background nothing is know

---

23. Lee, *War in Late Antiquity*, 83.
24. Theodosius died after falling from his horse while hunting; as already noted, Valentinian was assassinated by vengeful retainers of Aetius.
25. For a detailed study of Ricimer, see MacGeorge, *Warlords*, 167–268.

(461–5), and Anicius Olybrius, a senatorial aristocrat (472). The other western emperor from these years, Anthemius, an eastern aristocrat (467–72), was the candidate of the court in Constantinople, not Ricimer's choice, but his eastern promoters ensured they had Ricimer's acquiescence (probably through the promise of his marriage to Anthemius' daughter) before despatching Anthemius westwards. Ricimer's political power in this period is also evident in his removal of some of these emperors and in the interregna which invariably fell between their reigns – most strikingly in the substantial gap between the death of Severus in November 465 and the accession of Anthemius in April 467. It is perhaps worth adding that these events were mostly played out in Rome, since from the 440s onwards emperors once again spent more time there than in Ravenna.[26]

The limited surviving ancient sources for this period make it difficult to determine whether Ricimer was motivated by anything more than the desire to maintain his own position of dominance, but there can be no doubt that his elimination of successive emperors was detrimental to continuity of policy and to the prestige of imperial authority in the west. At the same time, it is important to recognise that the power he exercised was effectively limited to the Italian peninsula. On the one hand, the western Balkans was controlled by another general and protégé of Aetius, Marcellinus, who had rebelled against Valentinian III after the death of Aetius, until Marcellinus himself was murdered in 468, after which his nephew Julius Nepos assumed command of his forces.[27] On the other, Gaul was divided between the emerging Gothic kingdom in Aquitania, the Burgundians in the Rhone valley and Savoy, and the final outpost of imperial authority, in the Paris basin, where the general Aegidius, yet another protégé of Aetius, and his son Syagrius sought to maintain their independence during these years.[28]

Following Ricimer's death in August 472 (from natural causes),

26. A. Gillett, 'Rome, Ravenna and the last western emperors', *PBSR* 69 (2001), 131–67; M. Humphries, 'From emperor to pope? Ceremonial, space and authority at Rome from Constantine to Gregory the Great' in K. Cooper and J. Hillner (eds), *Religion, Dynasty and Patronage in Early Christian Rome, 300–900*, Oxford: Oxford University Press, 2007, 21–58, at 39–49.
27. For Marcellinus' career, see MacGeorge, *Warlords*, 17–63; for a divergent analysis of aspects of his career, see M. Kulikowski, 'Marcellinus "of Dalmatia" and the dissolution of the fifth-century empire', *Byzantion* 72 (2002), 177–91.
28. For Aegidius, Syagrius and the so-called 'kingdom of Soissons', see MacGeorge, *Warlords*, 71–164, and pp. 125–6 below.

the kingmaker role was briefly assumed by Ricimer's nephew, the Burgundian Gundobad, whose help Ricimer had called upon against Anthemius in early 472. Ricimer's final appointee, Olybrius, passed away a few months after Ricimer, and early in 473 Gundobad selected an official named Glycerius as his replacement. After little more than twelve months on the throne, however, Glycerius, apparently abandoned by Gundobad (who perhaps returned to Burgundian territories in Gaul), was overthrown by the general Julius Nepos from the western Balkans in mid-474. Nepos' own hold on power in turn lasted little more than twelve months, before one of his generals, Orestes, used his army to drive Nepos from Ravenna and proclaim his own son Romulus emperor in his place in October 475.

Orestes had already had an interesting career, serving as secretary to Attila the Hun and as an envoy from the Huns to Constantinople on two occasions in 449. It is not clear why he opted to make his son emperor, rather than taking the role for himself, unless perhaps he believed that his past association with Attila would make him unacceptable. At any rate, he was to be the last generalissimo wielding power behind the imperial throne, and a very short-lived one at that, for in August 476 troops in the Italian army (by now mostly of barbarian origin) mutinied when Orestes refused their request for grants of land. They then offered their support to one of their officers, a Hun named Odoacer who, ironically, was the son of Edeco, another former associate of Attila. In return for promising to fulfil their request for land, Odoacer was proclaimed king by the rebels, who then advanced against Orestes and killed him. Romulus was deposed, but allowed to live on account of his youth (hence the diminutive epithet 'Augustulus' applied to him in some sources), seeing out his days in relative comfort on the Bay of Naples like senatorial aristocrats of old. So it was that by a fortuitous but neat coincidence, the last western emperor bore the same name as the man credited with founding the city from which that empire derived. The only surprise is that no surviving ancient source comments on this uncanny symmetry – confirmation, perhaps, that for contemporaries, the events of 476 were not seen as having the momentous significance with which they have sometimes been instilled by modern scholars.[29]

29. For further discussion, see B. Croke, 'A.D. 476: the manufacture of a turning point', *Chiron* 13 (1983), 81–119.

The fact that Odoacer decided to have himself proclaimed king rather than adopting the role of kingmaker no doubt reflects the way in which imperial authority in the west had become devalued during the hegemony of Ricimer, as well as its geographical restriction to the Italian peninsula. Nevertheless, Odoacer's new departure did not represent a rejection of the idea of empire or of Roman ideals, for a senatorial embassy was soon sent to Constantinople seeking imperial sanction for Odoacer to rule Italy on behalf of the eastern emperor as a sort of client king. Unfortunately, the penultimate western emperor Julius Nepos had made good his escape from Orestes back to the western Balkans in 475, and he too sent envoys to Constantinople seeking imperial support for his claim to the western throne – a claim which was duly acknowledged (Malchus, *fr.* 14). However, since no resources were made available to him to make good his claim, Odoacer remained in control of Italy, maintaining both the security of the region against external threat and the position of the senatorial aristocracy[30] – until, in 489, he fell victim to the political machinations of Constantinople (see pp. 124–5 below).

Turning back, then, to developments in the eastern empire in the aftermath of Theodosius II's death (450), there was (in contrast to the west at the death of Valentinian in 455) a figure who had become increasingly powerful during the latter part of Theodosius' reign and in a position to influence the succession, in the person of the Alan general Aspar (pp. 93–4 above). Yet, surprisingly, there was a delay of nearly a month before a new emperor was proclaimed. The eventual successor was a relatively unknown fifty-eight-year-old former army officer named Marcian. Since he had served as an aide to Aspar and his father for fifteen years, he must have been Aspar's candidate, but the delay in his proclamation implies that Aspar had to engage in some serious negotiations. Some of those negotiations were no doubt with Theodosius' sister Pulcheria, whose subsequent marriage to the new emperor was important in helping to legitimate his rule, but they may too have involved another senior general, Flavius Zeno (p. 94 above), who was also in a strong position militarily in 450 and who subsequently benefited from Marcian's accession as well, in the form of being granted the prestigious rank of patrician.[31] If so, however, this potential rival to Aspar was not on

30. J. Moorhead, *Theoderic in Italy*, Oxford: Clarendon Press, 1992, 9–10, 28–30. As for Nepos, he was murdered by his own men at his villa near Salona in 480.
31. C. Zuckerman, 'L'Empire d'Orient et les Huns: notes sur Priscus', *T&M* 12 (1994), 160–82, at 172–6.

the scene for much longer, since he passed away perhaps as early as the end of 451.

Since Marcian's accession quickly resulted in the elimination of the eunuch Chrysaphius and the reversal of significant policies associated with him – notably, a tougher stance towards Attila (p. 120 below) and intervention in ecclesiastical affairs (pp. 144–6 below) – the new emperor can appear as a stronger figure than many other fifth-century incumbents of the imperial office. However, it has also to be borne in mind that Flavius Zeno and Pulcheria had both been opponents of Chrysaphius, so the changes may be more a reflection of their influence. As already noted, however, Zeno died early in Marcian's reign, and Pulcheria passed away in 453, leaving Aspar as the most important figure at court. He already held one of the two commands over the praesental field armies stationed near Constantinople, and in 453 his position was enhanced by the promotion of his son Ardabur as senior general in the eastern provinces. It is unsurprising, then, that when Marcian died in January 457 without an heir or a nominated successor, Aspar played the role of king-maker. Indeed, one later source reports that Aspar himself was offered the throne by the senate in Constantinople, but declined with the cryptic comment that 'I fear that a tradition in ruling might be initiated through me' – presumed to be a reference to his heterodox Arian religious affiliation.[32]

At any rate, Aspar selected an army officer in his mid-fiftiess named Leo, then commanding a unit of troops in one of the praesental armies. If not currently serving under Aspar, then presumably he must have done so previously. Certainly, Aspar chose him in the expectation that Leo would comply with his guidance, as indeed he did initially. He appears to have promised that his daughter Ariadne would marry Aspar's son Patricius, with a view to the latter succeeding Leo as emperor, and associates of Aspar were appointed to important positions in government. It is evident, however, that Leo developed a mind of his own, and although a son born in 463 died less than six months later, Leo nonetheless began to take steps to create the possibility of a future which diverged from that envisaged by Aspar. In 464 Leo appointed his brother-in-law Basiliscus as general of the field army in Thrace, in 465 Aspar's son Ardabur was dismissed from his military command after evidence

---

32. For references and discussion, see B. Croke, 'Dynasty and ethnicity: Emperor Leo I and the eclipse of Aspar', *Chiron* 35 (2005), 147–203, at 150, 190–1.

emerged of treasonable communication with Persia, and probably in 467 Leo married Ariadne not to Aspar's son Patricius, but to the commander of the *domestici* (a prestigious corps of officers), an Isaurian named Zeno. This man was not related to the general Flavius Zeno, but had adopted the name in place of his foreign-sounding birth name, Tarasicodissa, no doubt partly to deflect cultural prejudice at the imperial court, and partly to accrue by association some of the prestige which his fellow countryman had gained in the late 440s.[33] Zeno then held the consulship in 469 and was promoted to general of the field army in Thrace.[34]

Despite these setbacks, Aspar continued to pursue his family's interests with apparent success. In late 469, Zeno was transferred to Antioch to command the field army in the eastern provinces, thereby removing him from proximity to Leo in Constantinople, and the following year, Leo was pressured by Aspar into proclaiming Patricius as Caesar and heir (although, interestingly, on condition that Patricius adopted orthodox beliefs in lieu of Arianism before becoming emperor) and agreeing to his marriage to his younger daughter Leontia. This development, however, persuaded Leo of the need to act decisively to resolve matters definitively so as to protect his own family's interests. Perhaps fearing that Aspar might engineer his assassination in order to expedite Patricius' accession to the throne (as some later sources allege), Leo had Aspar, Ardabur and possibly Patricius murdered during a routine visit to the palace in 471.[35] This action may have gained Leo the unwelcome epithet of 'the butcher', but it did ensure that when he himself passed away in January 474, he was succeeded by his young grandson, Leo II, the son of Zeno and Ariadne, who had probably been made co-emperor in November 473.[36] In understanding why the eastern empire avoided the fate of the west, the contrast with Ricimer's relationship with his emperors during these same years is instructive: in Leo, the east had an emperor willing and able to act against a dominant generalissimo.

---

33. On Zeno's original name, see D. Feissel, 'Deux inscriptions d' Asie Mineure et les consuls de 448 and 452', *BCH* 108 (1984), 564–71, which supersedes R. M. Harrison, 'The emperor Zeno's real name', *Byz. Zeitschr.* 74 (1981), 27–8.

34. For detailed treatment of the events of this and the next paragraph, see Croke, 'Dynasty and ethnicity'.

35. One contemporary source (Candidus, *fr.* 1) appears to say that Patricius was wounded but escaped, but the text is only preserved via a summary, and Patricius is never mentioned again anyway.

36. B. Croke, 'The imperial reigns of Leo II', *Byz. Zeitschr.* 96 (2003), 559–75.

Leo II did not long outlive his grandfather, dying in November 474, aged seven – but not before his father Zeno had been appointed co-emperor (soon after Leo's accession). Despite the political convenience of young Leo's death for Zeno, there is not a whisper of foul play on his part in the sources, which, given his subsequent unpopularity, is highly significant with regard to his innocence; it is also worth remembering that child mortality was a much more common phenomenon in antiquity. However, while Zeno achieved what no other fifth-century generalissimo had – a sustained tenure of imperial power[37] – it proved to be an unusually difficult task for him to maintain control of the imperial throne. Zeno's acquisition of power provoked much bitterness among the relatives of Leo, whose wife Verina was quick to organise a coup, proclaiming her brother, the general Basiliscus, emperor in January 475. Zeno fled to Isauria, leaving Basiliscus for the next twenty months in control of Constantinople, where large numbers of Isaurians were massacred. However, Basiliscus alienated many inhabitants through his heterodox religious policies (p. 149 below), and also fell out with one of his most important supporters, another Isaurian named Illus (whose original backing for Basiliscus gives the lie to the idea that Basiliscus' overthrow of Zeno was primarily inspired by anti-Isaurian sentiment). Basiliscus had sent Illus to deal with the fugitive Zeno in Isauria, but when Basiliscus failed to keep certain (unspecified) promises, Illus changed sides and agreed to help restore Zeno to power (August 476). Basiliscus' elimination did not, however, deter (a now imprisoned) Verina from encouraging a second attempt to overthrow Zeno, when her son-in-law Marcian (husband to Leontia) almost succeeded in seizing Zeno and the imperial palace in 479.

Somewhat surprisingly, Zeno's chief internal opposition during the 480s came from Illus. Zeno had promoted Illus to important administrative and military posts in recognition of his help against Basiliscus, but Illus' stormy relations with the womenfolk of Leo's family destroyed the two men's co-operation. After Verina tried to have Illus assassinated in 478 for his betrayal of Basiliscus, Illus demanded Verina from Zeno and imprisoned her in his fortress in Isauria, and when Illus refused Ariadne's request to release her mother in 480, Ariadne too tried to have him killed. Eventually, Illus rebelled openly against Zeno in 484, proclaiming another Isaurian, Leontius, emperor (with the blessing of Verina, of all people – but

37. Constantius III was, of course, emperor for less than a year (above, pp. 81–2).

her hatred of Zeno was even greater than her hatred of Illus). Zeno's forces laid siege to Illus and Leontius in Isauria for four years until their betrayal led to their capture and execution; Verina died in the early stages of the war, while Zeno himself passed away in 491.[38]

By the final quarter of the fifth century, then, the empire had undergone a major political reconfiguration. In the western half, the reach of imperial power steadily contracted, particularly after the death of Aetius in 454 until, in 476, it disappeared completely. This was the outcome of the complex interplay of court politics with the challenges presented by various barbarian groups who managed to establish themselves in the western provinces over the course of the fifth century (Chapter 6 below). The experience of the eastern half of the empire during this same period shows, however, that there was nothing inevitable about such an outcome. Despite facing formidable frontier challenges of its own (Chapter 6 below) and considerable turmoil in court politics at the end of the fourth century and in the second half of the fifth, it continued as a viable entity, with the period when Theodosius II was emperor emerging as one of crucial significance for maintaining stability, even if Theodosius himself appears to have been a man of limited abilities. The final section of this chapter aims to shed further light on these developments by examining the nature of political power during the fifth century.

The dyamics of political power

The shift from mobile to largely palace-bound emperors following the death of Theodosius I had important consequences for the dynamics of political power in the late Roman world.[39] Most obviously, it restricted their interaction with the armed forces and created the space for ambitious generals to become dominant figures in the political life of both west and east during the fifth century (though earlier in the west than the east). That dominance was reflected not only in their direction of military affairs, but also in

38. For good analysis of Illus' career and relations with Zeno, see H. Elton, 'Illus and the imperial aristocracy under Zeno', *Byzantion* 70 (2000), 393–407.
39. Valuable discussions of the late Roman imperial court include C. Kelly, 'Emperor, government and bureaucracy', *CAH*[2] 13.138–83, M. McCormick, 'Emperor and court', *CAH*[2] 14.135–63, Millar, *Greek Roman Empire*, 192–234, R. Smith, 'The imperial court of the late Roman empire, c. AD 300–c. AD 450' in A. J. S. Spawforth (ed.), *The Court and Court Societies in Ancient Monarchies*, Cambridge, Cambridge University Press, 2007, 157–232, and M. Whitby, 'The role of the emperor' in D. Gwynn (ed.), *A. H. M. Jones and the Later Roman Empire*, Leiden: Brill, 2008, 65–96.

their active involvement in a range of non-military matters. In 419, it was the general Constantius to whom an embassy from Gaul directed its request for tax relief (Sid. Apoll. *Carm.* 7.210–11) and from whom African bishops sought aid concerning individuals who had sought asylum in a church in Carthage;[40] it was also Constantius who is found corresponding in the same year with the prefect of Rome concerning the disputed election of the city's bishop (*Coll. Avell.* 29–32). Aetius, too, was charged with enforcing the primacy of the bishop of Rome in 445 (*Nov. Val.* 17.4), intervened in arrangements for Rome's pork supply in 452 (*Nov. Val.* 36.1), and at the time of his murder in the imperial palace by Valentinian's hand was engaged with the emperor in 'evaluating proposals to raise money … [and] was explaining the finances and calculating the tax revenues' (John of Antioch, *fr.* 224.2 [Mariev]). In the east, Aspar initiated the construction of a large cistern in Constantinople in 459 to augment the city's water supply (*Chron. Pasch. s.a.* 459), intervened to try to alleviate the impact of the disastrous fire which swept through Constantinople in 464 (Candidus, *fr.* 1), and acted to protect Timothy, bishop of Alexandria, against the Emperor Leo's attempt to enforce the outcomes of the Council of Chalcedon (Theophanes, *Chron.* AM 5952; cf. p. 149 below).

The shift to the palace also created greater opportunities for others with a less obvious power base to try to exert influence in political life. The case of imperial eunuchs, whose role as chamberlains gave them direct, daily contact with the emperor, has already been noted with reference to figures such as Eutropius, Antiochus and Chrysaphius – all at the eastern court (pp. 90–1, 93 above) – to whom can be added, from the west, Heraclius, 'a eunuch who carried very great weight with the emperor' and who was instrumental in persuading Valentinian III to eliminate Aetius in 454 (John of Antioch, *fr.* 224 [Mariev]). Famously, when Porphyry, bishop of Gaza, sought official sanction for his efforts to close local pagan temples in the period 398–400, he directed his lobbying first to the eunuch chamberlain Eutropius and then, after the latter's fall from power, to Amantius, the eunuch steward of the Empress Eudoxia;[41]

---

40. August. *Epp.* 15*.2, 16*.2, 23A*.1, with R. Delmaire and C. Lepelley, 'Du nouveau sur Carthage', *Opus* 2 (1983), 477–87.
41. Marcus Diaconus, *V. Porphyrii* 26–7, 37–41. T. D. Barnes (*Early Christian Hagiography and Roman History*, Tubingen: Mohr Siebeck, 2010, 260–83) has presented strong arguments for doubting the historicity of this text, but they do not invalidate the assumptions underlying the text as to how court politics worked.

equally famously, when Cyril, bishop of Alexandria, was trying to influence imperial opinion in his favour in the context of the Christological controversies of the early 430s (pp. 138–40 below), he despatched material inducements to a range of individuals whom he regarded as being in the best position to assist his cause, including a number of palace eunuchs, one of whom received the largest amount of any recipient (200 lbs of gold).[42]

Porphyry's targeting of Eudoxia's steward, and Cyril's also directing some of his 'gifts' to attendants of the Emperor Theodosius' sister Pulcheria, reflect the fact that imperial females – wives, mothers, sisters – now also had more constant interaction with palace-bound emperors, and greater potential to sway them, if they were so minded. The fifth century certainly featured a number of prominent imperial females who have often been viewed as influential figures in affairs of state. In particular, Galla Placidia, widow of Constantius III and mother of Valentinian III, and Pulcheria, sister of Theodosius II, have been seen as exercising significant influence over their son and brother respectively, especially since both of the latter acceded to the throne as minors.[43] Their influence, however, should not be overstated. Pulcheria, after all, was only two years older than her brother, making it hard, in practice, to see her as such an influential figure in the earlier part of his reign when he was most susceptible to manipulation. Moreover, even once she was of age, she would have been competing against experienced civilian and military figures, such as Helion, master of the offices from 414 to 427, and Flavius Plintha, a senior general from 419 to 438 – 'at that time [mid-420s] one of the most powerful people at court' (Sozom. *Hist. eccl.* 7.17.14). Galla, of course, was not handicapped by youth at the time of Valentinian III's accession, but, though she no doubt disliked Aetius for having supported the usurper John in the mid-420s, and sought to counteract his power through Boniface, he was firmly in control from 432 onwards. Where imperial females did sometimes have an important role was in providing dynastic continuity through marriage to a successor, most obviously in Pulcheria's marriage to Marcian in 450, but also in the marriages

42. P. Battifol, 'Les présents de Saint Cyrille à la cour de Constantinople', *Bulletin d'ancienne literature et d'archeologie chretiennes* 1 (1911), 247–64; Millar, *Greek Roman Empire*, 219–21.
43. S. I. Oost, *Galla Placidia Augusta*, Chicago: University of Chicago Press, 1968; K. Holum, *Theodosian Empresses: Women and Imperial Dominion in Late Antiquity*, Berkeley: University of California Press, 1982.

of Ariadne (Fig. 8) to Zeno and to Anastasius (p. 161 below). In a similar vein is the Emperor Leo's widow Verina's proclamation of her brother Basiliscus as emperor in opposition to Zeno, and her support for Marcian's attempted usurpation. It is generally agreed that Pulcheria, at least, extracted concessions in return for her legitimation of Marcian's rule, by his agreeing to call a new church council (at Chalcedon) to endorse a shift in religious policy (p. 145 below).

Although the restriction of emperors to palace and capital city in the fifth century exposed them to different pressures, this shift also offered opportunities for projection of imperial power in different ways, particularly through architecture and the development of associated ceremonial rituals. The best evidence undoubtedly derives from Constantinople, where continuity of occupation and freedom from the direct impact of military conflict facilitated uninterrupted evolution in these areas. Nevertheless, Ravenna and then, from the 440s, Rome provide some indication of comparable trends in the west, even if the evidence is much sketchier. Although mapping the detailed layout and evolution of the imperial palace in Constantinople in late antiquity remains fraught with difficulties,[44] the permanent residence of the emperor there from the late fourth century was the catalyst for the investment of resources in the development of the large terraced site between the hippodrome and the waters of the Bosporus which was gradually filled by a complex of reception and dining halls, consultation chambers, residential quarters, courtyards and gardens, chapels, and bureaux for elements of the imperial administration most closely associated with the court, such as the master of the offices and his staff. In Ravenna, textual and archaeological evidence suggests the development of a palace complex in the south-eastern corner of the city in the first half of the fifth century, including a colonnaded courtyard and a large hall with an apse and marble paving, although this may have involved the adaptation and enlargement of a pre-existing urban villa.[45] As for Rome, it seems that damage to the Palatine during the Gothic sack of the city in 410 led to the development of a new palace on the Pincian hill including a semi-circular, marble-clad pavilion

44. J. Bardill, 'The Great Palace of the Byzantine emperors and the Walker Trust excavations', *JRA* 12 (1999), 216–30.
45. D. M. Deliyannis, *Ravenna in Late Antiquity*, Cambridge: Cambridge University Press, 2010, 55–8.

Figure 8 Ivory diptych leaf of the Empress Ariadne (26.5 × 12.7 cm), seated on a throne under a baldachin, holding a globe with a cross and wearing elaborate robes and jewellery. © Kunsthistorisches Museum, Vienna

offering views over the city centre, which is presumed to be where
emperors were based in the final decades of the western empire.[46]

Palaces were important statements of imperial power, but while
their exteriors could project that message to all who viewed them,
their interiors were accessible to a much smaller audience. However,
emperors also left their marks on the public spaces of the cities in
which they resided. In Constantinople, following the lead of his
father, Arcadius added his own forum on the main east–west
thoroughfare of the Mesē in which was placed the historiated
column depicting the defeat of Gainas in 400 (pp. 91–2 above).
While the Theodosian Walls constructed in 413 served a practical
protective purpose (p. 118 below), they were also potent symbols of
imperial capability, and Theodosius II also added a further semi-
circular forum beyond the Forum of Arcadius, with its own column
surmounted by a statue of the emperor. Marcian in turn added
another forum and column with statue, albeit on the route heading
north-west, while Leo placed his forum and column with statue
closer to the city centre, in the area behind the church of Hagia
Eirene.[47] As for Ravenna, the structures which date from the first
half of the fifth century and which must have involved imperial
initiative comprise the city walls and various churches, while in mid-
century Rome the imperial presence was reflected in renovations to
the amphitheatre and in church construction.[48]

The cities' public spaces were also important as the venues for
ceremonial rituals which increased in number and complexity during
this period, and played an important role in reinforcing imperial
authority. Imperial accessions had long been important occasions,
but had more often than not taken place in a military camp with
an audience necessarily limited to the troops who happened to be
present. In the second half of the fourth century, however, some
accessions began to take place in Constantinople, or at least in the
suburb of the Hebdomon where a military parade ground was
located, and this continued to be the pattern for Theodosius II,
Marcian and Leo in the fifth century. A detailed account of the
last of these survives, confirming military involvement in the initial
stages before Leo proceeded into the city, via public spaces, to

46. Humphries, 'Emperor to pope', 37.
47. F. A. Bauer, 'Urban space and ritual: Constantinople in late antiquity' in J. R. Brandt
and O. Steen (eds), *Imperial Art as Christian Art – Christian Art as Imperial Art*, Rome:
Bardi, 2001, 27–61, at 38–40.
48. Deliyannis, *Ravenna*, 52–4, 60–84; Humphries, 'Emperor to pope', 42–3.

various churches, the whole process accompanied by a succession of rituals, part military, part religious. Later in the fifth century, the focal point for accessions shifted to the hippodrome, where an even larger audience could be guaranteed.[49] Imperial marriages and funerals were also major ceremonial occasions, perhaps most prominently in this period the nuptials of Valentinian III and Theodosius II's daughter Eudoxia in Constantinople in 437.[50] Imperial visits to services in the city's churches and to inspect its granaries also offered opportunities for ceremonial display, as did news of military victories.[51] Explicit evidence from Ravenna is more limited, but includes at least one example of victory celebrations (over usurpers),[52] while there is evidence from Rome in the mid-fifth century of the formal celebration of the arrival of the emperor and of images representing him.[53]

But what about inhabitants of the empire who did not live in or near an imperial capital? How did emperors project their power to them? In an empire the size of the Roman, this was of course a long-standing problem, since even peripatetic emperors could still only be in one place at a time. Its solution, however, became even more relevant when that one place rarely changed. An important part of that solution was the empire-wide distribution of the imperial image, not only through the obvious medium of coinage, but also through imperial portraits, as an early fifth-century bishop noted:[54]

> Since the emperor cannot be present everywhere, it is necessary to set up a portrait of the emperor at tribunals, in marketplaces, at meetings and in theatres. In fact a portrait must be present in every place where an official acts, so that he might sanction whatever transpires; for the emperor, being human, cannot be everywhere. (Severianus of Gabala, *In Cosmogoniam* 6.5 [= *PG* 56.489] [tr. C. Ando])

49. For references and the account of Leo's accession, see Lee, *War in Late Antiquity*, 54–6.
50. See J. F. Matthews, *Laying Down the Law: A Study of the Theodosian Code*, New Haven: Yale University Press, 2000, 1–4, for a reconstruction of this event.
51. McCormick, 'Emperor and court', 158–60.
52. M. McCormick, *Eternal Victory: Triumphal Rulership in Late Antiquity, Byzantium and the Early Medieval West*, Cambridge: Cambridge University Press, 1985, 56–7.
53. Humphries, 'Emperor to pope', 43–5.
54. For detailed discussion of this subject, see C. Ando, *Imperial Ideology and Provincial Loyalty in the Roman Empire*, Berkeley: University of California Press, 2000, 215–28 (coinage), 228–53 (portraits).

Moreover those portraits were more than just mere pictorial representations: they were regarded as embodying the emperor and his presence. Athanasius of Alexandria imagined an imperial portrait explaining its relationship to the emperor as follows: 'The emperor and I are one, for I am in him and he is in me. What you see in me, this you see in him, and what you have seen in him, you see now in me' (*Contra Arianos* 3.5). Hence, the terror which descended on the city of Antioch in 387 when rioting there spilled over into the destruction of the imperial images (p. 215 below).

If imperial portraits embodied the emperor and allowed inhabitants of the empire to visualise him, then imperial laws were the medium through which they could hear the emperor's voice. Imperial laws were disseminated in written form, to be posted in public locations in communities throughout the empire and sometimes engraved on stone or bronze for more permanent display. This raises the issue of the extent of literacy; however, in addition to the likelihood that literate individuals would read the posted text for the benefit of others, it appears to have been normal practice for new laws to be read out aloud when first promulgated in a particular locality: 'A profound silence reigns when imperial documents are read aloud; there is not the slightest noise, as everyone listens very attentively to the commands contained in them' (John Chrysostom, *Hom. in cap. II Gen.* 14.2 [= *PG* 53.112)].[55] The reverence which this expectation of silence implies, along with other features of the process of delivering the law (such as the references to officials who received the text 'worshipping' or 'adoring' the law),[56] are indicative of how, irrespective of their actual content, the emperor's legal pronouncements were a crucial means for projecting and reinforcing his authority across the empire.

As with the despatch of imperial portraits, so the promulgation of laws throughout the empire was not a development specific to late antiquity. However, the fifth century does provide an important instance of an emperor exploiting the potential of law to communicate his authority in a novel and powerful way, through the issuing, in 438, of a law code bearing the name of Theodosius II. There were

55. For the promulgation of laws, including their reading out, see further Ando, *Imperial Ideology*, 104–8, and Matthews, *Laying Down the Law*, 181–99.
56. Matthews, *Laying Down the Law*, 181–2, suggests that 'this adoration was presumably expressed by the recipient's lowering his head and raising the document to his lips, much as an official would bend to touch the imperial purple in the court ceremonial of *adoratio purpurae*.'

precedents for such a project from the reign of Diocletian, but these earlier codes – those of the jurists Gregori(an)us and Hermogenianus – had focused on the narrower task of collecting imperial rescripts (responses to petitions), and they were identified by the names of the two jurists, rather than that of the emperor.[57] It is a measure of the larger task undertaken by Theodosius' law commission that it took a decade to gather, collate and edit the imperial laws, but this also made it a more significant achievement, through which the emperor could be seen to be systematising the law and imposing order in the legal realm.[58] Theodosius may not have been able to claim significant success in war-making, but he could claim to have trumped his forebears in that other important field of imperial endeavour, law-making.

The *Theodosian Code* also had a further dimension of relevance to the dynamics of political power in this period. Although it was compiled in Constantinople, it was intended for use in both parts of the empire as was made clear through its promulgation in the senate in Rome in 438.[59] In this way, the *Code* also served as an assertion of the unity of the empire, following close on the promotion of this idea by different means the previous year, through the marriage of Valentinian III and Theodosius' daughter Eudoxia.[60] While it must have been difficult for westerners not to feel that, for all the symbolism of unity, it was the east which had the upper hand in this relationship, it was also the case that the east was prepared repeatedly to commit military forces to aiding the west throughout much of the fifth century (p. 85 above and pp. 113, 116–17, 121–2 below).

---

57. J. Harries, *Law and Empire in Late Antiquity*, Cambridge: Cambridge University Press, 1999, 63–4.
58. For the work of the law commission, see Matthews, *Laying Down the Law*.
59. Matthews, *Laying Down the Law*, 1–9, 31–5.
60. It has been argued that the *Notitia Dignitatum*, a register of military and civilian offices in east and west in the late fourth/early fifth century, was likewise intended as an expression of imperial unity: P. Brennan, 'The *Notitia Dignitatum*' in C. Nicolet (ed.), *Les Litteratures techniques dans l'antiquité romaine*, Geneva: Fondation Hardt, 1996, 153–69.

CHAPTER 6

Barbarians and Romans

Goths, Vandals and Huns

During the half century following the death of Theodosius I, the empire had to contend with many barbarian groups, but the most significant were the Goths, the Vandals and the Huns. Each of these groups owed its ability to create serious difficulties for the empire, at least in part, to having forceful leaders in the persons of Alaric, Geiseric and Attila respectively. The analytical narrative which follows therefore focuses on imperial dealings with each of these men in turn.[1]

Gothic federates had formed an important component of Theodosius' expeditionary force to the west in 394 and had played a major role in the victory at the River Frigidus (p. 27 above). It was perhaps lack of recognition of that role which prompted some of these Goths, on their return to the Balkans in 395, to rebel against imperial authority, under the leadership of one of their officers, Alaric, who seems to have resented not being given a formal Roman command. No doubt supplemented by other Goths from the region, Alaric's forces plundered widely through the Balkans, and since the eastern field armies from the Balkan region had not yet returned from Italy, the authorities in Constantinople could do little to stop them. Stilicho did intervene with the substantial forces at his disposal, but since Rufinus feared that this was a pretext for Stilicho to march on Constantinople, Arcadius was persuaded to order Stilicho to relinquish those of his troops from the eastern field armies and return to Italy – which Stilicho duly did (at the cost, however, of Rufinus' life (p. 90 above). The following year, Alaric moved south into Greece, unopposed because eastern forces were preoccupied

---

1. For more detailed overviews of the often complex developments treated here, see P. Heather, *The Fall of the Roman Empire*, London: Macmillan, 2005; G. Halsall, *Barbarian Migrations and the Roman West, 376–568*, Cambridge: Cambridge University Press, 2007.

with a major Hunnic invasion across the Caucasus into Anatolia. In 397 Stilicho again intervened, but before he was able to deal a decisive blow against Alaric, he suddenly withdrew his forces to Italy – perhaps because Eutropius, fearful of Stilicho's intentions, instigated Gildo's rebellion in north Africa (the precise chronological relationship of these different events is, however, not entirely certain) (pp. 83–4 above). At the same time, Eutropius seems to have appeased Alaric by granting him some sort of command in the eastern army, usually thought to be that of senior general in the Balkans, as well as probably providing pay and rations for his forces. This would certainly help to account for the relatively quiescent state of Alaric's Goths over the next three to four years.[2]

That changed in late 401 when Alaric and his forces moved to the north-west Balkans and crossed the Julian Alps into northern Italy (facilitated, no doubt, by the recent destruction of the forts in this area during Theodosius' campaign against Eugenius and Arbogast).[3] Suddenly, Constantinople's Gothic problem had become Stilicho's. The most plausible explanation for Alaric's decision is that his agreement with Eutropius in 397 lapsed in 399 when the latter fell from power, and Eutropius' immediate successors were unwilling to continue arrangements; when the turmoil at Constantinople created by Gainas in 400 (above, p. 92) failed to produce a regime more amenable to Alaric's wishes, he may have calculated that he might achieve success more easily by turning his attention westwards.[4] Initially, that proved not to be the case, since Stilicho achieved sufficient success against Alaric in a battle at Pollentia in north-west Italy on Easter Day 402 to convince the Goths to withdraw back to the north-west Balkans, where they remained for the next few years. Perhaps the most important consequence of these events concerned the location of the imperial court. In the period before Pollentia, the Goths had threatened Milan, and although Honorius was not there at the time, it was enough to persuade him that Ravenna would make a better residence. While the defensive advantages of Ravenna were not as great as often assumed – among other things, it had no natural supplies of fresh water – it did offer greater security than

2. For discussion, see J. Matthews, *Western Aristocracies and Imperial Court, AD 364–425*, Oxford: Clarendon Press, 1975, 270–3; P. Heather, *Goths and Romans 332–489*, Oxford: Clarendon Press, 1991, 199–208.
3. N. Christie, *From Constantine to Charlemagne: An Archaeology of Italy, AD 300–800*, Aldershot: Ashgate, 2006, 325–6.
4. Heather, *Goths and Romans*, 206–8.

Milan, but above all its coastal location on the Adriatic facilitated communications with the east.[5]

Alaric's return to the north-west Balkans brought only temporary respite to Italy, for in 405 another substantial body of Goths and other barbarians, this time from outside the empire, crossed the middle Danube and advanced into northern Italy, where they plundered the countryside and besieged cities and towns. The decision of their leader Radagaisus to split his forces into three groups helped Stilicho to contain the threat, eventually cornering Radagaisus' group near Florence and starving them into submission. However, the imperial government was clearly struggling to find enough military manpower to cope with these different invasions, since Stilicho had to recall units from Britain and Gaul, and a law issued at Ravenna in early 406 took the very unusual step of offering slaves their freedom and money if they enlisted (Claud. *de bello Getico* 414–29, *Cod. Theod.* 7.13.16).

Pressures on Stilicho increased further when another body of barbarians, comprising Vandals, Sueves and Alans, crossed the Rhine into Gaul at the end of 406 (p. 115 below),[6] and a rebellion in Britain spread to Gaul under the leadership of the usurper Constantine in 407 (p. 84 above). All these developments prevented Stilicho from implementing a plan to take troops into the western Balkans (perhaps with a view to detaching from Constantinople a region which could help to relieve the west's shortage of recruits) – but not before he had persuaded Alaric to prepare the way by advancing there with his forces. When Stilicho then found himself unable to follow with Roman troops, Alaric marched back into Italy and demanded financial compensation for his efforts to the tune of 4,000 lbs of gold. While not a vast sum by the standard of senatorial incomes (cf. Olympiodorus, *fr.* 41,2), Stilicho's insistence in early 408 that the senate should find the money to pay Alaric met with fierce resistance as a matter of principle, and although Stilicho's

5. For differing emphases on the factors involved, see A. Gillett, 'Rome, Ravenna and the last western emperors', *PBSR* 69 (2001), 131–67, 159–65; Christie, *Constantine to Charlemagne*, 332–3; D. M. Deliyannis, *Ravenna in Late Antiquity*, Cambridge, Cambridge University Press, 2010, 46–8.
6. The proposal to advance the crossing to the end of 405 (M. Kulikowski, 'Barbarians in Gaul, usurpers in Britain', *Britannia* 31 [2000], 325–45) has been vigorously challenged by A. R. Birley, *The Roman Government of Britain*, Oxford: Clarendon Press, 2005, 455–60, and N. McLynn, 'Poetic creativity and political crisis in early fifth-century Gaul', *JLA* 2 (2009), 60–74, at 61 n.3.

request was eventually conceded, this episode played a major part in generating the opposition which eventually led to his downfall later that year (p. 84 above).

Those responsible for Stilicho's elimination did not retain their influence over Honorius for long, but since they were resolutely opposed to negotiating with Alaric, their short tenure of power was to have disproportionate consequences. When his attempt to negotiate some sort of *modus vivendi* with the new regime was rejected, Alaric tried to place pressure on Honorius by blockading Rome during the winter of 408/9. The resulting starvation induced the senate to send envoys to Ravenna pleading with the emperor to grant Alaric's demands – money, food and a senior command in the army. After provisionally agreeing to Alaric's terms in return for lifting the blockade, Honorius then reneged on a part of the terms (specifically the senior army command), prompting Alaric not only to besiege Rome again in late 409, but also to proclaim a leading senator, Priscus Attalus, as a rival emperor, from whom Alaric then received the appointment as senior general which Honorius could not bring himself to bestow.[7]

A now desperate Honorius initially offered to share power with Attalus, but when this proposal was rejected, he made ready to escape from Ravenna by sea to the east, until his resolve was restored by the unexpected arrival by ship of 4,000 troops from Constantinople. Eventually in the summer of 410 he offered further negotiations with Alaric, whereupon Alaric deposed Attalus and advanced towards Ravenna. While waiting nearby for negotiations to commence, however, Alaric and his retinue were attacked by an independent body of Goths led by a certain Sarus who had long been connected with the court of Honorius. Whether Sarus was acting on imperial orders or on his own initiative is unclear, but Alaric assumed the former, and immediately withdrew southwards, where he besieged Rome for a third time. This time, however, his aim was not to force Honorius back to the negotiating table, but rather to vent his frustration. In a little over a fortnight, the city was captured and then subjected to three days of plundering, before

7. It was around this time that Honorius is reported to have 'sent letters to the cities of Britain, urging them to fend for themselves' (Zos. 6.10.2), thereby signalling the formal end of Roman rule there. For further discussion, see D. Mattingly, *An Imperial Possession: Britain in the Roman Empire, 54 BC–AD 409*, London: Allen Lane, 2006, 529–39.

Alaric withdrew southwards, perhaps hoping to cross over to north Africa.[8]

Far from representing some great success for the Goths, therefore, Alaric's sack of Rome in 410 was, as commentators have noted, 'an irrelevance, forced on him by the failure of his other policies', and 'an admission of defeat'.[9] From an imperial perspective, too, the fact that Rome had long ceased to be the emperor's residence and the focal point of court politics meant that, at a practical level, the significance of the event was also much reduced. Nonetheless, there was no escaping its symbolic importance, as the first time that a foreign army had occupied the city since the Gallic sack of 387/6 BC – when Rome was still only one state among many in the Italian peninsula and was still more than a century away from acquiring the beginnings of a territorial empire. This helps to explain the famously apocalyptic reaction of one contemporary to news of the event, referring to it as the time 'when the brightest light of the world was extinguished, the Roman empire was decapitated, and the whole world perished in one city' (Jer. *Comm. in Ezech.* 1, *praef.*). At the same time, there was a ground swell of pagan opinion blaming the empire's adoption of Christianity for the fate of the city – a reaction which provoked Augustine to write his hugely influential apologetic work *De Civitate Dei (The City of God)*.[10] As for the city itself, it certainly experienced destruction of buildings, as well as loss of population – besides those killed or taken prisoner by the Goths, many wealthy inhabitants fled overseas to north Africa and the east, while numerous slaves seized the opportunity to escape. However, there is a limit to how much damage can be done to a city of Rome's size in three days, and the city did recover, with a succession of public structures in the city centre restored over the course of the next decade or so.[11]

As for the Goths, their attempt to cross to Sicily en route to Africa was thwarted by a storm which wrecked the fleet they had assembled, and while returning northwards, Alaric himself fell ill

8. For a superb, more detailed account of the complex twists and turns of the period 408–10, see Matthews, *Western Aristocracies*, 284–306.

9. Matthews, *Western Aristocracies*, 301; M. Kulikowski, *Rome's Gothic Wars from the Third Century to Alaric*, Cambridge: Cambridge University Press, 2007, 177.

10. For discussion of its genesis, see G. O'Daly, *Augustine's* City of God: *A Reader's Guide*, Oxford: Clarendon Press, 1999, 27–33.

11. Details in B. Lançon, *Rome in Late Antiquity* (tr. A. Nevill), Edinburgh: Edinburgh University Press, 2000, 39.

and died, whereupon his brother-in-law Athaulf was chosen to succeed him as leader. Under him the Goths eventually advanced into southern Gaul, where they fought against both Roman and Vandal forces. In an effort to strengthen his position vis-à-vis the Romans, he married Galla Placidia (the daughter of Theodosius I who had been captured at Rome in 410) in 414; intriguingly, at the ceremony not only the bride, but also the groom, was attired in Roman dress (Olympiodorus, *fr.* 24). It is reported that, under Galla's influence, Athaulf declared it his aim to 'restore and extend the Roman empire by the might of the Goths ... and to be remembered by posterity as the author of Rome's renewal' (Oros. 7.43.6–7). However, the opportunity to see what that might have meant in practice was foiled the following year when Athaulf was murdered by a resentful retainer. As a result of the energetic activities of the Roman general Constantius (pp. 84–5 above), who blockaded the Goths in northern Spain, Athaulf's successor Vallia was forced by the threat of starvation to come to terms in 416, agreeing to hand over Galla Placidia and to fight the Vandals and other barbarians in Spain in return for supplies of food. After two years of effective campaigning, he negotiated Roman agreement to the Goths' settling permanently in Aquitania, although he himself died before this agreement was implemented.[12] The arrangement suited the Roman authorities since Aquitania was geographically peripheral to the centres of political power in the west. Unlike Vallia, or indeed Athaulf, his successor Theoderic, a son-in-law of Alaric, was to enjoy an extended period as ruler of the Goths, from 418 until 451 – a longevity which enabled him to develop an increasingly independent Gothic state in south-western Gaul (p. 178 below).[13]

The Gothic sack of Rome may be the most enduring image associated with this period in the popular imagination, but it was another barbarian group who were to play the most significant role in determining the fate of the western empire – the Vandals. That role was not to become apparent for some decades following their crossing of the Rhine at the end of 406, but even during those intervening years before they invaded north Africa their presence in Gaul contributed to the fall of Stilicho, the rise of Constantius and the

12. For the major debate which this settlement (and that of other barbarian groups) has generated, see below, pp. 128–32.
13. For further detail on the events of this paragraph, see Matthews, *Western Aristocracies*, 307–28, Heather, *Goths and Romans*, 219–24.

trajectory of the Goths.[14] A decade or so later, in 418, their future
may have looked doubtful as they reflected on the recent destruction
of one sub-grouping of Vandals by Vallia's Goths while the other,
surviving sub-grouping found itself confined to the north-west of
the Iberian peninsula. However, the withdrawal of the Goths to
Aquitania, followed by the death of Constantius in 421 and the
extended period of instability in Italy after Honorius' death in 423
(p. 85 above), provided these surviving Vandals with the opportunity to move southwards into the wealthier regions of southern
Spain and consolidate their position there. Nonetheless, they are
unlikely to have been viewed by the imperial authorities as a serious
threat at this stage.[15]

The accession of a new Vandal ruler in 428 in the person of
Geiseric – 'among the German leaders of his time ... unquestionably
the ablest'[16] – prompted a bold initiative which opened up an alarm-
ing new scenario in the west: in 429 (probably), Geiseric led the
Vandals across the Straits of Gibraltar into north Africa, attracted no
doubt by the economic resources of the region and by the limited
Roman military presence.[17] Advancing eastwards, they soon encroached on the more heavily populated and wealthy region of
Numidia. In 431 a Roman army comprising forces from Italy and
the east arrived under the command of Aspar, but these forces
proved unable to defeat the Vandals and eventually came to terms
with them in 435. The Vandals were permitted to retain control of
part of Numidia and the regions further west, while also paying an
annual tribute to the imperial government which, crucially, retained
control of Carthage. However, Geiseric soon took advantage of
Aetius' preoccupation with affairs in Gaul to resume his eastward
advance until, in October 439, the Vandals captured Carthage. They
quickly mobilised the shipping resources of the city to attack Sicily
and provoke panic about a possible seaborne expedition against
Italy and even Constantinople.

14. P. Rousseau, 'Inheriting the fifth century: who bequeathed what?' in P. Allen
and E. M. Jeffreys (eds), *The Sixth Century: End or Beginning?*, Brisbane: Byzantina
Australiensia 10, 1996, 1–19, at 4–5.
15. For many years, the most detailed study of the Vandals has been C. Courtois, *Les
Vandales et l'Afrique*, Paris: Arts et métiers graphiques, 1955, but see now A. Merrills
and R. Miles, *The Vandals*, Oxford: Wiley-Blackwell, 2010, who emphasise the Vandals'
lacklustre military record prior to 422 (50–1).
16. J. B. Bury, *History of the Later Roman Empire from the Death of Theodosius I to
the Death of Justinian*, London: Macmillan, 1923, 1.246.
17. Merrills and Miles, *Vandals*, 52.

Even without this unexpected naval threat, the Vandal occupation of the north African provinces as far east as Carthage was a blow of incalculable importance to the western empire, for the provinces in question included the wealthiest in the western Mediterranean, based on their production of grain, olive oil and wine. Their occupation by the Vandals meant the loss of significant revenues for the government, with all that implied for its ability to maintain the army.[18] It is not surprising therefore that the government in Constantinople quickly began coordinating another rescue package, in the form of a major expeditionary force combining eastern forces from the lower Danube with western forces. In 441 this force assembled in Sicily, to be met by a request for negotiations from Geiseric, who then dragged them out over the ensuing months until the empire's opportunity was lost. Fortuitously for the Vandals, a Hunnic invasion on the lower Danube forced Constantinople to withdraw its forces from Sicily, and Ravenna then had to agree (in 442) to a far from satisfactory settlement with Geiseric which recognised Vandal possession of Carthage and adjacent regions in return for Vandal recognition of imperial control of the western regions of north Africa – effectively, the mirror image of the settlement of 435. The importance of this episode cannot be overstated, for had the expedition proceeded and managed to defeat the Vandals, the western empire's financial well-being would have been placed on a much sounder footing, with all that that implies for its ability to sustain its military efforts in the years to come. The actual outcome, on the other hand, left the west with a serious handicap which risked more and more becoming fatal the longer it was not reversed.

It was the Huns who were, to a significant degree, responsible for that outcome and who also presented the eastern empire with increasingly serious problems of its own during the first half of the fifth century. Unlike the Goths and Vandals – both Germanic-speaking groups who, despite their movement through parts of the empire in the early fifth century, were from socio-economic backgrounds involving settled villages and arable farming – the Huns were nomadic pastoralists from Central Asia. Their skill in horsemanship and archery gave them military potential, but the herding of animals which underpinned their way of life meant a social struc-

18. For the fiscal significance of the loss of north Africa, see C. Wickham, *Framing the Early Middle Ages: Europe and the Mediterranean, 400–800*, Oxford: Oxford University Press, 2005, 87–8.

ture involving dispersed, impermanent settlement which normally militated against the development of centralised political authority. However, their advent in the lower Danube basin in the late fourth century allowed them to establish hegemony over various settled barbarian groups living in the region – for even after Valens' admission of so many Goths to the empire in 376, there remained substantial numbers north of the Danube who soon fell under Hunnic rule. The resulting control of significant human and material resources facilitated the emergence of Hunnic leaders able to present significant challenges to Constantinople.[19]

The first warning of this worrying development came in 408 when the Hunnic leader Uldin, who had been responsible for the death of Gainas some years earlier (p. 92 above), invaded Thrace, albeit without being able to sustain the threat. This episode may have been enough to prompt the decision to construct impressive new land walls for Constantinople, completed in 413 (Fig. 9).[20] At about the same time, the imperial court was sufficiently concerned to use an embassy to the Huns as a cover for the assassination of a Hunnic leader named Donatus.[21] It was in 422, however, that the direct consequences of the Huns' proximity to the empire were first felt in a serious way. Relations with Persia were disturbed only twice during the fifth century, with short-lived conflicts occurring in 421–2 and 440,[22] and the Hunnic leader Rua took advantage of the first of these to invade Thrace and force Constantinople to purchase his withdrawal by promising an annual payment of 350 lbs of gold over the next fifteen years. Rua employed a similar tactic in 434 when significant numbers of imperial troops were absent from the

19. For good introductions to Hunnic society, see J. Matthews, *The Roman Empire of Ammianus*, London: Duckworth, 1989, 332–42, and C. Kelly, *Attila the Hun: Barbarian Terror and the Fall of the Roman Empire*, London: Bodley Head, 2008, 7–54, 238–48.

20. Lying 1.5 km to the west of the Constantinian wall (with substantial portions still extant), they increased the city's area by 5 km², reflecting its population growth, but their defensive priority is evident in their height (11 m), thickness (4.8 m), and provision of towers (96, c. 70 m apart) and advance wall and trench (details in W. Müller-Wiener, *Bildlexikon zur Topographie Istanbuls*, Tübingen: Wasmuth, 1977, 286–7).

21. The episode is briefly described in Olympiodorus, *fr.* 19, with some scholars arguing that Donatus was a Roman refugee, rather than a Hunnic leader; for discussion of this episode and Roman double-dealing more generally, see A. D. Lee, 'Abduction and assassination: the clandestine face of Roman diplomacy in late antiquity', *International History Review* 31 (2009), 1–23.

22. Details (with sources) in G. Greatrex and S. Lieu, *The Roman Eastern Frontier and the Persian Wars,* AD *363–630*, London: Routledge, 2002, 36–45.

Figure 9 A section of the Theodosian Walls, Constantinople. © Nevit Dilmen/
Wikimedia Commons

Balkans helping to defend Carthage against the Vandals, although
on this occasion the fortuitous death of Rua, apparently through a
lightning strike, afforded the empire some respite.

Rua's death, however, signalled the emergence into leadership of
his nephews Bleda and Attila, the latter of whom was to become a
formidable enemy of the empire over the next two decades. While
perhaps not as able as Geiseric, and certainly not as long-lived –
Attila died in 453, whereas Geiseric continued until 477 – Attila is
better known primarily because the pre-eminent historian of this
period, Priscus of Panium, wrote a detailed account of an embassy
to Attila in 449 in which he participated (Priscus, *fr.* 11, 2). Bleda
and Attila's first opportunity to aggrandise themselves at Constantinople's expense arose in the winter of 439/40 when, in anticipation
of the forthcoming expedition against the Vandals, Roman envoys
agreed to double the annual payment to 700 lbs of gold in return for
assurances of peace on the lower Danube. However, once those
forces assigned to the Vandal expedition had been withdrawn, the
Huns found excuses for reneging on their recent agreement and
began raiding Balkan communities. The recall of the imperial forces
from Sicily put an end to this and an uneasy truce ensued until 447,

when Attila (now sole ruler, following his murder of Bleda in 445) once more went on the offensive, this time with devastating effect. Imperial forces were unable to resist, and Constantinople had no choice but to grant Attila's demands, including a trebling of annual payments to 2,100 lbs of gold. Despite the burden this placed on imperial finances, resources were found to invest in the construction of the so-called 'Long Walls' in Thrace, with a view to enhancing the protection of Constantinople's hinterland, on which the city relied for its water supply via aqueduct. An attempt to solve the Hunnic problem by the expedient of assassinating Attila in 449 went badly awry, but the fallout was not as bad as it might have been, since Attila was beginning to shift his focus westwards.[23]

This shift, whose rationale remains unclear,[24] resulted in the Huns invading Gaul in 451 and advancing towards Orleans until confronted by Aetius, leading a coalition of Roman and barbarian forces, among whom Goths were most prominent. In the ensuing battle of the Catalaunian Plains, Aetius forced Attila to retreat, but not before suffering serious losses, including that of the Gothic ruler Theoderic. After regrouping over the winter, Attila invaded Italy the following year, capturing many of the major cities in the north, until a combination of food shortage, disease and harrying by Aetius induced him to withdraw. Any plans he may have had to return were forestalled by his sudden death in 453, apparently from a brain haemorrhage. While helpfully removing the source of some of the empire's most taxing problems in recent years, this fortuitous development was to generate another whole set of difficulties for the east arising from the break-up of Attila's empire.

Vandals, Goths and Franks

Of the three major barbarian leaders of the first half of the fifth century, only the Vandal leader Geiseric now survived, and while he lived (until 477), the Vandals continued to create significant difficulties for the empire. However, as already intimated, the death of Attila also created new instabilities in the Balkans, out of

23. For important revisions to the traditional chronology of the 430s and 440s, see C. Zuckerman, 'L'Empire d'Orient et les Huns: notes sur Priscus', T&M 12 (1994), 160–82, at 160–8; for a good overview of the basis of Attila's power, see M. Whitby, 'The Balkans and Greece 420–602 , CAH² 14.701–30, at 704–12.
24. Attila was, however, clearly well informed about western affairs via a steady stream of envoys, merchants and others: Rousseau, 'Inheriting the fifth century', 14.

which another, different group of Goths, led by Theoderic the Amal, emerged as a powerful force in imperial affairs. Finally, in the closing decades of the fifth century, a new barbarian group known as the Franks began to impinge forcefully on Gaul.

The settlement of 442 by which Valentinian III acceded to the Vandal occupation of Carthage and the more prosperous parts of north Africa also seems to have included provision for the betrothal of his elder daughter Eudocia to Geiseric's eldest son Huneric – a move which has interesting implications for Geiseric's attitude to the empire, and for the political capital to be gained from marriage into the imperial family. In the event, nothing further happened in this respect until Valentinian's death in 455. Upon receipt of this news, Geiseric led a large seaborne force to Italy and proceeded to sack the city of Rome in a much more comprehensive manner than Alaric's Goths had done in 410. Ironically, the booty he carried back to Carthage included treasures from the Roman sack of Jerusalem in 70, but also Valentinian's wife and daughters, and at some point after their arrival in Carthage, Eudocia was finally married to Huneric. This union produced a son, Hilderic, who was to play a crucial role in the eventual imperial conquest of north Africa by the Emperor Justinian in the sixth century (p. 259 below).

Valentinian's death does appear to have been the trigger for a more aggressive policy towards the empire generally on Geiseric's part, with Vandal forces occupying Sicily, Sardinia, Corsica and the Balearics. This in turn prompted the western emperor Majorian (457–61) to prepare another attempt to drive the Vandals from north Africa. However, Geiseric launched a pre-emptive strike which destroyed the fleet Majorian had prepared in ports along the south-east coast of Spain, and in the aftermath of this debacle Ricimer had Majorian arrested and executed (p. 94 above). For the next few years, Geiseric led his fleet in annual raids along the coastline of Sicily and Italy (Priscus, *fr.* 39, 1), but his extension of this raiding into the eastern Mediterranean, together with his persecution of orthodox Christians in north Africa (pp. 187–8 below), eventually provoked a response from Constantinople (Procop. *Wars* 3.5.22, 3.6.1). In 467 the Emperor Leo persuaded Ricimer to support the elevation of the eastern aristocrat Anthemius to the vacant imperial throne in the west in preparation for the largest expedition yet to regain north Africa from the Vandals. An armada from Constantinople under the command of Leo's brother-in-law Basiliscus combined with western forces to advance on Carthage.

Once again, however, Geiseric proved adept at using diplomatic delay to forestall the attack, and then deployed fireships to wreak havoc among the densely packed imperial fleet as it lay moored off the coast of north Africa. The cost of this disaster was put by contemporaries at somewhere between 7.5 and 9 million *solidi* – a truly enormous sum 'which probably exceeded a whole year's revenue' for the eastern empire.[25] This failure also had other significant repercussions. As well as effectively sealing the fate of the western empire, it left deep psychological scars in the memories of the elite in Constantinople for many years to come, ensuring that the Vandals escaped further external interference for more than half a century – a development further aided by the death of Geiseric in 477. While his successors continued to persecute orthodox Christians, in other respects they pursued less provocative policies towards Constantinople, giving their attention, as they had to, to the growing problems presented by local Moorish polities (p. 260 below).

In addition to leaving his successor Zeno with a near-empty treasury, Leo also bequeathed him a highly volatile situation in the Balkans. Following Attila's death in 453, the various barbarian groups who had been subject to his rule in the lower Danube basin seized the opportunity to rebel against Hunnic rule, successfully defeating Attila's sons in a battle at the River Nedao in 454. Of these newly free groups, the most important were Goths. During the late 450s and 460s, one group of these Goths settled in the former province of Pannonia in the north-western Balkans, while a second group settled in Thrace with a formal status as federate troops. Aspar made a point of cultivating ties of patronage with this second group, with the result that his assassination by Leo in 471 (p. 99) provoked a revolt on their part. Leo was only able to restore order in the region by agreeing in 473 to a number of concessions, including an annual payment of 2,000 lbs of gold and an imperial generalship for their leader Theoderic Strabo ('the squinter') – a mark of status much valued by barbarian leaders in this period because of the way it enhanced their authority among their own retainers. In the meantime, however, the other group of Goths had taken advantage of Leo's preoccupation with this revolt to advance from Pannonia to Macedonia, where the threat they posed

---

25. M. F. Hendy, *Studies in the Byzantine Monetary Economy, c. 300–1450*, Cambridge: Cambridge University Press, 1985, 223.

persuaded Leo to grant them land on which to settle and farm.[26]

As the chief beneficiary of Aspar's demise, Zeno could hardly expect Theoderic Strabo to view him favourably, so it is no surprise to find Strabo and his Goths supporting Basiliscus' usurpation in 475 (p. 100 above). During his enforced exile in Isauria, however, Zeno had begun to develop links with the other group of Goths as a counter-weight, and upon his regaining power in 476, he transferred the privileges previously enjoyed by Strabo and his Goths to this other group and their leader Theoderic the Amal.[27] This Theoderic was to be a figure of increasing importance in the decades to come, and it is logical to link his success, at least in part, to the formative experiences of his youth. He was the son of Theodemer, one of the leading Goths during the years immediately after Attila's death, and in the early 460s, at the age of seven or eight, Theoderic had been sent to Constantinople as a hostage, to guarantee an agreement between Leo and his father. The status of hostage in antiquity did not usually entail the degree of close constraint and deprivation associated with modern usage of the term, and Theoderic spent the next ten years in the imperial capital living a lifestyle appropriate to his elite status and receiving a formal Roman education in Greek (and perhaps Latin) language and literature – a process Theoderic must have viewed favourably, since a later panegyrist believed he would win his approval with the observation that 'Greece educated you in the lap of civilization (*civilitas*)' (Ennodius, *Pan.* 3). Theoderic will therefore have been well known at the imperial court and have developed a good understanding of imperial politics and culture, as indeed he himself acknowledged in a later letter to Zeno's successor: 'With divine help I learned in your republic the art of governing Romans with equity' (Cassiod. *Var.* 1.1).[28]

Zeno did not, of course, transfer Strabo's privileges to Theoderic the Amal without a *quid pro quo* – namely, that the Amal and his Goths act against Strabo and his Goths. However, when the Amal

26. Full details and discussion in Heather, *Goths and Romans*, 240–71.
27. Heather, *Goths and Romans*, 272–8.
28. For a good discussion of this case as part of a wider phenomenon, see J. Shepard, 'Manners maketh Romans? Young barbarians at the emperor's court' in E. Jeffreys (ed.), *Byzantine Style, Religion and Civilization*, Cambridge: Cambridge University Press, 2006, 135–58, who notes an important limitation to Theoderic's education, which evidently did not succeed in converting him from Arian to Nicene Christianity (although it may have been responsible for his later moderation in religious policy). See also J. Moorhead, *Theoderic in Italy*, Oxford: Clarendon Press, 1992, 13–14.

came increasingly to suspect that Zeno was simply playing the two groups of Goths off against one another, he broke off ties with the imperial court, forcing Zeno to reach an accommodation with Strabo (478). That accommodation, however, proved very short-lived, when Strabo backed the attempted usurpation of Marcian the following year (p. 100 above). After its failure, Strabo tried again to capture Constantinople in 481 on his own account, but was repulsed and, fortuitously for Zeno, died soon after in a freak accident. Although this might have been the cue for Zeno to focus his attention on the elimination of the other Theoderic, his developing difficulties with Illus in the early 480s (p. 100 above) prompted him instead to renew his association with Theoderic the Amal, albeit at the cost of granting the latter not only an imperial generalship, but even the consulship for the year 484. While the latter was certainly 'an unprecedented honour for a barbarian leader',[29] its novelty was no doubt tempered by knowledge of the Romanisation which Theoderic had undergone in his youth.

From his new position of strength, Theoderic proceeded to eliminate Strabo's son and successor Recitach, thereby paving the way for the amalgamation of Strabo's Goths with his own, but although he did assist Zeno in the early stages of his response to Illus' rebellion, Theoderic himself turned against Zeno in 486, perhaps fearing more double-dealing from the emperor. When Theoderic moved to attack Constantinople itself in 487, Zeno averted the immediate danger by buying him off with gold, but it was not until the following year that a definitive solution emerged when Theoderic decided to accept Zeno's proposal that he go west and seek greener pastures in Italy by overthrowing Odoacer, whose formal status had remained anomalous since 476 (p. 97 above) and who had been in communication with Illus during his revolt. Of course, as far as Zeno was concerned, it did not really matter which of the two won the ensuing contest: either way, Theoderic and his Goths would be removed from the Balkans and, Zeno hoped, the complexities of affairs in the eastern empire would be simplified immeasurably.[30]

In the event, it was Theoderic who prevailed. After hard-fought

---

29. Heather, *Goths and Romans*, 300.
30. For further details on the complicated events of this and the previous paragraph, see Heather, *Goths and Romans*, 278–308, with further valuable comment on the background to Theoderic's decision to invade Italy in Moorhead, *Theoderic*, 17–19.

victories in the field against Odoacer near Verona in 489 and Milan in 490, Theoderic besieged him in Ravenna. Eventually, in early 493, shortage of food forced Odoacer to negotiate his surrender, with assurances of his safety and perhaps even shared rule. Within less than a fortnight, however, Theoderic had murdered his rival during a banquet, apparently justifying his treachery with a claim of vengeance on behalf of relatives killed by Odoacer in years gone by.[31] It remained to be seen how far Theoderic would follow Odoacer's precedent with regard to maintaining Roman traditions and respecting the rights of the senatorial aristocracy (Ch. 9 below).

The post-imperial west within which Theoderic had to establish himself involved various barbarian groups who have previously featured – Vandals in north Africa, Goths and Burgundians in Gaul, and Sueves in Spain. There had, however, been an important new addition in recent decades – the Franks. Another Germanic-speaking group, they had been a presence on the lower Rhine from the later third century and received attention during the campaigning of the emperors Constantine and Julian in fourth-century Gaul. It may have been in the context of diplomatic dealings between the empire and the Franks during the fourth century that the Romans planted the idea that the Franks shared a common origin with them from the Trojans, an idea which found elaboration in later sources from the seventh century.[32] In the second half of the fourth century, Franks (like other barbarians) held high rank in the Roman army, notably Silvanus, Bauto, Richomer and Arbogast. There is also evidence for Franks serving as rank-and-file soldiers, most famously the unnamed individual commemorated on an epitaph as 'a Frankish citizen [and] a Roman soldier in arms'.[33]

While Goths, Vandals and Burgundians were active in Gaul in significant ways at various points during the first half of the fifth century, Franks barely register in the (admittedly patchy) sources. During the second half of the century, however, they become increasingly prominent, notably in the context of the last outpost of Roman authority in northern Gaul associated with the general Aegidius and his son Syagrius. Although Aegidius was unable to prevent Franks

---

31. Moorhead, *Theoderic*, 19–31.
32. I. Wood, *The Merovingian Kingdoms, 450–751*, Harlow: Longman, 1994, 33–5. Cf. Sid. Apoll. *Carm.* 7.501–2, where, in a speech delivered at Rome in 456, Sidonius claimed that the Romans and Goths shared a common ancestor in the person of Mars.
33. *CIL* 3.3576 = *ILS* 2814, from Aquincum on the middle Danube. For Frankish units in the fourth-century Roman army, see James, *Franks*, 39.

from seizing control of Cologne and Trier in the mid-450s, he had, by the early 460s, gained their support as allies against the expansionist Goths in Aquitaine, with the Frankish leader Childeric helping Aegidius to defeat the Goths in a battle at Orleans in 463. Following Aegidius' death in 465, Syagrius increasingly exercised independent power from his base at Soissons – he had little choice, given the turmoil in Italy (pp. 94–6 above) – so that one source later referred to him as 'king of the Romans' (Gregory of Tours, *Hist.* 2.27). In 482 Childeric (about whose activities nothing else is known) died and was buried at Tournai, where what appears to have been his grave was discovered in the seventeenth century, complete with rich grave goods including a seal ring bearing his name and the title *rex* ('king') (most of these finds were, unfortunately, subsequently stolen).[34] His son and successor, Clovis, soon began to pursue a more aggressive, expansionist policy in northern Gaul, resulting in the defeat and death of Syagrius in 487, and setting the stage for the conflict between Clovis' Franks and the Goths in southern Gaul which was to be so important in defining the future of France (pp. 178–80 below). From the perspective of the empire, however, the death of Syagrius was significant as extinguishing the last vestige of Roman authority in the west.[35]

Over the course of the fifth century, then, imperial power in the west contracted as various barbarian groups established themselves in different regions. The Gothic groups led by Alaric and Theoderic played major roles in these developments, but it was the Vandal occupation of north Africa, with its economic resources, which proved to be most significant. While the wealthy east was also an attractive target for barbarian groups, geography and other fortuitous circumstances combined to make the eastern empire less vulnerable. Egypt, the wealthiest region in the empire (pp. 233–4 below), was never exposed to serious external threat during the fifth century, while the empire's most powerful neighbour, Persia, was preoccupied with problems along its own northern frontier for much

---

34. For Childeric's tomb, see S. Lebecq, 'The two faces of King Childeric: history, archaeology, historiography' in W. Pohl and M. Diesenberger (eds), *Integration und Herrschaft: Ethnische Identitäten und soziale Organisation im Frühmittelalter*, Vienna: Österreichischen Akademie der Wissenschaften, 2002, 119–32.

35. For the early history of the Franks, see E. James, *The Franks*, Oxford: Blackwell, 1988, 34–84, and Wood, *Merovingian Kingdoms,* 35–41; for a significantly different chronology, see G. Halsall, 'Childeric's grave, Clovis' succession and the origins of the Merovingian kingdom' in R. Mathisen and D. Shanzer (eds), *Society and Culture in Late Roman Gaul*, Aldershot: Ashgate, 2001, 116–33.

of this period, leaving the other eastern provinces in peace.[36] This allowed Constantinople to focus on maintaining the lower Danube frontier, while also trying to provide aid to the west. As a result, it was inhabitants of the western half of the empire who were more likely to find themselves having to deal at first hand with the consequences of these significant and often rapid changes, as explored in the final section of this chapter.

Romans and barbarians in a changing world

For many ordinary inhabitants of the Roman empire in the fifth century, their encounter with barbarians obviously occurred in the context of warfare, whether it be barbarian raiders plundering farm-steads or more organised assaults on urban centres (cf. Fig. 10). Although Roman commentators on such events were often unable to resist the rhetorical opportunities which they offered for hyperbole and apocalyptic drama, there can be no doubting the significant loss or destruction of property and the incidence of violence, rape and death at the hands of foreigners in vulnerable parts of the empire during this period.[37] One particular dimension of this which involved ongoing interaction with barbarians was enslavement, the frequency of which is reflected in the increasingly common involvement of bishops in organising the ransoming of captives.[38] Interestingly, however, not all prisoners of war were keen to escape barbarian control. The historian Priscus, who participated in an embassy to the Huns in 449, famously reports encountering in Attila's camp north of the Danube a former inhabitant of the empire who was apparently very happy to remain where he was. A mer-chant who had been captured by the Huns when they sacked the Danubian town of Viminacium in the early 440s, he had become the slave of one of the leading Huns, and after proving his valour in battle and gaining much booty, he was given his freedom, married a barbarian woman, enjoyed a comfortable life and had no desire

36. Apart from the short-lived Roman–Persian conflicts in northern Mesopotamia in 421–2 and 440.
37. B. Ward-Perkins, *The Fall of Rome and the End of Civilization*, Oxford: Oxford University Press, 2005, 13–31; A. D. Lee, *War in Late Antiquity: A Social History*, Oxford: Blackwell, 2007, 133–46 (with 167–73 for provincials sometimes experiencing violence at the hands of Roman troops).
38. W. Klingshirn, 'Charity and power: Caesarius of Arles and the ransoming of captives in sub-Roman Gaul', *JRS* 75 (1985), 183–203; C. Rapp, *Holy Bishops in Late Antiquity*, Berkeley: University of California Press, 2005, 228–32.

to return to the empire with its heavy taxes and corrupt system of justice (Priscus, *fr.* 11.2 [lines 407–53]).[39] While it is hard to believe that this was a common experience or attitude, it provides an interesting caveat against making blanket assumptions.[40]

For those within the empire who retained their lives and freedom, there remained a variety of less violent contexts in which interaction with barbarian incomers occurred. As already noted (p. 115 above), some barbarian groups were induced to provide military resources for the empire in the first half of the fifth century, and one consequence of this was that landowners sometimes found themselves having to provide temporary billets for barbarian soldiers. Paulinus of Pella, a grandson of the eminent Gallic aristocrat Ausonius, referred to Goths billeted on landowners in the Bordeaux district who protected their hosts and their property against destruction by other, independent Goths in 414, while his own estate, which lacked a Gothic billet, was pillaged (*Eucharisticon* 281–90). In the middle of the century, another Gallic aristocrat, Sidonius Apollinaris, ruefully remarked on the experience of having to host a group of Burgundian soldiers in his house:

> [I find myself] situated among a lank-haired band of soldiers, having to endure conversation in Germanic, maintaining a serious expression while repeatedly complimenting the singing of a Burgundian glutton, his hair smeared with rancid butter ... *You* don't have to put up with the stink of garlic and onion emanating from ten breakfasts first thing in the morning ... or with the pre-dawn invasion of so many oversized giants that even the kitchen of Alcinous would struggle to cope! (*Carm.* 12)

Fortunately for Sidonius, billeting was only a temporary arrangement, but there are also references in the sources which suggest that barbarian groups in the fifth-century west received land on a more permanent basis. This is a subject with important implications for the character of Roman–barbarian relations in this period which continues to generate lively academic debate – a reflection, at least in part, of the difficulties of the extant sources. The seminal work in this debate is Walter Goffart's 1980 study *Barbarians and Romans,*

---

39. While Priscus' subsequent discussion with the man about the relative merits of life under imperial and barbarian rule has echoes of a formal rhetorical exercise, this need not cast doubt on Priscus' report of the encounter itself.

40. For other evidence, see E. A. Thompson, 'Barbarian invaders and Roman collaborators', *Florilegium* 2 (1980), 71–88.

Figure 10 Wooden carving of a besieged city being relieved (45 × 22 cm)
(Egypt, early fifth century). Roman infantry approach from the left, driving
away mounted barbarians who have been besieging the city, while the defending
garrison lines the top of the wall. The buildings of the city rise up behind them,
with three large figures on the left, who are perhaps protective saints.
© bpk/Skulpturensammlung und Museum für Byzantinische Kunst,
SMB/Jürgen Liepe

AD *418–584: The Techniques of Accommodation.*[41] An older strand
of scholarship had proposed a link between, on the one hand, late
Roman laws on the billeting of soldiers, which referred to troops
being given a third of a house (on a temporary basis), and, on the
other, provisions in early barbarian law codes which mentioned
the division of land into thirds, and on this basis it was suggested
that barbarian groups in the fifth-century west were granted
thirds of estates in regions where they settled as a sort of extension
of billeting principles.

    Although not without its critics, this view gained broad accept-
ance until the publication of Goffart's study, which was particularly
significant for two reasons.[42] First, he showed that the posited
link between Roman billeting practice and barbarian settlement
was untenable: essentially, billeting involved temporary use, whereas
fifth-century arrangements were more permanent. Secondly, and
most significantly, he argued that the references to 'thirds' in the
context of barbarian settlement related not to ownership of land,
but to receipt of the taxes due from that land. If right, this made
a significant difference as to who bore the brunt of the costs of
barbarian settlement, with further implications for the nature of
Roman–barbarian relations. If barbarian groups were given land,
then it was landowners who lost out, with resulting resentment
towards the incomers and the government; if, on the other hand, the
barbarians received a portion of the taxes on land, then it was the
imperial treasury which suffered. Imperial finance officials would
not be happy, but they were unlikely to protest.

    One of the attractions of Goffart's thesis is that it helps to explain
the surprising lack of evidence for complaints by landowners which
one might otherwise have expected if the settlement of barbarians
had involved expropriation of land on a large scale.[43] At the same

---

41. Goffart has more recently responded to critics and restated and refined his views in
Barbarian Tides: The Migration Age and the Later Roman Empire, Philadelphia: University of Pennsylvania Press, 2006, 119–86, and in 'The techniques of barbarian settlement
in the fifth century: a personal, streamlined account with ten additional comments', *JLA*
3 (2010), 65–98 (the latter particularly prompted by the next item).
42. For a clear overview of earlier scholarship and a careful assessment of Goffart's
1980 study, see Halsall, *Barbarian Migrations*, 422–47, supplemented by his 'The technique of barbarian settlement in the fifth century: a reply to Walter Goffart', *JLA* 3
(2010), 99–112.
43. Goffart, *Tides*, 183–6, summarises the half dozen instances of complaints by
property-owners against barbarians, arguing that their detail does not support an
assumption of widespread dispossession.

time, there has remained for many scholars an important obstacle to accepting Goffart's thesis – namely, that a number of sources seem to refer unequivocally to fifth-century barbarians receiving land.[44] Goffart has more recently sought to address this objection by arguing that the terms used for 'land' in the sources could have an array of connotations, ranging from ownership of land, to rental of land, to the fiscal liability of land, and that the sharp contrast drawn between 'land' and 'taxes' in many discussions of his thesis sets up a false opposition.[45] However, while recognition of the 'multivalency' of the term 'land' allows a more nuanced approach to the issue, it does not necessarily follow that every reference to 'land' in this context must refer to its fiscal liability, as Goffart would apparently have it.[46]

Goffart also argues for a consistent application of the same principles in all the different regions of the west where barbarians were settled in the fifth century – in his own formulation, 'one size fitted all'.[47] But a good case has recently been made for the possibility that arrangements varied from context to context, depending upon specific circumstances. By way of illustration, the earliest instance, the establishment of Goths in south-west Gaul in 418, took place at a time when imperial authority still carried weight, and the Roman general Constantius who oversaw the arrangements is unlikely to have instigated large-scale expropriation of landowners; in these circumstances, reassigning of tax revenues from land is a plausible scenario. The Vandals, on the other hand, acquired control of north Africa by conquest, in which situation the seizure of estates was much more likely to have occurred, perhaps supplemented by other arrangements. However, whereas they were not concerned to conciliate estate-owners (many of whom were absentee landlords anyway), it was much more important for Theoderic in Italy to win over the senatorial aristocracy (cf. p. 182 below), and so an arrangement involving tax revenues could well have carried greater appeal there.[48] This more flexible approach offers a better prospect of doing justice to the changing circumstances of the period and the

---

44. Halsall, *Barbarian Migrations*, 430–1.
45. Goffart, *Tides*, 126–7.
46. Halsall, 'Reply', 107 ('multivalency' is his term).
47. Goffart, 'Streamlined account', 93.
48. See Halsall, *Barbarian Migrations*, 436–47, for further detail, with Halsall, 'Reply', for his entertaining response to Goffart's critique; also Moorhead, *Theoderic*, 32–5, for the specific situation in Italy.

difficulties of the evidence, while also taking some account of Goffart's insights.

A rather different issue which is also relevant to the subject of Roman–barbarian relations in this period is that of religion. Most of the major barbarian groups which settled within the empire during the fifth century had converted to Christianity, but they usually adopted the Arian version at odds with the Nicene Christianity which prevailed within the empire from the reign of Theodosius I onwards.[49] It is ironic that a step which was presumably intended to aid the integration of barbarian incomers should have ended up being a potential source of division. The Goths are the only group about which any detail is known concerning the circumstances of their conversion, and since it occurred around the time of their entry to the empire in 376, it is unsurprising that it was the Arian version favoured by the Emperor Valens which they embraced (p. 33 n.29 above). On the other hand, it is unclear why other groups such as the Vandals who entered the empire rather later, when Arianism was no longer in receipt of imperial favour, also adopted Arian Christianity, unless perhaps they were simply following the Gothic example.[50] This divergence in creeds certainly had the potential to create barriers between barbarian immigrants and provincial inhabitants, especially if the barbarian leadership adopted an aggressive stance towards Nicene Christians, as was the case with the Vandals in north Africa. Even if much of the initial Vandal aggression was actually more to do with acquiring the church's wealth than with an excess of religious zeal,[51] it will still have militated against integration. On the other hand, there is much less evidence for open religious hostility from and towards the Goths in Gaul, which may have allowed greater scope for the slow but steady impact of another, integrative factor.

That factor was intermarriage, a high-profile example of which has already been noted – that of the Gothic leader Athaulf to the Roman princess Galla Placidia in 414 (p. 115 above). This instance

49. For the major exception of the Franks (whose conversion to Nicene Christianity did not occur until the early sixth century), see p. 189 below.
50. For the Vandals, see P. Heather, 'Christianity and the Vandals in the reign of Geiseric' in J. Drinkwater and B. Salway (eds), *Wolf Liebeschuetz Reflected*, London: Institute of Classical Studies, 2007, 137–46, at 143; for an overview of the inconclusive argument about the Ostrogoths (i.e., the Goths whom Theoderic the Amal led to Italy), see Moorhead, *Theoderic*, 89–90.
51. Merrills and Miles, *Vandals*, 181.

was of course primarily a political marriage, of which there are further examples during the fifth century,[52] but there is also evidence for the phenomenon occurring at lower levels of society where political considerations will have been irrelevant. At the same time, the subject of Roman–barbarian marriages has been seen as problematic because of an imperial law from the early 370s which seemed to forbid any such unions: 'For none of the *provinciales*, of any rank or status, may there be a marriage with a barbarian wife, nor may any female *provincialis* marry any of the *gentiles*' (*Cod. Theod.* 3.14.1). Although this is sometimes interpreted as reflecting official concerns about racial mixing or about the risk that such marriages might encourage disloyalty to the empire, the most plausible exegesis has focused on *provinciales* as a term referring to a particular category of citizen liable to serve on a provincial council and *gentiles* as a term referring to a specific category of barbarian settler liable to military service – in other words, legal statuses both of which entailed obligations to the state in one form or other. The concern of the law would then be to prevent mixed unions which might confuse the status of any offspring and potentially help them to evade their obligations, whether civic or military – which was undoubtedly a more general anxiety on the part of the late Roman authorities. If the law had this much more restricted focus, it strengthens the likelihood of increasingly widespread intermarriage between Romans and barbarians during the fifth century, with all that that implies for the growing integration of barbarians residing in imperial territory.[53]

---

52. Moorhead, *Theoderic*, 84–5.
53. R. Mathisen, '*Provinciales, gentiles*, and marriages between Romans and barbarians in the late Roman empire', *JRS* 99 (2009), 140–55.

CHAPTER 7

Church and state, piety and power

Politics and theology in the east from Chrysostom to Nestorius

The Council of Constantinople in 381 and the Emperor Theodosius'
subsequent combination of legislative rhetoric and episcopal consultation had ensured that supporters of Nicaea increasingly prevailed
in church affairs in the eastern half of the empire (pp. 44–7 above).
If, however, there was an expectation that this growing uniformity
signalled the end of significant disunity in the church, events after
Theodosius' death were to prove any such hope misplaced, as senior
bishops pursued their theological and political agendas, often in
conflict with one another. As previously, Alexandria and Antioch
were major players, joined now, however, by Constantinople, whose
prestige as imperial capital inevitably had ramifications for the status
of the city's bishop, as already shown by Canon 3 of the Council of
Constantinople in 381 (p. 46 above). That growing status was the
source of considerable animosity in Alexandria in particular, long
accustomed to regarding itself as the premier see of the eastern
Mediterranean. In view of this, it is perhaps unsurprising that the
two major crises of the next half century involved conflict between
bishops of those two cities.

The first of these crises focused on John Chrysostom, a native of
Antioch who became bishop of Constantinople in 398.[1] A former
student of the famous teacher of rhetoric, Libanius, he had made

1. For fuller detail on what follows, see T. E. Gregory, Vox Populi: *Popular Opinion in
the Religious Controversies of the Fifth Century AD*, Columbus: Ohio State University
Press, 1979, 31–80; J. H. W. G. Liebeschuetz, *Barbarians and Bishops: Army, Church
and State in the Age of Arcadius and Chrysostom*, Oxford: Clarendon Press, 1990, 166–
227; J. N. D. Kelly, *Golden Mouth: The Story of John Chrysostom*, London: Duckworth,
1995, 104–290; S. Elm, 'The dog that did not bark: doctrine and patriarchal authority
in the conflict between Theophilus of Alexandria and John Chrysostom of Constantinople' in L. Ayres and G. Jones (eds), *Christian Origins: Theology, Rhetoric and
Community*, London: Routledge, 1998, 68–93 (emphasising the important point that the
surviving sources were written by John's followers and sympathisers, thereby leaving a
hostile portrait of Theophilus).

a name for himself in his home city as a preacher of rare ability –
hence the (posthumous) epithet Chrysostom ('golden mouth') – and
it was this which brought him wider attention. Although his motives
for doing so are unclear, it was the influential eunuch Eutropius who
recommended John to the Emperor Arcadius in 397, and despite
the unwillingness of the inhabitants of Antioch to lose such a
prized asset and the attempt by Theophilus, the proactive bishop
of Alexandria who had played a part in the destruction of the
Serapeum in 391/2 (pp. 53–4 above), to have one of his own adherents appointed, John was duly confirmed as the new bishop of the
eastern capital. However, although his eloquent preaching and
abstemious lifestyle won him a large following among the urban
masses, his tenure was to last little more than five years, until, in
403, he was deposed by the 'Synod of the Oak' (so called after the
suburb of nearby Chalcedon where the bishops who opposed him
met). The prime orchestrator of the synod was Theophilus of
Alexandria, who proved adroit at turning the tables on a politically
naïve John after Theophilus himself had been summoned to Constantinople to answer charges relating to his treatment of a group of
Egyptian monks who had appealed to the emperor. The charges
brought against John were, however, of such a petty nature that
Theophilus only succeeded because John had gradually managed to
alienate a range of powerful individuals in and near the capital.

Spending, as he had, the early years of his adult life pursuing an
ascetic life near Antioch, it is no surprise to find that, soon after his
appointment, John set about urging the reform of various aspects of
church life in Constantinople which, in his view, fell short of the
highest Christian standards, such as the way in which some clergy
had unmarried women living under the same roof as housekeepers.
Needless to say, his attempts to curtail such practices, and his
dismissal of some clergy whom he regarded as unsuitable, created
resentment, as did his railing against the ill discipline of many of the
city's monks, one of whose leaders – a holy man named Isaac – had
close ties with several important figures at the imperial court. John's
intervention in neighbouring dioceses in Asia to eliminate corrupt
practices such as the sale of episcopal office was no doubt motivated
by similar laudable concerns, but this did not prevent him from earn-
ing the enmity of bishops in that region who regarded John as merely
seeking to extend the power of his see at their expense. John also
worked hard to cultivate good relations with the bishop of Rome,
but again this exposed him to criticism at court at a time when

political relations with a Stilicho-dominated west were strained (pp. 83–4 above). Moreover, while his preaching against the dangers of excessive wealth struck a chord with some of the capital's elite (notably the wealthy widow Olympias, who proceeded to give substantial assets to the church), it also caused offence in some circles. Crucially, his comments in a sermon on the vices of women in early 403 were interpreted by some of his enemies as veiled criticisms of the Empress Eudoxia – and were reported to her as such.

As a result, the highly dubious process by which John was deposed went unchallenged when presented for approval by the imperial court in mid-403, and within a few days John was escorted out of the city en route to a place of exile. However, popular expressions of anger at John's treatment in the capital were such that the emperor was forced to recall John, promising to hold another synod to formalise his reinstatement. Perhaps through the influence of his enemies, that promise kept being deferred over the next nine months, encouraging ever more violent behaviour by his supporters. This in turn allowed his opponents to argue that his continued presence in the capital was an unwelcome cause of public disorder and thereby persuade Arcadius to sanction John's permanent exile to the wilds of Isauria, and then, after three years, to an even more remote outpost on the north-east coast of the Black Sea – en route to which John's weakened body finally gave way. After his exile, and even after his death, his enemies continued to wage a campaign of persecution against prominent individuals among his supporters until advisers to Arcadius' young son and successor, Theodosius II, eventually agreed to the posthumous rehabilitation of John's reputation, for which the bishop of Rome had lobbied hard.[2]

That process of rehabilitation was not fully completed until John's remains were brought back to Constantinople in a magnificent ceremony in 438, by which time the second great ecclesiastical crisis of this period was well under way, with another bishop of Constantinople already deposed and exiled as a consequence. The bishop in question was Nestorius, also from Antioch and a student of one of John's friends, the eminent theologian Theodore of Mopsuestia. Appointed in 428, Nestorius soon found himself in conflict with Theophilus' successor, his nephew Cyril. Given Cyril's

2. For an interesting comparison of John's episcopal career with that of Ambrose, see J. H. W. G. Liebeschuetz, *Ambrose and John Chrysostom: Clerics between Desert and Empire*, Oxford: Oxford University Press, 2011.

previous record of involvement in Alexandria's religious politics, notably the expulsion of the city's Jewish community and seizure of their synagogues in 415, and the death of the celebrated female pagan philosopher Hypatia through mob violence in the same year (both episodes in the context of antagonism between Cyril and Orestes, the imperial prefect responsible for Egypt), political rivalry with Constantinople was bound to be a factor in the crisis.[3]

It is clear, however, that there were also important theological issues at stake. Those issues concerned the association between the divine and the human in Christ, and how best to conceptualise the nature of the bond between them, divergent views about which had developed within the theological traditions of Antioch and Alexandria. In the context of the fourth-century Arian controversy, Alexandrian theologians such as Athanasius were understandably keen to assert Christ's equality with the Father and therefore emphasised the over-riding importance of Christ's divinity, whereas Antiochene scholars such as Theodore of Mopsuestia were concerned not to lose sight of Christ's identification with mankind and so gave greater weight to his humanity. The specific point of disagreement which sparked the crisis in the late 420s was the appropriate terminology for describing Mary, the mother of Jesus, who had become an increasingly important focus of popular devotion during the fourth century.[4] Cyril took the view that the right term was *Theotokos* ('Mother of God') since this gave due emphasis to Christ's divinity, whereas Nestorius regarded *Christotokos* ('Mother of Christ') as more appropriate. The specific circumstances which set in train the fateful sequence of events leading to Nestorius' deposition in 431 and all that followed from that are described by a contemporary historian in a way which emphasises the strong element of misunderstanding involved:

> Nestorius had an associate whom he had brought from Antioch, a priest named Anastasius. He had the highest esteem for this man, and consulted him in the management of his most important affairs.

3. Cyril's precise role in these two episodes is the subject of debate: see S. Wessel, *Cyril of Alexandria and the Nestorian Controversy*, Oxford: Oxford University Press, 2004, 33–57; E. Watts, *City and School in Late Antique Athens and Alexandria*, Berkeley: University of California Press, 2006, 196–203.
4. For a good overview of the scholarly debate about the origins and early development of Marian devotion, see Averil Cameron, 'The cult of the Virgin in late antiquity: religious development and myth-making' in R. N. Swanson (ed.), *The Church and Mary* (= *SCH* 39), Woodbridge: Boydell, 2004, 1–21.

Preaching one day in church, Anastasius said, 'Let no one call Mary
Theotokos: for Mary was but a woman; and it is impossible that
God should be born of a woman.' These words created a great
sensation, and troubled many both of the clergy and laity, for they
had been taught to acknowledge Christ as God, and by no means to
separate his humanity from his divinity on account of the economy
of Incarnation ... But Nestorius, eager to establish Anastasius'
proposition – for he did not wish to have a man whom he esteemed
found guilty of blasphemy – delivered several sermons on the subject,
in which he assumed a controversial attitude, and totally rejected
the epithet *Theotokos*. The controversy on the subject was taken
in one spirit by some and in another by others, with the result that
the discussion which ensued divided the church, and resembled
the struggle of combatants in the dark, all parties uttering the most
confused and contradictory assertions. In this way, Nestorius
acquired the reputation among the masses of asserting the blas-
phemous dogma that the Lord was a mere man (Socrates, *Hist. eccl.*
7.32).[5]

For many in contemporary, post-Christian, western society, it
can be difficult to understand how disagreements over the seeming
niceties of theological terminology could generate such passions and
unwillingness to compromise. But for those involved at the time,
these were not just matters for academic debate, but issues with far-
reaching practical ramifications. For those like Nestorius who had
been trained in the Antiochene tradition, due emphasis on Christ's
humanity, his experience of the human condition and the choices he
made was essential if his death on the cross was to be relevant to the
salvation of mankind, whereas for those within the Alexandrian
tradition like Cyril, Nestorius' teaching risked suggesting that Christ
had two natures – one human, the other divine – and even that
he was no more than an inspired man, thereby jeopardising the
assurance of salvation. From Cyril's perspective,

by disputing the mode of God's involvement or engagement with
man in Christ, Nestorius questioned its purpose and so the whole of
the Christian message. For if man's creation, his present condition,
and future hope are all bound up with the divine grace which is
Christ, it will not do to think of Christ as ... a very inspired man ...

5. For a clear exposition of the grounds for regarding the disagreement about Marian
nomenclature as the occasion rather than the root cause of the controversy, see R. M.
Price, 'Marian piety and the Nestorian controversy' in Swanson, *The Church and Mary*,
31–8.

Grace must be unconditional and the Incarnation a binding of the Son of God with man in a union stronger than, because more basic than, any human act or choice. To divide the One Christ must be to divide man from life and grace. Because these were his convictions, he became passionate, angry and unfair to his opponents in controversy. No one would praise Cyril for his open-mindedness or his ability to hold in fruitful tension, for the Church's good, views which were at odds with one another and with his whole understanding of the faith. But he would not have wished ... for such praise.[6]

The shadow of the Emperor Julian may also have given the issue additional edge as far as Cyril was concerned, for in his notorious critique of Christianity, *Against the Galilaeans* (262d), Julian had specifically ridiculed Christian displays of devotion to Mary and the use of the term *Theotokos*, and it is surely significant therefore that Cyril wrote a detailed rebuttal of Julian's polemic, probably beginning work on it in the 420s.[7]

It is perhaps a measure of just how passionately held Cyril's convictions were that he was not prepared to rely solely on force of argument to defeat Nestorius, but also resorted to an array of political tactics to achieve victory. Those tactics included lobbying the emperor and members of the imperial family, and trying to win the support of the bishop of Rome. While he was successful with the latter, his initial approaches to the former proved counterproductive, since the Emperor Theodosius took umbrage at Cyril's writing separately to his wife Eudocia and sister Pulcheria, and accused Cyril of trying to sow dissension within the imperial family (*ACO* 1.1.1 pp. 73–4 [= Festugière110]).[8] So when Theodosius announced in November 430 that an ecumenical council was to be convened the following summer at the neutral but easily accessible location of Ephesus to resolve the Christological disagreements between Nestorius and Cyril, he is likely to have done so in the expectation

6. L. R. Wickham, *Cyril of Alexandria: Select Letters*, Oxford: Clarendon Press, 1983, xxxv. Cf. Wessel, *Cyril*, 2–4. For a robust defence of the orthodoxy of Cyril's Christology, see T. G. Weinandy, 'Cyril and the mystery of the incarnation' in T. G. Weinandy and D. A. Keating (eds), *The Theology of St Cyril of Alexandria*, Edinburgh: T&T Clark, 2003, 23–54 (a reference I owe to Dan Hames).
7. For further discussion, see R. L. Wilken, 'Cyril of Alexandria's *Contra Iulianum*' in W. E. Klingshirn and M. Vessey (eds), *The Limits of Ancient Christianity*, Ann Arbor: University of Michigan Press, 1999, 42–55.
8. There is no English translation of the documents relating to the Council of Ephesus (431), but a French translation of many relevant portions can be found in A. J. Festugière, *Éphèse et Chalcédoine: Actes des conciles*, Paris: Beauchesne, 1982.

that the outcome would be the censure of Cyril and vindication of Nestorius (towards whom Theodosius had thus far been well disposed). In the event, matters turned out rather differently, with respect to both the character of the council and its outcome.

The first factor which shifted the balance back in Cyril's favour was the practical constraints of long-distance travel within the empire, which prevented a major contingent of eastern bishops from Syria and adjacent provinces (who were bound to support Nestorius) from reaching Ephesus by the scheduled start date of 7 June 431. When the contingent had still not arrived a fortnight later, Cyril used this to justify beginning the council in their absence, despite having received word that they were now only a few days away, and despite the protests of Candidianus, the imperial commissioner appointed by Theodosius to oversee the operations of the council (*ACO* 1.1.1 p. 119 [= Festugière184–5], 1.1.4 pp. 31–3). In the absence of the eastern bishops, Cyril speedily proceeded to persuade a largely receptive audience to condemn and depose Nestorius, who, like John Chrysostom in 403, refused to attend the gathering on the grounds of its being improperly constituted. When the eastern bishops duly arrived a few days later and were presented with this *fait accompli*, they in turn declared Cyril deposed. After initially continuing to endorse Nestorius, the Emperor Theodosius then validated the deposition of both bishops, before eventually abandoning his support for Nestorius and withdrawing his confirmation of Cyril's deposition.

This final shift was partly a response to disorder in Constantinople instigated by the vociferous protests of monks whom Nestorius had offended early in his episcopacy,[9] but may also reflect the more subtle pressures brought to bear on the emperor by those courtiers and attendants who benefited from Cyril's notorious strategic targeting of substantial 'gifts' (cf. p. 103 above).[10] Nestorius, meanwhile, had decided there was no point in continuing to resist the inevitable and returned to Antioch, from where he was subsequently sent into exile in southern Egypt. Despite Cyril's emerging victorious, however, the Council of Ephesus did not produce any formal

9. Cf. Gregory, *Vox Populi*, 108–16.
10. It is worth noting how the eastern bishops also sought to bring pressure to bear on Theodosius by reminding him of the importance of maintaining church unity in order to ensure divine favour in the context of the current war against the Vandals in north Africa (*ACO* 1.1.7, p. 76) – an interesting instance of the potential links between military and religious history.

definition of orthodox Christology – hardly surprising, given the chaotic pattern of events surrounding the council, and the continued opposition of the eastern bishops to Cyril. Concerned not to risk alienating divine favour by tolerating a major schism in the church, the Emperor Theodosius eventually forced the two sides to accept an uncomfortable reconciliation involving significant compromises by both (433). The eastern bishops reluctantly acceded to Nestorius' condemnation and accepted the term *Theotokos*, while Cyril grudgingly accepted a formula of reunion which included phraseology redolent of Antiochene Christology. The reconciliation achieved was therefore more one of appearance than substance, with all that that implies for the potential for further disagreement, although in the event, renewal of open controversy did not occur until the years after Cyril's death in 444 (p. 143 below).

The developing authority of the bishop of Rome

Although the bishop of Rome made sure his views were known in Constantinople about the cases of John Chrysostom and Nestorius – critical of the treatment of the former, but endorsing that of the latter – he remained essentially a peripheral figure in these eastern crises. As events unfolded in the east during the late 440s, however, his role became more central – a development symptomatic of the increasing authority of the holder of that office, and a major theme in the religious politics of the fifth century.

The bishop of Rome had long enjoyed a position of prestige among the bishops of the western half of the empire by virtue of the see of Rome's being the only one in the west which could claim to be an apostolic foundation, and one, moreover, associated with such a prominent disciple as Peter. The historic status of the city of Rome, and its location as the primary residence of emperors until the third century, further enhanced the bishop's standing. Paradoxically perhaps, the withdrawal of emperors from Rome to imperial bases near the frontiers in the third and fourth centuries served to increase the authority of the bishop, as did Constantine's generous material endowment of the church in Rome. Nevertheless, it was only during the second half of the fourth century, in the episcopates of Damasus (366–84) and Siricius (384–99), that that prestige began to be consolidated into primacy in the west, through, for example, the issuing of decretals – definitive pronouncements on church policy – and the promotion of Rome as the ultimate court of appeal in episcopal disputes in the west – a development to which the Emperor Gratian lent his support by making available the machinery of the state for its enforcement (*Coll. Avell.* 13.11 [= Coleman-Norton 1.348]). That developing primacy was also reflected symbolically in the increasing use of the term *papa* with reference to the bishop of Rome – a title which combined connotations of pastoral concern with paternal authority[11] – and in the accoutrements of power on which the pagan historian Ammianus Marcellinus, living in Rome in the late fourth century, had occasion to comment, particularly the bishop's riding in a carriage and wearing splendid attire (27.3.14).[12] On the other hand, Ambrose's tenure as bishop of Milan (374–97) and the opportunities he had to exert influence at the court of Theodosius meant that the bishop of Rome was not yet able to take centre stage even in Italian affairs.

That changed during the first half of the fifth century. In 410 Bishop Innocent (401–17) famously developed Rome's claim to primacy in matters of church discipline in his letter to Decentius, bishop of the central Italian town of Eugubium, by arguing that because all churches in the west owed their existence to Rome (not in fact the case), 'they ought to observe what is safeguarded by the Roman church, which they undoubtedly acknowledge as their origin' (*Ep.* 25 = *PL* 20.552). The Pelagian controversy (concerning the relative importance of free will and divine grace in salvation) also gave Innocent the opportunity to assert Rome's claims to adjudicate on doctrinal matters. In a letter to bishops in north Africa in 417, he stated that 'nothing which is done even in the most remote and distant provinces should be taken as finally settled unless it has come to the notice of this see, that any just pronouncement might be confirmed by all the authority of this see, and that the other churches might understand from this ... what they should teach' (*Ep.* 29 = *PL* 20.583).[13]

The legitimation afforded by the apostle Peter also received

11. C. Pietri, *Roma christiana: Recherches sur l'église de Rome, son organisation, sa politique, son idéologie de Miltiade à Sixte III (311–440)*, Rome: École française de Rome, 1976, 1609–11.
12. The association of carriages with high imperial officials is noted (with references) by M. Humphries, 'From emperor to pope? Ceremonial, space and authority at Rome from Constantine to Gregory the Great' in K. Cooper and J. Hillner (eds), *Religion, Dynasty and Patronage in Early Christian Rome, 300–900*, Oxford: Oxford University Press, 2007, 21–58, at 52, and the same could be said with regard to attire.
13. For the Pelagian controversy, see B. R. Rees, *Pelagius: A Reluctant Heretic*, Woodbridge: Boydell, 1988.

increasing emphasis during the fifth century, above all by bishop Leo (440–61), who exploited the implications of the Roman law of inheritance to strengthen the significance of the bishop of Rome's claim to be Peter's heir,[14] as well as deploying other arguments concerning Peter's pre-eminence, such as the following: 'Even among the most blessed apostles, alike in honour, there was a certain distinction in power. Although they were all equal in being chosen, one was allowed to stand out above the others' (*Ep.* 14.11). There did remain limits to the recognition of Roman primacy in the west at this stage: while bishops in Italy, Gaul and Illyricum were usually content to take their lead from Rome in the late fourth and early fifth century, those in north Africa and Spain were more independent-minded.[15] However, given the overall direction of Roman claims, it is unsurprising to find Leo intervening forcefully when Christological disagreements in the east came to the fore again in the late 440s.

Politics and theology in the east: Chalcedon and its background

As already noted, the renewal of open controversy in the east did not occur until the years after Cyril's death in 444. With capable advocates of the Antiochene tradition such as Theodoret of Cyrrhus and Ibas of Edessa regaining the intellectual initiative during the mid-440s, other Antiochene loyalists targeted a prominent monastic leader in Constantinople, Eutyches. Eutyches appears to have laid himself open to attack by espousing an extreme version of Cyril's views which, his enemies claimed, denied Christ's humanity completely, and in November 448, he was condemned by a local synod presided over by Flavian, bishop of Constantinople since 446.[16] Eutyches, however, had a powerful patron in the form of his godson, the imperial eunuch Chrysaphius, who is usually presumed to have

14. W. Ullmann, 'Leo I and the theme of papal primacy', *JTS* 11 (1960), 25–52; J. Meyendorff, *Imperial Unity and Christian Divisions: The Church, 450–680 AD*, Crestwood, NY: St Vladimir's Seminary Press, 1989, 59–66, 148–58; Pietri, *Roma christiana*, 1515–23, for the evolution of ideas prior to Leo.
15. See, e.g., J. E. Merdinger, *Rome and the African Church in the Time of Augustine*, New Haven: Yale University Press, 1997, 183–99, for the case of Apiarius in the mid-420s.
16. Eutyches' chief accuser, Eusebius, bishop of Dorylaeum, had previously been a legal advocate, and made good use of his forensic training in this and other ecclesiastical contexts, as well noted by C. Humfress, *Orthodoxy and the Courts in Late Antiquity*, Oxford: Oxford University Press, 2007, 184–5.

played a part in the dramatic turnaround the following year when the Emperor Theodosius sanctioned another council at Ephesus (August 449), at which Eutyches was rehabilitated while Flavian, Theodoret and Ibas were all deposed from their episcopates. The strongly anti-Antiochene stance of this council was to a large extent due to the dominating influence of Dioscorus, Cyril's successor as bishop of Alexandria.

Dioscorus' success was, however, to be short-lived, not least because, unlike Cyril in 431, Dioscorus had not prepared the ground by gaining the support of the bishop of Rome. Perhaps this was less surprising given that Leo, the incumbent since 440, had, in the aftermath of Eutyches' condemnation in November 448, produced and circulated his own assessment of Eutyches' beliefs – his so-called *Tome* – confirming that condemnation and the distinction between the divine and the human in Christ. But Dioscorus guaranteed Leo's condemnation of the outcome of the second Council of Ephesus by his high-handed treatment of Leo's representatives, which, together with his use of intimidatory tactics towards any opposition, prompted Leo to brand the council a *latrocinium* ('a robbers' den').[17]

Leo quickly set about trying to gain imperial sanction for another council, to be held in Italy where he would be able to oversee proceedings. The western Emperor Valentinian III was agreeable, but of course the eastern Emperor Theodosius also needed persuading. Leo wrote to him directly, and induced Valentinian, his mother Galla Placidia and his wife Licinia Eudoxia to do so too, with Galla, interestingly, also writing to Theodosius' sister Pulcheria.[18] However, since Theodosius responded that 'nothing contrary to the rule of faith or of justice had been done there [at the second Council of Ephesus]',[19] it took the unexpected removal of Theodosius from the scene – he died on 28 July 450 following a fall from his horse while hunting – to facilitate greater receptivity in the east to the idea of

---

17. For the second Council of Ephesus and its background, see W. H. C. Frend, *The Rise of the Monophysite Movement*, Cambridge: Cambridge University Press, 1972, 29–45; Price and Gaddis, *Chalcedon* 1.25–37.

18. These letters are all preserved in Leo's correspondence (*Epp.* 55–8). For the significance of Galla's letter as 'the only example from Classical antiquity of a letter from a woman to a woman on a major matter of public policy', see F. Millar, *A Greek Roman Empire: Power and Belief under Theodosius II (408–450)*, Berkeley: University of California Press, 2006, 37–8, 231 (quotation).

19. Theodosius' responses to Valentinian, Galla and Eudoxia are preserved in Leo's correspondence as *Epp.* 62–4, with the phrase quoted appearing in 62, and a similar assertion in 63.

another council. Being of Balkan origin, the new Emperor Marcian was unlikely to be sympathetic to the Alexandrian tradition, but the prime mover for a new council was probably Pulcheria, who may well have made this a condition of her agreeing to marry Marcian and thereby legitimate his rule.[20] The council was to take place, however, not in Italy, but in the east where the court at Constantinople could keep a close eye on proceedings. The original location was to be the hugely symbolic city of Nicaea, site of the first ecumenical council in 325, but because of trouble with Attila and the Huns on the lower Danube, Marcian subsequently requested that it meet at Chalcedon, whose close proximity to Constantinople would allow Marcian to respond quickly to developments on the Danube frontier or at the council, as the need arose.

The council duly met during October 451, attended by about 370 bishops, nearly all from the eastern half of the empire; the most important westerners present were, of course, Leo's four representatives.[21] Its lengthy proceedings have been preserved, making it one of the events from Roman history about which the most detail is known.[22] These make a number of important points clear. First, many bishops who had endorsed the outcome of the recent second Council of Ephesus changed their position in the interim – some no doubt out of genuine conviction, but others surely from less creditable considerations of convenience.[23] Secondly, although the Emperor Marcian attended only one of the sixteen sessions in person, his arrangements for the council ensured that his agents remained in control of proceedings, making it, in a sense, no more free a forum for theological discussion than the recent second council at Ephesus had been.[24] Thirdly, the council provided an important symbolic stage on which to strengthen Marcian's legitimation as new emperor, most obviously at the sixth session when he and Pulcheria

20. Cf. R. W. Burgess, 'The accession of Marcian in the light of Chalcedonian apologetic and Monophysite polemic', *Byz. Zeitschr.* 86–7 (1993–4), 47–68, at 65.
21. For discussion of attendance numbers and ecumenicity at Chalcedon, see Price and Gaddis, *Chalcedon*, 3.193–203.
22. As emphasised by G. E. M. de Ste Croix (with M. Whitby), 'The Council of Chalcedon' in his *Christian Persecution, Martyrdom and Orthodoxy*, eds M. Whitby and J. Streeter, Oxford: Oxford University Press, 2006, 259–319, at 259. The proceedings are available in the translation and commentary by Price and Gaddis, *Chalcedon*; there is also a valuable collection of essays: R. Price and Mary Whitby (eds), *Chalcedon in Context: Church Councils 400–700*, Liverpool: Liverpool University Press, 2009.
23. De Ste Croix, 'Chalcedon', 303–17.
24. This is the main thesis of de Ste Croix, 'Chalcedon' (e.g., at 273–4).

were present to receive prolonged acclamations from the assembled bishops as the 'new Constantine' and the 'new Helena'[25] – acclamations which also implicitly asserted that the Council of Chalcedon was of comparable importance to that of Nicaea.

The most important outcomes of the council's deliberations were the condemnation and deposition of Dioscorus, the rehabilitation of Theodoret and Ibas,[26] the endorsement of Leo's *Tome*, and the formulation of a Definition concerning Christ which it was hoped would be acceptable to all moderate parties:

> Following, therefore, the holy fathers, we all in harmony teach confession of one and the same Son our Lord Jesus Christ, the same perfect in Godhead and the same perfect in manhood, truly God and the same truly man, of a rational soul and body, consubstantial with the Father in respect of the Godhead, and the same consubstantial with us in respect of the manhood, like us in all things apart from sin, begotten from the Father before the ages in respect of the Godhead, and the same in the last days for us and for our salvation from the Virgin Mary the *Theotokos* in respect of the manhood, one and the same Christ, Son, Lord, Only-begotten, acknowledged in two natures without confusion, change, division, or separation (the difference of the two natures being in no way destroyed by the union, but rather the distinctive character of each nature being preserved and coming together into one person and one hypostasis [i.e., oneness of inner being]), not parted or divided into two persons, but one and the same Son, Only-begotten, God, Word, Lord, Jesus Christ. (*ACO* 2.1.2 pp. 129–30 [325–6] = Price and Gaddis, *Chalcedon*, 2.204)

The recognition of two natures and references to Christ's humanity aimed to satisfy Leo and those in the Antiochene tradition, while the acknowledgement of Mary as *Theotokos* and the emphasis on union were intended to make the Definition acceptable to those loyal to the Alexandrian tradition. Indeed it has been argued persuasively that the Definition owed most to the theology of Cyril.[27] Despite this, however, it proved least acceptable to those loyal to his memory. The inclusion of the phrase 'in two natures' at the insistence of

---

25. *ACO* 2.1.2 pp. 140 [336] (line 27), 155 [351] (lines 12–14, 19, 25–6) = Price and Gaddis, *Chalcedon*, 2.216, 240.

26. Flavian had died soon after the council of Ephesus from injuries he received at the hands of Dioscorus' and Eutyches' supporters, and was referred to at Chalcedon as a martyr: *ACO* 2.1.3 p. 51 [410] (line 13) = Price and Gaddis, *Chalcedon*, 3.14.

27. R. Price, 'The theology of Chalcedon' in Price and Gaddis, *Chalcedon*, 1.56–75.

Leo's representatives and the Emperor Marcian at the final stage
of revision was enough to sow doubts in the minds of many
from the Alexandrian tradition – doubts which were reinforced
by the council's condemnation of Dioscorus and rehabilitation of
Theodoret and Ibas. These different elements 'gave plausibility to the
charge that the Definition, while pretending to honour Cyril, had in
fact betrayed him'.[28] That sense of betrayal meant that Chalcedon,
far from facilitating unity, became a monumental stumbling block to
its attainment (p. 148 below).

One further outcome of the council warrants comment, namely
Canon 28, which, taking its lead from Canon 3 at the Council of
Constantinople in 381 (p. 134 above), reiterated the primacy of the
see of Constantinople in the east, in second place after Rome:

> Primacy and exceptional honour shall be preserved for the most
> God-beloved archbishop of Senior Rome according to the canons,
> but the most sacred archbishop of imperial Constantinople New
> Rome is to enjoy the same privileges of honour, and he is to have
> power, on the basis of his authority, to consecrate the metropolitan
> bishops in the dioceses of Asiana, Pontica and Thrace. (*ACO* 2.1.3
> p. 98 [457] = Price and Gaddis, *Chalcedon*, 3.90)[29]

Understandably, this reinforced resentment among church leaders in
Alexandria towards Constantinople (cf. p. 134 above), but it also
demonstrated the limits of Rome's authority in the east. Although
this canon acknowledged the primacy of Rome, Leo was unhappy
with its reliance on political criteria at the expense of the see's
spiritual claims of Petrine descent. His objections were, however,
ignored.

Brave new world, post-Chalcedon

The Council of Chalcedon concluded in November 451, and in the
early months of the following year, the Emperor Marcian issued a
number of edicts confirming the council's outcomes, claiming that
'contention over the orthodox law of Christians has been brought to
an end, remedies have at last been found for culpable error, and the
discordant judgement of congregations has harmonised in a single
consensus and accord' (*ACO* 2.1.2 p. 120 [479] = Price and Gaddis,
Chalcedon, 3.128–9). Those claims, however, were made in the face

28. Price, 'Theology' in Price and Gaddis, *Chalcedon*, 1.74.
29. For further discussion, see Price and Gaddis, *Chalcedon*, 3.67–72.

of growing evidence that the council's outcomes were unacceptable to significant numbers in the eastern half of the empire. Indeed, Marcian's edicts of confirmation betray his awareness of opposition to Chalcedon in the imperial capital itself, where Eutyches had lived and where he continued to find support among the monastic population. That opposition seems to have found expression primarily in a war of words – one of the edicts stipulated that anti-Chalcedonian tracts were to be burned and their authors exiled – but further afield hostility took altogether more extreme forms.

In Palestine, where churches and monasteries had developed increasingly close ties with Alexandria during the first half of the fifth century, there was outrage that Juvenal, bishop of Jerusalem, who had supported Cyril at the first Council of Ephesus and Dioscorus at the second, should have publicly abandoned Dioscorus at the first session of Chalcedon and endorsed the council's conclusions. Anti-Chalcedonian monks intercepted the returning Juvenal at the port of Caesarea and made it so clear to him that he was not welcome in Jerusalem that he returned to Constantinople. At the same time, the Chalcedonian bishop of Ashkelon was forced to flee to Cyprus, while the bishop of Scythopolis was actually killed. The monks then set about appointing their own set of anti-Chalcedonian bishops.[30] Eventually, after a period of nearly two years during which he tried by persuasion to win over the monks, Marcian ordered local military units to arrest the anti-Chalcedonian leadership and install Juvenal as bishop once again.

This use of force in the face of anti-Chalcedonian opposition already had a recent precedent in Alexandria. A new bishop, Proterius, was appointed in place of Dioscorus, who had been deposed and exiled at Chalcedon, but despite his having been an associate of Dioscorus', Proterius incurred such a level of opposition from those loyal to Dioscorus and resentful at Proterius' assent to the outcomes of Chalcedon that the Emperor Marcian had to send military reinforcements from Constantinople to restore public order (Evagrius, *Hist. eccl.* 2.5). It is clear, however, that this did not resolve the problem, for Marcian's death in 457 was the signal for a recrudescence of violence against Proterius which resulted in his lynching and the election of the resolutely anti-Chalcedonian

---

30. The best-known of these was Peter the Iberian: C. B. Horn, *Asceticism and Christological Controversy in Fifth-Century Palestine: The Career of Peter the Iberian*, Oxford: Oxford University Press, 2006.

Timothy Aelurus in his place (Evagrius, *Hist. eccl.* 2.8). When Marcian's successor, the Emperor Leo, failed in his attempts at reaching a compromise with Timothy, he had Timothy arrested and exiled. Needless to say, while such exercise of force may have shown the Alexandrians that imperial power could not be flouted with impunity, it did not help to achieve the longer-term goal of winning hearts and minds.

Although Leo's successor Zeno also came to the imperial throne committed to upholding Chalcedon, the political insecurity he experienced during the early years of his reign (p. 100 above) had significant implications for imperial policy with regard to church affairs. First, Zeno's temporary displacement from Constantinople by Basiliscus between January 475 and August 476 resulted in a reversal of policy, with Basiliscus, keen to win quick support for his regime, issuing an encyclical in which the Council of Nicaea (325) was reaffirmed as the basis of faith and the innovations introduced by Chalcedon, including the *Tome* of Leo and Canon 28 on the primacy of the bishop of Constantinople in the east, were condemned (Evagrius, *Hist. eccl.* 3.4). Unsurprisingly, the bishop of Constantinople, Acacius, was unhappy about this last item and proceeded to rally opposition to Basiliscus in the capital, including that of the influential holy man Daniel the Stylite, who deployed character assassination to great effect by branding Basiliscus 'a second Diocletian' after the last great persecutor of the church (*V. Daniel* 73). Secondly, although the restored Zeno initially resumed his previous policy of upholding Chalcedon, he soon found, as Marcian and Leo had, that this resulted in violence and the need to use force. In 479 the new Chalcedonian bishop of Antioch, Stephen, was killed by anti-Chalcedonians, and his imperially approved successor Calendion was probably only able to take up his post with the assistance of imperial troops.[31]

Against this background, and continuing problems in persuading Alexandria to accept bishops who were not clearly anti-Chalcedonian, Zeno issued a doctrinal statement in 482 which, through a careful balancing act of studied ambiguity and omission, tried to find a middle way acceptable to both Chalcedonians and anti-Chalcedonians. The so-called *Henotikon*, or 'formula of union', was

---

31. For Stephen's death, see Evagrius, *Hist. eccl.* 3.10; for the likelihood that Calendion required military aid, see E. Stein, *Histoire du Bas-Empire* (tr. R. Palanque), Paris: de Brouwer, 1949–59, 2.20.

noteworthy both for its manner of formulation and for its content. Zeno had no theological pretensions, so clearly relied on advice from church leaders, especially the incumbent bishop of Constantinople, Acacius (472–89), but the *Henotikon* was nevertheless issued by the emperor without reference to any council of bishops, and as such, set an important precedent for state intervention in church affairs which became significant during the reign in the sixth century of the Emperor Justinian – an emperor who did fancy himself as a theologian (pp. 264–6 below). As for its content, the *Henotikon* condemned Nestorius, endorsed Cyril's more hard-line views, and made no reference to two natures – all features designed to win over anti-Chalcedonians – but it also condemned Eutyches and refrained from explicit rejection of Chalcedon.[32]

These compromises did not satisfy those at the extreme end of the spectrum in either camp, but they were enough to win the support of significant numbers of Chalcedonian and anti-Chalcedonian bishops in the eastern half of the empire. This stabilisation of church affairs in the east was very helpful for Zeno during a period when he faced enough challenges to his position on other fronts (p. 100 above), but it did come at a price. The *Henotikon* included the statement that 'we anathematize anyone who has thought, or thinks, any other opinion, whether at Chalcedon or at any synod' – a seemingly inconsequential element which was, however, easily interpreted as a pejorative comment on Chalcedon. The bishop of Rome certainly took this view, and also objected strongly to Acacius' re-establishing formal ties with the anti-Chalcedonian bishop of Alexandria without reference to Rome. The result was the severing of ties between the churches of Rome and Constantinople for more than three decades in what became known as the Acacian schism – an unfortunate outcome, but one with which Zeno was prepared to live.

State power and Christianisation

Although imperial intervention in Christological controversies was the most prominent way in which the state was involved in the religious life of the empire during the fifth century, emperors also continued to issue laws which discriminated against adherents of traditional pagan cults, and thereby promoted the ongoing

32. For the text, see Evagrius, *Hist. eccl.* 3.14, with discussion in Frend, *Monophysite Movement*, 174–83, and Meyendorff, *Imperial Unity*, 194–202.

Christianisation of the empire. Although some temples had been destroyed and Theodosius I had specifically prohibited sacrifice and related expressions of pagan religious devotion during the latter part of his reign (pp. 52–3 above), many shrines remained intact and the prohibition of sacrifice did not guarantee that it or other forms of devotion were not practised illicitly. Indeed, given the huge diversity of pagan cults throughout the empire, their antiquity and the limited ability (and, sometimes, unwillingness) of officials to enforce the relevant laws, traditional cults were bound to retain significant followings for the foreseeable future. The size and visibility of those followings will have been determined by a range of factors – whether a particular cult had achieved empire-wide recognition or was restricted to a particular locality, whether its rites were performed primarily in urban or rural contexts, and in public or private, and the extent to which local Christians were proactive in evangelisation.[33]

Emperors continued periodically to issue laws affecting pagans adversely in one respect or another. A law of 396 deprived pagan priests of any privileges they had previously enjoyed, while one of 408 sanctioned the removal of cult images from temples and shrines (*Cod. Theod.* 16.10.14, 19). A different strategy is evident in a law of 416 which excluded pagans from admission to service in the imperial bureaucracy, and in one of 468 which restricted the right to practise law to orthodox Christians (*Cod. Theod.* 16.10.21, *Cod. Iust.* 1.4.15). Nor was the ideological dimension neglected, with a law of 448 stipulating that the anti-Christian writings of the famous Neoplatonic philosopher Porphyry (234–c. 305) were to be burned (as also, intriguingly, were those of Nestorius) (*Cod. Iust.* 1.1.3). At the same time, a strand of pragmatism can be detected in some imperial decisions. A number of laws prohibited the destruction of temples if they were made available for other public uses (*Cod. Theod.* 16.10.15, 18, 19), and when the Christians of Gaza requested imperial sanction for the demolition of temples in their city, the Emperor Arcadius is said to have responded, 'I know that the city is prone to idolatry, but it is willing to pay its dues in public taxes, bringing in substantial amounts. Therefore, if we suddenly instill fear in them, they will take to flight and we will lose this great

---

33. For the usually neglected private dimension of religious practice in late antiquity, see K. Bowes, *Private Worship, Public Values, and Religious Change in Late Antiquity*, Cambridge: Cambridge University Press, 2008.

amount of tax income.'[34] Given the pressing military concerns which emperors faced for much of the fifth century, particularly in the west, it is less surprising that their measures against paganism were intermittent, and sometimes prioritised concerns for fiscal well-being and public order ahead of religious principles. Such pragmatism is likewise evident in the fact that avowed pagans continued to hold high office in the army until the middle of the fifth century (as also did individuals who adhered to heterodox Arianism).[35]

In practice, then, much of the responsibility for advancing the Christianisation of the empire rested not with the emperor or his officials, but with Christian leaders at the local level – most obviously bishops, but also holy men. So, for example, in central Egypt the abbot Shenute features in the surviving sources as an important activist in the destruction of pagan shrines and idols in the first half of the fifth century, while in western Anatolia another monk, Hypatius, is credited with aggressive evangelism of rural areas:[36]

> He had zeal for God and he delivered many parts of Bithynia from the error of idols. For whenever he heard that any district was showing reverence for a tree or something similar, he went there immediately, taking with him monks who were his disciples, and cut it down and burned it. In this way, then, they gradually became Christians. (Callinicus, V. *Hypatii* 30.1)

Of course, to a significant degree the prominence of such individuals is a function of the survival of hagiographical accounts of their lives, but those accounts nonetheless include much circumstantial detail which lends credence to an overall picture of gradual religious

---

34. Marcus Diaconus, *V. Porphyrii* 41 (tr. C. Rapp) (still an intriguing comment to place in the mouth of a Christian emperor, even if the historicity of this text is open to doubt [p. 102 n.41 above]). Cf. the similar reasoning invoked by the (Christian) praetorian prefect Taurus in the context of the controversy over Nestorius in the early 430s: when instructed to compel Cilician bishops to recognise the pro-Nestorian John of Antioch, he countered that any attempt to do so would result in such disturbances that the collection of taxes in the province would be jeopardised: *ACO* 1.4 p. 155 (lines 18–23). For further discussion of pagans in the fifth century, see K. W. Harl, 'Sacrifice and pagan belief in fifth- and sixth-century Byzantium', *P&P* 128 (1990), 7–27.
35. For details, see A. D. Lee, *War in Late Antiquity: A Social History*, Oxford: Blackwell, 2007, 190, 192–3.
36. For Shenute, see F. R. Trombley, *Hellenic Religion and Christianization, c. 379–527*, 2nd edn, Leiden: Brill, 2001, 2.207–19, and D. Frankfurter, *Religion in Roman Egypt: Assimilation and Resistance*, Princeton: Princeton University Press, 1998, 68–9, 265–6. For Hypatius, see Trombley, *Christianization*, 2.76–96.

change at the grassroots level. At the same time, it is apparent that the advance of Christianity often entailed compromises and syncretism whereby elements of the pagan past were incorporated into local expressions of Christianity.[37] Perhaps the most obvious example of this phenomenon was the conversion of temples into churches, rather than their destruction.[38] The slaughter of animals at saints' shrines and feasting thereon in rituals not so different from pagan sacrifice was also permitted in some places as a strategy for integrating the local peasantry into church life, best documented at the tomb of the martyr Felix at Nola in southern Italy in the early fifth century.[39] Also noteworthy is the way in which traditional forms of oracular practice based on the drawing of lots or the random selection of a passage from a holy text were adapted by some Christians in the form of the so-called *sortes sanctorum* ('lots of the saints') and the *sortes Biblicae* ('lots of the Bible'), evidence for which emerges in the fifth century.[40] Given such developments, it is unsurprising to find Augustine, in his capacity as bishop of Hippo in north Africa in the early fifth century, lamenting the fact that the church was increasingly filled with individuals whose Christian commitment was shallower than in the past.[41]

The other major religious category in the empire – adherents of Judaism – also experienced mixed fortunes at the hands of the imperial government during the fifth century, but they still enjoyed greater official protection of their rights than pagans did. Although the construction of new synagogues was prohibited by law in the early decades of the fifth century (*Cod. Theod.* 16.8.22 [415], 25, 27 [423]), the right of existing structures to protection was regularly reasserted (*Cod. Theod.* 16.8.20 [412], 21 [420], 25–7 [423]), and repair of synagogues was also officially permitted (*Nov. Theod.* 3.3,

37. See generally R. MacMullen, *Christianity and Paganism in the Fourth to Eighth Centuries*, New Haven: Yale University Press, 1997, 103–49, Frankfurter, *Religion in Roman Egypt*, 265–84.
38. R. P. C. Hanson, 'The transformation of pagan temples into churches in the early Christian centuries', *Journal of Semitic Studies* 23 (1978), 257–67 (reprinted in his *Studies in Christian Antiquity*, Edinburgh: T & T Clark).
39. D. Trout, 'Christianizing the Nolan countryside: animal sacrifice at the tomb of St Felix', *JECS* 3 (1995), 281–98.
40. P. W. van der Horst, '*Sortes*: sacred books as instant oracles in late antiquity' in L. V. Rutgers et al. (eds), *The Use of Sacred Books in the Ancient World*, Leuven: Peeters, 1998, 143–73; W. E. Klingshirn, 'Defining the *sortes sanctorum*: Gibbon, du Cange and early Christian lot divination', *JECS* 10 (2002), 77–130.
41. E.g., August. *Enarrationes in Psalmos* 7.9, with further references and discussion in P. Brown, *Augustine of Hippo*, London: Faber, 1967, 234.

5 [438]). Like pagans, Jews were also prohibited from employment in government service and from practising law (*Nov. Theod.* 3.2, 5–6 [438], *Cod. Iust.* 1.4.15 [468]), but unlike those of pagans, the right of Jews to worship freely remained unchanged as far as the law was concerned.[42] However, just as the imperial government had difficulty enforcing prohibitions on pagan sacrifice, so too it was unable to guarantee protection of Jewish rights against the activities of Christian leaders at the local level. This is most graphically illustrated by the famous account of the conversion of the Jewish community on the island of Minorca in 418, where what effectively developed into a Christian assault on the local synagogue resulted in its destruction and, in the ensuing days, the agreement of a demoralised Jewish community to convert to Christianity.[43] At the same time, Minorca's peripheral location must have significantly reduced the possibility of official intervention to uphold Jewish rights in a way which would have been more likely in a major urban centre.[44]

Alternative sources of religious power

This account of the empire's religious history during the fifth century has necessarily focused on bishops and emperors, since their influence on many developments was understandably significant. However, as already intimated at various points, bishops were not the only individuals with religious clout in late antiquity. Beyond the institutional hierarchy of the church lay alternative sources of religious power which drew their energy and authority from the pursuit of ascetic ideals in one form or another. Although becoming a monk was often inspired by a desire to reject worldly power and values, the prestige which many ascetics acquired by virtue of the rigours to which they subjected themselves meant that that intention could be subverted, as their reputation for holiness gave them an influence which was even more potent. This helps to explain how,

42. Millar, *Greek Roman Empire*, 123–9.
43 For good discussions of this episode, see E. D. Hunt, 'St Stephen in Minorca: an episode in Jewish–Christian relations in the early 5th century AD', *JTS* 33 (1982), 106–23, and S. Bradbury, *Severus of Minorca: Letter on the Conversion of the Jews*, Oxford: Clarendon Press, 1996 (including an edition and translation of the relevant text).
44. For another case of Jewish conversion to Christianity en masse in this period, see Socrates, *Hist. eccl.* 7.38 (Crete in the 430s), with discussion in M. Schuol, 'Die Taufe der Juden auf Kreta', *Historia* 60 (2011), 219–54.

paradoxically, it was possible for none other than the Emperor Theodosius II to be presented as an individual who pursued a monastic regimen: 'Such was his fortitude in undergoing hardships that he would courageously endure both heat and cold, fasting very frequently, especially on Wednesdays and Fridays, which he did from an earnest endeavour to observe closely all the prescribed forms of the Christian religion; his palace was little different from a monastery' (Socrates, *Eccl. hist.* 7.22). Presumably it was thought that promotion of such an image would help to offset the handicap of a reputation for being an 'unwarlike' emperor who 'lived a life of cowardice', as another contemporary historian disdainfully described him (Priscus, *fr.* 3, 1).

The saint or holy man has long been recognised as a figure of importance in the social and religious history of late antiquity, with his role as independent arbitrator and patron in communities attracting particular attention.[45] Perhaps the most famous holy man of the fifth century was Simeon the Stylite (d. 459), so called because of his practice of standing atop a *stylos* or pillar in the depths of the Syrian countryside (cf. Fig. 11). Although he seems originally to have adopted this extreme form of asceticism in an effort to escape the steady stream of petitioners who came to seek his guidance and prayers for their problems, this strategy served only to make him more famous and attract even larger crowds, while also spawning a host of imitators. Simeon's solution to his unwanted celebrity was to ration the time he devoted to dealing with petitioners to the period between mid-afternoon and sunset; outside those hours, his location atop his pillar allowed him to 'disconnect' himself from the masses and devote himself to prayer.[46] The sorts of issues which exercised his petitioners are perhaps best reflected in the communal letter from the inhabitants of the village of Panir, appended to the Syriac version

45. For earlier discussion of the saint in late antiquity, see N. H. Baynes, 'The thought-world of East Rome' in his *Byzantine Studies and Other Essays*, London: Athlone, 1955, 24–46. However, it was P. Brown, 'The rise and function of the holy man in late antiquity', *JRS* 61 (1971), 80–101, which provoked intensive study of the phenomenon, reflected in the special issue of *JECS* 6 (1998), 343–539, and J. Howard-Johnson and P. Hayward (eds), *The Cult of the Saints in Late Antiquity and the Middle Ages*, Oxford: Oxford University Press, 1999.

46. The term is that of R. Lane Fox, who remarks that 'pillars gave stylites the freedom of choice which we now enjoy from answer-phones' ('The *Life of Daniel*' in M. J. Edwards and S. Swain [eds], *Portraits: Biographical Representation in the Greek and Latin Literature of the Roman Empire*, Oxford: Clarendon Press, 1997, 175–225, at 216).

Figure 11 Basalt panel from a chancel screen in a church (84.5 × 76 cm) (Syria, fifth century), depicting St Simeon the Stylite on his column. A bird, perhaps a dove, places a wreath on his head, while a monk climbs a ladder with a censer, perhaps reflecting the reverence which the saint inspired. © bpk/Skulpturensammlung und Museum für Byzantinische Kunst, SMB/Jürgen Liepe

of his *Life*, in which they express their concern about illegal changes to land boundaries, labourers being cheated of their wages, excessive interest charges on loans, bribery of judges and sexual violence against women; their hope seems to have been that if Simeon spoke out against such practices, his charismatic authority would persuade those in positions of power to act justly.[47] However, the ultimate proof of his status was the way in which emperors are said to have sought his help in resolving knotty issues, such as the reconciliation of the eastern bishops with Cyril in the aftermath of the first Council of Ephesus (p. 141 above) and reiteration of the outcomes of the Council of Chalcedon at the start of the Emperor Leo's reign in 457 (Evagrius, *Hist. eccl.* 2.10).

Simeon's most famous successor as a stylite was Daniel (d. 493), whose decision to establish himself at the heart of empire, on the

47. *V. Simeon syr.* 130–2 with discussion in Lane Fox, '*Life of Daniel*', 212–13.

coast near Constantinople, provided even more opportunity for the influence of a holy man to be exhibited at the highest levels of society. His reputation was reflected in a 'pillargram' – an epigram penned by a prominent poet of the period and inscribed on his column:

> Standing 'twixt earth and heaven a man you see
> Who fears no gales that all about him fret.
> Daniel's his name, great Simeon's rival he.
> Upon a double column firm his steps are set.
> Ambrosial hunger, bloodless thirst support his frame
> And thus the Virgin Mother's Son he doth proclaim.[48]

So it was that, alongside administering healings and exorcisms to family members of prominent figures in Constantinople, the *Life* of Daniel presents him as playing a role in political life from time to time – mediating in treaty negotiations between the Emperor Leo and the ruler of the Caucasian Lazi, responding to requests from the Leo for advice in dealing with the Vandals and with affairs in Thrace, and condemning the Christological stance of the usurper Basiliscus (p. 149 above).[49]

Although it is understandable that an individual ascetic like Daniel should have had a high profile in Constantinople, leaders of monastic communities in the capital also proved capable of wielding influence, particularly during the Christological controversies of Theodosius II's reign. As already noted (p. 135 above), Isaac, founder of the earliest monastic community in the capital, played a part in the fall of John Chrysostom, while Eutyches, head of another monastic community, had an important role in the calling of the second Council of Ephesus in 449 and the condemnation of Flavian, the bishop of Constantinople (pp. 143–4 above).[50] In between these two episodes, Isaac's successor as head of his community, Dalmatius, intervened very publicly against Nestorius during the first Council of Ephesus by leaving his monastery for the first time in forty-eight years and, in the company of his monks, processing to the imperial

---

48. *Anth. Pal.* 1.99 = *V. Daniel* 36 (tr. E. Dawes and N. H. Baynes), by Cyrus of Panopolis; 'pillargram' is Lane Fox's term ('*Life of Daniel*', 178).
49. *V. Daniel* 51, 56, 65, 70–1, with discussion in Lane Fox, '*Life of Daniel*'.
50. On these episodes, see also D. Caner, *Wandering, Begging Monks: Spiritual Authority and the Promotion of Monasticism in Late Antiquity*, Berkeley: University of California Press, 2002, 169–76, 194–9 (Isaac), 223–41 (Eutyches); P. Hatlie, *The Monks and Monasteries of Constantinople, ca.350–850*, Cambridge: Cambridge University Press, 2007, 66–70.

palace, where the Emperor Theodosius received him.[51] It was the role of Isaac, Dalmatius and Eutyches in these events which no doubt prompted the determination of bishops to assert their authority over monks, as embodied in the fourth canon of the Council of Chalcedon. While this canon acknowledged the honour which monks were due, it expressed concern about the way in which some had 'used the monastic cover to throw church and civil affairs into confusion', and decreed that henceforth a new monastery could not be established without the approval of the local bishop and that 'those who pursue a monastic life in each city and village [shall] be subordinate to their bishop'.[52] Enforcement of such a canon may not always have been easy, but its issuing demonstrates the awareness and concern of the church hierarchy about asceticism as an alternative focus of popular religious loyalties, and their determination to restrict its challenge.

Emperors in late antiquity, then, faced novel problems in the area of religion compared with their predecessors in earlier centuries. In principle, Christian monotheism had the potential to be a unifying force which also simplified the religious landscape of the empire, but in practice matters proved much less straightforward. Bishops and holy men emerged as figures who could exercise greater influence than any pagan priest had ever been able to wield, and doctrinal differences within the church created fissures which threatened the unity of the empire.[53] Juggling the competing demands of different religious constituencies must sometimes have seemed almost as great a challenge for emperors as dealing with ambitious generals or recalcitrant barbarians.

51. Caner, *Monks*, 212–23.
52. For further discussion, see Caner, *Monks*, ch. 6.
53. Cf. G. Fowden, *Empire to Commonwealth: The Consequences of Monotheism in Late Antiquity*, Princeton: Princeton University Press, 1993, 106–8.

CHAPTER 8

Anastasius and the resurrection of imperial power

Securing power

Like Theodosius II in 450 and Marcian in 457, Zeno died without having nominated a successor. Unlike on those earlier occasions, however, there was no powerful general in April 491 ready to impose his choice – a circumstance which allowed scope for other parties to intervene, and provides further insights into the mechanics of power at the imperial court in Constantinople. Those insights are aided by the survival of a detailed description of the interregnum among the sixth-century chapters embedded in a tenth-century handbook on court ceremonial (Constantine Porphyrogenitus, *De Caerimoniis* 1.92). Inside the palace, senators and senior courtiers met the patriarch Euphemius and the Empress Ariadne, while members of the urban populace and soldiers present in the capital gathered in the adjacent hippodrome ready to make their views known. When Ariadne and various officials appeared in the imperial box to calm the hippodrome crowd, they were met by chants stipulating the criteria which they regarded as important in selecting a new emperor – that he be Roman, orthodox and not given to greed. The first criterion no doubt reflected a desire to avoid any further turmoil of the sort engendered in recent decades by Zeno's Isaurian connections, while the second and third reflected a concern to ensure religious and financial stability.

After Ariadne had reassured the crowd that their wishes would be taken into account, she withdrew to the palace, where a further meeting of senior figures resulted in the decision to entrust the choice to Ariadne.[1] This was the proposal of the chamberlain Urbicius, who emerges from these events as another example of a eunuch exercising considerable influence in court politics. In his case, that

---

1. R. J. Lilie, 'Die Krönung des Kaiser Anastasios I', *Byzantinoslavica* 56 (1995), 3–12, argues that the choice was actually made by senior courtiers in the name of Ariadne.

influence must have derived primarily from a very long track record
of experience stretching all the way back to the reign of Theodosius
II, probably unmatched by any other individual present during the
deliberations following Zeno's death. His decision to champion
Ariadne's cause presumably reflects recognition not so much of her
status as widow of the unpopular deceased emperor, but rather of
the link she provided back to Zeno's predecessor, her father Leo – a
link which perhaps offered the best prospect of assuring a smooth
transfer of power and a return to political stability.

Ariadne's choice was Anastasius, a court functionary whose name
(closely related to the word for 'resurrection') was in most respects
to prove a good omen for the empire's fortunes in the coming
decades.[2] He was at this time one of the chiefs of the thirty-strong
corps of so-called silentiaries, a role of more importance than its
usual glossing as 'usher' might suggest. Silentiaries were present
at meetings of the imperial consistory (advisory council of senior
officials) and were sometimes used by emperors to undertake
sensitive missions, especially in relation to ecclesiastical affairs.[3]
Even so, a silentiary was not an obvious candidate for imperial
office – unless he happened to be one of the four specifically attached
to the person of the empress, which is the likely context in which
Ariadne came to know Anastasius (he is said to have enjoyed
'freedom of speech' with her: Ps.-Zachariah Rhetor, *Chron.* 7.1a).
Although he was already at least sixty years old, he did come from
Latin-speaking Dyrrhachium on the western coast of the Balkans
and so could be regarded as satisfying the first popular requirement
of being a Roman (whatever that might mean by this stage of the
empire's history – but perhaps in the immediate context, the crucial
consideration was that he was not from Isauria, or anywhere
nearby),[4] and although he is not known to have had prior financial
experience, he certainly proved to be skilled in this sphere – or
at least, in selecting financially able individuals for the relevant
administrative posts. There was room for doubt, however, about the
third qualification – theological orthodoxy – since Anastasius had

---

2. For studies of Anastasius' reign, see F. Haarer, *Anastasius I: Politics and Empire in
the Late Roman World*, Cambridge: Francis Cairns, 2006; M. Meier, *Anastasios I: Die
Entstehung des byzantinischen Reich*, Stuttgart: Klett-Cotta, 2009.
3. Jones, *LRE*, 571–2.
4. For a good discussion of this issue, see G. Greatrex, 'Roman identity in the sixth
century' in S. Mitchell and G. Greatrex (eds), *Ethnicity and Culture in Late Antiquity*,
London: Duckworth, 2000, 267–92.

a reputation for being something of a maverick when it came to doctrinal issues. Certainly the patriarch Euphemius felt it was necessary for Anastasius to sign a declaration of Chalcedonian orthodoxy before Euphemius would agree to crown him emperor. On the other hand, Anastasius' general reputation for piety seems to have been sufficient for the urban populace, who appear to have welcomed his election.

Anastasius' formal accession involved a number of stages which took place in the palace and the hippodrome. After donning the relevant imperial garments, he appeared in the imperial box in the hippodrome where he was raised on a shield and crowned with a torque, after which troops assembled in the hippodrome raised their standards and, together with the urban populace, acclaimed him. Returning to the palace, Anastasius was then crowned by the patriarch, before returning to the imperial box where he promised the troops the standard accession donative of five gold coins and a pound of silver per man. Many of the elements of this ceremonial reflect the traditional acknowledgement of the importance of the army's support – especially important for an emperor like Anastasius without any military background – but also notable is the role of the church in bestowing its approval on the new emperor. His legitimacy was further enhanced by his marriage to Ariadne a month or so after his accession – a matter which was no doubt discussed and agreed as part of negotiations during the interregnum.

Securing power was, however, to involve a great deal more than these events during the spring of 491, important though they undoubtedly were. For there were various powerful individuals who did not welcome Anastasius' elevation to the throne, a number of whom, rather confusingly, bore the name Longinus – symptomatic of their common Isaurian origin. The first Longinus was Zeno's brother, who had held a senior military post and the consulship in the final years of Zeno's reign and who, understandably, entertained hopes of succeeding his brother. Anastasius was clearly aware of the danger from this quarter and acted quickly to have Longinus exiled to southern Egypt. The second Longinus was from Cardala in Isauria and had held the senior post of master of offices during the second half of Zeno's reign: Anastasius dismissed him, whereupon he fled to Isauria, where a revolt against Anastasius had already broken out, one of whose leaders was a third Longinus, from Selinus. The following year substantial forces advanced from Isauria towards Constantinople, but they suffered a decisive defeat in battle at Cotyaeum in Phrygia, with a number of the rebel leaders captured and executed. Nonetheless, the mountainous terrain of Isauria meant that Anastasius' victorious generals, John the Scythian and John the Hunchback, took another six years to capture the remaining leaders.[5]

Anastasius' generals were rewarded with consulships in 498 and 499, but Anastasius made sure that it was he who accrued most of the credit for the effective elimination of the Isaurians from imperial politics, seeking to capitalise on the ensuing popularity by a variety of strategies. There was a (no longer extant) six-book epic entitled the *Isaurika* by an Egyptian poet, Christodorus (*Suda*, *s.v.* Christodorus), and commemorative building in the form of a substantial addition to the palace – the so-called *Chalkē* or Bronze Gate – as recorded in a contemporary poem:

> I am the house of Anastasius, the emperor, slayer of tyrants, and I alone far excel all cities of the earth … I surpass the celebrated wonders of the Italian land. Beauty of the Capitolian temple, give place to your betters, even though your roof of bronze dazzles the eye … The pyramids are not capable of vying with me, or the colossus of the Pharos – I alone surpass a great legion of buildings. My prince himself, after his victory over the Isaurians, completed me, the house of the dawn, shining with gold, on all sides exposed to the breezes of the four winds. (*Anth. Pal.* 9.656 [tr. W. Paton])

And there were victory celebrations in Constantinople, with one panegyrist making explicit comparison with triumphs of the Republican period:

> This very place rightly displayed trophies to you and placed on view the fettered and defeated tyrants who were driven to your feet in the middle of the circus spectacles. Once in the same manner while the Latin people watched, Aemilius Paullus, that bravest of men, riding in his chariot, dragged King Perseus to the Tarpeian citadel and placated Jupiter, the lord of the Capitoline temples [167 BC]. (Priscian, *De laude Anastasii* 171–7 [tr. P. Coyne with revisions])

Although the two Johns had proved reliable commanders during the Isaurian war, Anastasius' age and lack of military experience clearly left him feeling vulnerable on this front, since there is a noticeable pattern during his reign of senior military commands often being held by relatives. Anastasius' sister had three sons, two

---

5. Details of the Isaurian war in Haarer, *Anastasius*, 21–8; Meier, *Anastasios*, 75–84.

of whom (Hypatius and Pompeius) held commands during his reign, as did one of his brother's son-in-laws (Sabinianus), another relative of unspecified relationship (Ioannes) and one of Ariadne's relatives (Diogenianus).[6] A similar pattern is observable in Anastasius' distribution of the consulship, which, while only an honorific position, continued to carry considerable kudos. Of the nineteen consuls whom Anastasius is known to have appointed in the eastern empire (in addition to the three times when he held the office himself), eight were close relatives (his brother, brother-in-law, nephews or great-nephews). Family members are less obviously present in the upper echelons of the civilian bureaucracy (although his brother-in-law Secundinus was prefect of Constantinople in the early 490s), but a significant number of those appointed were in broad sympathy with Anastasius' heterodox theological views (p. 172 below). These include the most influential praetorian prefect of his reign, Marinus of Apamea, his long-serving master of the offices, Celer, and the deputy praetorian prefect from Egypt, Apion; the same consideration is also relevant to another prominent general, Patricius.[7] Anastasius' strategy did not forestall the possibility of a challenge to his position entirely – there was to be a very serious one, generated precisely by his ecclesiastical policies – but that did not occur until the final years of his reign, after many years of internal stability (p. 173 below).

'The most careful and stewardly of all emperors'

Those years of stability gave Anastasius and his officials the opportunity to revive imperial finances after the disaster of Leo's Vandal expedition in 468 and the turmoil of Zeno's reign, both of which had had seriously adverse effects on the fiscal health of the eastern empire. There can be no doubting their success in this respect, since by the end of Anastasius' reign the imperial treasury had accumulated a very significant surplus, prompting one commentator (who attaches a figure of 320,000 lbs of gold to the surplus) to describe

---

6. Alan Cameron, 'The house of Anastasius', *GRBS* 19 (1978), 259–76, at 260–1; A. D. Lee, *War in Late Antiquity: A Social History*, Oxford: Blackwell, 2007, 71.
7. This is not to deny the willingness of these individuals to demonstrate flexibility in their convictions under Anastasius' successor, as noted by G. Greatrex, 'Flavius Hypatius, *quem vidit validum Parthus sensitque timendum*: an investigation of his career', *Byzantion* 66 (1996), 120–42, at 124–9.

him as 'the most careful and stewardly of all emperors'.[8] Moreover
this surplus was achieved despite significant outlays and the loss of
a long-established revenue stream. The outlays included two major
wars – the suppression of the Isaurian revolt (491–8), and renewed
war with Persia (502–5) (pp. 168–71 below) – and significant tax
remissions to communities adversely affected by the latter, as well as
to others which experienced natural disasters.[9] Anastasius was also
active in sponsoring a range of building projects, many of which, it
should be added, were of practical benefit in relation to trade and
defence – most famously, the construction, in the aftermath of the
Persian war, of the frontier fortress at Dara (suitably renamed
Anastasiopolis).[10]

As for the loss of a revenue stream, Anastasius took the decision
in 498 to abolish the infamous tax on traders and artisans known
in Latin as the *collatio lustralis* ('the five-yearly collection') and in
Greek as the *chrysargyron* ('the gold and silver [tax]'), originally
introduced by Constantine to help fund donatives to the army. The
deficit was then made up from some of the resources previously overseen by the financial office within the imperial administration known
as the *res privata*, responsible for the emperor's personal property
and for land acquired by the emperor through confiscation and a
range of other mechanisms (see pp. 227–8 below). The rents from
these lands covered the costs of the imperial household, as well as
being the source of gifts by the emperor to individuals or institutions
such as the church – and some of this income was now redirected so
as to offset the loss of the *chrysargyron*.[11] Anastasius' decision to
abolish the tax may have been motivated in part by a belief that its
removal would facilitate commercial activity, but he must also have
been aware of the political capital he stood to gain among the urban
inhabitants of the empire. A vivid sense of the popularity of the
decision is conveyed by a contemporary account from the Mesopotamian city of Edessa:

---

8. The description and figure appear in Procop. *Anecdota* 19.5, 7, although caution has
been advised against taking too literally a figure whose 'primary rhetorical purpose was
to denigrate the financial competence of the future Emperors Justin I and Justinian':
P. Sarris, *Economy and Society in the Age of Justinian*, Cambridge: Cambridge University Press, 2006, 201.
9. Haarer, *Anastasius*, 221–2.
10. Haarer, *Anastasius*, 230–45.
11. Haarer, *Anastasius*, 194–9; Meier, *Anastasios*, 121–4.

> The edict of the emperor Anastasius arrived this year, remitting the gold which tradesmen paid every four years and freeing them from the tax ... The whole city rejoiced. They all dressed up in white from the greatest to the least, and carrying lighted candles and burning censers, to the accompaniment of psalms and hymns, they went out to the martyrs' shrine of St Sergius and St Simon, thanking God and praising the emperor. There they held a eucharist, and on coming back into the city they extended the feast of joy and pleasure for a whole week, and decreed that they would celebrate this feast every year. (Ps.-Joshua Stylites, *Chron.* 31 [tr. F. R. Trombley and J. W. Watt with changes])

Anastasius himself was certainly not slow to capitalise on the popularity of this measure in Constantinople by staging a public incineration of the relevant tax records in the hippodrome.[12]

With regard to the various outlays noted above, a range of factors enabled Anastasius not only to offset these, but to compile a substantial surplus. The first was the termination of substantial recurrent payments. Zeno made an important contribution on this front in his final years: by inducing Theoderic to take the Goths westward to Italy in 489, he removed an important drain on imperial resources, since the Goths had periodically been given significant payments during the 470s and 480s. Anastasius made a further important saving early in his reign when, following the outbreak of rebellion in Isauria, he abolished the annual payment to that region which Illus had forced Zeno to institute in 484 – a substantial amount, even if one accepts the lower of the figures provided by the ancient sources.[13] He also resisted pressure from the Persian king Kavad, in the context of the Isaurian revolt, that he should resume payments of gold to assist with the defence of the northern frontier against nomadic incursions, as emperors earlier in the fifth century had done (Ps.-Joshua Stylites, *Chron.* 8–10, 23). This was ultimately to be one of the factors contributing to the initiation of war by Persia in 502 (p. 169 below), which in turn entailed significant expense for the empire, but since Anastasius also offered to lend Kavad the money he can hardly be accused of trying to provoke war or of naivety about the risks involved.

Anastasius proceeded to build on these savings by various changes

---

12. Priscian, *De laude Anastasii* 162–71, Evagrius, *Hist. eccl.* 3.39.
13. John of Antioch, *fr.* 239.4 (Mariev) gives a figure of 1,400 lbs of gold per annum, whereas Evagrius, *Hist. eccl.* 3.35, gives a figure of 5,000 lbs of gold per annum.

to the empire's fiscal system. The most important change concerned the phenomenon of *adaeratio* – that is, the commutation of taxes assessed in kind into payments in gold coin. While the system of payment of taxes in kind formalised by Diocletian (p. 4 above) had circumvented the problems of inflation, it also entailed significant logistical problems, particularly those of transporting large quantities of grain to the parts of the empire where troops were concentrated. This created pressure to revert to a system where taxes were levied in coin, a process which began in the western empire in the second half of the fourth century. For reasons which remain unclear, the shift in the eastern empire took longer and was more gradual, despite the fact that it had clear benefits from the government's perspective, and it was only during Anastasius' reign that the bulk of the land tax was converted to gold (a proportion was still levied in kind for the needs of troops in the local area). Besides avoiding the logistical problems noted, the main benefits from the government's perspective were that it reduced wastage of tax revenue, which was an obvious problem when taxes were collected in the form of a perishable substance like grain, and, correspondingly, it made it much easier for the government to build up a financial surplus. The real puzzle is why none of Anastasius' fifth-century predecessors was more proactive on this matter.[14]

A second important change was introduced in relation to the actual collection of taxes. This had traditionally been the responsibility of the local elite of each community, the so-called *curiales* or city councillors, whose control of this operation gave them plenty of scope to allocate the tax burden in ways advantageous to themselves and to extract an additional proportion which went straight into their own pockets (p. 201 below). To improve the efficiency of this system, Anastasius introduced a new category of official called *vindices* ('defenders'). Their role was not, as some ancient sources suggest, to undertake the actual collection – there was only one *vindex* per community and he did not have a staff – but rather to supervise and audit the work of the *curiales*. The institution of *vindices* attracts criticism in some sources, but this no doubt reflects the resentment of the local elites at the curtailment of their opportunities for self-aggrandisement (e.g., Evagrius, *Hist. eccl.* 3.42); other sources acknowledge that Anastasius acted to protect the

14. Jones, *LRE*, 460–2; S. Barnish, A. D. Lee and M. Whitby, 'Government and administration', *CAH*[2] 14.165–206, at 194–7.

interests of peasants against *curiales*, while also increasing imperial revenues (Priscian, *De laude Anastasii* 193–5, Lydus, *Mag.* 3.49).[15]

These reforms of the fiscal system were complemented by reform of the empire's bronze coinage. Constantine had been responsible for introducing a stable gold coinage in the form of the *solidus*, but smaller denominations were needed for the everyday transactions of the vast majority of the empire's inhabitants. Since silver coins increasingly went out of circulation in the fifth century, this role came to be performed solely by the small bronze coins known as *nummi*. The official exchange rate at the beginning of the fifth century specified that the *solidus* was worth 5,400 *nummi* (equivalent to approximately 25 lbs of bronze). Over the course of the fifth century, that exchange rate rose inexorably, despite attempts to maintain the original rate, until by Anastasius' reign, it had trebled. Besides the risk that these inflationary pressures would jeopardise the stability of the *solidus* – which, with Anastasius' sanctioning of more widespread *adaeratio*, was now even more important to imperial finances – there was also the sheer practical problem of people having to use ever more cumbersome quantities of *nummi* in their transactions. The quality of *nummi* was also poor, making it easy to produce counterfeits and so deprive the government of revenues. In order to ease these different problems, a new bronze coinage was introduced in 498. It was issued in a helpful range of sizes – a 40 *nummi* coin known as the *follis*, a 20 *nummi* coin (half-*follis*) and a 10 *nummi* coin – which helped address the problem of bulky transactions; moreover, the various denominations were clearly marked and well produced, which inspired public trust and made it more difficult for counterfeiters. Having established the new coinage and helped to stabilise inflationary pressures, a second reform was introduced in 512 when the weight of the coinage was doubled (and a new 5 *nummi* coin was introduced), thereby helping to put the inflationary trend into reverse.[16]

Although Anastasius deserves credit for initiation and oversight of these various reforms which were so important to the revival of the

15. A. Laniado, *Recherches sur les notables municipaux dans l'empire protobyzantin*, Paris: Collège de France, 2002, 27–36; Haarer, *Anastasius*, 207–11; Meier, *Anastasios*, 130–7.
16. M. F. Hendy, *Studies in the Byzantine Monetary Economy, c. 300–1450*, Cambridge: Cambridge University Press, 1985, 475–8; K. W. Harl, *Coinage in the Roman Economy, 300 BC to AD 700*, Baltimore: Johns Hopkins University Press, 1996, 178–9, 192–3; Haarer, *Anastasius*, 202–6.

fortunes of the eastern empire, acknowledgement must also be given to his officials who were instrumental in their implementation. The most famous of these was Marinus, from Apamea in Syria. Although he did not achieve the rank of praetorian prefect until the final years of Anastasius' reign, it is apparent that he was an influential figure for some time before this, with the introduction of the *vindices* particularly being attributed to him (Lydus, *Mag.* 3.49). Likewise, John, from Paphlagonia, held the important financial post of count of the sacred largesses in 498, in which capacity he was responsible for the reform of the bronze coinage (Malalas, *Chron.* 400). What is particularly interesting about both men, as well as one of Marinus' predecessors in the office of praetorian prefect, Polycarp, is that they had all begun their careers working at lower levels in the financial administration of the empire (*PLRE* 2, *s.v.* Ioannes 45, Marinus 7, Polycarpus). As such, they did not possess the traditional classical education which was the normal prerequisite for holding high office, but Anastasius clearly placed a greater priority on relevant experience, with beneficial consequences for the empire.

War with Persia

Anastasius was certainly no warmonger and the conflict with Persia in the second decade of his reign was relatively short-lived, but it nonetheless warrants attention for various reasons. First, it marked the renewal of serious, sustained fighting with the empire's most powerful neighbour after more than a century virtually free of significant military action between the two.[17] As such, it set the tone for relations during the sixth century, which were to be characterised by major bouts of warfare. Secondly, it is a war into which unusually vivid insights are provided by an invaluable contemporary narrative source of a kind rarely available in antiquity – the *Chronicle* traditionally (but incorrectly) attributed to Joshua Stylites. The value of this source derives from its author's having been a contemporary observer of events in northern Mesopotamia, and from his writing an account unconstrained by the usual dictates of genre: since he wrote in his native language of Syriac (a dialect of Aramaic), he felt no compulsion to follow classical models in the manner of other narrative historians of late antiquity, such as Ammianus and

17. For the two brief, inconclusive wars during the reign of Theodosius II, see p. 118 above.

Procopius. He certainly had his own agenda in relation to Christianity and the judgement of God, but his descriptions of warfare – especially its impact on non-combatants – convey a sense of unadorned immediacy which gives them great value.

As previously noted, it was the Persian king Kavad who instigated the war after Anastasius refused his request for money to help with the defence of Persia's northern frontier against Asiatic nomads whose activities had, in the past, also impinged on the Roman empire. As Kavad had previously issued such demands a number of times since Anastasius' accession without acting on his threat of war, the emperor perhaps assumed that the latest such demand in 502 was another attempted bluff. At any rate, it seems that Roman forces and defences were not as well prepared as they could have been when Kavad invaded and quickly captured a number of towns, before laying siege to the important fortress of Amida on the upper Tigris. That eventually fell during the winter of 502/3 after a three-month siege. Anastasius despatched a large field army in the spring of 503, but its effectiveness was impeded by dissension between its various commanders, only rectified the following year when Anastasius appointed his master of the offices Celer as overall commander. As a result, Roman efforts had a greater impact in 504, but control of Amida was only regained the following year when Kavad finally sought a settlement, so that he could return to Persia and deal with renewed attacks from northern nomads.[18]

Neither side, then, gained much from the war, but it did alert Anastasius to the need for greater investment in the region's defences, including the construction of a new frontier fortress at Dara as a forward defensive post in the north Mesopotamian plain which effectively filled the gap left by the loss of Nisibis in 363 (Figs 12–13). On the other hand, Dara was to be the source of considerable disagreement between the two powers in the years after Anastasius' reign – the Romans came to regard it as essential to the empire's defence, while the Persians saw it as an aggressive staging post for possible Roman invasions of Persia – so that part of the legacy of the war was circumstances which made a renewal of war more likely in the future.

For many of the inhabitants of northern Mesopotamia caught up in the warfare, however, the events of the war were far from incon-

18. G. Greatrex, *Rome and Persia at War, 502–532*, Leeds: Francis Cairns, 1998, 73–119.

Figure 12 View of the walls of Dara, northern Mesopotamia. © C. Lillington-Martin

clusive. Consider the following account of the experience of rural dwellers at the hands of Kavad's Arab allies:

> On the twenty-sixth of this month [November 502], [the Lakhmid Arab ruler] Nu'man also arrived from the south and entered the territory of the Harranites. He ravaged and plundered it, and took away captive men, cattle and goods from the whole territory of the Harranites. He even came as far as Edessa, ravaging, plundering, and taking captive all the villages. The number of people whom he led away into captivity was 18,500, not counting those who were killed, and the cattle, goods and spoil of all kinds. The reason so many people were in the villages is that it was the vintage season, when not only the villagers, but also many Harranites and Edessenes, had gone out for the vintage and were thus taken captive. (Ps.-Joshua Stylites, *Chron.* 52 [tr. Trombley and Watt])

Meanwhile the inhabitants of a number of the towns of the region underwent the exigencies of siege, including the hardships of hunger, disease and, if these or Persian weapons did not kill them, enslavement and enforced emigration to Persia. Even those communities not besieged by the Persians found themselves having to billet Roman troops, which often proved to be as taxing an experience:

> When those who came to our assistance ostensibly as saviours were going down and coming up, they looted us in a manner little short of enemies. They threw many poor people out of their beds and slept in

Figure 13 The granaries at Dara, northern Mesopotamia. Unusually, these granaries were placed underground; they are estimated to have had the capacity to store enough grain to support 25,000 people for a year – an important provision in a frontier fortress like this. © Nevit Dilmen/Wikimedia Commons

> them, leaving their owners to lie on the ground at a time of cold weather. They ejected others from their houses, going in and living in them. Others' cattle they led away by force as if plundering an enemy. They stripped some people's clothing off them and took it away. They used rough treatment on others for the sake of obtaining anything whatever. In the streets they denounced and insulted others for the smallest reason. They brazenly plundered the meagre provisions which everyone had ... In full view of everyone they had their way over the women in the streets and houses. (Ps-Joshua Stylites, *Chron.* 86 [tr. Trombley and Watt])

Such was the frequent experience of war on the part of civilians during late antiquity.[19]

Religion and politics

The skills which enabled Anastasius to excel in the management of inanimate tax registers and coinage proved not to be easily transferable when it came to dealing with flesh-and-blood bishops and

19. See further Lee, *War in Late Antiquity*, 133–46.

clerics, although that probably says more about the intractable nature of the theological issues involved than about Anastasius' aptitude for such matters. After all, his predecessors had struggled to manage these matters with any great success, just as his successors were to. He endeavoured to steer a middle course, but particularly during the final years of his reign, he found that growing polarisation of opinion placed him in some very awkward situations from which he managed to extract himself only with great difficulty.[20]

Although he had had to sign an official endorsement of Chalcedonian orthodoxy prior to his accession, the new emperor essentially continued to uphold Zeno's compromise *Henotikon* during the early years of his reign as the best strategy for retaining the loyalty of the different parts of the empire. When the bishop of Constantinople, Euphemius, became too vociferous in his public endorsement of Chalcedon, however, and threatened to upset this delicate balance, Anastasius had him replaced in 496 by an elderly cleric named Macedonius who, initially at least, was prepared to give his formal approval to the *Henotikon*. Before long, however, the balance was threatened from the other side by the activities of various anti-Chalcedonian leaders, notably Philoxenus of Hierapolis and Severus of Sozopolis,[21] both of whom spent extended periods of time in Constantinople in the early years of the sixth century in order to lobby against Flavian, bishop of Antioch, a moderate Chalcedonian who, in the interests of harmony, had lent his support to the *Henotikon*. For some time, Anastasius continued to steer a middle course, but as Macedonius became increasingly open in his allegiance to Chalcedon while Philoxenus and Severus became increasingly strong in their criticism of the *Henotikon*, Anastasius seems to have decided it was impossible to maintain his balancing act. In 511, he deposed Macedonius, while the following year he allowed the deposition of Flavian in Antioch and his replacement by Severus.[22]

20. For Anastasius' religious policy, see Haarer, *Anastasius*, 115–83; Meier, *Anastasios*, 250–311.
21. For their theology, see R. C. Chesnut, *Three Monophysite Christologies: Severus of Antioch, Philoxenus of Mabbug, and Jacob of Sarug*, Oxford: Oxford University Press, 1976.
22. For recent discussion of the depositions of Euphemius and Macedonius, see J. Dijkstra and G. Greatrex, 'Patriarchs and politics in Constantinople in the reign of Anastasius (with a re-edition of O. *Mon. Epiph.* 59)', *Millennium* 6 (2009), 223–64.

These changes of personnel were not popular with laity who supported the principles of Chalcedon, but they took place without serious disturbance. However, another action of Anastasius' in 512 did have grave repercussions. Towards the end of the year, he ordered that the liturgy used in the churches of Constantinople be emended to include phraseology associated with anti-Chalcedonian views – a decision which provoked rioting in the city, the toppling and dragging of statues of Anastasius through the streets, and demands for an aristocrat (Areobindus) to be made emperor. Order was only restored when Anastasius appeared in the imperial box at the hippodrome without his diadem and dramatically offered to relinquish the imperial office. Given the recent behaviour of the urban populace, one would have expected them to accept Anastasius' offer with alacrity, but the emperor's pointed display of humility proved sufficient to satisfy the crowd and resolve the immediate crisis – another indicator of Anastasius' skills as a ruler.

The resolution of this crisis, however, provided only temporary respite from turmoil, for the following year Anastasius found himself facing an even more serious challenge to his position arising from his religious policy. That challenge was led by an army officer named Vitalian, a native of Thrace and commander of a unit of federate troops in the northern Balkans. In 513 he instigated a military mutiny against the government in Constantinople on the basis of soldiers' dissatisfaction with the failure of promised supplies to arrive and of the unpopularity of the senior general in that region, Hypatius. However, Vitalian also declared his support for Chalcedonian principles against Anastasius. While there may be a temptation to regard this as a tactical ploy to win wider support, there is good reason to see it as a genuine motivation on Vitalian's part, for he twice advanced close to Constantinople (in 513 and 514), only to withdraw after Anastasius twice promised to approach the bishop of Rome with a view to the latter's acting as mediator in relation to the religious issues which concerned Vitalian; and even after Anastasius' death in 518, Vitalian continued to be a strong advocate of reconciliation with the church in the west.[23] Before that, however, there was a further setback for Vitalian when, in 515, Anastasius turned from negotiation to confrontation and his forces managed to defeat those of Vitalian, who fled into hiding until the end of Anastasius' reign.

23. Cf. Meier, *Anastasios*, 309–10.

Anastasius' successor

The latter years of Anastasius' reign, then, had seen increasing religious turmoil, but he had in other respects proved to be a very capable ruler who restored political and financial stability to the eastern empire after the upheavals of Zeno's reign, and thereby established the foundation for the initiatives of the Emperor Justinian (Chapter 12 below). Anastasius was already at least sixty years old at the time of his accession, so his death in 518 cannot have been unexpected. Despite his advanced years, however, he had taken no steps to identify a clear successor – an issue whose importance one would have thought had been highlighted by the threat from Vitalian. Certainly, he had no children of his own, but he did have a number of nephews from among whom he might have selected a successor. Perhaps he did not regard any of them as having sufficient competence, or perhaps he feared triggering family in-fighting if he singled out one of them in this way. At any rate, at the time of his death, one – Hypatius – was absent in Antioch, fulfilling his duties as senior general in the eastern provinces, while his brother Pompeius, senior general in Thrace, was in Marcianople – not as far from Constantinople as Antioch, but still about 200 miles' journey. Neither, therefore, was on the spot and in a position to influence events in the capital. Nor, on this occasion, was there an imperial widow to take the lead, since Ariadne had died in 515. As with the events leading up to Anastasius' accession in 491, however, there is a detailed account of the manoeuvrings that followed the emperor's death in 518 (Constantine Porphyrogenitus, *De Caerimoniis* 1.93) which, once again, provides insight into the workings of palace politics at a time of transition.

A central role in proposals for Anastasius' successor seems to have been taken by the various bodies of palace guards, who were obviously in a strong position to influence events. One group, the *excubitores*, began by suggesting one of their officers, otherwise unknown, named John, but this was met by hostility from the crowds in the hippodrome, prompting a more plausible counter-proposal from the other major group of palace guards, the *scholae palatinae*, who nominated the senior general Patricius – only for him to meet with disapproval from the *excubitores*. The palace eunuchs also made their opposition known to both of these proposed candidates by refusing to release the imperial garments, perhaps encouraged in this by the senior eunuch Amantius, who, according to another source, tried unsuccessfully to promote a candidate of his own (Evagrius, *Hist. eccl.* 4.2). Eventually, the senate sought to resolve the deadlock by putting forward Justin, the commander of the *excubitores*, and when his name was welcomed by the crowds in the hippodrome with acclamations of him as 'the new Constantine', he was duly crowned by the patriarch. Nevertheless, this version of events leaves some unanswered question, above all why the *excubitores* should initially have nominated the officer John rather than their commander Justin. Perhaps it was, as has been suggested, a case of Justin's deliberately orchestrating events to create a deadlock which his candidacy could then resolve. There were also allegations that Justin had used bribery to win support for his cause.[24]

Justin had certain things in common with Anastasius – both came from the Balkans, and both were in their sixties when they became emperor – but the differences were more important. First, as his command of the *excubitores* implies, Justin had a military background: he joined the army during Leo's reign to escape rural poverty, rising to be an officer in Anastasius' Isaurian and Persian wars, and as commander of the *excubitores* he played an important role in the defeat of Vitalian's attack on Constantinople in 515, which may have contributed to the popular welcome of his nomination in 518.[25] Secondly, although Justin had remained loyal to Anastasius during his conflict with Vitalian, he was nonetheless a supporter of Chalcedon – another important factor in his favour as far as the populace of Constantinople was concerned.[26] Given these differences, it may perhaps seem strange to include Justin's reign in a chapter primarily devoted to Anastasius – and even more so in view of the fact that Justin is often portrayed as the puppet of his famous successor, his nephew and adopted son Justinian, to whose lengthy reign (Part IV below) Justin's is typically seen as a prelude.

24. J. B. Bury, *History of the Later Roman Empire from the Death of Theodosius I to the Death of Justinian*, London: Macmillan, 1923, 2.17–18, not accepted, however, by A. A. Vasiliev, *Justin the First*, Cambridge, MA: Harvard University Press, 1950, 81–2, who takes a more benign view of Justin. See also G. Greatrex, 'The early years of Justin I's reign in the sources', *Electrum* 12 (2007), 99–113, at 99–105.
25. Cf. Greatrex, 'Flavius Hypatius', 135.
26. V. Menze, *Justinian and the Making of the Syrian Orthodox Church*, Oxford: Oxford University Press, 2008, 18–30, presents a pragmatic Justin as only supporting the Chalcedonian position from the time of his accession, but this seems unlikely given his geographical origin, the events of his accession, and the strength of his support for Chalcedon once emperor.

This latter idea, however, is open to serious doubt, while alongside the undoubted shifts in policy after 518, there were also important continuities between the reigns of Anastasius and Justin.

Those continuities primarily took the form of personnel. There were unquestionably changes, but these mostly involved the removal of those most closely associated with Anastasius' final, unpopular years, and their replacement either by Justin's relatives (e.g., his nephews Germanus and Justinian) or by individuals who had previously served under Anastasius in the earlier part of his reign and then fallen out with him (e.g., Apion, Diogenianus, Philoxenus). The most striking instance of this was Vitalian, who quickly emerged from hiding to become a senior general and a very important figure in the early years of Justin's regime. Even individuals who had been prominent in the final years of Anastasius' reign, such as Patricius and Celer, can be found playing roles under Justin, as also his relatives Hypatius and Pompeius. 'The conservatism of Justin's administration is not surprising: considering his age – 66 or 68 – on ascending the throne: his trust was reserved for those with whom he himself had served, the only exception being his relatives.'[27]

Anastasius' chief financial adviser, Marinus, was also restored to his post of praetorian prefect for a period early in Justin's reign, and is credited with having had painted on the walls of a public bath house (presumably in Constantinople) a mural depicting Justin's career from his humble beginnings to his election as emperor. The explanation he is said to have offered for this action is a useful reminder of the prejudice which Justin faced:

> I have employed pictures for the information of the observant and for the edification of those with discernment, so that the great men, the rich men and the children of important families not trust in their power, their wealth and the importance of their noble families, but in God, 'who raises the unfortunate man from the dung pile and places him at the head of the people' [Psalm 113.7], 'and rules in the human kingdom, to give it to whomever he wishes, to set the lowest of humanity over it' [Daniel 5.21], and he chooses those of humble families in the world, and the despised, and those who are nothing, in order to remove those who are something. (Ps-Zachariah Rhetor, *Chronicle* 8.1a [tr. R. R. Phenix and C. B. Horn])

The most familiar expression of that prejudice is the notion that Justin was no more than Justinian's puppet. This can be traced

27. Greatrex, 'Flavius Hypatius', 139–40.

to the influence of the invective of Procopius in his *Secret History* (*Anecdota*), where Justin is portrayed as a doddering, illiterate nonentity, in contrast to the scheming and ambitious Justinian. It is a scenario which is not borne out by careful consideration of other evidence for these years.[28] Vitalian was clearly the most important influence at the court until his murder in 520, and although Justinian may have had a hand in that, his involvement is by no means certain, and it could equally have been Justin acting against a threat to his position. Thereafter, Justinian's position strengthened, but only gradually and, it seems, at the insistence of the senate against the apparent resistance of Justin. Meanwhile, Justin can be observed taking a full and active role in various areas of government. The most significant of these was religious policy. The leading advocates of anti-Chalcedonian views, Severus and Philoxenus, were promptly dismissed from their sees and exiled, and Justin acted swiftly to open dialogue with the bishop of Rome, Hormisdas (514–23), initiating correspondence with him within three weeks of his accession with a view to ending the Acacian schism (p. 150 above) and aligning the government in Constantinople firmly with Chalcedonian orthodoxy. The ensuing flurry of communications between Constantinople and Rome (*Coll. Avell.* 141–65) culminated in a papal embassy to Justin's court in March 519 during which relations were formally restored. The papal envoys participated in a synod at which those who had supported the *Henotikon* were condemned – not only Acacius, the bishop of Constantinople, and those of his successors who had endorsed it, but also the Emperors Zeno and Anastasius. While this outcome reflected Justin's personal convictions, it also had the political benefit of winning the support of the inhabitants of Constantinople and the Balkans whom Anastasius' policy had alienated – reflected most immediately in their acclamation of Justin as a 'new Constantine'.[29] At the same time, however, it endangered imperial relations with those parts of the eastern empire which were anti-Chalcedonian in sympathy, above all the economically fundamental provinces of Egypt – a problem with which Justin's successors would have to wrestle at length.

---

28. See the important discussion by B. Croke, 'Justinian under Justin: reconfiguring a reign', *Byz. Zeitschr.* 100 (2007), 13–56.
29. This is recorded as early as 15 July 518, when Justin made clear his intention to restore relations with Rome (*ACO* 3.27); the same acclamation had already featured a few days earlier at his accession: Constantine Porphyrogenitus, *De Caer.* 1.93 (p. 430).

CHAPTER 9

Rome's heirs in the west

Ruling a post-imperial world

By the final quarter of the fifth century, the western half of the Roman empire had given way to a collage of kingdoms controlled by different barbarian groups – the outcome of an untidy process stretching back over the preceding half century or so (Chapter 6 above). The Vandals can be regarded as having established themselves as an independent political entity by 442, when, following their capture of Carthage in 439, Valentinian III formally ceded control of Carthage and adjacent provinces to Geiseric and his people, while Theoderic the Goth's founding of his kingdom in Italy – usually referred to as the Ostrogothic state – clearly dates from his elimination of Odoacer in 493. The other Gothic kingdom in the west – the Visigothic – emerged from the Goths whom Alaric had led westwards in the early fifth century and whom the Roman authorities settled in Aquitania in 418, but it cannot be assigned a foundation date so easily. Throughout the first half of the fifth century, these Goths had to compete for power against continued attempts to uphold imperial authority in Gaul, above all by Aetius, and it was only in the early 470s, as imperial power in the west contracted back to Italy, that the Gothic leader Euric was able to establish an independent Visigothic kingdom in the southern half of Gaul and in northern Spain.[1] In a similar though less protracted manner, the Frankish kingdom emerged as the result of gradual, but poorly documented, expansion out of northern Gaul from the 480s onwards, culminating in Clovis' establishment of Frankish control over most of Gaul through his victory over Visigothic forces at the battle of Vouillé (near Poitiers) in 507, with the defeated Goths

---

1. For the emergence of the Visigothic kingdom, see P. Heather, *The Goths*, Oxford: Blackwell, 1996, 181–91; for the history of the names 'Visigoth' and 'Ostrogoth' in this period, see P. Heather, *Goths and Romans 332–489*, Oxford: Clarendon Press, 1991, 331–3.

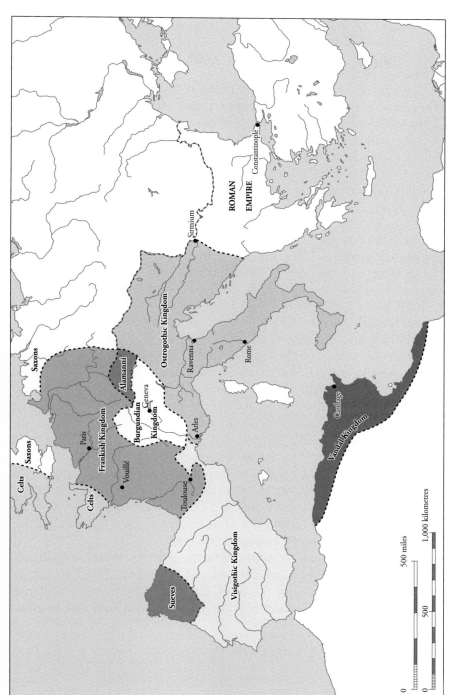

Map 7 The barbarian kingdoms in the 520s

shifting the focus of their kingdom to Spain. A Burgundian kingdom also maintained an independent existence in south-east Gaul in the later fifth and early sixth century until it succumbed to Frankish expansion in the 530s.

Contrary to what one might perhaps have expected, there was considerable continuity of administrative structures in these kingdoms which replaced the empire in the west. This was most evident in Italy, where Odoacer and Theoderic successively retained all the senior posts from the imperial bureaucracy – praetorian prefect, master of the offices, quaestor and so on – together with the officials subordinate to these; Theoderic even created an additional praetorian prefect for the small region of south-east Gaul which he added to his kingdom in the early sixth century. Data from Vandal Africa is less plentiful, but holders of the office of proconsul (i.e., provincial governor) are known from the mid-fifth century, even if the post can no longer have entailed the power it did under emperors, while there is also evidence of individuals continuing to hold lesser positions deriving from the imperial bureaucracy into the early sixth century. The less stable development of the Visigothic kingdom from southern Gaul to Spain makes it more difficult to discern continuities in the regions under its control in the fifth and early sixth centuries, but once it was more securely established in Spain, it is evident that a framework involving provinces and governors remained in place. As for the Franks, Clovis was said, in a contemporary source, to have 'taken over the administration of [the northern Gallic province of] Belgica Secunda' (*Epistolae Austrasicae* 2) after his defeat of Syagrius in the 480s (p. 126 above), which might be taken to imply administrative continuity; if that was the case, however, then the division of his kingdom between his four sons following his death in 511 will have made that difficult to sustain, since the division does not appear to have followed provincial boundaries, except in south-east Gaul.[2]

An important area of administrative activity where significant continuities can be observed is taxation. Once again, the Ostrogothic kingdom in Italy provides the most detailed insights, with evidence for the continuing collection of traditional taxes in kind and in gold.

---

2. Jones, *LRE*, 253, 257, 259–60, 261; P. S. Barnwell, *Emperor, Prefects and Kings: The Roman West, 395–565*, London: Duckworth, 1992, 71–128, 155–65. The seal ring of Clovis' father, Childeric (p. 126 above), implies some sort of document-based Frankish administrative structure.

However, taxation broadly within the framework established by the empire also continued in the regions under Vandal, Visigothic and Frankish rule.[3] This has prompted a further important question: how were these taxes spent? Under Roman rule, they had helped above all to maintain the empire's standing army, as well as paying for the imperial bureaucracy. Presumably some of the taxes collected under barbarian rule helped to pay those holding the administrative posts already noted. However, the major consumer of fiscal resources in the past – the imperial army – had ceased to exist. In place of the imperial army, of course, kings called upon the military service of adult male barbarians, and while in some regions these troops may initially have been supported by receiving a portion of the revenues owed by estates (pp. 129–32 above), ownership of land by barbarian soldiers became the primary means for supporting the kingdoms' armies.[4] Kings had other ways of using their fiscal income, such as gifts to encourage the loyalty of the barbarian elite and construction projects to advertise their cultural pedigree (pp. 183–6 below). However, the fact that the main call on tax income no longer existed has been seen as helping to explain the indications that, with the passage of time, kings became less assiduous in enforcing the collection of taxes.[5]

While administrative continuities in part reflect the fact that, far from wishing to destroy all vestiges of Roman rule, barbarian kings looked to the empire as a model (it was not as if they had any obvious alternative on which to draw), these continuities also reflect the practical problem of numbers. The order of magnitude of barbarian incomers has been vigorously debated, but there can be little doubt that even on the most generous of estimates, they still must have been significantly outnumbered by provincial inhabitants – and therefore had good reason to leave existing arrangements in place, as far as possible.[6] Likewise, it was generally in their interests to draw on the expertise of local elites to assist them in meeting the

3. Jones, *LRE*, 254, 257, 261–2; C. Wickham, *Framing the Early Middle Ages: Europe and the Mediterranean, 400–800*, Oxford: Oxford University Press, 2005, 89–90, 96–8, 107–8.
4. Wickham, *Framing*, 90–1, 100, 106.
5. Wickham, *Framing*, 91–2, 100, 107–8.
6. Perhaps the best-known figure given in ancient sources – the 80,000 Vandals who are said to have crossed into Africa in 429 – is generally treated with scepticism: A. Merrills. and R. Miles, *The Vandals*, Oxford: Wiley-Blackwell, 2010, 48; more generally G. Halsall, *Barbarian Migrations and the Roman West, 376–568*, Cambridge: Cambridge University Press, 2007, 144–5.

novel challenges of ruling the mixed populations of their kingdoms. Although some aristocrats chose to relocate, most commonly to Constantinople, but sometimes within the west,[7] many stayed where they were and some were alert to the potential advantages of co-operation with the new regimes. Odoacer and Theoderic (who had himself held the consulship in the east in 484) certainly went out of their ways, by symbolic gestures, to reassure the senatorial aristocracy in Italy that their social position and prerogatives would be respected. Both kings continued to appoint senators as consuls in the west and as prefects of the city of Rome, Odoacer restored senators' seats in the Colosseum, and Theoderic regularly sought the formal assent of the senate when making new appointments.[8] A number of senators held high office under Odoacer and/or Theoderic, whether as praetorian prefect, master of the offices or quaestor. Of these, the most consistent servants of the new regimes were Liberius and the two Cassiodori, father and son, whose aristocratic pedigree was not as venerable as that of the most illustrious families,[9] but individuals from the latter did also hold office at various points, notably members of the Anician clan.[10]

Rulers of the other kingdoms could not expect to draw on quite such eminent talent, but they still found willing aides among the provincial elites. The Visigothic king Euric was assisted in the 470s and 480s by Leo, a Gaul of senatorial status who was knowledgeable about Roman law and known for his eloquence (*PLRE* 2.662–3), while the court of the Vandal ruler Huneric (477–84) included as one of its officials a Victorinianus who was of senatorial rank (Victor of Vita, *Hist. persecut.* 3.27). Sidonius Apollinaris famously wrote to Syagrius, great-grandson of a fourth-century consul, expressing his amazement that Syragrius had acquired such fluency in Burgundian German that 'in your presence the barbarian

7. R. Mathisen, *Roman Aristocrats in Barbarian Gaul*, Austin: University of Texas Press, 1993, 58–66 (Gaul), 146–9 (other regions).

8. J. Moorhead, *Theoderic in Italy*, Oxford: Clarendon Press, 1992, 9, 145, 147–54 (who detects, however, a change in Theoderic's policy during the years 511–21, when he 'open[ed] up this most coveted office [the consulship] to a wider spectrum of society').

9. J. J. O'Donnell, 'Liberius the patrician', *Traditio* 37 (1981), 31–72; J. J. O'Donnell, *Cassiodorus*, Berkeley: University of California Press, 1979 (also available online at: www9.georgetown.edu/faculty/jod/texts/cassbook/toc.html).

10. Fl. Nar. Manlius Boethius (praetorian prefect in the mid-480s), Fl. Anicius Probus Faustus (master of the offices in the mid-490s, quaestor 503–505/6, and praetorian prefect 509–12) and Anicius Manlius Severinus Boethius (master of the offices in the early 520s).

is afraid to perpetrate a barbarism in his own language'; this, and his legal knowledge, in turn had facilitated his acting as an arbitrator in disputes, prompting Sidonius to dub him 'the new Solon of the Burgundians' (*Ep.* 5.5).

Projecting royal power

Another important dimension of royal rule was how the barbarian kings themselves acted as rulers and how they projected their power. Unsurprisingly, here too they drew heavily on Roman traditions, as Theoderic was keen to emphasise in a letter to the Emperor Anastasius: 'our kingdom is an imitation of yours, modelled on your design, a copy of the only empire' (Cassiod. *Var.* 1.1.3).[11] Theoderic's claim is borne out by the following account of his activities from an anonymous author probably writing soon after Theoderic's death (526):

> He gave games in the circus and the amphitheatre, so that even by the Romans he was called a Trajan or a Valentinian, whose times he took as a model ... To the people of Rome and to the poor of the city he gave each year 120,000 measures of grain, and for the restoration of the palace and the rebuilding of the city walls he ordered 200 pounds [of gold] to be given each year from the tax on wine ... At Ravenna he restored the aqueduct which the emperor Trajan had constructed and thus brought water to the city after a long period without. He finished the palace, ... and built baths and a palace at Verona ... and restored the aqueduct which had long since been destroyed ... Also at Ticinum he built a palace, baths, and an amphitheatre, besides new city walls. (*Anonymous Valesianus* 60, 67, 71 [tr. J. Rolfe with revisions])

The key theme here is euergetism, in the long-established forms of 'bread and circuses' for the populace of Rome and of building projects for public benefit in major cities – above all, maintaining the water supply and the associated amenity of baths, and seeing to the upkeep of city defences. Drawing on more recent imperial exempla since Constantine, Theoderic was also an active builder of churches,

---

11. This is not to suggest that Theoderic, or indeed any of the other barbarian kings, tried to present themselves as emperors, at least in their dealings with Constantinople, even if they sometimes seem to have encouraged their subjects to 'assimilate [them] into the category of emperor': see Moorhead, *Theoderic*, 39–51, who deploys this felicitous phrase at 48.

especially in his capital, Ravenna, albeit for use by Arian Christians,[12] while, no doubt also following in Constantine's footsteps, he founded a city bearing the name Theodericopolis (location unknown).[13]

Theoderic may also have issued a law code,[14] and he certainly carried on issuing coins in all three metals, an activity which had an important practical economic function, but carried significant symbolic capital as well. Gold coins continued to bear the image and name of the reigning emperor in Constantinople, reflecting the unquestioned assumption that gold was 'an imperial metal that should always carry an emperor's name', while also 'implying that it was authorised by the emperor'; silver coins also bore the emperor's image and name, but with the addition of the name or monogram of the king on the reverse, thereby becoming 'an overtly regal coinage issued under the auspices of the emperor'.[15] Continuing another long-standing tradition, Theoderic was the recipient of panegyrics by senators – the younger Cassiodorus (in 507) and Boethius (in 522) – and by the Gallic aristocrat-turned-cleric Ennodius (probably in 507), who included the claim that Theoderic's reign had witnessed Rome, 'the mother of cities', regaining her youth (*Pan.* 56).[16]

Even though he refrained from making it his capital and probably only visited it once (in 500), the presence of the city of Rome within his kingdom still gave Theoderic the greatest scope to exploit the imperial past to his advantage. Nonetheless, the rulers of the other kingdoms took opportunities to proclaim their credentials as worthy successors. Some of them issued law codes modelled to varying degrees on the *Theodosian Code* (Euric and Alaric II for the

12. M. J. Johnson, 'Towards a history of Theoderic's building program', *DOP* 42 (1988), 73–96; I. Wood, 'Theoderic's monuments in Ravenna' in S. J. Barnish and F. Marazzi (eds), *The Ostrogoths from the Migration Period to the Sixth Century*, Woodbridge: Boydell Press, 2007, 249–63; D. M. Deliyannis, *Ravenna in Late Antiquity*, Cambridge, Cambridge University Press, 2010, 106–87.

13. Moorhead, *Theoderic*, 43.

14. For debate over the *Edictum Theoderici*, see Moorhead, *Theoderic*, 76; P. Amory, *People and Identity in Ostrogothic Italy, 489–554*, Cambridge: Cambridge University Press, 1997, 78 n.187; S. Lafferty, 'Law and society in Ostrogothic Italy: evidence from the *Edictum Theoderici*', *JLA* 3 (2010), 337–64.

15. M. Blackburn, 'Money and coinage' in *CMH* 1, 660–74, with the quotations at 661, 674 and 664. Unusually, Odoacer had issued a silver coin bearing his name and image, but significantly, he was not shown wearing any regalia which might suggest imperial aspirations (663).

16. The panegyrics of Cassiodorus and Boethius are not extant, but are referred to in Cassiod. *Libellus* 10–11, 17–18.

Visigothic kingdom, Gundobad for the Burgundian, Clovis for the Frankish),[17] while a succession of Vandal kings were recipients of panegyrical poems preserved in the *Latin Anthology*.[18] All the major kingdoms continued to issue coinage in one form or another. The Visigothic kings issued gold coinage from their capital at Toulouse until the defeat by Clovis in 507 forced a relocation to Spain, where minting resumed. The Burgundians issued coins in all three metals, with the silver and bronze including the monograms of kings from the late fifth and early sixth century. Unusually, the Vandals did not mint any gold coinage, but they continued issuing silver and bronze coins, initially using imperial designs, but in the late fifth century bearing the name and image of the king alone – one example of the way in which the Vandal kingdom sometimes pursued a more independent line (another being their use of Punic motifs on some of their coinage, possibly to help evoke the idea of a new Carthaginian empire).[19] The Franks issued coins in all three metals during the first half of the sixth century, with the gold bearing the image of an emperor, except, notoriously, in the case of Theudebert (533–47), who minted gold coins showing himself in imperial guise with an imperial-sounding legend ('Our master, Theodebertus, victor') – an action which attracted the attention (and indignant criticism) of the contemporary Roman historian Procopius (*Wars* 7.33.5–6).[20]

Theoderic's building activities can also be paralleled in other kingdoms, albeit on a much more sporadic basis. The Vandal king Thrasamund (496–523) built or restored a bath complex in the suburb of Carthage known as Alianae, whose features were celebrated in a series of poems,[21] while the poet Luxorius praised a new palace constructed by Hilderic (523–30) in Carthage:

> The remarkable edifice of King Hilderic gleams, erected with skill, toil, talent, riches, wealth. From it the sun itself takes rays which it can spread to this place. Another dawn is believed to arise from the

17. T. M. Charles-Edwards, 'Law in the western kingdoms between the fifth and the seventh century' in *CAH*² 14.260–87.
18. Y. Hen, *Roman Barbarians: The Royal Court and Culture in the Early Medieval West*, London: Palgrave Macmillan, 2007, 74–8, 81; Merrills and Miles, *Vandals*, 221–3. Sidonius Apollinaris also wrote a poem for a friend in 476 which incorporated panegyrical comments on the Visigothic king Euric; the poem is included in *Ep.* 8.9.5; cf. J. Harries, *Sidonius Apollinaris and the Fall of Rome, AD 407–485*, Oxford: Clarendon Press, 1994, 240–1.
19. Merrills and Miles, *Vandals*, 73.
20. Blackburn, 'Money and coinage', 664–9.
21. Merrills and Miles, *Vandals*, 223–4.

marble. Here the flawless pavement is thought to be thick snow
spread about. When your feet stand upon it, you think they could
sink into it. (*Carm.* 90 [tr. M. Rosenblum])

While not a case of founding *de novo*, Huneric renamed the city of
Hadrumetum as Hunericopolis.[22] Burgundian kings constructed at
least three new churches in Geneva, which served as their capital for
much of the existence of their kingdom,[23] and Clovis was credited
with building a church of the Holy Apostles in Paris, in which he was
himself subsequently buried (Gregory of Tours, *Hist.* 2.43) – perhaps
thereby seeking to emulate the emperors in Constantinople (p. 73
above).[24] Evidence for royal Visigothic construction in their fifth-
century Gallic capital of Toulouse is very limited because of the
continuous occupation of the site,[25] but the repair of city walls and
of a bridge at Emerita (Mérida) in Spain was completed in 483, 'in
the time of Euric, powerful king of the Goths',[26] while in the mid-
sixth century Leovigild was to build the new city of Reccopolis
(named after one of his sons) in the centre of the Iberian peninsula
(John of Biclaro, *Chron. s.a.* 578).[27] As for public entertainment,
Frankish kings are reported as enjoying watching chariot races in the
circus at Arles (Procop. *Wars* 7.33.5) and building amphitheatres in
Soissons and Paris (Gregory of Tours, *Hist.* 5.17). Archaeological
and literary evidence indicates that the circus in Carthage remained
in use throughout the Vandal period;[28] and while the involvement of
Vandal kings in maintaining the circus and the events staged in it
is not explicitly attested, the interest of the Vandal elite as spectators
is (Procop. *Wars* 4.6.7). With intentional irony, Huneric even
presented his persecution of Nicene Christians as being based on

22. Moorhead, *Theoderic*, 43 n.46.
23. C. Bonnet and J.-F. Reynaud, 'Gèneve et Lyon, capitales burgondes' in G. Ripoll and
J. M. Gurt (eds), *Sedes Regiae (ann. 400–800)*, Barcelona: Reial Acadèmia de Bonas
Lletres, 2000, 241–66.
24. B. Ward-Perkins, 'Constantinople: a city and its ideological territory' in G. P.
Brogiolo, N. Gauthier and N. Christie (eds), *Towns and their Territories between Late
Antiquity and the Early Middle Ages*, Leiden: Brill, 2000, 325–45, at 329–30.
25. J. Guyon, 'Toulouse, la première capitale du royaume wisigoth' in Ripoll and Gurt,
Sedes, 219–40.
26. Text in J. Vives, *Inscripciones cristianas de la España romana y visigoda*, 2nd edn,
Barcelona: Consejo Superior de Investigaciones Científicas, 1969, no. 363.
27. It has been suggested that the name may also have been intended to evoke
royal connotations (from *rex*): C. Martin, *La Géographie du pouvoir dans l'Espagne
visigothique*, Lille: Press Universitaire du Septentrion, 2003, 269 (a reference I owe to
Andy Merrills).
28. Merrills and Miles, *Vandals*, 210.

imperial behaviour by closely modelling his edict of 484 on that issued by the Emperor Honorius against the Donatists of north Africa in 412.[29]

Kings and bishops

The persecution of Nicene Christians during the Vandal period is a reminder of the ongoing importance of religious issues, despite the reconfiguration of political power. Indeed, given that, unlike western emperors of the fifth century, the new rulers were nearly all Arian and that Arianism had had only a limited presence in the west since the late fourth century, their advent effectively introduced a novel factor into the scenario.[30] Its impact, however, varied considerably from kingdom to kingdom.

The Vandals were the most active proponents of Arianism and discriminators against Nicene Christianity. A number of fifth-century texts present the Vandal kings as avid persecutors who inflicted great cruelty on Nicene Christians, the foremost of these texts being Victor of Vita's *History of the Persecution*, probably written in the 480s. There can be no doubting that Nicene Christians suffered under Vandal rule, while a range of evidence indicates that significant numbers of Nicene clergy and laypeople 'converted' to Arianism.[31] Nonetheless, it is important to register a number of caveats and qualifications. First, not all Vandal kings were staunch persecutors. Geiseric, Huneric and Thrasamund certainly were, but Hilderic was not, as also probably Gunthamund. Secondly, persecution is a broad term which can refer to a wide range of discriminatory actions with varying degrees of severity. Vandal kings undoubtedly exiled many Nicene clergy, with much associated hardship, and they also confiscated much property from Nicene churches

29. Wickham, *Framing*, 88–9. The well-known description of the daily round of the Visigothic king Theoderic II (453–66) by Sidonius (*Ep.* 1.2), who presents him as a model ruler, should not necessarily be taken at face value, given that it is likely to have been written and publicised at a time when political circumstances required the promotion of a favourable image of the king: see H. Sivan, 'Sidonius Apollinaris, Theoderic II and Gothic–Roman politics from Avitus to Anthemius', *Hermes* 117 (1989), 85–94.
30. Amory, *Ostrogothic Italy*, 237–47, draws attention to evidence for the continuity of Arianism in the Balkans and Italy during the fifth century, but also acknowledges (257) that it 'certainly counted only a tiny minority of Italians as believers' at the start of Theoderic's reign.
31. For details, see Moorhead, *Theoderic*, 90, and Merrills and Miles, *Vandals*, 187, 195.

and their members. Persecution, though, is a term most commonly associated with the ultimate penalty of execution – martyrdom – and Victor's account certainly gives the impression that many martyrs died as a result of the policies of Geiseric and Huneric. However, a concern to dramatise the difficulties facing Nicene Christians in north Africa may have led him to exaggerate the number of martyrs. A third qualification concerns regional variation: Nicene Christians in Carthage and its hinterland appear to have suffered more than those in other regions of the kingdom. Finally, it is worth bearing in mind that the discriminatory actions of some Vandal kings were not necessarily motivated primarily by religious fervour: particularly during Geiseric's reign, the economic benefits of acquiring the property of Nicene churches appear to have been the priority.[32]

Visigothic kings appear to have been much more cautious about encroaching on Nicene interests, at least until the reign of Euric (466–84). Euric is reported to have prevented the appointment of new Nicene bishops in at least nine cities, and to have exiled a number of episcopal incumbents. This prompted the contemporary Sidonius Apollinaris to portray him as something of a religious fanatic (*Ep.* 7.6) and the later historian Gregory of Tours to write of 'the serious persecution of Christians in Gaul' at that time (*Hist.* 2.25). However, Euric's actions are likely to have been motivated by political, rather than religious, considerations. In the difficult circumstances of the early 470s when he had gone to war against the western Emperor Anthemius, Euric had reason to be concerned about the loyalties of the cities in his kingdom, and especially the potential danger that Nicene bishops could become the focus of attempts by cities to defect to the imperial cause.[33] Otherwise, the impression is generally one of peaceful co-existence between Nicene and Arian Christians in the Visigothic realm.

Peaceful co-existence was also the norm in the Ostrogothic kingdom of Theoderic, who is praised in one near-contemporary source for not harming the Nicene church, despite being an Arian (*Anonymous Valesianus* 60). The fact that these years generated so little in the way of anti-Arian polemic from Nicene leaders in Italy has

---

32. For the various points in this paragraph, and further references, see P. Heather, 'Christianity and the Vandals in the reign of Geiseric' in J. Drinkwater and B. Salway (eds), *Wolf Liebeschuetz Reflected*, London: Institute of Classical Studies, 2007, 137–46; Merrills and Miles, *Vandals*, 177–203. There is a convenient translation of Victor of Vita by J. Moorhead (Liverpool: Liverpool University Press, 1992).
33. Mathisen, *Aristocrats*, 32–3; Harries, *Sidonius*, 234–5.

been seen as providing circumstantial corroboration,[34] as also has Theoderic's enlightened treatment of the Jewish communities in his kingdom. In a letter to the Jews of Genoa, he stated that 'we cannot command adherence to a religion, since no one is forced to believe against their will' (Cassiod. *Var.* 2.27.2 [507/11]), and he took steps to defend Jewish interests after violence against them in Rome and Ravenna.[35] Even when serious disputes arose over the election of the bishop of Rome, Theoderic appears to have refrained from exploiting the situation to his advantage.[36] It was only in the final years of Theoderic's reign that this balance was disturbed, first by the resolution of the Acacian schism between the churches in Rome and the east, and then with the execution of the prominent senator Boethius (p. 194 below).

The major exception to rule by Arian kings was the Frankish king Clovis, who famously converted to Catholic (i.e., Nicene) Christianity.[37] That conversion has been the subject of considerable debate, with regard both to its date – was it after his defeat of the Alamanni in 496 (or perhaps 506), or after his defeat of the Visigoths, in 508? – and to Clovis' prior religious affiliation – was he converting from pagan practices, or had he flirted with Arianism? The debate has focused on the interpretation of the relevant passage from Gregory of Tours' *History* (2.27), written in the late sixth century, and on a contemporary letter to Clovis from Avitus, bishop of Vienne (*Ep.* 46). Recent discussions which have focused on the contemporary evidence of Avitus have provided good reason to think that the most likely scenario was baptism in 508, after victory against the Visigoths and after Clovis had shown interest in Arianism.[38] The fact that Clovis' Burgundian wife of many years, Chlothild, was already a Catholic Christian was presumably an important factor in his eventual decision. Whatever Clovis' original religious allegiance, however, his adoption of Catholic Christianity was very significant for the future of his kingdom, as he no doubt

34. Moorhead, *Theoderic*, 93–4.
35. Moorhead, *Theoderic*, 97–100.
36. Moorhead, *Theoderic*, 91–2, 138–9.
37. Sigismund, king of the Burgundians (516–23), also converted to Catholic Christianity at some point before becoming king, and Rechiarius, king of the Sueves (448–55), is reported to have been a Catholic.
38. D. Shanzer, 'Dating the baptism of Clovis: the bishop of Vienne vs the bishop of Tours', *Early Medieval Europe* 7 (1998), 29–57; D. Shanzer and I. Wood, *Avitus of Vienne: Letters and Selected Prose*, Liverpool: Liverpool University Press, 2002, 362–73 (including a translation of *Ep.* 46).

appreciated. By aligning himself with the religious commitment of the majority of inhabitants of Gaul, he made it much easier for those inhabitants, especially the elite, to accept a Frankish regime. One small but significant indication of this was his later being characterised as 'a new Constantine' (Gregory of Tours, *Hist.* 2.31).

If Clovis' original religious allegiance was to some form of paganism, it will presumably have been to cult practices of Germanic origin. However, there is also evidence of the continued survival of Roman pagan practices in the barbarian kingdoms which warrants brief comment. First, there is a range of documentary evidence from Vandal north Africa attesting the continued appointment of individuals to the position of *flamen perpetuus*, a priesthood associated in Roman times with the imperial cult. It is obviously puzzling that this position should continue publicly in the late fifth and early sixth century, when Christian emperors had dissociated themselves from the imperial cult by the late fourth century and when the region in question was no longer under imperial rule. The most plausible resolution of this conundrum is that the position no longer carried any religious associations, and was now viewed as a civic office, which the Vandal kings allowed members of the Romano-African elite to hold as an avenue for the continued expression of civic pride and self-importance.[39]

A second practice relates to the city of Rome and the celebration of the Lupercalia. The Lupercalia was an ancient festival whose rituals were closely associated with the foundation myths of Rome. Aristocratic youths were organised into two teams of Luperci, named after Romulus and Remus, who assembled at the Lupercal – the sacred site below the Palatine where the baby twins were said to have been suckled by the wolf. There a goat and a dog were sacrificed, and the skin of the goat was cut up to provide loin-cloths for the Luperci and strips of hide to act as whips. After a feast which included much consumption of wine, the Luperci ran around the city centre striking anyone they met with their goatskin whips, amidst much hilarity. Since it was believed that any women so struck would become pregnant, it seems that the festival was in origin a rite to promote fertility, though it may also have involved an element of

---

39. Merrills and Miles, *Vandals*, 212–13, summarising A. Chastagnol and N. Duval, 'Les survivances du culte imperial dans l'Afrique du Nord à l'époque vandale', *Mélanges d'histoire ancienne offerts à William Seston*, Paris: De Boccard, 1974, 87–118.

ritual purification.[40] Theodosius I had of course banned sacrifice in the early 390s (pp. 52–3 above), but it is apparent that the Lupercalia continued to be celebrated publicly during the fifth century, albeit in a modified form. The clearest indication of its continuation is a letter by Gelasius, bishop of Rome in the early 490s, apparently railing against the persistence of the festival. While this has often been seen as *prima facie* evidence for the tenacity of pagan religious traditions despite the Christianising efforts of church and state, the most plausible interpretation of this episode is one which relates it to the Roman tradition of street theatre – it seems that the festival was now performed by professional actors – and to the social ambitions of the Roman aristocrats who staged it: their undoubted Christianisation had not eradicated their enduring appetite for the self-promotion which such an occasion offered.[41]

Kings and emperor

For much of the fifth century Constantinople had shown a willingness to intervene in the west to uphold imperial rule. In 410 a small force had been sent to Ravenna to aid the Emperor Honorius against Alaric (p. 113 above), while in 425 a more substantial expedition had placed Valentinian III on the western throne after the turmoil following Honorius' death in 423 (p. 85 above). Another expedition had tried, unsuccessfully, to turn back the Vandal advance in north Africa in the early 430s, while yet another was poised in 441 to recover Carthage from them, only for Attila's activities on the Danube to force the abandonment of the attempt (p. 117 above). The nadir came, of course, in 468, when the largest of these forces, sent by the Emperor Leo, was destroyed by Geiseric (p. 122). Leo's effective successor, Zeno, was so preoccupied with internal problems – indeed, with sheer survival – that the west was of little concern to him. He did take the initiative early in his reign to seek a settlement with the Vandals which seems to have ensured peaceful relations during his and Anastasius' reigns (Malchus, *fr.* 5, Procop. *Wars* 3.7.26). However, Zeno was certainly in no position to intervene when Odoacer deposed the last western emperor, Romulus, in 476, and his persuading Theoderic to invade Italy in 489 was more about removing one of his biggest internal problems than about

40. J. A. North, 'Caesar at the Lupercalia', *JRS* 98 (2008), 144–60, at 147–53.
41. N. McLynn, 'Crying wolf: the pope and the Lupercalia', *JRS* 98 (2008), 161–75.

reasserting imperial authority in the west by proxy. Anastasius was therefore effectively the first emperor to confront the vastly changed circumstances of the west and the novel situation of dealing with the successor kingdoms.

Since he was the most recently established king and since his kingdom included the city of Rome, Theoderic had most reason to be concerned about Anastasius' attitude, and indeed most of the relevant material relates to the Ostrogothic kingdom. It is clear that Theoderic was concerned to have the approval of Constantinople, for he sent a senatorial embassy early in Anastasius' reign seeking confirmation of his position. Anastasius was not prepared to acknowledge him at that point, which made for a period of strained relations, only resolved in 497 when a second embassy, led by a leading senator, secured some form of recognition, although in what capacity is unclear.[42] Nonetheless, with the passage of time and a growing sense of security, Theoderic became less concerned about causing upset in Constantinople, and in 504 – perhaps taking advantage of Anastasius' preoccupation with his Persian war (p. 169 above) – he intervened in the Balkans, seizing control of the city of Sirmium. While the city was actually in the hands of Gepids at the time, it lay in territory which was strictly speaking part of the eastern empire. Soon after, the Ostrogothic force which had captured Sirmium from the Gepids also took on and defeated an army led by an eastern Roman general.[43]

Anastasius' eventual response to Theoderic's aggression was measured, but sufficient to make clear to him that the empire was by no means a spent force. First, in late 507 or early 508, he reminded Theoderic of the military capabilities of the empire by despatching a fleet of 200 ships carrying 8,000 troops to carry out raids along the coast of Apulia, in southern Italy (*Chron. Marc. s.a.* 508). Secondly, later in 508, he reminded Theoderic of the long reach of imperial diplomacy by sending envoys to the Frankish king, Clovis, fresh from his victory over the Visigoths. These envoys bore official documentation bestowing an honorary consulship on the king, following which Clovis paraded through the city of Tours distributing gold and silver to the populace in a manner reminiscent of a triumphing

---

42. Moorhead, *Theoderic*, 36–9.
43. Moorhead, *Theoderic*, 174–5; F. Haarer, *Anastasius I: Politics and Empire in the Late Roman World*, Cambridge: Francis Cairns, 2006, 91–3.

Roman general.[44] At some point in the early sixth century, Anastasius also bestowed on the Burgundian prince Sigismund an official title (possibly that of master of the soldiers, which his father and grandfather had also held)[45] – perhaps another attempt to discomfort Theoderic. Even if this last item was not directly relevant, however, Anastasius' other steps appear to have had the intended effect, for later in 508 Theoderic wrote to Anastasius expressing his desire for peace in deferential terms (the overblown language is typical of late Roman bureaucratese):

> We are obliged, most merciful emperor, to seek peace, since we know that there are no reasons for anger between us … It is in accord with your power and honour that we who have already benefited from your affection should seek concord with you. You are the fairest ornament of all realms, you are the life-preserving defence of the whole world, to whom all other rulers rightly look up with reverence, because they know that there is in you something which is unlike all others – especially ourselves, who with divine help learned in your state (*res publica*) the ability to govern Romans with justice. (Cassiod. *Var.* 1.1.1–2 [tr. T. Hodgkin with revisions])

That relations were restored is implied by the fact that the name of Theoderic's appointee for western consul in 508 appears in eastern documentation in the final months of the year, after that for 507 was ignored.

The accession of Justin in 518 and the ending of the Acacian schism soon after (p. 177 above) has sometimes been seen as a worrying development for Theoderic's relations with Constantinople, since it removed a major obstacle to co-operation between non-Gothic, Nicene Christian inhabitants of Italy and the east, thereby increasing the possibility of disloyalty to Theoderic's regime. While this should not necessarily be assumed to have been the case,[46] Theoderic's actions in the mid-520s strongly suggest that he was increasingly worried about disloyalty on the part of members of the senatorial aristocracy. Perhaps in 524, one of Theoderic's courtiers brought an accusation against an eminent senator, Albinus, to the effect that he had written to the Emperor Justin in a way which

---

44. Gregory of Tours, *Hist.* 2.37–8, with M. McCormick, 'Clovis at Tours, public ritual and the origins of medieval ruler symbolism' in E. Chrysos and A. Schwarcz (eds), *Das Reich und die Barbaren*, Vienna: Böhlau, 1989, 155–80.
45. Shanzer and Wood, *Avitus*, 143–4.
46. Moorhead, *Theoderic*, 198–200.

was hostile to Theoderic's kingdom. Albinus denied the charge, and received the support of another eminent senator, Boethius, who was at that time Theoderic's master of the offices. When Albinus' accuser then produced witnesses against both Albinus and Boethius, Theoderic had the two senators arrested (*Anonymous Valesianus* 86). Albinus' fate is unknown, but Boethius was subsequently executed, along with his father-in-law Symmachus.

Their deaths are puzzling, since the action seems out of character with the prevailing tenor of Theoderic's reign and the victims unlikely targets. Both men came from distinguished lineages – Boethius a member of the Anician clan, Symmachus the great-grandson of the famous orator of the late fourth century – and both men had further distinguished themselves through their own scholarly endeavours. Symmachus was the author of a (no longer extant) history of Rome in seven books, while Boethius was a learned student of Greek philosophy who embarked on a grand project to translate all the works of Aristotle and Plato's dialogues into Latin, with a view to demonstrating that there was greater agreement between them than usually assumed.[47] Much uncertainty surrounds their fate – whether (and if so, by whom) they were tried, the underlying reasons for their deaths, even the manner of their execution – but it is possible that they were the victims of a power struggle at Theoderic's court.[48] In the long term, Boethius' posthumous reputation was secured by the profound philosophical dialogue he wrote while in prison, entitled *The Consolation of Philosophy*, which, despite its eschewing explicit Christian reference, was to have an extraordinarily wide influence on medieval thinkers.[49] More immediately, however, his and Symmachus' executions must have engendered disaffection with the Gothic regime among the senatorial aristocracy. They must also have caused disquiet in Constantinople, even if there does not seem to have been any immediate reaction from the east. Theoderic's effective successor, Amalasuintha, the mother of his young grandson Athalaric, took pains to write (in Athalaric's name) a conciliatory letter to the Emperor Justin in 526 (Cassiod. *Var.* 8.1) and to restore the confiscated property of

47. The case for regarding Boethius as more than just an unoriginal transmitter of others' ideas is made in J. Marenbon, *Boethius*, Oxford: Oxford University Press, 2006.
48. Moorhead, *Theoderic*, 219–35.
49. M. Gibson (ed.), *Boethius: His Life, Thought and Influence*, Oxford: Blackwell, 1981; J. Marenbon (ed.), *The Cambridge Companion to Boethius*, Cambridge: Cambridge University Press, 2009.

Boethius and Symmachus to their families (Procop. *Wars* 5.2.5), suggesting that she was alert to the precariousness of the kingdom's position vis-à-vis the empire – an instinct which was to prove all too justified within less than a decade (see p. 262 below).

Part III

Longer-term trends

CHAPTER 10

Urban continuity and change

Cities and civic elites

Cities and their amenities were one of the distinctive features of the Roman empire.[1] To be sure, the empire's main eastern neighbour in late antiquity, Persia, was also urbanised, partly as a result of the long tradition of urban settlement in the Middle East, and the fresh injection of city-founding brought by Alexander the Great and his successors, but also through the building activities of the Sasanian kings themselves.[2] However, this was the exception among the empire's neighbours during the late Roman period, the remainder of which were still at considerably earlier stages of development. In his accounts of Roman military expeditions beyond the Rhine and Danube in the mid-fourth century, Ammianus refers to barbarian villages of rudimentary wooden structures which Roman troops destroyed with ease (e.g., 18.2.15); according to Priscus (*fr.* 11.1 [lines 356–72]), Attila's main settlement north of the lower Danube

---

1. There is an ever-expanding body of literature on the city in late antiquity. An outstanding overview is S. T. Loseby, 'Mediterranean cities' in P. Rousseau (ed.), *A Companion to Late Antiquity*, Oxford: Wiley-Blackwell, 2009, 139–55, while K. G. Holum, 'The classical city in the sixth century' in M. Maas (ed.), *The Cambridge Companion to the Age of Justinian*, Cambridge: Cambridge University Press, 2005, 87–112, provides another good summary within a more restricted timeframe; C. Wickham, *Framing the Early Middle Ages: Europe and the Mediterranean, 400–800*, Oxford: Oxford University Press, 2005, 591–692, offers a more detailed survey with a particular focus on the economic dimension. Important monographic treatments include J. H. W. G. Liebeschuetz, *The Decline and Fall of the Roman City*, Oxford: Oxford University Press, 2001, and H. G. Saradi, *The Byzantine City in the Sixth Century*, Athens: Society of Messenian Archaeological Studies, 2006. There are many conference volumes relating to the subject, including J. Rich (ed.), *The City in Late Antiquity*, London: Routledge, 1992, N. Christie and S. Loseby (eds), *Towns in Transition: Urban Evolution in Late Antiquity and the Early Middle Ages*, Aldershot: Scolar Press, 1996, and J.-U. Krause and C. Witschel (eds), *Die Stadt in der Spätantike: Niedergang oder Wandel?*, Stuttgart: Franz Steiner, 2006 (which includes many papers in English).
2. J. Howard-Johnston, 'The two great powers in late antiquity: a comparison' in Averil Cameron (ed.), *The Byzantine and Early Islamic Near East* III: *States, Resources and Armies*, Princeton: Darwin Press, 1995, 157–222, 181–2, 198–211.

was 'a very large village' which included a palace and a bath house, but the palace was made of timber and the modest bath house had been constructed by a Roman prisoner with stone imported from Roman territory (presumably *spolia* – plundered building materials – comprising dressed blocks). One would be justified in wondering whether these historians' descriptions were influenced by prejudiced stereotypes of barbarian capabilities, but in this case archaeological investigation has corroborated the essential lack of any settlement in *barbaricum* remotely comparable to a Roman city, in either size or the presence of monumental public structures.[3]

None of this is to say that most of the empire's own inhabitants were city dwellers, for it remained the case that the bulk of the empire's population lived in rural contexts. However, since, for administrative purposes at any rate, cities were conceived of as comprising the sometimes extensive rural hinterland of villages, hamlets and dispersed settlement surrounding the built-up urban core, the city was also a focal point for rural inhabitants, even if many rarely had occasion to visit the city proper. Historical circumstances meant that the distribution of cities across the empire was uneven. Broadly speaking, there were heavier concentrations in the east than the west, although Italy and north Africa were exceptions to this. Late Roman emperors did continue the long-established practice of founding new cities which bore their name – most famously, Constantinople. In theory, these expanded the empire's stock of cities, but in practice many (such as the most famous) simply involved the 'rebranding' of already existing cities, albeit sometimes in conjunction with restoration work after major damage arising from war or earthquake. While, then, there can be no denying the broader historical significance of the investment by Constantine and his successors specifically in Constantinople, imperial foundations in late antiquity more generally did little to change the overall number or distribution of cities.[4]

---

3. M. Todd, *The Early Germans*, 2nd edn, Oxford: Blackwell, 2004, 62–75; M. Kulikowski, *Rome's Gothic Wars from the Third Century to Alaric*, Cambridge: Cambridge University Press, 2007, 87–94 (who notes the existence of the occasional larger dwelling making some use of stone and terracotta tiles – but still in a village context).

4. Imperial foundations are detailed in Jones, *LRE*, 718–22, to which can be added the elevation of Didyma, in western Anatolia, from village to city status in 527/33 with the new name of Justinianopolis, as attested in an important inscription discovered in 1991 (*AE* 2004.1410).

During the late Republican period, the Roman ruling class had absorbed from the Greeks a cultural appreciation of the benefits of *polis*-centred life, but they were also quick to grasp the practical advantages of the Mediterranean's network of cities as a convenient infrastructure to assist effective governance of a vast empire. For this purpose, the crucial institution in a city was its council (*curia* in Latin, *boulē* in Greek), the members of which constituted the civic elite (*curiales* or *decuriones* in Latin, *bouleutai* or *politeuomenoi* in Greek). Varying in number depending on the size of the city, these were local landowners whose wealth and connections made them the ideal candidates to oversee the administration of their city and to shoulder the responsibilities and burdens that this entailed. These localised administrative duties included ensuring adequate availability of staple foods and water, maintenance of public buildings, preservation of public order, and the staging of religious festivals and games. City councils could use city revenues to help fund such matters (e.g., rents from civic land), but these were rarely sufficient to cover everything and there was an expectation that councillors would draw on their personal resources to supplement civic funds. Indeed in the early empire there developed a culture in which rivalry between members of the local elite expressed itself in competitive display and generosity to their community – so-called 'euergetism' – as attested in the numerous inscriptions which memorialised their gifts, whether it be helping to purchase grain, fund games or construct a new theatre. From the perspective of the emperor, however, the most important function of city councils was to oversee and underwrite the collection of imperial taxes from their city's rural hinterland. It was their assumption of this role which enabled emperors during the Principate to make do with a tiny total number of administrators (in the low hundreds) – an arrangement aptly characterised as 'government without bureaucracy'.[5]

The curial order were prepared to take on this role partly because it was accepted that, in collecting imperial taxes, they could extract more than the emperor required and pocket the difference. They also benefited from minimal interference by central government in the internal affairs of cities, which allowed councillors to run local affairs and to engage in political and social rivalry with their peers.

---

5. P. Garnsey and R. Saller, *The Roman Empire: Economy, Society and Culture*, London: Duckworth, 1987, 20–40.

By the fourth century, however, the balance between the benefits of
status and the burdens of responsibility involved in performing
curial duties had begun to shift inexorably away from the former
towards the latter. This was at least partly due to the expansion of
central government resulting from the reforms of Diocletian and
Constantine. The number of administrators grew significantly, into
the tens of thousands, as the central bureaucracy expanded and the
number of provinces was increased by the subdivision of existing
ones. This facilitated closer oversight of provincial and civic affairs,
and above all of the levying of taxes, for which, with a larger army
to support, there was even greater demand. The scope for city councillors to enrich themselves through the tax collection process
accordingly contracted, while cities lost control of civic lands and
local taxes to the imperial treasury. With the material and less
tangible incentives for curial service receding, many of those liable
for service sought ways to escape; one of the themes of the fourth
century was the attempts of successive emperors to maintain
numbers on the city councils by, for example, insisting on the
hereditary nature of curial obligations.[6] Yet, ironically, emperors
were also responsible for creating escape routes, through the expansion of the central bureaucracy and the establishment of the new
senate at Constantinople, both of which drew on city councillors
and gave immunity from curial duties. Service in the army or the
church offered further modes of egress.

The correspondence and speeches of the rhetorician Libanius
provide some of the best evidence for the phenomenon as it affected
the city of Antioch in the second half of the fourth century. At
various points he comments on the sharp decline in the number of
city councillors, no doubt with an element of rhetorical exaggeration
– 'Instead of the six hundred of days gone by, there aren't even sixty
now' (*Or.* 2.33) – while elsewhere he remarks on the difficulties of
councillors in finding a wife of any wealth, since no prospective
father-in-law wanted to risk their daughter's dowry being consumed
by the demands of curial obligations (*Or.* 2.36). At the same time,
many of Libanius' students – often the sons of city councillors – were
keen to escape their looming obligations and sought entry to the

---

6. Valentinian and Valens did also try to ease the strains on city councils by restoring
one third of the revenues from former civic estates for the specific purpose of repairing
public buildings: N. Lenski, *Failure of Empire: Valens and the Roman State in the Fourth
Century* A.D., Berkeley: University of California Press, 2002, 295–6.

imperial bureaucracy, which Libanius, proud teacher that he was, assisted by writing letters of recommendation.[7]

While repeated imperial legislation to restrict avenues of escape and require absconding councillors to surrender their property to the council might suggest that emperors were fighting a losing battle, there is other, admittedly patchy, evidence from the fourth and fifth centuries indicating that the laws were not consistently ignored.[8] An inscription from the reign of Valentinian I, for example, records one man's restoration of a basilica at Cuicul in Numidia 'for the completion of his required curial obligation (*munus*)' (*ILS* 5535), while a fifth-century saint's life reports the conversion of Rabbula, a leading councillor in a Syrian city (probably Chalcis), whose first step towards an ascetic life involved his giving to the council the property on which it had a claim.[9] Furthermore, *curiales* were not such an endangered species as to be on the verge of extinction: as already noted (p. 166 above), the Emperor Anastasius' institution of *vindices* to oversee tax collection did not, as sometimes assumed, replace the involvement of councillors in this process, and they continue to feature in the extant sources for the eastern half of the empire throughout the sixth century.[10]

Nonetheless, the city council as the body responsible for civic administration was increasingly superseded by more informal arrangements, with leadership in cities being assumed by a less clearly defined elite of what modern scholars have come to refer to as 'notables', comprising all or some of the following: *honorati* – that is, locals of senatorial rank (in its expanded and diluted form [p. 64 above]); imperial officials based in the city; some city councillors (probably the wealthiest); and – most strikingly – clergy, above all the local bishop.[11] The growing dominance of these notables partly reflected changing patterns of land ownership, as indicated by the collective terms often used in the sources to refer to

7. J. H. W. G. Liebeschuetz, *Antioch: City and Imperial Administration in the Later Roman Empire*, Oxford: Clarendon Press, 1972, 174–82.

8. A. Laniado, *Recherches sur les notables municipaux dans l'empire protobyzantin*, Paris: Collège de France, 2002, 3–26.

9. *Life of Alexander Akoimetos* 11, 20, with general discussion of this source and a translation in D. Caner, *Wandering, Begging Monks: Spiritual Authority and the Promotion of Monasticism in Late Antiquity*, Berkeley: University of California Press, 2002, 126–57, 249–80.

10. Laniado, *Notables*, 63–87.

11. Liebeschuetz, *Decline*, 104–36; Laniado, *Notables*, 131–223.

them – *possessores* in Latin, and its Greek equivalent, *ktētores*.[12] Some city councillors were prepared to escape their obligations by selling their land and using the proceeds to facilitate their appointment to a post in the imperial bureaucracy, creating opportunities for other notables to expand their local land-holding and influence.[13] In one sense, bishops could be seen as an exception to this pattern, since even if they did not always relinquish all their property at ordination as the church encouraged them to do – many bishops came from a curial background – they were unlikely to add to what they already owned; in another sense, however, they epitomised this new urban elite, since they held office independently of the curial order, and they controlled (sometimes significant) local church resources which necessarily gave them influence in their community.[14]

The first clear indication of the shift of power from council to notables is a law issued in the west in 409 regarding appointments to the civic post of *defensor civitatis* ('defender of the city', who acted as a judge in minor civil cases), previously a decision of the city council, but now to be determined by the bishop, clergy, *honorati*, *possessores* and *curiales* (*Cod. Iust.* 1.55.8). This law was reiterated by the Emperor Anastasius in the east in 505 (*Cod. Iust.* 1.55.11), and a number of inscriptions from Corycus in Cilicia at about the same time also record imperial rulings confirming that the *defensor* and other civic posts were to be appointed by the bishop, clergy and *ktētores*.[15] In the post-imperial west, the *curiales* (and indeed the council) retained a presence in some of the law codes and other documentation of early barbarian rulers, but the most important figures in cities were the bishop, the *possessores* and the *comes civitatis* ('count of the city') – a royal official with responsibility for maintaining public order and overseeing the levying of taxes.[16] This reconfiguration of civic elites represented an important change in the leadership and administration of cities during late antiquity, both

---

12. The most detailed evidence on changing patterns of land-holding is from Egypt, for which see J. Banaji, *Agrarian Change in Late Antiquity: Gold, Labour and Aristocratic Dominance*, rev. edn, Oxford: Oxford University Press, 2007, 101–70; terminology is discussed in Laniado, *Notables*, 171–200.
13. Liebeschuetz, *Antioch*, 182–6.
14. C. Rapp, *Holy Bishops in Late Antiquity*, Berkeley: University of California Press, 2005, 211–34.
15. *MAMA* 3.197 with discussion in Liebeschuetz, *Decline*, 55–6, 110–11.
16. Liebeschuetz, *Decline*, 124–36; S. T. Loseby, 'Decline and change in the cities of late antique Gaul' in Krause and Witschel, *Stadt*, 67–104, at 83–97.

symbolically and because the less formal organisation of the notables is likely to have made it more difficult for emperors and kings to hold them to account in the way that had been possible with city councils.[17]

Urban fabric and amenities

Changes in the fortunes and character of civic elites are ones which can be traced primarily through legal and other documentary sources. Another important dimension of urban continuity and change is the physical character of cityscapes, for which the primary evidence comprises inscriptions and the archaeological remains of buildings and urban spaces. There is now a vast (and ever-increasing) volume of relevant data, to which it is impossible to do justice within the constraints of a study such as this. The intention here is rather to sketch the outlines of the most important developments. In doing so, a fundamental theme is the difficulties of generalisation. These difficulties are twofold. First, the haphazard survival of evidence from individual sites and the finite resources available for their archaeological investigation mean that it is rarely possible to gain a comprehensive overview of the development of a city. Secondly, it is difficult to generalise more broadly because of regional variation, not only between east and west, but also between areas within those broader designations. Patterns of development in Anatolia were not necessarily the same as in the Balkans, just as those in north Africa could be quite different from those in Gaul, while the pace of change was also variable – a reflection of differing geographical and historical circumstances and differing cultural traditions. Nor was the experience of cities even within the same area necessarily uniform.

By way of illustration, it is instructive to consider some of the most intensively studied sites from around the empire. Turning first to the east and more specifically to Palestine, the material remains from Scythopolis indicate that the city reached the peak of its development and prosperity in the late fifth and early sixth century, while excavations at the coastal city of Caesarea show

---

17. Liebeschuetz, *Decline*, 123, 407 (although in the west, the proliferation of counts was designed to counter this). Laniado (*Notables*, 211–14) has argued for the existence of a 'conseil des notables', but the evidence he adduces is extremely thin; cf. J. H. W. G. Liebeschuetz, 'Transformation and decline: are the two really incompatible?' in Krause and Witschel, *Stadt*, 463–83, at 470–1.

significant expansion of the city's area in the fifth century, a range
of evidence for the upkeep and repair of public buildings and infrastructure throughout the sixth century, and a flourishing economy
during this period.[18] In western Anatolia, a wealth of epigraphic
and archaeological evidence from Aphrodisias points to growing
prosperity from the mid-fifth to the mid-sixth century and significant
investment in public buildings, while the commercial quarter of
Sardis appears to have been thriving in the sixth century.[19] At
Sagalassos in central Anatolia, on the other hand, the picture is
less uniformly positive. Important public buildings, such as the Neon
Library and the baths, were refurbished in the second half of the
fourth century, while a large urban villa was also constructed in this
period. On the other hand, the library was destroyed c. 400 and
not rebuilt, and a defensive wall was also constructed at this time,
defining an area a third of the size of that occupied during earlier
centuries. Other indications that the fifth century was a less prosperous period in the city's history include the complete disappearance of inscriptions honouring members of the local elite, and the
abandonment of the city's main pottery workshop. A severe earthquake c. 500 did major damage to the city's infrastructure, and
although there was some rebuilding, it is apparent that the fifth and
sixth centuries here were not a period of prosperity akin to that
enjoyed by cities in Palestine and western Anatolia.[20]

In the Balkans, the picture is even bleaker. Corinth, which once
prided itself on one of the most spacious civic centres in the empire,
experienced significant earthquake damage in 365 and again in 375,
and although a certain amount of restoration work was done in their
aftermath, the city was sacked by Alaric's Goths in 395 (p. 110
above); while some new structures were built (from *spolia*) in the
fifth century, most public buildings were not restored, honorific
inscriptions disappeared from the agora (the focal point of public

18. Y. Tsafrir and G. Foerster, 'Urbanism in Scythopolis-Bet Shean in the fourth to
seventh centuries', *DOP* 51 (1997), 85–146, at 99–106; A. Raban and K. G. Holum
(eds), *Caesarea Maritima: A Retrospective after Two Millennia*, Leiden: Brill, 1996;
K. G. Holum et al. (eds) *Caesarea Papers 2*, Portsmouth, RI: *JRA* Supp. 35, 1999.
19. C. Roueché, *Aphrodisias in Late Antiquity: The Late Roman and Byzantine Inscriptions*, 2nd edn: http://insaph.kcl.ac.uk/ala2004, Introduction 18; C. Ratté, 'New research
on the urban development of Aphrodisias in late antiquity' in D. Parrish (ed.), *Urbanism
in Western Asia Minor*, Portsmouth, RI: *JRA* Supp. 45, 2001, 116–47; J. S. Crawford,
The Byzantine Shops at Sardis, Cambridge, MA: Harvard University Press, 1990.
20. M. Waelkens et al., 'The late antique to early Byzantine city in southwest Anatolia
– Sagalassos and its territory: a case study' in Krause and Witschel, *Stadt*, 199–255.

life) after the early fifth century, the city wall enclosed a much reduced area of only 1.5 km², and by the sixth century the agora was being used for burials.[21] Meanwhile, Nicopolis ad Istrum, in the northern Balkans, was destroyed, presumably by the Huns, and although the city was subsequently rebuilt in the later fifth century, it was located on a new site adjacent to the original city, covering an area only a quarter the size.[22]

Moving westwards, inscriptions and archaeology from urban centres across north Africa show local elites continuing to invest in public buildings and infrastructure throughout the fourth and early fifth century.[23] While the advent of the Vandals in the middle of the fifth century did not for the most part entail the destruction of the fabric of cities (cf. pp. 185–6 above), it is apparent that civic centres increasingly ceased to be maintained in traditional fashion. At Belalis Maior (Henchir al-Faouar), to the west of Carthage, rooms around the forum were modified by the addition of partition walls, there was a build-up of soil over the forum pavement, and the area began to be used for burials;[24] at Thuburbo Maius, inland to the south-west of Carthage, the forum area was gradually occupied by housing and oil presses;[25] and at the Tripolitanian city of Sabratha the forum area 'was eventually turned into a cemetery ... [and] the adjacent temple of the Unknown Divinity was overlain with dense housing and workshops'.[26] The return of imperial rule during the reign of Justinian brought fresh investment, but as far as secular structures are concerned, this was mostly spent on fortifications to defend communities against Moorish tribesmen, as described by the

21. E. A. Ivison, 'Burial and urbanism at late antique and early Byzantine Corinth (c. AD 400–700)' in Christie and Loseby, *Towns in Transition*, 99–125; Saradi, *Byzantine City*, 239–42.
22. A. G. Poulter, *Nicopolis ad Istrum – The Roman, Late Roman and Early Byzantine City: Excavations 1985–1992*, London: JRS Monographs 8, 1995.
23. C. Lepelley, *Les cités de l'Afrique romaine au Bas-Empire*, Paris: Études augustiniennes, 1979–81, with his recent updating 'La cité africaine tardive, de l'apogée de IVe siècle à l'effondrement du VIIe siècle' in Krause and Witschel, *Stadt*, 13–32; also A. Leone, *Changing Townscapes in North Africa from Late Antiquity to the Arab Conquest*, Bari: Edipuglia, 2007, 82–96.
24. A. Mahjoubi, *Recherches d'histoire et d'archéologie à Henchir el-Faouar (Tunisie)*, Tunis: Publications de l'Université de Tunis, 1978.
25. L. Maurin, 'Thuburbo Maius et la paix vandale', *Cahiers de Tunis* 15 (1967), 225–54.
26. D. J. Mattingly and R. B. Hitchner, 'Roman Africa: an archaeological review', *JRS* 85 (1995), 165–213, at 212.

contemporary historian Procopius in Book 6 of his *Buildings* and corroborated by inscriptions and archaeological evidence.[27]

Continuous occupation of many ancient urban sites in the Iberian peninsula has made it more difficult to trace the evolution of cities in this region during late antiquity. At one of the more accessible, Emerita (Mérida), to the west in Lusitania, there is a range of material evidence for substantial investment in private housing throughout the fourth century and into the fifth, even if some of these structures increasingly encroached on public space; on the other hand, some of these residential quarters experienced major damage during the middle decades of the fifth century, a period when the city is known, from literary sources, to have been fought over by imperial and barbarian forces. At Tarraco (Tarragona) on the Mediterranean coast, the civic centre was maintained into the fifth century until, in the 440s, the paving was removed from a section of the forum, which became a pit for domestic rubbish, again implying the encroachment of private housing into public space. Elsewhere, at Caesaraugusta (Zaragoza), in the north, there is evidence for the deterioration of the city's infrastructure rather earlier, in the later fourth century, when, for example, all the city's sewers became silted up, and it is thought that this pattern was in fact more typical of cities in the region.[28]

In Gaul, the southern half of the region had been exposed to Roman influence for longer than the north, and so there was a stronger tradition of urbanism in the former. Nonetheless, a number of southern cities saw the construction of walled enclosures during the fourth century which encompassed much reduced portions of the urban settlements of earlier centuries and, significantly, excluded the established civic centres. In the case of Bordeaux, this shift in the city's centre of gravity was due to the pull of the river port, while in the case of Périgueux, it can be attributed to the desire to save money and labour by incorporating the city's amphitheatre into the wall-circuit.[29] While the influence of such practical considerations is understandable, shifts of this sort are nonetheless symbolic of changing priorities. Even at Arles, which particularly benefited

27. D. Pringle, *The Defence of Byzantine Africa from Justinian to the Arab Conquest*, Oxford: British Archaeological Reports, 1981; Leone, *Changing Townscapes*, 187–98.
28. M. Kulikowski, *Late Roman Spain and its Cities*, Baltimore: Johns Hopkins University Press, 2004, 85–129, with an overview in his 'The late Roman city in Spain' in Krause and Witschel, *Stadt*, 129–49.
29. Loseby, 'Cities of late antique Gaul', 73–5, 80–1.

from imperial patronage during the fourth century and became an administrative centre at the end of that century, the forum lost its paving and accompanying portico during the first half of the fifth century as simple commercial structures encroached on this public space; although the circus seems to have remained in sufficiently regular use for Frankish kings to watch chariot races there in the mid-sixth century (Procop. *Wars* 7.33.5), private housing was erected around its exterior.[30] A striking departure from this pattern was Marseille, which remained prosperous throughout the fifth and sixth centuries. There was little, if any, contraction of its city wall or of intramural habitation, and even evidence of extramural expansion; and archaeological and textual evidence confirms its role as a thriving emporium, channelling goods from Africa and the eastern Mediterranean up the Rhone valley. It was, however, the exception, which owed its good fortune primarily to its liminal location between the Mediterranean and the emerging Frankish kingdom, and its excellent harbour.[31]

Turning finally to Italy, the city of Rome itself remained in many respects unique and, together with cities which functioned as imperial capitals in the fourth or fifth centuries (Milan, Ravenna) or as royal capitals in the sixth century (Ravenna, Verona, Pavia), cannot be taken as a guide to more general trends in the physical evolution of Italian cities. In many of those cities which did not benefit from imperial, royal or senatorial patronage, it seems, on the one hand, that the traditional forum and paved street grid were nonetheless preserved at least through to the sixth century, but, on the other hand, that private investment in public buildings ceased at the end of the fourth century or in the early fifth century.[32] While Italian cities did not experience the growth which many eastern cities did during the fifth and sixth century, neither did they suffer the contraction which cities did in other regions of the west – at least, not until the imperial campaigns of the 540s against the Goths, followed closely by the Lombard invasion in the late 560s.[33]

---

30. M. Heijmans, *Arles durant l'antiquité tardive*, Rome: École française de Rome, 2004, 367–71.
31. S. T. Loseby, 'Marseille: a late antique success-story?', *JRS* 82 (1992), 165–85.
32. B. Ward-Perkins, *From Classical Antiquity to the Middle Ages: Urban Public Building in Northern and Central Italy, AD 300–850*, Oxford: Oxford University Press, 1984, 14–37, 179–86.
33. T. S. Brown, *Gentlemen and Officers: Imperial Administration and Aristocratic Power in Byzantine Italy, AD 554–800*, Rome: British School at Rome, 1984, 39–45.

This brief overview of a selection of sites from different parts of
the empire demonstrates the dangers of generalisation about the fate
of cities during late antiquity. While cities in the east tended to fare
better for longer than those in the west, there were exceptions in
both halves of the empire, often depending on the vulnerability of
a particular location to military or geophysical dangers, or alterna-
tively its favourable position vis-à-vis trade routes. These examples
also hint at some of the problems raised by employing the term
'decline' in the context of the urban history of late antiquity.
Clearly some cities were expanding and enjoying enhanced levels of
prosperity well into the sixth century. However, even for those cities
which were not so fortunate, the use of the term 'decline' can still be
challenged, on a number of grounds. The term is loaded with much
unhelpful baggage, and it is such a broad term which can be applied
to so many diagnostic features of urban well-being of varying
degrees of significance that its value as a descriptive term is
questionable.[34] Dissatisfaction with the term has in turn prompted
scholars increasingly to deploy alternative terminology, such as
'demonumentalisation' for changes to civic centres. Moreover, the
diagnostic features used to assess urban well-being are themselves
often more ambiguous in their implications than is often recognised.
Take the case of the construction of city walls, often seen as symptomatic of urban decline because they are assumed to have been
erected in response to military threats, because their construction
frequently included the use of *spolia* (which is taken to imply haste
in the face of such threats), and because they often enclosed a much
more restricted area of the city. However, while military insecurity
undoubtedly must have been a factor in many instances, fortifications could also be a statement of civic pride; there are instances
where *spolia* have been deployed in city walls with great care and
discrimination; and the walls did not necessarily mark the extent of
human habitation, since (as archaeological evidence often shows)
in some cases there were unoccupied areas within the walls, while
it was perfectly possible for some of a city's populace to live in
extramural suburbs.[35]

---

34. Cf. Wickham, *Framing*, 672–3, who lists eight different features which might be
characterised as symptomatic of urban decline, though need not indicate 'urban weak-
ness'. For a vigorous defence of the terminology of 'decline', see Liebeschuetz, *Decline*,
and 'Transformation and decline'.
35. Loseby, 'Cities of late antique Gaul', 76–9; Waelkens et al., 'Sagalassos', 220;
Kulikowski, *Late Roman Spain*, 210.

Running in tandem with all these developments was another over-arching trend with important implications for the debate about urban change – the Christianisation of cityscapes. The most visible manifestation of this was obviously the construction of churches, with leading citizens who might in the past have displayed their philanthropy to their community through contributing to new civic structures now redirecting their resources towards the construction of churches and related buildings such as hospices. Church resources were, of course, also directed into such structures, as well as related charitable activities – care for widows, orphans and the poor – which contributed to the growing prominence and influence of bishops in cities.[36] The other side of this development was the increasing neglect of temples, or even their destruction and subsequent replacement by churches. Again, the pace of change varied, as also its impact on urban topography. It has been observed that in the west, there was a tendency for churches to be built away from the traditional civic centre, with the result that the classical configuration of cities was lost more quickly than in the east, where churches tended to replace temples in the civic centre. While this marked a significant change to the civic centre, it also had the effect of preserving the broader layout of the city.[37]

Christianity also had potential implications for buildings related to public entertainment, such as theatres, amphitheatres and circuses/hippodromes, since Christian bishops and clergy usually regarded the events staged at such venues as antipathetic to Christian values and a distraction from church attendance. The plays, mimes and dancing presented in the theatre perpetuated familiarity with the deities of classical myth and exposed audiences to storylines and performances of questionable morality (cf. p. 13 above), while the chariot-racing held in the circus or hippodrome, and the gambling which accompanied it, was evidently an obsessive preoccupation for many (cf. Figs 14–15). Augustine told his congregation that 'the absurdity of spectacles' was 'a fever of the soul' comparable to avarice, lust and hatred (*Serm.* 9.8.10 [= *PL*

36. P. Brown, *Poverty and Leadership in the Later Roman Empire*, Hanover, NH: University Press of New England, 2002; R. D. Finn, *Almsgiving in the Later Roman Empire: Christian Promotion and Practice, 313–450*, Oxford: Oxford University Press, 2006.
37. B. Ward-Perkins, 'Reconfiguring sacred space: from pagan shrines to Christian churches' in G. Brands and H.-G. Severin (eds), *Die spätantike Stadt und ihre Christian-isierung*, Wiesbaden: Reichert, 2003, 285–90; Kulikowski, *Late Roman Spain*, 220–40.

Figure 14 A gambling machine, with reliefs of chariot racing (77 × 55 × 57 cm) (marble, Constantinople, c. 500). This was an appropriate device to find at the hippodrome where money was wagered on the outcome of the chariot races; here coloured balls would be rolled down the tracks and through the holes, with gamblers placing bets on which ball would emerge first at the back. The relief at the base shows a four-horse chariot in pursuit of another, with further reliefs on the sides depicting other aspects of the races. © bpk/Skulpturensammlung und Museum für Byzantinische Kunst, SMB/Jürgen Liepe

38.83]),[38] while John Chrysostom, preaching in Antioch, emphasised the distortion of priorities they induced:

> There are those who are in a state of excited distraction over the spectacle of horse racing and are able to state with complete accuracy the names, the herd, the pedigree, the place of origin, and the rearing of the horses, as well as their age, their performance on the track, which horse drawn up against which other horse will be victorious, which horse will begin best from which starting-gate, and which charioteer will be victorious over the course and outrun the opposition. And no less than these, there are those who devote their time to the theatre and display even greater madness over those who behave in an unseemly manner in the theatre – I mean dancers and

38. On Augustine's response to the challenge of spectacles, see further R. A. Markus, *The End of Ancient Christianity*, Cambridge: Cambridge University Press, 1990, 107–23, and D. G. Van Slyke, 'The devil and his pomps in fifth-century Carthage: renouncing *spectacula* with spectacular imagery', *DOP* 59 (2005), 53–72.

Figure 15 A contorniate with inlaid decoration depicting a four-horse chariot (4.3 cm diameter) (later fourth century), found in the amphitheatre at Trier. Contorniates were bronze medallions with raised edges, usually bearing images associated with success in the games, and are thought to have been distributed by aristocrats to the urban populace during such events. The name in the upper label, Pvrfyri (Porphyry), may refer to the charioteer, while that in the lower label, Fontanus, may be the name of the lead horse. © Rheinisches Landesmuseum Trier

> those who perform mimes – detailing their ancestry, place of origin, upbringing and all the rest. But if we ask them how many and what letters Paul wrote, they do not know the number; or if some know the number, they are quite at a loss when asked the cities which were the recipients of the letters. (*In illud, Salutate Priscillam* 1 [= PG 51.188])

Despite ecclesiastical opposition, however, the continued popularity of spectacles meant that the structures in which these events were staged were generally maintained for much of late antiquity, whether from imperial or (in the post-imperial west) royal funds, or by local patrons, so preserving one of the distinguishing features of the classical cityscape.[39] In addition to providing a time-honoured distraction from sources of dissatisfaction among the urban masses, these events also presented an opportunity for the populace of a city

39. Ward-Perkins, *From Classical Antiquity*, 92–118.

to voice their complaints to the emperor or his officials through the
mass chanting of acclamations, and for a response to be given[40] –
thereby demonstrating the continuing relevance of cities to the
political dynamics of the late Roman world. Such opportunities
to voice popular discontent could serve as a valuable safety valve
for rising tensions, although as the next section shows, it was not a
guaranteed solution.

'City-destroying civil strife'

Bouts of mass unrest were an inevitable phenomenon in cities of the
Roman world. Food shortages were perhaps the most predictable
stimulus, with the largest city – Rome – potentially the most vulnerable in this respect.[41] As long as Rome was the emperor's primary
residence during the first two to three centuries AD, measures were
in place to minimise the risks of hunger-induced public disorder, but
with emperors ceasing to reside in Rome for most of the fourth
century and much of the fifth, there was no longer the same impera-
tive to guarantee supplies. It is hardly surprising, then, that food
riots appear to have become a much more common phenomenon
in the city in this period, with the prefect of the city shouldering
the responsibility and bearing the brunt of the anger of hungry
inhabitants.[42] Nor was Constantinople immune from such problems,
at least initially, despite becoming a permanent imperial residence
from the late fourth century onwards. In 409, rioting over food
shortages resulted in the burning of the headquarters of the prefect
of the city and the dragging of his carriage through the city streets;
the government quickly found 500 lbs of gold to purchase emer-
gency supplies of grain, and subsequently established a permanent
reserve of gold to deal with any future food crisis in the capital.[43]

---

40. Alan Cameron, *Circus Factions: Blues and Greens at Rome and Byzantium*, Oxford:
Clarendon Press, 1976, 157–83; C. Roueché, *Performers and Partisans at Aphrodisias in
the Roman and Late Roman Periods*, London: *JRS* Monographs 6, 1993.
41. The heading of this section is taken from *IAph2007* 8.407 (from a fragmentary
inscription at Aphrodisias honouring an individual [perhaps a governor] who, probably
during the fifth century, 'drove out city-destroying civil strife': discussion in Roueché,
Aphrodisias, V.37).
42. P. Garnsey and C. Humfress, *The Evolution of the Late Antique World*, Cambridge:
Orchard Press, 2001, 110–14; cf. also pp. 62–3 above.
43. Marcellinus, *Chron. Marcell. s.a.* 409, *Chron. Pasch. s.a.* 412, *Cod. Theod.* 14.16.1
(409), 14.16.3 (434), with discussion in Garnsey and Humfress, *Evolution*, 112–13.
Malalas, *Chron.* 488, records a shortage of bread in 556 which led to chants against the
emperor in the hippodrome, though not, apparently, to violence.

Nor was grain the only commodity of importance: in 515 shortages of bread and oil in Alexandria led to rioting and the lynching of the senior imperial official in the city (Malalas, *Chron.* 401–2, *Exc. de Insid. fr.* 41).

Since the main burden of taxation fell on the inhabitants of rural areas, it was less common for fiscal demands to be a source of urban disturbances. Nonetheless, it did provoke one famous episode, in Antioch, when, in 387, it was announced that taxes were to be levied on the city. Although the episode is comparatively well documented (particularly from a series of sermons by John Chrysostom and speeches by Libanius), the sources are vague about the taxes in question, but the reaction suggests they represented some sort of significant additional imposition. In the ensuing rioting, the wooden portraits and bronze statues of the imperial family outside the residence of the governor were pulled down, mutilated and dragged through the streets, and public buildings were torched. Imperial troops then intervened, arresting and executing rioters identified as ringleaders, while reports were sent to the emperor in Constantinople. Destruction of imperial portraits and statues, which embodied the emperor's presence in the city, was tantamount to treason (cf. p. 108), so Theodosius' response was awaited with trepidation. Following the arrival of imperial commissioners, the public baths, theatres and hippodromes were closed, the city was deprived of its metropolitan status, and the city councillors were arrested, tried and sentenced to death, on the grounds that they bore the ultimate responsibility for what had happened. Significantly, it was the bishop of Antioch who led a delegation from the city to the capital to plead for the emperor's clemency, while local monks interceded with the commissioners; their efforts were successful, with the lives of the councillors spared and the city pardoned.[44]

There is no surprise in hunger and taxes giving rise to urban unrest in late antiquity, since these had been factors in earlier periods of Roman history. However, there were also a number of novel factors contributing to civic disturbances in late antiquity. In particular, there were many instances of religiously inspired disorder, on the one hand, and, on the other, many instances of violence arising from the activities of the so-called circus 'factions' – both factors which had been far less prominent in earlier periods.

---

44. D. R. French, 'Rhetoric and the rebellion of AD 387 in Antioch', *Historia* 47 (1998), 468–84.

While the element of intolerance in polytheistic Roman religion of the pre-Constantinian period should not be underestimated,[45] exclusionist religious attitudes intensified during late antiquity and generated much urban unrest. That intensification derived partly from Christianity's monotheistic theology, partly from competition between different groups within the church, and partly from the polarisation of attitudes provoked by Julian's attempt to undo the effects of Constantine's support for the church.[46] It manifested itself in public confrontations between pagans and Christians, most famously the events resulting in the destruction of the Serapeum in Alexandria in 391/2 (p. 54 above), but also in incidents which are perhaps less well known such as an episode in Sufes in north Africa in 399, when the destruction of a statue of Hercules by Christians resulted in rioting by local pagans during which sixty Christians died (August. *Ep.* 50),[47] and the fracas in Alexandria in 486 between pagan and Christian students which resulted in the sacking of an extramural shrine of Isis.[48] It was also evident in violent confrontations between rival Christian groups.[49] Episcopal elections provided recurrent flashpoints. In Rome there were disturbances between the supporters of different candidates, most famously in 366 when more than a hundred died in the violence (Amm. Marc. 27.3.13, *Coll. Avell.* 1), but also in 418 (*Coll. Avell.* 14–37). There were also public disturbances in Constantinople after the deposition of John Chrysostom in 403 (Sozom. *Hist. eccl.* 8.22); and the appointment of a pro-Chalcedonian bishop to Alexandria in 451 led to rioting which required the intervention of imperial troops, who nonetheless proved unable to prevent the lynching of the bishop in

---

45. P. Garnsey, 'Religious toleration in classical antiquity' in W. J. Sheils (ed.), *Persecution and Toleration* (= *SCH* 21), Woodbridge: Boydell, 1984, 1–27.

46. For discussion of some of the issues, see H. A. Drake, 'Intolerance, religious violence, and political legitimacy in late antiquity', *Journal of the American Academy of Religion* 79 (2011), 193–235; also M. Gaddis, *'There is no crime for those who have Christ': Religious Violence in the Christian Roman Empire*, Berkeley: University of California Press, 2005.

47. Cf. also August. *Epp.* 90–1, 103–4, for similar violence between pagans and Christians in the city of Calama in 408.

48. E. J. Watts, *Riot in Alexandria: Tradition and Group Dynamics in Late Antique Pagan and Christian Communities*, Berkeley: University of California Press, 2010.

49. The ongoing controversy between Catholic and Donatist Christians in north Africa generated much violence, particularly associated with the so-called *circumcelliones*, but their activities focused on rural areas, rather than cities: see B. D. Shaw, *Sacred Violence: African Christians and Sectarian Hatred in the Age of Augustine*, Cambridge: Cambridge University Press, 2011.

457 (Evagrius, *Hist. eccl.* 2.5, 8). The frequent exiling of heterodox
bishops by emperors in this period seems to have been a strategy for
removing them from their support base, so reducing the likelihood
of their becoming a focus for urban unrest.[50]

The other new source of urban unrest in late antiquity was the
circus 'factions'. In earlier centuries, there had been four factions,
identified by different colours – red, white, blue and green – and they
had been responsible for providing horses and chariots for racing in
the circus (Latin) or hippodrome (Greek) of major cities. By the fifth
century, however, a number of important changes had occurred.
First, two of the factions – the red and white – had become much less
important, with the blue and green the dominant groups. Secondly,
the factions had become responsible not only for the provision of
chariot-racing, but also for other forms of public entertainment,
such as productions for the theatre (plays, mimes, pantomimes).
Thirdly, the role of the factions increasingly extended beyond
provision of entertainment to the orchestration of popular opinion
in the form of chanting and acclamations at the hippodrome and
other venues, as well as during imperial accessions. Fourthly,
although there was a notorious hippodrome-related riot in Thessalonica in 390,[51] it was only from the 440s onwards that the Blues
and the Greens became involved in regular episodes of violence in
major cities in the eastern empire. The following account of an
episode during the reign of Anastasius (probably from the year
507) illustrates some of these developments, and the destruction that
could result:

> During his reign, the supporters of the Greens at Constantinople
> appealed to the emperor, while the chariot-races were being held, for
> the release of some people who had been arrested by the city prefect
> for throwing stones. The emperor did not yield to them but grew
> angry and ordered troops to attack them, and there was great
> disorder. The supporters advanced against the palace guard, and
> approached the imperial box and they threw stones at the emperor
> Anastasius. Among them was a man named Maurus who threw a
> stone at the emperor, who stood up and dodged it. The palace guard,
> having seen the man's boldness, went for him and dismembered him
> limb by limb, and so he breathed his last. The crowd, which was
> hemmed in, set fire to the Chalke, as it is known, of the hippodrome,

---

50. Garnsey and Humfress, *Evolution*, 143–5.
51. Details and references in N. B. McLynn, *Ambrose of Milan: Church and Court in a
Christian Capital*, Berkeley: University of California Press, 1994, 315–30.

and the colonnade was burned as far as the imperial box, and also the public colonnade, as far as the Hexahippion and the Forum of Constantine, was completely burned and destroyed, collapsing throughout its length. After many had been arrested and punished, there was quiet, when Plato, who was patron of the Green faction, was appointed as city prefect. (Malalas, *Chron.* 394–5 [tr. E. Jeffreys et al., with revisions])

Scholars originally tried to account for this sort of violence by seeing the factions as championing a particular Christological stance – Blue Chalcedonians, Green anti-Chalcedonians – or a particular social group – Blue aristocrats, Green non-aristocrats – but it has been recognised for some time now that such identifications do not account for all the evidence.[52] However, the proposed alternative – that the violence was simply a case of sporting hooliganism between rival partisans – has also been seen as too simplistic an explanation.[53] It has been argued by some that the rise of the factions reflected the decay of traditional civic institutions and the emergence of government by the notables,[54] but this was irrelevant to Constantinople, where many of the factional disturbances occurred, and the most plausible analysis relates factional violence to the patronage of the factions by prominent figures, above all emperors whose authority needed affirmation, starting with Theodosius II (408–50).[55] As he was an emperor with no military credentials who spent nearly all his life in the imperial palace, patronage of the Greens during the 440s offered him an opportunity to harness the potential of the faction to influence the urban populace of Constantinople and other eastern cities.[56] Needless to say, this could be a dangerous game which sometimes got out of hand, as Justinian in particular was to discover in 532 (pp. 247–50 below).

52. This was the achievement of Cameron, *Circus Factions*; see also Rouché, *Partisans and Performers*.
53. Liebeschuetz, *Decline*, 253, 259, notes, e.g., that factional violence did not always involve Blues against Greens: sometimes the two groups co-operated, or one remained neutral, and sometimes they did show religious preferences.
54. Liebeschuetz, *Decline*, 213–18, 248–57.
55. In the episode quoted above, it is an aristocrat, Plato, who is described as patron of the Greens, reflecting the fact that, unusually for an emperor in this period, Anastasius took a deliberate decision early in his reign not to support either the Blues or Greens (Malalas, *Chron.* 393).
56. M. Whitby, 'The violence of the circus factions' in K. Hopwood (ed.), *Organised Crime in Antiquity*, London: Duckworth, 1999, 229–53; M. Whitby, 'Factions, bishops, violence and urban decline' in Krause and Witschel, *Stadt*, 441–61.

Cities, education and culture

Cities were synonymous with civilisation in the Roman world not only because of the architecture which adorned them and provided facilities such as bathing complexes and entertainment buildings, but also because they were the focal point for the maintenance of classical literary culture through education.[57] Judging by the evidence surviving from Roman Egypt, elementary education could be available in rural communities (though this should not be taken to mean that basic literacy was widespread), but education at a level beyond this could only be acquired in an urban context. This remained the case during late antiquity, as did the assumption that learning was a characteristic of urban society, reflected in the comment of a well-educated inhabitant of fifth-century Gaul: 'the educated are as far superior to rustics as humans are to beasts' (Sid. Apoll. *Ep.* 4.17.2). For those whose families had the resources, education beyond the basic level involved two main stages: first, studying under a grammarian to acquire, on the one hand, a sound grasp of the grammar and pronunciation of literary language and, on the other, close familiarity with the canonical poetic texts; and secondly, studying under a rhetorician to acquire detailed knowledge of rhetorical texts and handbooks, followed by practical instruction and experience in composing and delivering speeches. A prosopography of grammarians in late antiquity confirms that they were to be found in cities and towns, while, judging by what is known of the careers of individual rhetoricians and a law of the Emperor Gratian concerning arrangements in Gaul (*Cod. Theod.* 13.3.11), teachers of rhetoric usually practised in provincial capitals.[58] Ideally, this education would equip the student to a high level in both Greek and Latin, but increasingly during late antiquity this could not always be taken for granted.[59]

As has often been observed, the educational curriculum was a very narrow one, but it served to distinguish and unify the empire's elite through the specialised knowledge acquired, as well as the friend-

---

57. For good overviews of the subject in late antiquity, see Averil Cameron, 'Education and literary culture' in *CAH*[2] 13.665–707, and R. Browning, 'Education in the Roman empire' in *CAH*[2] 14.855–83.

58. Prosopography: R. A. Kaster, *Guardians of Language: The Grammarian and Society in Late Antiquity*, Berkeley: University of California Press, 1988, 20–1, 463–78; rhetoricians: Jones, *LRE*, 998.

59. For the status of Latin in the sixth-century east, see the references at p. 256 n.25 below.

ships and contacts made during student days.[60] In late antiquity, this
education became the usual prerequisite for service in the imperial
bureaucracy, and thus was the entrée to some degree of influence and
guaranteed remuneration. Gaining such an education for their son(s)
therefore became the goal of ambitious parents from more modest
backgrounds, of whom the future bishop and theologian Augustine
is perhaps the most famous example. Born in the north African town
of Thagaste to a father who owned only a little land and a few
slaves, Augustine moved first to the regional centre of Madauros,
then to Carthage, to acquire the education which eventually became
his passport to better things in Rome and Milan. The imperial
government and city councils did provide funding for some posts
for grammarians and rhetoricians – the Emperor Theodosius II,
for example, famously established more than thirty such posts in
Constantinople in 425 (*Cod. Theod.* 14.9.3, *Cod. Iust.* 11.1.9.1) –
but students were also expected to pay fees to their teacher, which
limited the pool of potential students significantly. Augustine's
education was delayed for a year while his father saved enough
money to send him on from Madauros to Carthage, and when his
father died soon after, Augustine was only able to continue his
studies there due to the generosity of a wealthy neighbour (August.
Conf. 2.3.5, *C. acad.* 2.2.3).

   The most detailed insights into the world of advanced education
from the perspective of the teacher emerge from the writings of
the fourth-century rhetorician Libanius, the son of an Antiochene
decurion, who studied in Antioch and Athens, and briefly held teaching posts in Athens and Constantinople before returning to Antioch,
where he established a reputation as one of the pre-eminent teachers
in the empire. His speeches and voluminous correspondence
illuminate both the educational process and his relationships with
students, which endured well after they had completed their
studies.[61] The student's perspective is perhaps best represented by
Zachariah's biography of the anti-Chalcedonian bishop Severus,
which recounts student life in the late fifth century in Alexandria
and Berytus (Beirut) – the latter a major centre for the study of law –

---

60. P. Brown, *Power and Persuasion in Late Antiquity*, Madison: University of
Wisconsin Press, 1992, ch. 2; E. Watts, *City and School in Late Antique Athens and
Alexandria*, Berkeley: University of California Press, 2006, 7–11.
61. R. Cribiore, *The School of Libanius in Late Antique Antioch*, Princeton: Princeton
University Press, 2007. For a western, Latin perspective, there is much evidence about
Bordeaux as an educational centre in the fourth-century: see Kaster, *Guardians*, 100–6.

especially clashes between pagan and Christian students and their teachers.[62]

As these incidents imply, education was not immune from the religious controversies of late antiquity; indeed, education was itself a culturally contested area. The Emperor Julian's ban on Christian teachers, though short-lived, politicised education as a religious issue and forced Christian leaders, many of whom had themselves been the beneficiaries of a traditional classical education, to review their attitudes. In doing so, they could draw on earlier pronouncements on the subject, but those pronouncements did not speak with a unified voice and anticipated an east/west divergence. In the early third century, the north African lawyer and theologian Tertullian had famously posed the rhetorical question, 'What has Athens to do with Jerusalem?' (*De praescr. haeret.* 7), whereas the Alexandrian theologian Origen did not regard pagan learning as posing an inevitable threat to Christian principles.[63] This latter 'sense of easy and sophisticated superiority' informed the views of leading Christian figures in the east during the fourth, fifth and sixth centuries, perhaps most famously in Basil of Caesarea's *Address to Young Men: How They Might Profit from Greek Literature.* Not an uncritical endorsement of classical literature or education, it nonetheless allowed a place within the formation of Christians for such study, since it could provide an outline of virtue which Christian teaching could then develop in detail.[64] Although the Emperor Justinian (527–65) was to take a strong line against the teaching of philosophy in Athens (p. 276 below), the prevailing attitude on the part of Christian leaders in the east was to remain one of accommodation with traditional literature and learning.

In the west, on the other hand, there was much greater ambivalence, reflected most famously in Jerome's report of a dream in which he stood before the heavenly judge and was told, 'You are a Ciceronian, not a Christian!' (*Ep.* 22.30). The fullest discussion of the subject was developed by Augustine in his *De Doctrina*

62. There is a recent translation of the life (which is preserved only in a Syriac version) by L. Ambjörn (Piscataway, NJ: Gorgias Press, 2008), with discussion of the author and work in G. Greatrex et al., *The Chronicle of Pseudo-Zachariah Rhetor: Church and War in Late Antiquity*, Liverpool: Liverpool University Press, 2011, 4–8, 15–18.
63. Kaster, *Guardians*, 74.
64. Text and commentary in N. G. Wilson, *St. Basil on the Value of Greek Literature*, London: Duckworth, 1975; discussion in Kaster, *Guardians*, 77–8, N. McLynn, 'The manna from uncle: Basil of Caesarea's Address to Young Men' in C. Kelly et al. (eds), *Unclassical Traditions* I, Cambridge: Cambridge Philological Society, 2010, 106–18.

Christiana ('On Christian education'). While not as hostile or uncompromising in his attitude to classical learning as Tertullian, he was much more dismissive of its value than eastern commentators. Although western Christians of aristocratic background, such as Sidonius Apollinaris, remained comfortable with their cultural inheritance, the prevailing attitude in Christian circles in the west was much more guarded and sceptical.[65] Even so, it was not this attitude which was primarily responsible for the shrinkage of educational opportunities in the west during the fifth and sixth century, nor was it a by-product of the new barbarian elites who gradually came to control the west, since they were for the most part appreciative of classical literary culture (Theoderic the Ostrogoth had, after all, been educated in Constantinople).[66] It was, rather, a consequence of political and economic uncertainty, the fragmentation of centralised imperial authority, and the deterioration of city and personal finances. Against this background, ecclesiastical institutions – above all, monasteries – increasingly emerged as the focal point for education. The classical heritage was not lost sight of, but it was firmly subordinated to Christian priorities. Perhaps the most explicit articulation of this approach was that of the Roman senator and servant of the Gothic regime in Italy, Cassiodorus. After being prevented by Justinian's invasion of Italy in 535 (pp. 262–3 below) from establishing the Christian educational institution he had envisaged at Rome, he eventually realised a version of his plan on his estate, Vivarium, in Calabria. Beginning in the early 550s, he founded two monasteries which included a library and a *scriptorium* for translating works from Greek into Latin. He also wrote his *Institutions*: the first part focused on guidance in reading and understanding the Bible, while the second part preserved a summary of what he considered to be important aspects of the classical literary heritage. He thereby provided both a practical model and an accompanying handbook which were to prove influential in the medieval west.[67]

---

65. Kaster, *Guardians*, 80–95; text and translation of Augustine, *De Doctrina Christiana*, by R. P. H. Green (Oxford: Oxford University Press, 1996).
66. Cf. Y. Hen, *Roman Barbarians: The Royal Court and Culture in the Early Medieval West*, London: Palgrave Macmillan, 2007, and pp. 184–6 above.
67. J. J. O'Donnell, *Cassiodorus*, Berkeley: University of California Press, 1979 (www9.georgetown.edu/faculty/jod/texts/cassbook/toc.html), 177–222; translation and discussion of the *Institutions of Divine and Secular Learning* by J. W. Halporn and M. Vessey (Liverpool: Liverpool University Press, 2004).

CHAPTER 11

Economic patterns

Contexts, evidence and issues

Longer-term economic trends form the often indistinct backdrop to the more colourful *histoire événementielle* of political, military and religious affairs during late antiquity, but their importance should not therefore be underestimated.[1] Indeed, for the vast majority of the empire's inhabitants, whose life revolved around gaining a livelihood from cultivation of the land, micro-economic survival was their daily *histoire événementielle*, played out at a localised level. At the same time, it is understandable that, in the attempt to understand the momentous changes which the Roman empire experienced during late antiquity, the primary focus of scholarly attention in this field should be macro-economic patterns. In the past there was a tendency to present a fundamentally pessimistic view of the state of the late Roman economy, particularly when compared with the prosperous condition of the empire in the early centuries AD. The increased burden of taxation from the early fourth century onwards was regarded as having rendered agricultural production less profitable, prompting widespread abandonment of land (the so-called *agri deserti*); another supposed symptom of straitened economic circumstances was imperial legislation tying individuals and their descendants to their occupation, including an important category of

---

1. Helpful overviews of economic developments during different phases of late antiquity include the following: P. Garnsey and C. R. Whittaker, 'Rural life in the late Roman empire' and 'Trade, industry and the urban economy' in *CAH*² 13.277–337; B. Ward-Perkins, 'Land, labour and settlement' and 'Specialized production and exchange' in *CAH*² 14.315–91; S. T. Loseby, 'The Mediterranean economy' in *CMH* 1, 605–38, and 'Post-Roman economies' in W. Scheidel (ed.), *The Cambridge Companion to the Roman Economy*, Cambridge: Cambridge University Press (forthcoming); in rather more detail, C. Wickham, *Framing the Early Middle Ages: Europe and the Mediterranean, 400–800*, Oxford: Oxford University Press, 2005, 259–302, 383–588, 693–824. P. F. Bang, 'Trade and empire: in search of organizing concepts for the Roman economy', *P&P* 195 (2007), 3–54, helpfully sets the late Roman economy in the context of wider debate about ancient economic history.

agricultural workers (*coloni*); and it was taken for granted that inter-regional commerce was minimal.[2] In recent decades, however, this pessimistic view has been revised towards a more nuanced, and increasingly more positive, assessment.

The old paradigm was one based primarily on textual evidence. The shift to a more positive view has been due, on the one hand, to the introduction of an ever-increasing volume of archaeological data into the picture, and, on the other, to a greater awareness of the limitations of the textual evidence. Some of that evidence comprises anecdotes taken from narrative sources such as histories and saints' lives. On the subject of trade, for example, Ammianus Marcellinus (29.4.4) records an episode from the early 370s when Roman forces operating beyond the Rhine chanced upon traders leading slaves for sale, while Procopius (*Wars* 3.24.11) refers to an incident when a merchant ship set sail from Carthage on the day the city was captured from the Vandals by Belisarius' Roman forces, and brought unusually rapid news of that momentous event to Spain. Both episodes are of potential interest to economic historians, but they highlight one of the problems which such anecdotal evidence often presents, namely a frequent lack of sufficient detail: Ammianus does not specify the origins of the traders or the slaves, the number of slaves, or their destination, while Procopius does not mention the origin or cargo of the merchant ship. Further issues are the bias of anecdotal evidence for trade towards luxury goods,[3] and the uncertainty about an anecdote's typicality, which renders generalisation hazardous; 'it functions best as a record of possibility'.[4]

Other categories of textual evidence potentially offer a sounder basis for generalisation, but are still not without their problems. The bulk of the evidence for the status of *coloni* (p. 232 below) and the phenomenon of *agri deserti* (p. 235 below) derives from legal sources, above all the law codes of Theodosius II (p. 109 above) and of Justinian (p. 251 below). While these might appear to be a more helpful genre of source, because they are not literary and present

---

2. For an overview of older scholarship, see B. Ward-Perkins, 'Jones and the late Roman economy' in D. Gwynn (ed.), *A. H. M. Jones and the Later Roman Empire*, Leiden: Brill, 2008, 193–209.

3. Wickham, *Framing*, 701.

4. S. T. Loseby, 'The ceramic data and the transformation of the Roman world' in M. Bonifay et al. (eds), *LRCW2: Late Roman Coarse Wares, Cooking Wares and Amphorae in the Mediterranean*, Oxford: British Archaeological Reports, 2007, 1–14, at 4 (with further valuable discussion of these issues).

imperial pronouncements with general application, they still need to be handled with care. The individual laws may have been responding to exceptional situations, the normative character of the codes could oversimplify existential complexities, and the process of editing and systematisation involved in codification may have 'imposed a false coherence upon the evidence and obscured the circumstances surrounding many of the texts'.[5]

The most valuable category of textual material for the economic history of the period is documentary evidence, especially papyri. Inscriptions have some contribution to make, such as the customs tariff from Anazarbus in Cilicia which records tolls on a range of products in the fifth or sixth century (*SEG* 37 [1987] 1257), or a reference, in a petition to the Emperor Justinian, to new land at Miletus reclaimed from the sea, presumably through the deposit of alluvial soil in the delta of the River Maeander, which should now be subject to taxation (*AE* 2004.1410); but these still tend to be isolated examples.[6] More plentiful are papyrus documents, mostly, but not exclusively, from Egypt.[7] Of particular significance are the fourth-century land registers from the Hermopolite nome,[8] the 'archive' of papyri relating to the estates of the Apion family near the Middle Egyptian city of Oxyrhynchus – more than 250 texts comprising letters, petitions, contracts, accounts and receipts, mostly from the sixth century[9] – and the sixth-century land and tax registers from the Middle Egyptian village of Aphrodito.[10] While some of these texts have been known for a century or more, there was a tendency of old to regard Egypt as exceptional and so downplay their wider significance, while many of the texts have only been

5. C. Grey, 'Revisiting the "problem" of *agri deserti* in the late Roman empire', *JRA* 20 (2007), 362–76, at 374.
6. The various important inscriptions recording portions of Diocletian's Prices Edict and the different categories of inscription relating to the Diocletianic census derive, of course, from the period before the starting date of this volume.
7. Late Roman papyri have also been recovered from Nessana in the Negev and from Petra: for these and others, see H. M. Cotton et al., 'The papyrology of the Roman Near East: a survey', *JRS* 85 (1995), 214–35.
8. A. K. Bowman, 'Landholding in the Hermopolite nome in the fourth century AD', *JRS* 75 (1985), 137–63; R. S. Bagnall, 'Landholding in late Roman Egypt: the distribution of wealth', *JRS* 82 (1992), 128–49.
9. P. Sarris, *Economy and Society in the Age of Justinian*, Cambridge: Cambridge University Press, 2006, 24–8.
10. J. Gascou and L. MacCoull, 'Le cadastre d'Aphrodito', *T&M* 10 (1987), 103–51; C. Zuckerman, *Du village à l'empire: autour du registre fiscal d'Aphrodito (525/526)*, Paris: Centre de recherché d'histoire et civilisation de Byzance, 2004, with review-discussion by J. G. Keenan in *BASP* 42 (2005), 285–97.

published and analysed more recently.[11] To the papyri can be added a number of caches of wooden tablets from different parts of northern Africa: forty-five found in southern Algeria in the early twentieth century which record the legal transactions of tenant farmers in the late fifth century (the so-called *Tablettes Albertini*), and eight tablets found in the 1980s at the village of Kellis in the Dakhleh Oasis to the west of the upper Nile which preserve, in more than 1,700 lines of text, a mid-fourth-century agricultural account book.[12]

For all the valuable insights which these documentary texts offer, however, their contribution to an understanding of the late Roman economy remains less significant than that of archaeological data. There are two particular areas of archaeological investigation which have added enormously to an understanding of macro-economic patterns. First, large-scale field surveys have provided a much better sense of the distribution of rural settlement in various parts of the empire during late antiquity, which in turn has major implications for the vitality or otherwise of the regional rural economy.[13] Secondly, analysis of ceramic evidence has been of critical importance on a number of fronts. Certain types of good-quality tableware, above all African Red Slip (ARS) ware, have been found in significant quantities in locations around the Mediterranean far removed from their places of manufacture, as also have the amphorae in which olive oil and wine were shipped. Both categories of pottery shed important light on interregional exchange networks, while the former is invaluable for insights into an aspect of the manufacturing economy, and the latter for major agricultural products. What makes ceramic evidence particularly significant is that it is found throughout the empire and in sufficiently large quantities to make statistical analysis meaningful, while extensive study of typology and

---

11. For a reiteration of the importance of not treating Egypt as exceptional, see R. S. Bagnall, 'Evidence and models for the economy in Roman Egypt' in J. G. Manning and I. Morris (eds) *The Ancient Economy: Evidence and Models*, Stanford: Stanford University Press, 2005, 187–204.
12. C. Courtois et al. (eds), *Tablettes Albertini: Actes privés de l'epoque vandale*, Paris: Arts et métiers graphiques, 1952, with discussion in A. Merrills and R. Miles, *The Vandals*, Oxford: Wiley-Blackwell, 2010, 159–62; R. S. Bagnall et al. (eds), *The Kellis Agricultural Account Book (P. Kell. IV Gr.96)*, Oxford: Oxbow, 1997.
13. For an overview of recent work, see A. Chavarría and T. Lewit, 'Archaeological research on the late antique countryside: a bibliographic essay' in W. Bowden et al. (eds), *Recent Research on the Late Antique Countryside*, Leiden: Brill, 2004, 3–51.

composition means that the approximate date and provenance of some wares can now be determined with relative confidence.[14]

Of course, there remain important limitations in the utility of archaeological evidence: wooden settlement structures in the countryside are much less easy to detect, amphorae were not the only type of container used in late antiquity – perishable materials such as wood, skins and sacking were also employed – and since some important products were themselves perishable, such as grain and cloth, and were not transported in amphorae, their circulation is effectively irretrievable. Recognition of these limitations should not, however, be allowed to detract from the overall significance of archaeological evidence for understanding the late Roman economy. Large-scale field survey and sophisticated analysis of ceramics are both developments of recent decades which were not available to scholars working within the old pessimistic paradigm, and it is the gradual injection of the results of this work into the debate about the economy during late antiquity which has played the most important role in changing perspectives.

The late Roman countryside

Patterns of land-holding in the late Roman countryside were very varied, arising from the influence of the past, of power relations and of climate and topography. Most conspicuous were the large estates of the wealthy, and the largest land-holder of all was, of course, the emperor. The imperial office had been acquiring land from the time of Augustus, starting with the public lands of the Republic, and regularly supplemented thereafter by bequests and confiscations. Constantine added temple lands and Constantius II the public lands of cities. Julian reversed these measures, but they were soon reinstituted by Valentinian and Valens, although a third of civic lands was subsequently returned to cities. The size of imperial land-holdings is unknown, but the few provinces or city territories for which a figure is known or can be calculated suggest holdings of the order of 15 per cent of the relevant area. Administration of the imperial lands was overseen by the count of the *res privata*, and the income which accrued from rents was at the personal disposal of the emperor,

---

14. Loseby, 'Ceramic data', 1–3; B. Ward-Perkins, *The Fall of Rome and the End of Civilization*, Oxford: Oxford University Press, 2005, 184–7; Wickham, *Framing*, 702–6.

allowing him to exercise patronage through the bestowal of material largesse.[15]

The senatorial aristocracy of Rome were also major land-holders in the west, with many of them owning estates in Italy and across the western provinces (pp. 66–7 above). Perhaps the most famous example from this period was Melania the Younger, descendant of a consul (Antonius Marcellinus, 341), and possessor of property in Italy, Sicily, north Africa, Spain and Britain which apparently generated an annual income of 120,000 *solidi* – until she sold it all, gave the proceeds to charity and became an ascetic in Palestine in the early fifth century (*PLRE* 1.593). Families such as Melania's had usually accumulated their land-holdings over many generations, but late antiquity witnessed the emergence alongside them of a new landed elite, in the form of those who gained aristocratic status and rewards through service in the imperial bureaucracy (p. 78 above). This so-called 'service aristocracy' was particularly prominent in the east, and it is in the east that there is the best evidence for their acquisition of property (no doubt in part through imperial generosity), usually in the locale where they had their roots. The best-known case is that of the Apiones, successive generations of whom held high imperial office during the fifth and sixth centuries, while at the same time building up substantial land-holdings in the vicinity of the Egyptian city of Oxyrhynchus.[16] Another new player in the arena of large-scale land-holding was the church. Constantine famously gave a substantial number of estates in Italy to the church to provide an income for the upkeep of church buildings and services, and in due course, as the elite increasingly aligned themselves with Christianity, they followed the imperial lead in bequeathing landed property to the church.[17]

The evidence for estates is primarily textual. Archaeological field surveys, on the other hand, have been important in helping to gauge

---

15. Jones, *LRE*, 411–27; M. Decker, *Tilling the Hateful Earth: Agricultural Production and Trade in the Late Antique East*, Oxford: Oxford University Press, 2009, 30–3.

16. Sarris, *Economy and Society*, 17–24, with a response to critics in 'The early Byzantine economy in context: aristocratic property and economic growth reconsidered', *Early Medieval Europe* 19 (2011), 255–84. For similar estates elsewhere in Egypt and the east, see respectively Sarris, *Economy and Society*, 90–5, 115–30, J. Banaji, *Agrarian Change in Late Antiquity: Gold, Labour and Aristocratic Dominance*, rev. edn, Oxford: Oxford University Press, 2007, 134–70, and Decker, *Tilling*, 51–4.

17. Jones, *LRE*, 781–2, with a detailed study of the core land-holdings of the Roman church by F. Marazzi, *I 'Patrimonia Sanctae Romanae Ecclesiae' nel Lazio (secoli IV–X)*, Rome: Istituto storico italiano per il medio evo, 1998.

Figure 16 Sixth-century houses from the village of Serjilla in the Limestone Massif east of Antioch. © Heretiq/Wikimedia Commons

the density and character of smaller-scale rural settlement in different parts of the empire, which in turn has provided important clues concerning the condition of the rural economy in late antiquity. One of the earliest such surveys was that of the so-called Limestone Massif to the east of Antioch, where substantial remains of many hundreds of late Roman villages survive (Fig. 16). The sheer number of villages and the quality of the stonework in their housing are clear indicators of economic prosperity, which the original investigator linked to the archaeological evidence for oil production (Fig. 17). More recent and detailed investigation of some of the villages has led to the recognition that other crops and livestock were also part of the local economy, which was therefore more broadly based than once thought. Nonetheless, it does seem likely that it was the production and export of olive oil which generated the wealth for the construction of the villages, whose inhabitants appear to have been independent peasant farmers.[18]

18. Helpful summaries with references in Wickham, *Framing*, 443–9, and Decker, *Tilling*, 168–73.

Figure 17 A press house for processing olive oil, Serjilla, in the Limestone Massif east of Antioch. Note the round basin towards the rear for crushing olives, and the square tank recessed into the floor on the right for collecting the oil.
© Bernard Gagnon/Wikimedia Commons

To the south, survey work in the region of the Hauran, which formed the hinterland of the city of Bostra, has also shown the existence of many late Roman villages comparable to those of the Limestone Massif, prospering on the basis of cereal cultivation in the volcanic soil of the region.[19] Further south again, it has become apparent through survey work in the northern part of the Negev, supplemented by the papyrus documentation found at Nessana, that this seemingly unpromising semi-arid landscape supported an extensive network of villages and farmsteads in late antiquity, based on

19. Summary in C. Foss, 'Syria in transition, AD 550–750', *DOP* 51 (1997), 189–269, at 245–8.

the cultivation of cereals, olive trees and vines which was made possible by various sophisticated irrigation strategies.[20] Returning northwards and to the west of Syria, the coastal hinterland of Lycia in southern Anatolia also sustained an extensive array of villages in late antiquity. Their prosperity seems to have derived primarily from their supplying coastal cities such as Xanthos, Patara and Myra with timber for shipbuilding and stone for urban development, together with agricultural produce for their populations.[21] There is, then, an overall picture of widespread prosperity in the eastern Mediterranean based on a highly integrated economy which responded to the opportunities and challenges of specific local circumstances.

In north Africa, surveys of the Segermes Valley and Kasserine region have provided the best available evidence for the character of settlement in the countryside, which seems to have comprised a mixture of modest villas, villages and small farms. Large numbers of oil presses have been found at a number of sites, implying significant levels of surplus production of olive oil, and this appears to have continued well into the period of the Vandal occupation. The scale of production implies that a significant proportion was intended for export.[22]

Rural settlement in the northern provinces of the west tended to be dispersed, with the most prominent feature in the fourth century being villas – that is, a rural dwelling associated with an estate. These appear to have experienced a resurgence after the setbacks and contraction of the third century. Some villas were used as opportunities to display the wealth of their owner, through marble and mosaic decoration, and the addition of facilities such as a bath house – so-called 'palatial' features;[23] others were less pretentious in scale and adornment.[24] This resurgence of villas proved to be longer-lived in some regions than others, and when change came, it could take different forms. At one end of the spectrum – that of least disruption – 'palatial' features disappeared, but the basic structures continued to be used, perhaps with alterations such as subdivision of

20. R. Rubin, 'The Romanization of the Negev, Israel: geographical and cultural changes in the desert frontier in late antiquity', *Journal of Historical Geography* 23 (1997), 267–83; Wickham, *Framing*, 452–4; Decker, *Tilling*, 193–202.
21. C. Foss, 'The Lycian coast in the Byzantine age', *DOP* 48 (1994), 1–52, esp. 47–8.
22. Merrills and Miles, *Vandals*, 156–9, for a useful summary and references.
23. The expression is that of P. Van Ossel and P. Ouzoulias, 'Rural settlement economy in northern Gaul in the late empire: an overview and assessment', *JRA* 13 (2000), 133–60, at 145.
24. Chavarría and Lewit, 'Archaeological research', 24–30.

rooms; at the other extreme, many sites were completely abandoned, while in between there were variations on the continued occupation of the site; these usually involved little if any attempt to maintain the original buildings and the use of alternative, simpler forms of habitation. With regard to regional patterns, change broadly began earliest in Britain and northern Gaul, in the late fourth century, in much of Spain during the fifth century, but in southern Gaul (above all Aquitaine), much of Italy and Mediterranean Spain not until the sixth century.[25] As villas disappeared, they seem most commonly to have been succeeded by small villages, but increasing use of wood rather than brick or stone for building can make them more difficult to detect in the archaeological record, and more scattered patterns of settlement were also possible.[26]

While the broad trend of regional change from the north-west peripheries of the empire to central parts might be thought to confirm the assumption that it was linked to the impact of war and the movement of barbarian groups into the western provinces, the chronology of villa change does not in fact fit with the familiar land-marks of late Roman military history. While some villas were undoubtedly destroyed by invaders, change in Britain and northern Gaul was already under way before the end of the fourth century, while the villas of the regions closer to the Mediterranean core gener-ally survived the upheavals of the fifth century. In a comparable way, the villages of the Limestone Massif in Syria, of the Hauran and the Negev, and of the Lycian littoral do not seem to have suffered directly as a result of the Persian and then Arab invasions of the early seventh century.

It has already been noted that the inhabitants of the villages in the east appear to have been independent peasant farmers. The law codes, however, also refer to rural workers with a range of other, dependent legal statuses. Of these, the one which has generated the most debate is that of *colonus* – the registered tenant whose freedom has traditionally been seen as becoming increasingly restricted over the course of late antiquity, to the point where his status was little better than that of a slave or precursor to the medieval serf. While there does seem to have been an increase in the incidence of registered tenancy as a result of the fiscal reforms introduced by Diocletian in the late third century and the need for landowners to

25. Wickham, *Framing*, 473–5.
26. Chavarría and Lewit, 'Archaeological research', 35–7; Wickham, *Framing*, 481–95.

ensure that imperial tax demands could be met, modern discussion had often bestowed a false coherence on what was in practice a much more complex situation involving an array of different statuses and levels of economic well-being. Caution is needed before drawing conclusions about the existence of 'the colonate' as a clearly defined social category, let alone about its being symptomatic of a decline in agricultural productivity.[27]

During the late Republic, an important component of the agricultural workforce had been slaves. With diminishing opportunities for expansionist warfare during the early centuries AD, it has often been assumed that slaves must have been a relatively insignificant factor by late antiquity. Such a contrast, however, is probably too stark. Significant slave use in the Republican period was by and large geographically restricted to the Italian peninsula and Sicily, while slave reproduction is likely to have helped compensate for fewer war captives during the Principate. During late antiquity there were occasional significant influxes of war captives, most famously after the defeat of Radagaisus' forces by Stilicho in 406 (Orosius 7.27.16), and slave trading continued, as evidenced by the episode on the Rhine frontier noted by Ammianus (p. 224 above) and also in one of the 'new' letters of Augustine in which he describes the kidnapping activities of Galatian slavers in north Africa (*Ep.* 10*).[28] Although some of Melania's estates seem to have made use of significant numbers of slaves (*V. Melaniae* [L] 18), it is difficult to gauge to what extent the traded slaves were employed in agricultural, rather than domestic, contexts. Perhaps all that can be said is that they do not appear to have been cheap in late antiquity, which will have acted as a constraint on significant employment, but some use of them continued to be made in parts of the late Roman countryside.[29]

What then was this land and labour producing? The traditional Mediterranean staples had long been grain, grapes and olives, and this remained the case during late antiquity. Certain regions continued to have deserved reputations for being particularly

27. C. Grey, 'Contextualizing *colonatus*: the *origo* of the late Roman empire', *JRS* 97 (2007), 155–75; Wickham, *Framing*, 520–7.
28. A 'new' letter because one of an important collection only discovered in the 1970s: see H. Chadwick, 'New letters of St Augustine', *JTS* 34 (1983), 425–52.
29. Jones, *LRE*, 792–5; C. Grey, 'Slavery in the late Roman world' in K. R. Bradley and P. A. Cartledge (eds), *The Cambridge World History of Slavery*, vol. 1, Cambridge: Cambridge University Press, 2011, 482–509; K. Harper, *Slavery in the Late Roman World, AD 275–425*, Cambridge: Cambridge University Press, 2011. A major study of the subject by Noel Lenski is in preparation.

productive, most obviously, for grain, Egypt and north Africa. In addition to feeding its own population, north Africa continued to ship significant quantities to Rome until the Vandal conquest in the mid-fifth century, while Egypt was responsible for supplying Constantinople; its resources were also drawn upon during emergencies, such as when an army of more than 60,000 men assembled near Antioch in 362–3 for Julian's invasion of Persia, and when a Roman army of more than 50,000 men was based in northern Mesopotamia during Anastasius' war with Persia (502–5) (p. 169 above). As for olive oil, by the fourth century, Spanish production had fallen behind that of north Africa in the west, while, as already noted, the Limestone Massif in Syria was an increasingly important source of oil in the east. Even agriculture in the Dakhleh Oasis appears to have become geared towards the production of surplus olive oil, albeit on a more modest scale, according to the evidence of the agricultural account book from Kellis.[30] Meanwhile, Palestine emerged as a producer of high-quality wine which found markets well beyond the Levant.[31]

Of course, all regions of the empire needed to maintain a certain level of agricultural productivity in late antiquity because of the empire's fiscal system, which, since the reforms of Diocletian, required the main tax to be paid in kind. However, various developments during the fifth century encouraged the intensification of agriculture and the production of surpluses. One of these developments was the gradual shift of the fiscal system away from payments in kind to their commutation into payments in cash (the technical term for which was *adaeratio*) (p. 166 above). This shift had obvious benefits for the imperial government – cash was easier to move around the empire than foodstuffs, and it also allowed the imperial treasury to accumulate financial reserves – but it meant too that producers had to sell their produce in order to acquire the cash needed to pay their taxes, and in this way they became more integrated into their regional economy. Another related development was growing confidence in the stability of the *solidus* – the gold coin introduced by the Emperor Constantine in the early fourth century.[32] Together, these developments facilitated the monetisation of the agricultural economy, which in turn gave producers the incentive

---

30. Bagnall, 'Evidence and models', 196–7.
31. For Palestinian wine, see Decker, *Tilling*, 137–40.
32. Banaji, *Agrarian Change*, esp. ch. 3.

to produce more. Needless to say, owners of large estates were in the best position to capitalise on these opportunities, since they had the greatest scope for specialisation and for economies of scale, as the evidence concerning the Apiones' lands in Egypt would seem to confirm. At the same time, the increasing productivity of large estates must also have contributed significantly to wider economic growth.[33]

Technological improvements also played a part. While the screw press was known as early as the first century, it appears only to have come into widespread use during late antiquity, at least in the eastern Mediterranean, where its application facilitated oil and wine production on a commercial scale.[34] More intensive application of various forms of irrigation technology also facilitated the agricultural exploitation of marginal lands in the eastern provinces, such as the Negev.[35] This phenomenon, incidentally, provides important counter-evidence against older assumptions of widespread abandonment of land in late antiquity, in addition to the problems presented by the legal evidence for the so-called *agri deserti*.[36] In the face of the archaeological evidence and more sensitive readings of the textual sources, *agri deserti* – long an important element in the pessimistic paradigm – have increasingly been recognised as having much more limited significance.

Late Roman trade

Many of the fundamental parameters of economic activity in the late Roman world were favourable to the maintenance of trade on a significant scale between the different regions of the empire. The political unity of the Mediterranean for much of the period, the existence of a common and stable coinage, a good infrastructure of roads and harbours, and modest customs duties all had the potential to create conditions conducive to commercial exchange beyond the local level. Despite these features,[37] the prevailing scholarly view until recent decades was, as already intimated, one which tended

---

33. Sarris, *Economy and Society*; 'Early Byzantine economy'.
34. T. Lewit, 'Absent-minded landlords and innovating peasants? The press in Africa and the eastern Mediterranean' in L. Lavan et al. (eds), *Technology in Transition*, AD *300–650*, Leiden: Brill, 2007, 119–39.
35. Decker, *Tilling*, chs 6–7.
36. On the legal evidence, see Grey, 'Revisiting *agri deserti*'.
37. Acknowledged, but minimised, by one influential sceptic: Jones, *LRE*, 824–7.

towards scepticism about the existence of interregional commercial exchange of any significance in this period. That belief derived, in part, from tenuous attempts at quantification based on anecdotal textual evidence, such as the deduction that trade contributed about 5 per cent to imperial revenues in late antiquity, and therefore to the economy of the empire, on the basis of a comparison of figures for the land tax revenue from two locations in sixth-century Egypt alongside figures for the tax revenue from traders and craftsmen from one location in late fifth-century Mesopotamia.[38]

More fundamental, however, were the assumed implications of the empire's fiscal system in late antiquity (the *annona*), involving as it did state responsibility for the redistribution of bulk agricultural products, above all grain and olive oil. Large quantities of these products, which represented the most significant form of government revenue, had to be moved from producers, the most important of whom were located in the southern regions of the Mediterranean basin (especially Egypt and north Africa), to military units located particularly to the north and east of the Mediterranean, to civilian administrators scattered throughout the empire, and to the major urban centres of Rome and Constantinople, in order to support their populations (pp. 61, 76 above).[39] The law codes indicate that this massive, recurrent logistical operation was undertaken primarily through the agency of *navicularii* (shipmasters), individuals of means who were obligated to provide the imperial government with ships of appropriate capacity. Because the system accounted for such significant quantities of the bare necessities of life and was based on state compulsion, it was assumed that this left little scope for interregional commercial enterprise to flourish.

This pessimistic conclusion has, however, increasingly been seen to be at odds with the implications of the growing quantities of ceramic evidence.[40] That ceramic evidence has certainly corroborated the importance of the *annona* in the movement of staples, in

38. Jones, *LRE*, 465, critiqued by Garnsey and Whittaker, 'Trade', 314.
39. The increasing commutation of taxes in kind to money taxes (*adaeratio*) during the fifth century will have had some impact on these patterns with regard to the supply of the army and the civilian administrators, but the movement of large quantities of grain from Egypt to Constantinople continued unchanged throughout, as also from north Africa to Rome until the Vandal conquest in the 430s.
40. Jones, *LRE*, was notorious for its general (surprising) neglect of archaeological evidence, but it is difficult to believe that a scholar of his acumen and experience would have ignored the material data now available and its implications for this subject.

so far as can reasonably be expected: since grain was not usually conveyed in pottery containers, the presence of this important product cannot be confirmed in this way, but late Roman oil amphorae from north Africa have been found in large quantities in Rome and its port at Ostia, and from Syria and the Aegean in Constantinople,[41] while oil amphorae from the Aegean are also strongly represented at late Roman military sites along the lower Danube frontier.[42] What is significant, however, is, first, that olive oil (and wine) amphorae have been found in large quantities at many sites which have no obvious connection with the operation of the *annona*, and secondly, that African Red Slip (ARS) tableware – a valued product which nevertheless had no direct link to the *annona* – has also been found in large quantities right around the Mediterranean basin and beyond. These two substantial categories of ceramics leave no doubt that commercial exchange was taking place on a significant scale during late antiquity.

The mechanism by which that commercial exchange took place was not, however, completely separate from the state-organised transport of staples. Rather, it seems to have been a case of the *navicularii* taking advantage of their role in the *annona* to engage in interregional private commerce at the same time, through carrying wine, ARS tableware and/or other products in their holds alongside government grain and oil. Analysis of the relevant legislation in the *Theodosian Code* indicates that, in addition to a range of incentives offered to *navicularii* for their involvement in the system (e.g., exemption from service on city councils, subsidies for shipbuilding costs), the imperial government sanctioned generous time allowances for their voyages, sufficient to accommodate stops at ports en route for their private activities, and freedom from customs duties on their transactions.[43] This is consistent with the limited anecdotal evidence, such as the following:

> So when the grain fleet from Alexandria reaches that point [the island of Tenedos, near the entrance to the Hellespont], if the wind blows favourably for them, those having this business in charge

---

41. Wickham, *Framing*, 708, with references.
42. O. Karagiorgou, 'LR2: a container for the military *annona* on the Danubian border?' in S. Kingsley and M. Decker (eds), *Economy and Exchange in the East Mediterranean during Late Antiquity*, Oxford: Oxbow, 2001, 129–66.
43. M. McCormick, 'Bateaux de vie, bateaux de mort', *Settimane di studio* 45 (1998), 35–122, at 65–93 (the most important legislation appears in *Cod. Theod.* 13.5).

> bring their ships into the harbours of Byzantium [i.e., Constantinople] in a short time; then, after discharging their cargoes, they depart with all speed, so that before the winter season they may complete a second or even a third voyage. And those of them who wish to do so, also take on a return cargo of merchandise from that place before they sail back. (Procop. *Aed.* 5.1.10–11 [tr. H. B. Dewing])

That return cargo can only have been products for private sale back in Alexandria or en route.

The existence of the *annona* was therefore of central importance for the development of interregional private commerce during late antiquity, since it effectively acted as a form of state subsidy for merchants and allowed for lower circulation costs.[44] At the same time, however, it seems that the demise of the empire in the west during the mid-fifth century and the end of the *annona* system in the western Mediterranean did not result in the rapid collapse of interregional trade in all parts of the west. Perhaps unsurprisingly in view of its peripheral location, Britain does appear to have experienced a speedy loss of commercial links with the empire, while the commercial integration of northern Gaul and central Spain began to undergo a downturn during the fifth century. Regions with access to the Mediterranean, on the other hand, continued to maintain a good level of involvement in interregional trade, even after the Vandal conquest of north Africa, since good evidence for African tableware and oil amphorae continues in coastal locations from eastern Spain, southern Gaul and Italy throughout the fifth century.[45] There will no doubt have been some readjustments in the immediate aftermath of the Vandal conquest and the disappearance of the *annona* in the west, but it seems that the patterns of exchange which had developed within the framework of the *annona* system were well enough established to survive the removal of its support for some time. It is even possible that the more limited fiscal demands of the Vandal kings gave north African producers and shippers greater room for manoeuvre and so contributed to the continuation of substantial levels of trade, albeit within a more restricted geographical orbit.[46]

Since the eastern Mediterranean did not experience any significant disruption to the *annona* system, it is unsurprising that the ceramic

44. C. Wickham, 'Marx, Sherlock Holmes and late Roman commerce', *JRS* 78 (1988), 183–93, at 193.
45. Loseby, 'Post-Roman economies'.
46. Merrills and Miles, *Vandals*, 148–51.

evidence indicates flourishing patterns of trade there throughout the fifth and sixth centuries. This prosperity will have been further facilitated by the continuing growth of Constantinople as a metropolis, with all that that implies for economic demand. It is also unsurprising that, with the changes in the west, eastern products, such as Levantine wine, should increasingly have penetrated western markets. Following Justinian's conquest of north Africa in the 530s (p. 260 below), this region was soon once again functioning within the *annona* system, albeit with its grain and oil now heading for Constantinople, rather than Rome, and this appears to have assisted the continuing involvement of the region in wider Mediterranean trade.[47] The picture which emerges, therefore, is one of a much more buoyant economic situation during late antiquity than the Mediterranean's political and military travails might otherwise have led one to expect, such that the definitive downturn of economic activity occurred only during the seventh century.

47. Loseby, 'Post-Roman economies'.

Part IV

The age of Justinian

CHAPTER 12

Justinian and the Roman past

Justinian the outsider

In the early months of 527, concern about the health of the Emperor Justin (now in his mid-seventies) (p. 177 above) prompted the senate to urge him to clarify the succession. On 1 April, Justin did so by elevating his nephew and adopted son Justinian to the rank of co-emperor. Four months later, Justin passed away, leaving Justinian, at the age of forty-five, as sole emperor – a remarkable outcome for someone from such apparently unpromising origins in the rural Balkans.[1] Born Petrus Sabbatius, the son of Justin's sister, he benefited from his uncle's example, and perhaps also from his influence at court, by moving to Constantinople during Anastasius' reign and securing a position in one of the units of the palace guard. Although another capable nephew of Justin, his brother's son Germanus, had also followed in his uncle's footsteps, it was Petrus whom Justin decided at some point between 505 and 518 to adopt, a fact reflected in his taking the additional name Justinianus.

As son of the reigning emperor, Justinian will have entertained the justifiable expectation of succeeding to the throne in due course, but as previously noted (p. 177 above), this does not mean that he was the effective power behind the throne during Justin's reign: he had to compete for influence with other powerful individuals – notably the senior general Vitalian and the chief legal adviser Proculus – and there is also good reason to think that Justin resisted moves for

1. Overviews of Justinian's reign include J. Moorhead, *Justinian*, London: Longman, 1994, P. Maraval, *L'Empereur Justinien*, Paris: Presses Universitaires du France, 1999, Averil Cameron, 'Justin I and Justinian', *CAH*² 14.63–85, K. L. Noethlichs, 'Iustinianus', *RAC* 19 (2001), 668–763, and M. Meier, *Justinian: Herrschaft, Reich und Religion*, Munich: Beck, 2004; for a more detailed survey, see J. A. S. Evans, *The Age of Justinian*, London: Routledge, 1996, while essays on a range of aspects can be found in M. Maas (ed.), *The Cambridge Companion to the Age of Justinian*, Cambridge: Cambridge University Press, 2005.

him to advance too quickly.[2] Moreover, despite his status as the
emperor's son, he must also have been conscious of the fact that his
background, and indeed that of Justin, meant that they struggled to
gain acceptance among the empire's elite and were the object of a
certain amount of disdain, as reflected, for example, in Procopius'
cruel caricature of Justin (*Anecdota* 6.1–17). Justinian's efforts to
counteract such prejudice are most readily evident in 521, the year
in which he held the consulship – an occasion for self-advertisement
which he exploited to the full. To the Constantinopolitan elite he
distributed (in accordance with traditional practice) precious ivory
diptychs decorated with motifs associated with the late Republic
and Principate, and inscribed as follows: 'Flavius Petrus Sabbatius
Justinianus, senator, count and commander of the cavalry and
infantry, and consul ordinary: these gifts, slight indeed in value but
rich in honours, I as consul offer to my fellow senators.'[3] For the
Constantinopolitan populace he organised (again in accordance
with traditional practice) public entertainment, but on a scale which
outdid his predecessors by some distance:

> The consul Justinian made this consulship the most famous of all
> eastern ones by being considerably more generous in his largesses.
> For 288,000 gold coins were distributed to the people or spent on
> spectacles or on their properties. He exhibited simultaneously in the
> amphitheatre twenty lions and thirty panthers, not counting other
> wild beasts. Above all, after already donating the chariots, he
> provided caparisoned horses in the hippodrome, one final race being
> the only thing denied the clamouring populace. (*Chron. Marcell.* s.a.
> 521 [tr. B. Croke])

Within a few years of this, however, Justinian took another step
which risked alienating whatever support he had managed to build
up in the capital – his marriage to Theodora. Whereas Marcian's
marriage to Pulcheria and those of Zeno and Anastasius to Ariadne
had played an important part in legitimating their claim to the
throne by linking them to a member of the imperial family,

---

2. B. Croke, 'Justinian under Justin: reconfiguring a reign', *Byz. Zeitschr.* 100 (2007),
13–56.
3. W. F. Volbach, *Elfenbeinarbeiten der Spätantike und des frühen Mittelalters*, 2nd edn,
Mainz: Römisch-germanischen Zentralmuseum, 1952, 29–30 (items 25–7); *ILS* 1307
(text). For the motifs, see A. Cutler, 'The making of the Justinian diptychs', *Byzantion* 54
(1984), 75–115, at 101. For the form and function of diptychs, see K. Bowes, 'Ivory lists:
consular diptychs, Christian appropriation and polemics of time in late antiquity', *Art
History* 24 (2001), 338–57.

Justinian's choice of partner seems almost intended deliberately to flout expectations. His determination to marry her irrespective of the handicaps such a move entailed can only be explained by genuine love. Those handicaps were social and religious.

First, Theodora had previously been an actress, a career which had always carried a strong social stigma in Roman society because it was assumed that, in addition to performing on the stage, actresses sold their sexual favours. As a result, Roman law regarded them as little better than prostitutes and unable to escape the taint of their profession even after they left it. Despite this, however, actresses could still exercise allure, whether through their physical attractiveness or the wealth which they sometimes accrued, prompting the first emperor, Augustus, to introduce a ban on senators marrying women of that profession. The increasing influence of Christian values during late antiquity does not seem to have changed attitudes significantly: although some theologians argued baptism could effect a clean break from the past for former actresses, others were reluctant to extend grace to such women and increased the stigma by emphasising their individual moral responsibility.[4] In the case of Theodora, the most detailed account of her early life is presented by Procopius in his infamous *Secret History* (*Anecdota*), but since he seems so set on exploiting the negative associations of the theatre and reports so much salacious detail about Theodora's behaviour, it is tempting to dismiss his account as a flagrant attempt to blacken her reputation.[5] However, while there is good reason to take much of what Procopius retails with a pinch of salt – 'exaggeration is a first desideratum in invective'[6] – there can be no doubt that, as a result of whatever circumstances, Theodora had at some point worked as

---

4. D. R. French, 'Maintaining boundaries: the status of actresses in early Christian society', *Vig. Chr.* 52 (1998), 293–318; R. Webb, 'Female entertainers in late antiquity' in P. Easterling and E. Hall (eds), *Greek and Roman Actors: Aspects of an Ancient Profession*, Cambridge: Cambridge University Press, 2002, 282–303.

5. Among many discussions of Procopius' treatment of Theodora, see: Averil Cameron, *Procopius and the Sixth Century*, London: Duckworth, 1985, 67–83; J. A. Evans, *The Empress Theodora: Partner of Justinian*, Austin: University of Texas Press, 2002; C. Foss, 'The Empress Theodora', *Byzantion* 72 (2002), 141–76; L. Brubaker, 'Sex, lies and textuality: the *Secret History* of Prokopios and the rhetoric of gender in sixth-century Byzantium' in L. Brubaker and J. Smith (eds), *Gender in the Early Medieval World: East and West, 300–900*, Cambridge: Cambridge University Press, 2004, 83–101.

6. P. Allen, 'Contemporary portrayals of the Byzantine empress Theodora (AD 527–548)' in B. Garlick et al. (eds), *Stereotypes of Women in Power*, New York: Greenwood, 1992, 93–103, at 96.

a prostitute, for another, much more favourably disposed source matter-of-factly refers to her as being 'from the brothel' (John of Ephesus, *Lives of the Eastern Saints* 13 [PO 17.189]). With such a controversial element in her background, it was inevitable that she would face prejudice of the sort reflected in Procopius.

As for the religious handicap, Theodora was a committed anti-Chalcedonian, which was bound to make her unpopular with the overwhelmingly pro-Chalcedonian populace of Constantinople. Again, love seems the only explanation as to why the otherwise firmly pro-Chalcedonian Justinian should have been so determined to marry her. His plans, however, had to be put on hold in the face of staunch opposition from Justin's wife, the Empress Euphemia, and it was only after her death at some point in the early 520s – and a change in the law to allow senators to marry former actresses – that the marriage could proceed.[7]

The new emperor and empress both acted promptly to strengthen their position through the distribution of largesse. Justinian assumed the consulship for the second time in January 528, which provided another opportunity to curry favour with the populace of Constantinople through staging entertainments and giving out money – 'such a quantity as no other emperor had done when consul' (*Chron. Pasch. s.a.* 528). In a similar vein later that year Theodora made a journey to the hot springs at Pythion, near Nicomedia (about 140 km to the east of Constantinople), en route to which 'she showed much liberality to the churches, poor-houses and monasteries' (Theophanes, *Chron.* AM 6025). On the other hand, she is said to have been accompanied by 4,000 people, many of them palace staff and attendants, but also a number of high officials and members of the aristocracy, who are likely to have been irked at having to follow in her wake and observe her making such a public display of her new-found status and resources.

That sense of disquiet can only have increased in the coming months and years as Justinian began to install his appointees to senior positions in the bureaucracy and army, which reflected a break with the pattern of the regimes of Anastasius and Justin. In place of established members of the elite, Justinian began to promote younger individuals from more obscure, provincial backgrounds – in

---

7. For Euphemia's opposition and the change of law, see Procop. *Anecdota* 9.47–51; the law is preserved in *Cod. Iust.* 5.4.23 (520/3), with discussion by D. Daube, 'The marriage of Justinian and Theodora: legal and theological reflections', *Catholic University Law Review* 16 (1967), 380–99.

other words, people like himself. During 528–9, two of his former bodyguards – Belisarius (from the Balkans) and Sittas (probably of Gothic origin) – received rapid promotion to be generals responsible for the eastern provinces and for Armenia respectively, while the Thracian brothers Buzes and Cutzes were advanced to joint command of the frontier forces in the province of Phoenice Libanensis (the southern half of modern Syria). On the civilian side, Justinian appointed a Pamphylian lawyer, Tribonian, to be quaestor (i.e., his senior legal adviser) in 529, while a Cappadocian named John who had risen through the ranks of the financial administration was made praetorian prefect of the east at the start of 531. Some idea of the prejudice these men faced can be gained from Procopius' jaundiced appraisal of them: while conceding that John was 'the most able man of his day' and 'very adept at devising solutions to problems', Procopius could not refrain from berating him for his lack of an elite education and traducing his character with allegations of greed, gluttony and lust; as for Tribonian, 'he possessed natural ability and in educational attainments was inferior to none of his contemporaries', but was nonetheless fatally flawed by avarice (Procop. *Wars* 1.24.11–16, 3.10.7).

Events in early 532, less than five years after his accession, were to show that Justinian could not take for granted his hold on power. On Tuesday 13 January, rioting broke out in Constantinople and continued for most of the ensuing week, resulting in the destruction by fire of much of the city centre and initiating a sequence of events which nearly resulted in Justinian's overthrow. This famous episode – the so-called Nika riot (after the Greek word for 'Conquer!' which the rioters adopted as their watchword) – was triggered by the dissatisfaction of partisans of the circus factions (pp. 217–18 above), but then grew in scale and significance as other factors fed into the turmoil. It is worth noting at the outset, however, that the factional violence which sparked the crisis was something for which Justinian must bear some of the responsibility, for it seems that, during Justin's reign, he actively encouraged the aggressive activities of the Blues as a way of intimidating others who might have been rivals for the imperial throne. Once he became emperor, however, he initiated a crackdown on the factions which they evidently resented and chafed against.[8]

8. G. Greatrex, 'The Nika riot: a reappraisal', *JHS* 117 (1997), 60–86, at 66–7; M. Whitby, 'The violence of the circus factions' in K. Hopwood (ed.), *Organised Crime in Antiquity*, London: Duckworth, 1999, 229–53, at 244–5.

The specific incident which roused the anger of the partisans in January 532 arose from the determination of the prefect of the city, Eudaemon, whose responsibilities included the maintenance of public order, to punish members of the Blues and Greens for murder. In the course of seven of them being executed on Saturday 10 January, two escaped and sought refuge in a church. During the races held at the hippodrome the following Tuesday, the factions began chanting for the two escapees to be pardoned, but when Justinian gave no response, members of the two factions combined – a somewhat unusual step, given that they were normally at logger-heads – and began rampaging through the city centre, setting the prefect's headquarters on fire. The rioting continued the following day, accompanied by a new demand that Justinian dismiss three prominent officials – the city prefect Eudaemon, the praetorian prefect John the Cappadocian and the quaestor Tribonian. However, Justinian's announcement later that day that he was granting their request and replacing the three officials proved insufficient to quell the violence, which took an even more worrying turn the following day (Thursday 15 January) when the rioters went to the home of one of the Emperor Anastasius' nephews, Probus, declaring their intention to proclaim him emperor; when it emerged that he was not there, however, they expressed their frustration, rather perversely, by setting his house on fire.

The rioting continued through Friday and Saturday, during which Anastasius' other nephews, Hypatius and Pompeius, who had hitherto been inside the imperial palace with Justinian, left the palace. Sunday 18 January was the most momentous day of the whole episode. The rioters somehow found Hypatius and proceeded to proclaim him emperor in the hippodrome. On learning this, Justinian is reported to have wavered and contemplated flight, until dissuaded by Theodora. He then ordered the military units which had been summoned from the hinterland of Constantinople some days before to proceed to the hippodrome and restore order – which essentially meant massacring rioters (perhaps as many as 30,000) and capturing Hypatius and Pompeius, who were executed the following day, their corpses thrown into the sea and their property confiscated.[9]

---

9. The most detailed treatments of these events are J. B. Bury, 'The Nika riot', *JHS* 17 (1897), 92–119 (still valuable, despite its age), and Greatrex, 'Nika riot', on some of whose arguments, however, note the reservations in Whitby, 'Violence' (esp. 250 n.66).

Although the Nika riot began with factional violence, the sources indicate that there were other factors which contributed to the way events unfolded. The demand for the dismissal of the three senior officials on Wednesday 14 January is significant. While Eudaemon's name is readily explicable in relation to the partisans' original objectives, John and Tribonian were less obvious targets. The inclusion of John's name is explained by some sources with reference to his tax policies, which fell heavily on provincials and prompted an influx of dissatisfied individuals to the capital (Lydus, *Mag.* 3.70, Ps.-Zachariah Rhetor, *Chron.* 9.14a); however, since John had been in office as praetorian prefect for less than a year by January 532, it is unlikely that his policies would yet have had time to have such an impact and more likely that these authors were retrojecting later developments.[10] It may simply have been a case of John's attracting the rioters' anger because he was a figure closely identified with Justinian, as also with Tribonian. The latter, however, had been in office for more than two years by the time of the Nika riot, and during that period a plethora of laws had been issued relating to the law of inheritance and succession which, it has been plausibly proposed, must have generated resentment amongst those with the most to pass on – the aristocratic elite.[11] The targeting of Tribonian, and John, may therefore be the first sign of elite opposition to Justinian seeking to manipulate and direct factional violence to their own ends – initially, to unseat a number of Justinian's most important officials responsible for policies detrimental to aristocratic interests, and then, as Justinian continued to prevaricate, to unseat Justinian himself and replace him with one of their own, namely Anastasius' nephew Hypatius.[12]

In the end, control and deployment of military force proved decisive in reasserting imperial authority. However, the Empress Theodora is also credited with a decisive intervention on Sunday 18 January, when she is said to have stiffened Justinian's resolve at a point where, on learning of Hypatius' proclamation as emperor, he

---

10. Cf. Greatrex, 'Nika riot', 61 n.5.
11. T. Honoré, *Tribonian*, London: Duckworth, 1978, 53–4.
12. Cf. Alan Cameron, *Circus Factions: Blues and Greens at Rome and Byzantium*, Oxford: Clarendon Press, 1976, 186, 278–80; M. Whitby, 'Factions, bishops, violence and urban decline' in J.-U. Krause and C. Witschel (eds), *Die Stadt in der Spätantike: Niedergang oder Wandel?*, Stuttgart: Franz Steiner, 2006, 441–61, at 443–4. Eighteen senators had their property confiscated for supporting Hypatius (Theophanes, *Chron.* AM 6024), which, while not a large number (Greatrex, 'Nika riot', 80 n.99), is nonetheless significant.

contemplated flight (Procop. *Wars* 1.24.32–8). The means by which
she did so, however, was through a speech, and since this is a rare
occasion on which Procopius presents Theodora in a positive light,
it increases the likelihood that he invented this episode, partly to
provide a dramatic rhetorical setpiece to enhance his narrative of the
riot, partly to provide another illustration of Theodora transgressing
gender roles, and partly to evoke female courage as a way of reinforcing the impression of Justinian's lack of leadership.[13]

There is nonetheless other evidence which suggests that Theodora
could sometimes exercise influence in political life. According to a
source favourably disposed towards her, it was she who insisted on
the execution of Hypatius and Pompeius against Justinian's desire to
spare the two men (Ps.-Zachariah Rhetor, *Chron.* 9.14b), while one
of Justinian's laws from 535, concerned with combating the use
of bribery to obtain public office, begins by acknowledging that, in
giving thought to these matters, he had 'taken as partner in their
consideration our most pious wife given to us by God' (*Nov.* 8.1).
Another independent indication that she was perceived as having
political influence is a number of letters she received from Gothic
rulers in Italy during the early 530s (Cassiod. *Var.* 10.10, 20, 23).
She certainly worked assiduously to promote the interests of anti-
Chalcedonian groups (p. 281 below), and although much of the
detail of Procopius' account of her role in the downfall of John the
Cappadocian in 541 (*Wars* 1.15.13–44) may be questionable,[14] her
playing some part finds corroboration in another source (Lydus,
Mag. 3.69). While, therefore, care should be exercised in taking at
face value what is often misogynistic comment, there were clearly
occasions and contexts where Theodora was able to exercise some
influence – and, indeed, may even have done so in tacit concert with
Justinian.[15]

Justinian the re-former

Following the restoration of order after the Nika riot, it was not long
before Justinian also restored John the Cappadocian and Tribonian

13. Cf. Cameron, *Procopius*, 69; M. Meier, 'Zur Funktion der Theodora-Rede im
Geschichtswerk Prokops', *Rh. Mus.* 147 (2004), 88–104.
14. Cameron, *Procopius*, 69.
15. Cf. C. Pazdernik, '"Our most pious consort given us by God": dissident reactions to
the partnership of Justinian and Theodora, AD 525–548', *Classical Antiquity* 13 (1994),
256–81; Foss, 'Theodora', 170–5.

to senior posts. John is attested as praetorian prefect again by October 532, and although Tribonian did not regain high office until November 533 (this time as master of the offices, rather than as quaestor), this delay was more apparent than real, since even after his dismissal in January 532 he remained fully occupied as chairman of the legal commission set up in 530, a role for which it was not essential that he be quaestor. Clearly, Justinian was not going to allow the experience of the Nika riot to deter him from pursuing the policies which he had initiated prior to January 532. He might, however, have to present them in ways which made them more palatable, particularly to the elite.

This was more necessary with respect to his administrative reforms than to his legal projects, since the practical benefits of the latter were obvious. The first of the legal projects had commenced within six months of Justinian's becoming sole emperor, when, in February 528, he established a commission of ten to produce a codification of imperial laws from the reign of the Emperor Hadrian (117–38) to the current time. This was not, of course, a novel idea, since a similar publication had been produced during the reign of Theodosius II in 438 (pp. 108–9 above). This helps to explain why Justinian's commission completed its work so speedily, in little more than twelve months, although this ought not to detract from its achievement: while there existed further collections of some imperial laws issued after 438, copies of those generated by Leo, Zeno, Anastasius and Justin had to be recovered from archives. Moreover, unlike Theodosius' code, Justinian's aimed to remove contradictions and inconsistencies between different imperial pronouncements. Through this process of editing and homogenising, Justinian hoped to make it easier for judges and lawyers to ascertain the state of the law on a particular issue, and thereby expedite the resolution of litigation.[16]

This, however, was only the first step in a more ambitious scheme. In addition to imperial edicts, law courts also drew upon the authoritative opinions of jurists of the late Republic and Principate as a source of law.[17] The writings of these jurists were vast in quantity,

16. For Justinian's stated aims, see the imperial laws establishing the commission, and promulgating the new code (*Const. Haec* [13 February 528] and *Const. Summa* [7 April 529]), which preface the text of the code.
17. Skilled jurists continued to write and practise in late antiquity; for possible practical reasons for their writings not being included in Justinian's *Digest*, see P. Garnsey and C. Humfress, *The Evolution of the Late Antique World*, Cambridge: Orchard Press,

and their systematisation had proved too forbidding a challenge
for Theodosius II's law commission. In December 530, however,
Justinian established a second commission of sixteen individuals
under the chairmanship of Tribonian (he had been a member of the
first commission, on which he must have performed impressively),
with the task of editing and organising the jurists' writings into
a user-friendly compendium. The resulting volume, the so-called
Digest, was still a weighty tome, but nonetheless a boon for the legal
profession, since it reduced more than three million lines of text to
about 150,000 (*Const. Tanta* 1); its completion in only three years
has been described as 'one of the most brilliant feats of organisation
in the history of civil administration'.[18]

That Justinian himself regarded the compilation of the *Code* and
the *Digest* as important achievements is apparent from the language
used in the following description of them, written a few weeks
before the promulgation of the *Digest*:

> The solemn pronouncements of the emperors were in disarray. We
> collected them into a clear, systematic series [i.e., the *Code*]. Then we
> turned our attention to the rolls of the classical law, that boundless
> ocean of learning, and passing by heaven's favour, as it were, through
> the midst of the deep, we soon completed a task which seemed over-
> whelming [the *Digest*]. (Justinian, *Institutes* preface [21 November
> 533] [tr. P. Birks and G. McLeod])

This description appears in the preface to the third element in
Justinian's grand scheme – a textbook for law students. Although
slight in size compared to the *Digest*, it reflects Justinian's concern
with the practicalities of the law. Like the *Code* and the *Digest*,
the *Institutes* also reflects his interest in self-promotion. The *Code*
bore Justinian's name, the *Digest* was 'our *Digest*', both law books
officially superseded all the earlier legal texts on which they were
based, and the *Institutes* was for the use of first-year law students,
who were henceforth to be known as 'New Justinians' (*Const.
Omnem* 2).[19]

The epilogue to Justinian's programme of reorganising and
systematising the textual basis of legal knowledge was the publi-

---

2001, 64–7 – though the preference for jurists of earlier centuries may also reflect
Justinian's interest in the Roman past.
18. Honoré, *Tribonian*, 186.
19. For an overview of Justinian's legal projects, see C. Humfress, 'Law and legal
practice in the age of Justinian' in Maas, *Justinian*, 161–84, at 161–71.

cation, twelve months later in November 534, of a revised edition of the *Code* incorporating the laws which he had issued during the seven years since his accession. Law-making continued after this date, of course, with these measures referred to as *leges novellae* ('new laws') or 'novels', but although Justinian announced his intention to produce a compilation of these in the mid-550s (*Nov. App.* 7.11), that plan was never realised, perhaps partly because he was unable to find another lawyer with the organisational skills and energy of Tribonian, who had died in the early 540s. Justinian's novels, however, were preserved in private collections and provide detailed insight into the programme of administrative reform implemented by John the Cappadocian during the 530s.

This programme involved the gradual reorganisation of provincial administration in various ways – the elimination of an intermediate tier of officials between governors and praetorian prefect in certain regions of the empire, the amalgamation of civil and military responsibilities in non-frontier provinces, and the strengthening of the authority of provincial governors by enhancing their status and remuneration. The first of these was presumably intended to save money and simplify the chain of command between centre and province, the second to improve the effectiveness of provincial government by reducing the scope for conflict between imperial officials, and the third to reassert imperial authority in the provinces, as well as to reduce corrupt practices by governors and thereby stem the flow of dissatisfied provincials to Constantinople and other major urban centres seeking redress, as a result of which 'uprisings in the cities and public disturbances occur'.[20] Concern about this particular problem is also reflected in the creation of a new official for Constantinople in 539 known as the *quaesitor*, whose job was, as his title implies, to inquire into the reasons of anyone visiting the capital and ensure that they returned home once their business was complete, so that 'this our great city shall be freed from confusion' (*Nov.* 80.9) – a step taken, no doubt, partly to minimise the chances of another Nika riot.

One change in provincial administration, however, had a more personal rationale: the transformation of Justinian's humble birthplace in the depths of the Balkans into a major administrative centre bearing the name Justiniana Prima, replete with new buildings

20. Jones, *LRE*, 280–3, for further detail on the reforms; the quotation is from the preface of *Nov.* 8. (535).

worthy of a city (Procop. *Aed.* 4.1.19–27).[21] This, rather than Sirmium or Thessalonica, was to be the base of the praetorian prefect of Illyricum, and it was also to have its own archbishop (*Nov.* 11 [535]). It is tempting to see this project as indicative of Justinian's nagging sense of inferiority about his lowly origins.

One further important instance of provincial reorganisation was the creation of the new post of *quaestor exercitus* (quaestor of the army), with responsibility for what at first sight appears to be an eclectic mix of provinces – Scythia, Moesia, Caria, Cyprus and the Cyclades (i.e., the islands of the Aegean). Despite the gist of the law only surviving in a later summary (*Nov.* 41 [536]), the rationale of this arrangement is clear: Scythia and Moesia were frontier provinces on the lowest reaches of the lower Danube which habitually struggled to produce enough food to support the military units concentrated there; the other three provinces were all safe, wealthy and easily accessible by sea; and the quaestor's primary responsibility was to oversee the transfer of resources from the latter to the former by ship (the cheapest and fastest mode of moving bulk goods). In other words, his dispersed group of provinces was effectively a mini praetorian prefecture created to solve a specific problem – another intriguing instance of a willingness on the part of Justinian and his advisers to be flexible and innovative.[22]

Innovation was, however, a dirty word in elite circles in sixth-century Constantinople, not least because change usually threatened their interests. It is one of the charges which Procopius levels against Justinian in his *Secret History*:

> Established customs were swept away wholesale, as if he had been invested with the mantle of imperial majesty on condition that he would change all things to new forms. Long-established offices were abolished, and new ones set up to run the state's business; the laws of the land and the organization of the army were treated in the same way, not because justice required it or the general interest urged him to it, but merely so that everything might have a new look and might be associated with his name. (*Anecdota* 11.1–2 [tr. G. Williamson and P. Sarris])

21. For the archaeological remains, see B. Bavant, 'Caričin Grad and the changes in the nature of urbanism in the central Balkans in the sixth century' in A. G. Poulter (ed.), *The Transition to Late Antiquity on the Danube and Beyond* (= Proc. Brit. Acad. 141), Oxford: Oxford University Press, 2007, 337–74.
22. Further detail, discussion and references in A. D. Lee, *War in Late Antiquity: A Social History*, Oxford: Blackwell, 2007, 109–11.

Procopius could not, of course, voice such criticisms openly, although this did not prevent him from cleverly placing very similar sentiments in the mouths of Gothic envoys addressing the Persian king Khusro in his publicly available *Wars*; the envoys disparage Justinian as 'an innovator by nature' and 'unable to abide by the settled order of things' (2.2.6). Justinian was undoubtedly alert to such attitudes among the elite, not least in the aftermath of the Nika riot, and sought to pre-empt them, partly by proceeding with reforms in a series of small steps, and partly by prefacing the various laws with appeals to precedents from the Roman past which offered apparent legitimation for his policies.[23] He may well also have seen the revival of traditional Roman titles as a way of reasserting central imperial control vis-à-vis vested interests.[24] Typical of this 'anti-quarian' strategy is the way in which the law to combine civil and military authority in the Anatolian province of Lycaonia was introduced:

> We have thought it right to adorn the nation of Lycaonia with a greater form of government than its present one since we have considered those first beginnings from which comes the present nation of the Lycaonians, according to those who have written about ancient matters. They have informed us that the Lycaonian nation is most closely akin to the Roman people and, on the basis of the same evidence, practically wedded to it. Long ago Arcadia in Hellas was ruled by Lycaon, and he began the settlement of the territory of the Romans. After he had seized the land of the Oenutrians he gave a beginning to the Roman Empire. We are speaking of times far more ancient than those of Aeneas and Romulus. When a colony was established there he seized a large portion of Pisidia, which he named after himself, calling the land Lycaonia. Hence it is only just that the administration of this province should be ornamented by investing it with a sign of ancient Roman magistracies. And now its current administrators, that is, the civil and military governors, should be joined into one office and decorated with the title of praetor. That title is part of the patrimony of Roman government, and it was in use in the great city of the Romans before the title consul. (*Nov.* 25 preface [535] [tr. M. Maas])

There were, however, some changes which were impossible to

---

23. M. Maas, 'Roman history and Christian ideology in Justinianic reform legislation', *DOP* 40 (1986), 17–31.
24. C. Roueché, 'Provincial governors and their titulature in the sixth century', *AnTard* 6 (1998), 83–9.

mask, one of which went to the heart of Roman identity –
namely, language. As the Roman empire had expanded during the
Republic, it had absorbed an increasingly exotic array of cultures
and languages, but the pre-eminent language of government had
remained Latin, and this continued to be the case during the fourth
century, despite the growing importance of Constantinople. There
were signs of the balance beginning to tilt towards Greek during the
fifth century, but the fact that Anastasius, Justin and Justinian were
all native Latin speakers from the Balkans must have helped to reinforce the status of the empire's original language. However, from the
530s onwards, laws were increasingly issued in Greek rather than
Latin, a shift for which the middle-level bureaucrat John Lydus
bitterly blamed John the Cappadocian (*De mag.* 3.68) – no doubt
reflecting the chagrin of a native Greek speaker who had spent much
money and time on acquiring a knowledge of Latin in order to
further his career. To be sure, this was an inevitable change for which
Justinian cannot be held culpable – as a law of 535 noted, 'we have
composed this law not in the ancestral tongue [i.e., Latin], but in the
familiar Greek language, so that, through ease of understanding, it
might be known to everyone' (*Nov.* 7.1) – and one to which the
Constantinopolitan elite will presumably not have objected, but it
remains a significant counter-current to Justinian's protestations of
his reverence for the Roman past.[25]

Justinian the imperialist

In the early years of his reign, Justinian promoted an image of
imperial rule based on the twin foundations of the rule of law and
the supremacy of Roman military power. So, for example, the consti-
tution confirming the publication of the first edition of the *Code*
began with the following assertion:

> The maintenance of the integrity of the government depends upon
> two things – namely, the force of arms and the observance of the
> laws – and, for this reason, the fortunate race of the Romans
> obtained power and precedence over all other nations in former

25. On Latin in the late Roman east, see G. Dagron, 'Aux origins de la civilisation
Byzantine: langue de culture et langue d'état', *Rev. Hist.* 241 (1969), 23–56; B. Croke,
Count Marcellinus and his Chronicle, Oxford: Oxford University Press, 2001, 86–93;
Averil Cameron, 'Old and new Rome: Roman studies in sixth-century Constantinople'
in P. Rousseau and M. Papoutakis (eds), *Transformations of Late Antiquity*, Farnham:
Ashgate, 2009, 15–36.

times, and will do so forever, if God should be propitious, since each
of these has ever required the aid of the other: for, as military affairs
are rendered secure by the laws, so also are the laws preserved by
force of arms. (*Const. Summa* 1 [529])[26]

In doing this, Justinian was essentially affirming age-old Roman
values, but just as he had a claim to have done more than recent
emperors to reinvigorate Roman law through the creation of the
Code and *Digest*, so too he could claim, by the mid-530s, to have
done more than any emperor for a long time successfully to reassert
the Roman tradition of imperial expansion. The best opportunities
for that reassertion were, of course, in the western Mediterranean,
but the initial focus of his military endeavours was of necessity in the
east, where relations with Persia had deteriorated in recent years and
required stabilising.

Renewed hostility on the part of the Persian king Kavad is attributed by Roman sources to the Emperor Justin rebuffing the somewhat unusual request that he adopt Kavad's third son Khusro in
order to guarantee his succession to the Persian throne (Justin's
advisers were concerned that implementation of the proposal might
leave Khusro with a legal claim to the Roman throne as well).
Certainly, the now elderly Kavad may have had reason to be
concerned about ensuring the successor of his choice, but the episode
may also have been a case of his fishing for an excuse for war. At any
rate, he soon invaded the Caucasian kingdom of Lazica, which had
in recent years established a client relationship with Constantinople,
confirmed through conversion to Christianity.[27] Perhaps in anticipation of direct conflict in northern Mesopotamia, one of Justinian's
first actions as sole emperor was to try, in 528, to strengthen the
frontier fortifications by the construction of another fortress like
Dara, to its south at a place called Thannuris (Minduon). However,
not only did Persian forces intervene to drive off Roman forces and
prevent further work on the site (Procop. *Wars* 1.13.1–8) – unsurprising, in view of their objections to the construction of Dara by the
Emperor Anastasius – but in 530 Kavad launched a major invasion
with a view to capturing Dara itself. By this time, Belisarius was
senior general in the eastern provinces, and first made a name for
himself by his successful defence of the fortress in the battle that

26. See also the preface to the *Institutes*.
27. Procop. *Wars* 1.11–12, Malalas, *Chron.* 412–14, with detailed discussion in
Greatrex, *Rome and Persia*, 130–47.

The258The age of Justinian

ensued before its walls.[28] The following year, however, another Persian invasion from a different direction, up the course of the Euphrates, briefly threatened Antioch until Belisarius' forces obliged the Persians to withdraw the way they had come – only for the two sides to engage near the frontier at Callinicum with heavy losses on both sides. Conflicting accounts in contemporary sources make it difficult to ascertain where the blame lay for what was a blow to Roman prestige in the region, but an official inquiry resulted in Belisarius' dismissal and return to Constantinople, where, however, he was fortuitously on hand a few months later to help rescue the emperor and his own reputation during the Nika riot (above, p. 248).[29]

Kavad's death soon after the battle of Callinicum – he was in his early eighties – and the succession of Khusro offered the opportunity for a new start in Roman–Persian relations. No doubt keen to concentrate his energies on securing his hold on power, Khusro proved receptive to the proposal of a peace settlement. Negotiations during the winter of 531/2 resulted in the 'endless peace' – so-called, because unlike previous agreements between the two states, no time limit was placed on the duration of this one: each side surrendered forts captured in recent warfare in Lazica and Armenia, but the Romans also agreed to pay the Persians 11,000 lbs of gold.[30] This was a very substantial quantity of gold – by far the largest recorded single payment to any foreign people or state during late antiquity.[31] Justinian's willingness to accede to this demand without demur indicates how eager he was to stabilise relations with Persia, and that eagerness is only explicable with reference to his planning for the invasion of Vandal north Africa which was launched the following summer and which, if successful, could be expected to recoup such an outlay many times over.

Why did Justinian initiate the Vandal expedition? This question has prompted a range of answers. At the 'minimalist' end of the spectrum, it has occasionally been suggested that it was the Nika riot of January 532 (p. 247 above), and Justinian's need to rehabilitate

---

28. Procop. *Wars* 1.13.9–14.55, with Greatrex, *Rome and Persia*, 168–92.
29. The conflicting accounts are Procop. *Wars* 1.18 (exculpating Belisarius and deferring mention of his dismissal until a later chapter) and Malalas *Chron.* 461–6 (in which Belisarius emerges much less favourably), with discussion in G. Greatrex, *Rome and Persia at War, 502–532*, Leeds: Francis Cairns, 1998, 194–207.
30. Details in Greatrex, *Rome and Persia*, 213–21.
31. See the tabulation of data in Lee, *War in Late Antiquity*, 121.

his reputation in the aftermath of the loss of human life and imperial prestige it entailed, which first prompted him to contemplate a bold overseas venture.[32] At the other extreme is the view that the Vandal expedition was but the first step in a long-cherished plan to recover the western provinces and restore the pre-eminence of the empire throughout the Mediterranean world.[33] While the fallout from the Nika riot no doubt supplied additional motivation, the idea of invading north Africa clearly predates the riot by some time. When the Vandal ruler Hilderic, who had established friendly relations with Constantinople during the 520s, was deposed and imprisoned by his younger relative Gelimer in May 530, Justinian sent success- ive embassies to Carthage demanding, first, Hilderic's restoration, and then, when that request was rebuffed by Gelimer, his release and dispatch to Constantinople – with the threat of war if Gelimer also rejected this request (which he did) (Procop. *Wars* 3.9). But was this the origin of Justinian's western ventures, with the rapid and unexpected success of the Vandal expedition subsequently encourag- ing Justinian's ambitions to expand and embrace the conquest of Italy and Spain, or was it a case of circumstances facilitating the realisation of long-standing and far-reaching ambitions?

There are two considerations which lend support to the latter idea. First, there is no doubt that religious policy was very important in Justinian's priorities, and that one of his chief aims was to rule an empire united in adherence to Chalcedonian Christianity (p. 265 below). Most obviously, this involved trying to win over the anti- Chalcedonian constituency in Egypt and other eastern provinces, but it could well also have extended to removing heterodox Arian rulers in the west.[34] Secondly, the imperial laws establishing the commissions to work on the *Code* and the *Digest* in 528 and 530 express Justinian's determination to achieve challenging goals in a way which is consistent with aspirations to recover the western provinces.[35] However, both of these arguments rely on circum- stantial evidence, which leaves open the possibility that Justinian's ambitions developed as events unfolded during the first half of the 530s.

32. Cf. P. Brown, *The World of Late Antiquity*, London: Thames and Hudson, 1971, 150–2; A. Louth, 'The eastern empire in the sixth century' in *CMH* 1, 93–117, at 101.
33. Cf. Jones, *LRE*, 270; Honoré, *Tribonian*, 18.
34. Cf. *Nov.* 78.4.1 (539): 'It was out of concern for liberty that we undertook such extensive wars in Africa and the west, both for right belief about God and for the freedom of our subjects'; also *Cod. Iust.* 1.27.1 (534).
35. This is the argument of Honoré, *Tribonian*, 17–20.

When Justinian first announced to his advisers his intention of invading Vandal north Africa, the response was unenthusiastic, with John the Cappadocian voicing concern about the risks involved – no doubt mindful of the failure of the Emperor Leo's expedition in 468 and (in his capacity as praetorian prefect) of the expense entailed by such a venture. Inspired, however, by a dream which emphasised the need to rescue the orthodox Christians of north Africa from their Arian overlords – or so he claimed – Justinian persisted with his plans, and in the summer of 533 dispatched a seaborne force from Constantinople.[36] Two features of this force were, however, odd. First, it was commanded by Belisarius, whose reputation as a general had suffered a serious setback at the battle of Callinicum in 531 (even if his responsibility for that debacle is open to doubt). The solution to this conundrum must surely lie in the debt Justinian owed Belisarius for his subsequent role in the crushing of the Nika riot. The other odd feature is the size of the force, which, at only 10,000 infantry, 5,000 cavalry and 1,000 allied troops, suggests that Justinian (perhaps mindful of John's warnings) may, after all, have been hedging his bets against the possibility of failure.[37]

In the event, the expedition achieved dramatically rapid success, capturing Carthage in September following a battle to the south of the city, inflicting a second defeat on Vandal forces in December, and capturing Gelimer in March 534.[38] Since Gelimer had had Hilderic murdered as Belisarius' forces approached Carthage, Justinian was spared the dilemma of whether to restore Hilderic to the throne and was able to claim north Africa for the empire. At least part of the explanation for Belisarius' success lay in the fact that Gelimer was busy fighting Moorish tribesmen when the Roman expedition set out, while the bulk of the Vandal navy was preoccupied with a revolt in Sardinia – both circumstances of which it seems there was

36. For John's opposition and Justinian's dream, see Procop. *Wars* 3.10; for the ingenious suggestion that Procopius' presentation of this episode was a veiled critique of Justinianic policy, see R. Scott, 'The classical tradition in Byzantine historiography' in M. Mullett and R. Scott (eds), *Byzantium and the Classical Tradition*, Birmingham: Centre for Byzantine Studies, 1981, 61–74, at 73–4.
37. While this figure is not untypical of the size of armies in this period, a significantly larger force of 52,000 was sent again Kavad's Persians in 503 (Ps-Joshua Stylites, *Chron.* 54), while a force of 30,000 operated in Armenia in 543 (Procop. *Wars* 2.24.16), and one would have expected a force of comparable magnitude for such a momentous initiative.
38. For further detail on the events of the campaign, see Evans, *Justinian*, 126–33.

knowledge in Constantinople prior to the expedition's departure.[39] Despite awareness of these favourable circumstances, there was still a justifiable sense of amazement at the speed and apparent ease with which the expedition's objective had been accomplished (cf. *Institutes* preface, Procop. *Wars* 4.7.18–21).

It may well have been this which prompted Justinian to take another unexpected step. Following Belisarius' return to Constantinople later in 534, Justinian staged what was billed as a revival of the traditional triumph. However, while a victorious general who was not a member of the imperial family parading through the streets of an imperial capital with a display of booty and notable prisoners was indeed an event which had not been witnessed since the reign of Augustus, the Justinianic version included a number of crucial modifications. Rather than riding in a chariot, as of old, Belisarius proceeded from his home to the hippodrome on foot, just like the defeated Gelimer, and upon reaching the hippodrome, Belisarius prostrated himself before Justinian, just like the defeated Gelimer. Justinian was clearly keen to satisfy popular demand for Belisarius to be honoured while ensuring that no one was left in any doubt as to his status relative to the emperor.[40]

Justinian also honoured Belisarius by bestowing on him the consulship for the following year (535). It seems, however, that this granting of what had long been a largely symbolic office was an action which Justinian came to regret. Belisarius had returned from Carthage to Constantinople with substantial quantities of booty from the Vandal treasury (including items from the temple in Jerusalem which Titus had brought to Rome in 70 and which had then been carried off by the Vandals during their sack of Rome in 455). Although the bulk of this must have gone into the imperial coffers, it is clear that Belisarius was allowed to retain some of it, presumably in accordance with the ancient custom of the victorious general's right of control over triumphal booty, for he is reported

39. Roman landowners from north Africa who had recently fled to Constantinople are said to have informed Justinian about the Vandals' problems with the Moorish tribes as part of their lobbying for an invasion (Ps.-Zachariah Rhetor, *Hist. eccl.* 9.17a), while the leader of the revolt in Sardinia is said to have sought aid from Constantinople at about the same time (Procop. *Wars* 3.10.25–11.2).
40. The triumph is described in Procop. *Wars* 4.9, with discussion in M. McCormick, *Eternal Victory: Triumphal Rulership in Late Antiquity, Byzantium and the Early Medieval West*, Cambridge: Cambridge University Press, 1985, 65–6, 125–7. Despite his declining to renounce his Arian faith in favour of orthodoxy, Gelimer and his family were well treated and given an estate in Galatia (Procop. *Wars* 4.9.13–14).

to have distributed his Vandal gold freely among the populace of Constantinople in the traditional manner of consuls dispensing largesse (Procop. *Wars* 4.9.15–16; cf. 5.5.17–19). Justinian evidently did not appreciate this particular revival of ancient practice. No doubt fearing that the combination of Belisarius' popularity and his control of military resources could become a threat to the throne – there had already been malicious allegations in the aftermath of the Vandal expedition that Belisarius was contemplating rebellion (Procop. *Wars* 4.8.1–8) – the emperor issued a law in 537 prohibiting holders of the consulship other than the emperor from giving out gold to the public (*Nov.* 105). Even this measure appears not to have assuaged Justinian's fears, for after 541 he no longer honoured anyone with the consulship – a striking shift in policy for a man who had been in other respects so keen to emphasise his respect for the Roman past.[41]

Whatever concerns Justinian was beginning to entertain about Belisarius, he could hardly entrust his next initiative – the invasion of Gothic Italy – to anyone other than the man who had defeated the Vandals with such ease. As with the Vandal expedition, circumstances conveniently helped both to justify and to facilitate the Italian expedition. Following the death of Theoderic in 526, he was succeeded by his ten-year-old grandson Athalaric, but on account of his youth, his mother and Theoderic's daughter, Amalasuintha, acted as regent (p. 194 above). She was a Romanophile, but her efforts to give her son a Roman education were thwarted by the Gothic aristocracy. Following Athalaric's premature death in 534, Amalasuintha sought to retain effective power by having Theoderic's nephew Theodahad declared king, but he soon proved unwilling to be a mere cipher and imprisoned her; the following year she was murdered. Since Amalasuintha had been on friendly terms with Justinian (even aiding the Vandal expedition by allowing the fleet to stop and restock in Sicily), the emperor was able to present her death as an anti-Roman action which justified imperial intervention, and in late 535 Belisarius invaded Sicily.

From there he advanced rapidly up the Italian peninsula, capturing Naples and Rome during the course of 536. Meanwhile,

---

41. Further discussion in Alan Cameron and D. Schauer, 'The last consul: Basilius and his diptych', *JRS* 72 (1982), 126–43; also Roueché, 'Provincial governors', 88, who suggests that Justinian may not have seen the preservation of the consulship as symbolically important because, as stated in the preface to *Nov.* 105, the powers of the consul had been transferred to the office of emperor.

Theodahad's ineffective response to the invasion led the Gothic army to depose him in favour of Vitigis, a man unconnected with Theoderic's family but with military experience, which he attempted to demonstrate by besieging Belisarius in Rome throughout 537, without success. In 538 Belisarius resumed his northward advance, eventually negotiating the surrender of Ravenna in May 540.[42] Belisarius duly escorted Vitigis and the Gothic royal treasure to Constantinople, where victory celebrations were, however, much more muted than in 534. The Gothic booty was put on display for members of the senate and the conquest of Africa and Italy was commemorated in a famous mosaic on the ceiling of the Bronze Gate entrance to the palace (Procop. *Wars* 7.1, *Aed.* 1.10.11–20). A second public triumph for Belisarius was, however, too great a political risk as far as Justinian was concerned – and, in the event, would have been premature anyway (p. 286 below).

---

42. For more detail on this (first) phase of the war in Italy, see Evans, *Justinian*, 136–51; J. Moorhead, 'The Byzantines in the west in the sixth century' in *CMH* 1, 118–39, at 124–7.

CHAPTER 13

Justinian and the Christian present

Justinian as a Christian emperor

While a number of Justinian's predecessors had been noted for their
piety – most famously, Theodosius II – none of them had regarded
Christianity as integral to their imperial responsibilities to the degree
that Justinian did. One simple illustration of the difference can be
found in the relative priority given to legislation on religious matters
and the church in the law codes of these two emperors. The code
which bore Theodosius' name devoted substantial space to this area
of legislation, but not until its final book, whereas, in a telling shift
of emphasis, it was dealt with in the opening sections of the first
book of Justinian's code. Moreover, the first section of Book I of
the latter concerned itself more specifically with doctrinal matters,
as clearly signalled by its title: 'Concerning the great Trinity and the
Catholic faith, and that no one should dare to dispute about it in
public' (*Cod. Iust.* 1.1). It was a logical extension of this approach
when Justinian subsequently decreed that the canons of the great
ecumenical church councils – Nicaea (325), Constantinople (381),
Ephesus (431) and Chalcedon (451) – should have the same status as
imperial laws (*Nov.* 131.1 [545]).

It was not, however, only a case of his giving such prominence
to ecclesiastical matters in the legal sphere: what was additionally
distinctive was the way in which he involved himself directly and
personally in this area. First, while he, like all emperors, generally
left the drafting of laws and official documents to officials with legal
training, one of the rare exceptions to this in his case was when
such texts concerned the definition of Christian dogma, in the
composition of which his individual style, with its distinctive
turns of phrase and lack of refinement, has been detected.[1] Second,

---

1. A. M. Honoré, 'Some constitutions composed by Justinian', *JRS* 65 (1975), 107–23,
at 122.

Justinian was the first Christian emperor to write theological discourses (often in the form of letters)[2] – an activity for which the most recent precedent of sorts was, interestingly, the Emperor Julian's various works of 'pagan theology'.[3] Thirdly, Justinian involved himself in theological debate: in 532 he invited theologians of various persuasions to discuss their differences, and although he did not participate directly in their discussions, he did talk privately with the separate delegations afterwards (below p. 280); later in his reign he was criticised for spending too much time talking over issues of dogma with clergy at the expense of more immediately pressing matters of policy such as the conduct of the Gothic war in Italy (Procop. *Wars* 7.35.11).[4]

It is intriguing to consider the origins of his personal interest in theological matters. Clearly, an important contributing factor was his consciousness of the need to maintain divine favour towards the empire by doing all he could as emperor to ensure respect for correct belief and for the church's personnel.[5] However, his interest in theological matters predated his accession to the throne by some way: his personal involvement in the negotiations with the bishop of Rome over the ending of the Acacian schism and related matters, reflected in the numerous letters he sent during the early years of Justin's reign (*Coll. Avell.* 147, 162, 187–8, 191, 196, 200, 235, 243), implies a long-standing concern with the intricacies of ecclesiastical and doctrinal affairs which appears somewhat surprising given his rural origins.[6] One can only surmise that his interest in such matters

2. For a detailed overview of the various texts which fall under this heading (with full bibliographical references), see K.-H. Uthemann, 'Kaiser Justinian als Kirchenpolitiker und Theologe', *Augustinianum* 39 (1999), 5–83; some of these (difficult) texts are translated in K. P. Wensche, *On the Person of Christ: The Christology of Emperor Justinian*, Crestwood, NY: St Vladimir's Seminary Press, 1991.

3. As noted by J. Moorhead, *Justinian*, London: Longman, 1994, 120.

4. In all this, Justinian stands in marked contrast to the militarily oriented Valentinian I, who is reported to have distanced himself from any involvement or intervention in ecclesiastical matters on the grounds that 'church affairs lay outside his scrutiny' (Sozomen, *Hist. eccl.* 6.21.7).

5. E.g., 'Our greatest solicitude is for the true dogmas pertaining to God and for the honour of his priests; if they are maintained, we are confident that through it God will shower much good on us; that we shall not only firmly retain what we have, but further obtain what we do not yet have' (*Nov.* 6 pr. [535]).

6. Justinian's sudden shift of theological position during these negotiations has been seen by some as showing that 'Justinian was not concerned about the theological issues *per se* ... [but was rather] a pragmatic power broker looking for a deal that would do the job' (P. T. R. Gray, 'The legacy of Chalcedon: Christological problems and their significance' in M. Maas (ed.), *The Cambridge Companion to the Age of Justinian*, Cambridge:

developed during the initial years after he joined his uncle in Constantinople, no doubt intensified by exposure to the prominence of theological issues in imperial politics during the final years of Anastasius' reign – the crisis of 512 and the challenge mounted by Vitalian (p. 173 above).

Building the kingdom of God on earth

Justinian expressed his Christian ideals in a variety of ways which will be explored in this chapter, but the most tangible of these was the construction of churches and other religious buildings. Obviously he was not the first emperor to engage in this activity – Constantine had established a firm precedent two centuries previously – but, as with his more generally committed approach to religious matters, Justinian does seem to have pursued this activity to a greater extent than any of his predecessors. This is evident in the sheer number of churches whose construction he is credited with funding – more than thirty in Constantinople and its environs alone, according to Procopius (*Aed.* 1.1–9).[7] An early indicator of his ambitions on this front was provided by the church dedicated to Saints Sergius and Bacchus which he and Theodora built in the grounds of the Palace of Hormisdas in the 520s, whose impressively carved and carefully composed dedicatory inscription provides a telling illustration of the opportunities for self-advertisement which such pious projects also offered:[8]

Cambridge University Press, 2005, 215–38, at 228); cf. also V. Menze, *Justinian and the Making of the Syrian Orthodox Church*, Oxford: Oxford University Press, 2008, 39–41, 251–4. However, Richard Price has offered the following observation on this episode: 'The suddenness of the change may suggest that he was a pragmatic broker, indifferent to theological niceties, but keen to propitiate miaphysite [i.e., anti-Chalcedonian] opinion; but his main motive at this stage, when his own position was not yet secure, was not to be upstaged by Vitalian. The consistency with which he subsequently defended Cyrillian Chalcedonianism goes against the view that in religious matters he was a mere politician' (*The Acts of the Council of Constantinople of 553*, Liverpool: Liverpool University Press, 2009, 9–10).
7. Much of the journal *AnTard* 8 (2000) is devoted to articles on aspects of Procopius' *Buildings*, including an invaluable one by D. Feissel ('Les édifices de Justinien au témoignage de Procope et de l'épigraphie', 81–104), correlating the surviving epigraphic evidence for Justinian's building activities with Procopius' claims.
8. Arguments for dating its construction to the 520s, rather than later, are presented by B. Croke, 'Justinian, Theodora and the Church of Saints Sergius and Bacchus', *DOP* 60 (2006), 25–63.

Other sovereigns have honoured dead men whose labour was unprofitable, but our sceptered Justinian, fostering piety, honours with a splendid abode the servant of Christ, Creator of all things, Sergius. Neither the burning breath of fire, nor the sword, nor any other constraint of torments disturbed him; but he endured to be slain for the sake of Christ, the God, gaining by his blood heaven as his home. May he in all things guard the rule of the sleepless sovereign, and increase the power of the God-crowned Theodora whose mind is adorned with piety, whose constant toil lies in unsparing efforts to nourish the destitute. (*CIG* 4.8639 [tr. C. Mango])

Impressive as this church was, however, it proved to be merely a precursor to the building of the structure which remains one of Justinian's enduring legacies – the church of Hagia Sophia (Holy Wisdom) in Constantinople, to which Procopius justifiably gives pride of place and the most space in his survey of the emperor's building activities (*Aed.* 1.1.20–78).

Situated as it was near the hippodrome and palace, the previous incarnation of this church, built in the early fifth century at the behest of Theodosius II, was one of the casualties of the destruction of property which accompanied the Nika riot in January 532. Not for the first time – the example of Nero comes to mind – an emperor saw the devastation of the centre of an imperial capital as an opportunity to implement grandiose plans which he hoped would leave his mark on the cityscape (in the event, Justinian's efforts proved to be much more durable and influential than Nero's). The new church which arose between 532 and 537 was designed on an unprecedented scale – it was to be another millennium before a larger church was built anywhere in Europe (Seville Cathedral) – and deployed novel engineering techniques which involved the construction of a massive dome, resulting in a breath-taking interior space (Figs 18–20):

Rising above this circle is an enormous spherical dome which makes the building exceptionally beautiful. It seems not to be founded on solid masonry, but to cover the space with its golden dome suspended from heaven. All of these elements, marvellously fitted together in mid-air, suspended from one another and reposing only on the parts adjacent to them, produce a unified and most remarkable harmony in the work ...

The entire ceiling has been overlaid with pure gold which combines beauty with ostentation, yet the light reflected from the marble prevails, shining out in rivalry with the gold ... Who could

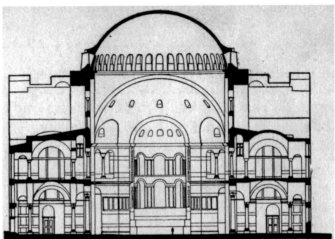

Figures 18–19 Cross-sections of Hagia Sophia in Constantinople. © Salzenberg/ *Simpson's History of Architectural Development* vol. II, C. Stewart, Pearson Education Ltd

recount the beauty of the columns and the marbles with which the church is adorned? One might imagine that one has chanced upon a meadow in full bloom. For one would surely marvel at the purple hue of some, the green of others, at those on which the crimson blooms, at those which flash with white, at those, too, which Nature, like a painter, has varied with the most contrasting colours. When- ever one goes to this church, one understands immediately that this work has been fashioned not by human power or skill, but under the influence of God. And so the mind is lifted up to God and floats aloft, thinking that he cannot be far away but must love to dwell in

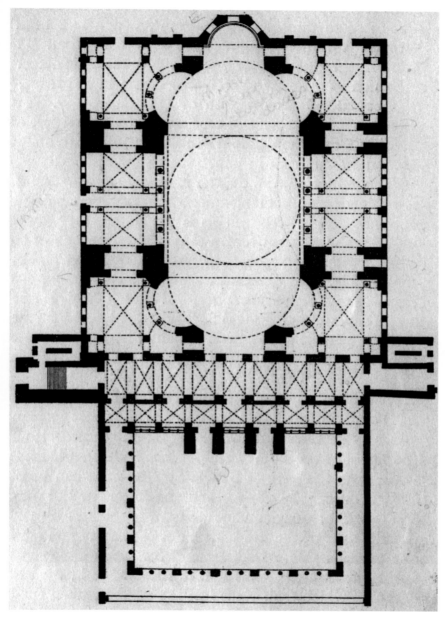

Figure 20 Floor plan of Hagia Sophia in Constantinople. © Salzenberg/*Simpson's History of Architectural Development* vol. II, C. Stewart, Pearson Education Ltd

Figure 21 Interior of Hagia Sophia, Constantinople. © Cinzia Maggiore/
Tony Parry

this place which he himself has chosen. (Procop. *Aed.* 1.45–7, 54, 59–61 [tr. H. B. Dewing with revisions])

While the enthusiam of Procopius' panegyrical description might prompt a certain scepticism, personal autopsy of the interior of the church bears out the overall thrust of his account, even given all the changes which the structure and decoration have undergone since Justinian's day (Fig. 21).[9] Moreover, the impressive array of coloured marbles was the subject of more detailed description by another contemporary author, who emphasises their origin from all parts of the Mediterranean – surely intended as a visual statement of Justinian's imperial ambitions.[10]

While there is no reason to doubt the significance of Hagia Sophia as an expression of Justinian's piety or of his desire to make a name for himself, there appears to have been a further important political motivation underlying its construction. By becoming the largest and most impressive church in Constantinople, Justinian's Hagia Sophia pushed into second place another remarkable church which had been completed a decade and a half earlier – a church dedicated to a military martyr, St Polyeuctus. Although it no longer stands, its remains were excavated by archaeologists in the 1960s and revealed a substantial basilica-style structure, richly decorated with coloured marbles, intricately carved columns and beautiful sculptures, as well as – most importantly – major portions of a superbly executed inscription, the complete text of which proved to be preserved in the collection of epigrams known as the *Greek Anthology* (1.10) (Fig. 22).[11] This identified the individual responsible for funding the church's construction as a prominent member of the Constantinopolitan elite, Anicia Juliana, probably descended from one of the most powerful Roman senatorial families of the fourth century

9. For its architectural significance and influence, see R. J. Mainstone, *Hagia Sophia: Architecture, Structure and Liturgy of Justinian's Great Church*, London: Thames and Hudson, 1997.
10. Paul the Silentiary, *Description of Hagia Sophia*, 617–46, with discussion by B. Ward-Perkins, 'Constantinople: a city and its ideological territory' in G. P. Brogiolo, N. Gauthier and N. Christie (eds), *Towns and their Territories between Late Antiquity and the Early Middle Ages*, Leiden: Brill, 2000, 325–45, at 327–9.
11. The most convenient discussion of St Polyeuctus is the beautifully illustrated volume by M. Harrison, *A Temple for Byzantium: The Discovery and Excavation of Anicia Juliana's Palace Church in Istanbul*, London: Harvey Miller, 1989. See also J. Bardill, 'A new temple for Byzantium: Anicia Juliana, King Solomon, and the gilded ceiling of the church of St. Polyeuktos in Constantinople' in W. Bowden et al. (eds), *Social and Political Life in Late Antiquity*, Leiden: Brill, 2006, 339–70.

Figure 22 Part of a peacock arch from the Church of St Polyeuctus, Constantinople, 520s. The text on the arch is part of the epigram preserved in the *Greek Anthology*, which celebrates the piety and pedigree of the church's patron, Anicia Juliana. The peacock, whose feathers alone remain, was associated with eternal life in late antiquity, though also had older associations with Hera, queen of the gods, while the grapes evoked Christ as the true vine, while also perhaps containing echoes of Dionysus. © Institute of Archaeology; photographer Elizabeth Harrison

and certainly descended from the fifth-century western emperors Valentinian III and Olybrius. As one would expect of any self-respecting aristocrat, she used the church's inscription to remind its users of her remarkable pedigree, while also making clear the pious nature of the enterprise. She herself had been married to Flavius Areobindus, one of Anastasius' generals during his Persian war, consul in 506 and the individual whom the populace touted as a possible imperial replacement for Anastasius during the crisis of 512 (p. 173 above); their son Olybrius had also held the consulship.

Anicia Juliana was, then, a woman of real substance, in both status and resources, and the combination of the inscription and the church's remains has led scholars to the very plausible conclusion that the construction of her church was a powerful and most public expression of her disgruntlement with the fact that a court functionary (Anastasius) and a Balkan peasant (Justin) had successively occupied the imperial throne, rather than more obviously suitable candidates such as her husband or son.[12] Justinian's Hagia Sophia can in turn be seen as the riposte of the new ruling family, safe-guarded against any attempt to over-trump it not only by its massive dimensions but also by Justinian's introducing, soon after, pro-cedural requirements which made it more difficult for anyone else to construct a church or other religious building in future (*Nov.* 67 [538], Procop. *Aed.* 1.8.5).[13]

If religion and politics were inextricably intertwined in the case of Hagia Sophia, however, this ought not to encourage undue scepticism about the primacy of religious motivations in Justinian's funding of some of his other building projects. In particular he is credited with helping to construct numerous monasteries (Procop. *Aed.* 5.9 *passim*) and, often in tandem with such institutions, hospices for the poor and sick. Under the latter heading, there is his rebuilding of the hospice of Samson in the centre of Constantinople, as well as the adding of two new hospices in the capital, complete with endowments (Procop. *Aed.* 1.2.14–17), and he was also respon-sible for the construction or expansion of hospices for the poor and sick in various provincial centres.[14]

Continuing Christianisation

The channelling of imperial resources into such charitable projects, as well as into monastic foundations, must have played a part in the ongoing process of Christianising the empire – for it was a fact that two centuries after Constantine, there remained significant numbers

---

12. That the church was a statement directed not only against Justin but also against Anastasius is the implication of recent work on the church's brickstamps, which point towards earlier start and finish dates for St Polyeuctus than Harrison proposed, namely c. 512 and c. 520 (J. Bardill, *Brickstamps of Constantinople*, Oxford: Oxford University Press, 2004, 62–4, 111–16).

13. Juliana's inscription included a reference to her church having 'surpassed the wisdom of renowned Solomon', which takes on added significance if an eighth-century report of Justinian's words at the dedication of Hagia Sophia is to be believed: 'Solomon, I have overcome you!' (*Patria Constantinopolitana* 3.57). The speed with which work on Hagia Sophia began after the Nika riot (23 February 532) implies that Justinian was already planning a church on this scale prior to the riot (as noted by J. A. S. Evans, *The Age of Justinian*, London: Routledge, 1996, 216), which is in turn consistent with the idea of the church as a response to Anicia Juliana.

14. In Pythia (Pontus), Jerusalem, Jericho, Bostra (Arabia), Apamea, Corycus (Cilicia) and Perge (Pamphylia) (Procop. *Aed.* 5.3.20, 5.6.25, 5.9.4, 22, 27, 34–5, 38, with epigraphic corroboration of that in Jerusalem: Feissel, 'Édifices', 100 [no. 64]).

of individuals who continued to adhere to traditional cults or were members of major non-Christian religious communities. With regard to the former category, the greatest numbers continued to be in rural areas, as became particularly apparent through the activities of John of Ephesus in some of the more remote countryside of western Anatolia. During the course of a thirty-year enterprise, from the mid-530s to the end of Justinian's reign, he claimed to have facilitated the conversion and baptism of some 80,000 individuals previously still adhering to traditional pagan cults. While the figure has prompted some scepticism, its plausibility has been well argued with reference to the length of time and the size of the area involved. Importantly, too, the emperor himself is said to have supported John's activities with funds for the construction of churches and monasteries.[15]

One particularly puzzling episode in the conversion of rural regions relates to the temple of the goddess Isis at Philae in the deep south of Egypt, which is reported to have been destroyed on Justinian's orders early in his reign, with its cult statues despatched to Constantinople (Procop. *Wars* 1.19.36–7). Although the army officer entrusted with the task may well have sent the temple's cult statues to Constantinople, the temple itself cannot in fact have been demolished, since it remains standing to this day, with inscriptions indicating, rather, that it was converted into a church at some point in late antiquity. In fact, cult inscriptions abruptly ceased in the 450s, implying that the cult had come to an end well before Justinian's reign, while the most plausible scenario for the conversion of the temple building into a church places it in the years immediately following Justinian's reign.[16] Given the distance of Philae from Constantinople, on the southern frontier of the empire, it would certainly have been difficult to verify Justinian's claim that he had had the temple destroyed, especially if what purported to be the cult's statues were displayed in the capital as proof of the cult's termination. As reported by Procopius, this particular episode looks like an exercise primarily concerned with reinforcing Justinian's credentials as a Christian ruler early in his reign.

15. F. R. Trombley, 'Paganism in the Greek world at the end of antiquity: the case of rural Anatolia and Greece', *Harv. Theol. Rev.* 78 (1985), 327–52, at 329–32. See also Menze, *Justinian*, 262–5, for some intriguing suggestions about Justinian's patronage of John's activities in the context of the emperor's attempts to resolve differences between Chalcedonian and anti-Chalcedonian Christians.
16. J. H. F. Dijkstra, *Philae and the End of Ancient Egyptian Religion*, Leuven: Peeters, 2008.

While imperial initiatives may have played a part in evangelistic endeavour, however, much of it relied on the initiative and resourcefulness of individuals. The biographies of holy men from this period are an important resource for gaining insights into the ongoing process of evangelisation, including both the compromises sometimes involved and the practical educational dimension. As previously noted with reference to the early fifth century (p. 153 above), a Christianised version of animal sacrifice was sometimes sanctioned, and there is also evidence of this from the activities of St Nicholas during Justinian's reign among remote communities of southern Anatolia, where the following is one of a number of such episodes:

> The clergy from Plenios came in a procession with the Christ-beloved people with crosses and met Nicholas at the chapel of St George. He followed them from there with seven calves. After they went into the chapel ... he slaughtered (lit. 'sacrificed') the seven calves. The crowds assembled and two hundred couches were laid. Nicholas also brought one hundred measures of wine and forty measures of wheat. All ate and were filled, and gave thanks to God who gave grace to his servant Nicholas. (*V. Nicholai* 55 [tr. F. R. Trombley])[17]

Another saint's life, that of Simeon 'the mountaineer', who was also active during Justinian's reign in mountainous regions near the upper Euphrates, highlights the importance of education and literacy in sustaining the influence of Christianity. Simeon is said to have selected a number of both boys and girls from these communities (albeit not without some opposition from their families) whom he taught to read and write so that they were able to read the Bible. It took time and commitment on his part, but in due course these disciples were in turn able to teach others (John of Ephesus, *Lives of the Eastern Saints* 16 [PO 17.246–7]).

While greater numbers of the unchurched were present in rural regions, the smaller numbers who retained loyalties to traditional cults in cities were nonetheless an important focus for Justinian because they were often members of the elite. This in itself was sufficient reason to target them, but it may also have been recognised that, as landowners, they were potential obstacles to effective evangelisation of rural regions where they owned estates[18] – a

17. For comparable evidence from Egypt, see D. Frankfurter, 'Syncretism and the holy man in late antique Egypt', *JECS* 11 (2003), 339–85.
18. Cf. M. Whitby, 'John of Ephesus and the pagans: pagan survivals in the sixth

suggestion strengthened by the fact that the punishment of suspected crypto-pagans often included the confiscation of their property. Early in his reign, Justinian conducted a purge of prominent individuals in the capital believed to be adherents of traditional cults (Malalas, *Chron.* 449), with further such crackdowns in major urban centres at various points subsequently.[19]

The most controversial of these actions was the supposed closure in 529 of the Athenian Academy, the philosophical school established by Plato a millennium earlier.[20] This has often been seen as indicative of a general and proactive anti-intellectualism on the part of Justinian, but on the most recent and persuasive interpretation it looks as though he was probably responding to the concerns of Christians in Athens and that this measure had the more restricted aim of ending the teaching there of Neoplatonic philosophy, which had in recent years, under the leadership of Damascius, become more uncompromisingly pagan and had attracted increasing numbers of students.[21] Although Justinian's edict can only have prevented public lectures, as distinct from private sessions with an inner circle of students, it marked the beginning of the end, reinforced by a pair of laws in 531 which prohibited pagan institutions from receiving bequests and pagans from receiving a municipal salary for teaching (*Cod. Iust.* 1.11.9–10). It was presumably these laws which prompted Damascius and half a dozen colleagues to make their famous, if ill-informed, decision to emigrate to Persia 'since the official religion of the Roman empire was not to their liking', whereas they had heard that Persia was 'the land of "Plato's philosopher king" in which justice reigned supreme' (Agathias 2.30.3). Enthusiastically welcomed by Khusro but soon disabused of their overly optimistic expectations, they were allowed to return

century' in M. Salamon (ed.), *Paganism in the Later Roman Empire and in Byzantium,* Cracow: Byzantina et Slavica Cracoviensia 1, 1991, 111–31, at 130–1.

19. Malalas, *Chron.* 491 (Constantinople, 562); *Life of the Younger Symeon the Stylite* 161 (Antioch, c. 555).

20. The assumption that the Academy still existed in sixth-century Athens has been challenged, with a number of scholars arguing that the focus of Justinian's actions was, rather, the Neoplatonic school at Athens (which saw itself as the heir to Plato's Academy): see E. Watts, 'Justinian, Malalas and the end of Athenian philosophical teaching in AD 529', *JRS* 94 (2004), 168–82, at 168 n.1 for references.

21. E. Watts, *City and School in Late Antique Athens and Alexandria*, Berkeley: University of California Press, 2006, 111–42, noting at the same time (232–56) the survival of a more moderate form of pagan philosophical teaching in Alexandria into the early seventh century.

to the Roman empire with protected status as part of the peace settlement of 532 (p. 258 above).[22]

The Jews continued to be an important non-Christian community within the empire. Justinian did not outlaw Judaism, but it is surely significant that he did not retain in his code the law of Theodosius I which asserted the religion's legality (*Cod. Theod.* 16.8.9), while the Jews' legal rights were eroded from early in his reign: they were deprived of the right to disinherit any children who converted to Christianity, and to give testimony in a court of law against Christians (*Cod. Iust.* 1.5.13 [527/8], 21 [531]). His disdain for them is evident in comments such as the following: 'Let them experience the dishonour which they have also wished for their souls' (*Nov.* 45 pr.). A more aggressive stance was taken towards the Samaritans, an ancient offshoot of Judaism, who had a history of rebellion against imperial authority. In particular an undated measure from his reign ordered their synagogues to be destroyed (*Cod. Iust.* 1.5.17), which may have been what provoked a fresh and costly revolt in northern Palestine in 529 (Malalas, *Chron.* 445–7).[23]

While it is clear that Justinian's reign did not mark the end of non-Christian practices and beliefs within the empire, there is nonetheless reason to think that this period was one when significant steps were taken towards the suppression of vestigial traditional cults, the conversion of the unchurched, and the continuing marginalisation of Jews and Samaritans, with much of the impetus coming from the emperor himself.[24]

Religion and foreign relations

Another interesting feature of the religious history of this period is the way in which Christianity came to play an increasingly

22. The widely accepted view that they took up residence in the firmly pagan city of Carrhae (Harran) in the Roman province of Mesopotamia has been persuasively challenged: E. Watts, 'Where to live the philosophical life in the sixth century? Damascius, Simplicius and the return from Persia', *GRBS* 45 (2005), 285–315; R. Lane Fox, 'Harran, the Sabians and the late Platonist "movers"' in A. Smith (ed.), *The Philosopher and Society in Late Antiquity*, Swansea: Classical Press of Wales, 2005, 231–44.

23. For a good overview of Jews and Samaritans in the sixth century, see N. de Lange, 'The Jews in the age of Justinian' in Maas, *Justinian*, 401–26, with further detail on Samaritans in H. Sivan, *Palestine in Late Antiquity*, Oxford: Oxford University Press, 2008, 107–42.

24. Cf. M. Whitby, 'John of Ephesus and the pagans: pagan survivals in the sixth century' in M. Salamon (ed.), *Paganism in the Later Roman Empire and in Byzantium*, Cracow: Byzantina et Slavica Cracoviensia 1, 1991, 111–31.

prominent role in foreign relations. It has already been noted how Justinian's concern to promote Chalcedonian orthodoxy may have contributed to his decision to mount expeditions aimed at over-throwing the Arian regimes of the Vandals in north Africa and of the Goths in Italy (p. 259 above). He can also be observed appealing to a common Christian allegiance as the basis for co-operation against common enemies. In the late 520s, when war with Sasanian Persia had resumed (p. 257 above), he sent an envoy to the southern reaches of the Red Sea to try to persuade the Christian kingdom of Axum (Ethiopia) to assist the Romans to circumvent the Persian stranglehold on the silk trade from the east, and to convince the Christian kingdom of the Himyarites (Yemen) to open up a second front against Persia, with the envoy particularly emphasising the Romans' 'likemindedness of belief' with both peoples (Procop. *Wars* 1.20.9–13). This initiative led to nothing, not least because the emperor had underestimated the distances and practical difficulties involved, but it is an early indication of his willingness to make use of Christianity for diplomatic ends. Similar thinking is evident in the west in the mid-530s when he sent a letter to the Frankish king Theudebert proposing an alliance against the Goths on the basis of their common commitment to 'the orthodox faith which rejects the beliefs of the Arians' (Procop. *Wars* 5.5.8–10). Even if Theudebert's subsequent actions indicated that, despite his enthusiastic response, the advancement of Frankish interests was his priority, the episode once again shows that Justinian was alert to the wider relevance of religion.

Justinian's interests, however, extended beyond trying to consolidate ties with neighbouring peoples who were already affiliated with Christianity. He was also 'the first emperor to perceive the political benefits of missionary activity beyond the frontiers'.[25] This was particularly relevant along the empire's eastern frontier, where the presence of Persia, with the allegiance of its kings to Zoroastrianism, presented a clear choice to the rulers of the various minor principalities which lay between the two great powers, particularly in the Caucasus. Justinian's activities in this respect may well have been prompted by an event during Justin's reign when Tzath, the ruler of the Caucasian region of Lazica, which was then a client state of Persia, fell out with the Persians and turned to the Roman empire for

25. G. Greatrex, 'Byzantium and the east in the sixth century' in Maas, *Justinian*, 477–509, at 491.

support. Upon arriving at the imperial court in Constantinople, he asked to become a Christian, and was duly baptised, married a Roman woman of aristocratic descent and returned to Lazica with ceremonial robes bearing the image of Justin (Malalas, *Chron.* 413). Early in Justinian's reign, another Caucasian people neighbouring Lazica, the Tzani, were persuaded to convert to Christianity, as too were the Abasgi in the late 530s (Procop. *Wars* 1.15.24–5, 8.3.18–21). Although not so directly relevant to the frontier with Persia, Grod, ruler of the Huns in the Crimean peninsula, on the north coast of the Black Sea, was brought into a client relationship with Constantinople in the late 520s, with baptism providing important ceremonial confirmation of the new relationship, as too was Grepes, ruler of the Heruls; in both cases, Justinian himself acted as baptismal sponsor.[26] Likewise the Nubians to the south of Egypt were converted to Christianity during Justinian's reign through the efforts of missionaries from the empire;[27] although not such a strategically important frontier, this nevertheless promised benefits in terms of greater security from raiders.[28]

A final detail worth mentioning is Justinian's inclusion in the peace negotiations with Persia in 561/2 (p. 288 below) of consideration of religious issues, as a result of which the Persians agreed to allow the Christians living in Persia freedom of worship, provided they refrained from proselytising Persians who adhered to Zoroastrianism (Menander, *fr.* 6.1 [lines 399–407]). It is difficult to know what to make of this, since Justinian was in no position to guarantee the behaviour of Christians in Persia. Perhaps this element of the peace was primarily to enhance his reputation as defender of the Christian faith among his own subjects – or perhaps he anticipated that it might prove to be a useful *casus belli* against Persia in the future.

Reconciliation within the church: mission impossible?

As previously noted (pp. 147–50 above), the decisions taken at the Council of Chalcedon in 451 failed to resolve the Christological

---

26. Details in Malalas, *Chron.* 427–8, 431–2, including the unfortunate aftermath of Grod's overenthusiastic imposition of Christianity on his subjects.
27. According to the main source for this episode, Justinian and Theodora sent rival missions to Nubia with a view to winning them to Chalcedonian and anti-Chalcedonian Christianity respectively: see Evans, *Justinian*, 250, for details.
28. Greatrex, 'Byzantium and the east', 491.

controversies of the Theodosian period. This was partly a result of the necessary ambiguities of the Definition concerning Christ, but another important factor was Chalcedon's rehabilitation of two Nestorian sympathisers in the persons of Theodoret of Cyrrhus and Ibas of Edessa. Although that rehabilitation had been granted reluctantly at Chalcedon and only on the grounds that their deposition at the second Council of Ephesus in 449 had been uncanonical, it is understandable that those loyal to the theology of Cyril of Alexandria should have viewed their rehabilitation as effectively granting approval of their pro-Nestorian theological views as well. It was this element of Chalcedon which was to become the focus of Justinian's efforts to reconcile the various parties. In considering those efforts, it is important to bear in mind that anti-Chalcedonians were not generally viewed as heretics who were outside the church, but as schismatics within the church, and that Justinian's aim was probably not to win unconditional anti-Chalcedonian acceptance of Chalcedon, but rather to reduce their objections to Chalcedon to a point where they would be willing to return to communion with Chalcedonian bishops.[29]

Justinian seems to have been first alerted to the significance of Chalcedon's rehabilitation of Theodoret and Ibas as a result of discussions he organised in 532 involving representatives of the Chalcedonian and anti-Chalcedonian positions.[30] The very fact of his organising these discussions is indicative of his willingness to explore ways of finding common ground – according to a record of the discussions, their purpose was to find 'some means for the peace of the churches'[31] – and although the discussions only lasted for two days and did not lead to agreement on any points, they did help to clarify where central points of disagreement lay. In particular, when asked to indicate their objections to Chalcedon, the anti-Chalcedonians responded that, in addition to 'the innovation of two natures, ... above all else the fact that they [the bishops at Chalcedon] accepted Ibas ... [and] they also accepted the wicked Theodoret, without his having changed his evil belief'.[32]

In 534 or 535, the leading anti-Chalcedonian theologian, Severus of Antioch, whom Justinian had invited from exile in Egypt to

29. Price, *Council of Constantinople*, 8–9, 20–3.
30. For an overview of the discussions, see Menze, *Justinian*, 58–67.
31. S. Brock, 'The conversations with the Syrian Orthodox under Justinian (532)', *Orientalia Christiana Periodica* 47 (1981), 87–121, at 114.
32. Brock, 'Conversations', 98–100.

Constantinople, finally agreed to come, and in 535 the new bishop of Constantinople, Anthimus, who had participated in the discussions of 532, began informal negotiations with Severus and other leading anti-Chalcedonian figures. However, Anthimus' sympathetic stance towards the anti-Chalcedonians caused increasing disquiet among clergy and laity in Constantinople, as well as Chalcedonian bishops in Syria and Palestine, and when the bishop of Rome, Agapetus, arrived in Constantinople in March 536 on an unrelated matter – he was part of an embassy from the Gothic regime in Italy aiming to dissuade Justinian from proceeding with his invasion of that region – he responded to Chalcedonian appeals to intervene (which had reached him even before he left Italy) by refusing to take communion with Anthimus. Anthimus promptly resigned his episcopal office, and Agapetus consecrated a local clergyman, Menas, as his successor (the first time a bishop of Rome had ordained a bishop of Constantinople). Menas was instructed by the emperor to convene a local synod to investigate Anthimus' case; that synod duly condemned Anthimus, along with Severus and other anti-Chalcedonian figures.[33] Justinian himself endorsed the synod's decisions in a law of his own in August 536 (*Nov.* 42), although it is worth noting that neither the synod nor Justinian's law went so far as to condemn anti-Chalcedonian views as heresy.[34]

While Severus and his associates returned to Egypt, where they could be assured of a sympathetic welcome, Anthimus joined a growing number of anti-Chalcedonians who remained in the capital and took advantage of the shelter in the Palace of Hormisdas offered by the Empress Theodora, who was, as previously noted (p. 246 above), anti-Chalcedonian in her sympathies. As a result of her privileged position and access to resources, the imperial palace complex came to harbour a substantial enclave of anti-Chalcedonian clergy and monks (numbering around 500 individuals at one stage).[35] However, Theodora could not have done this without Justinian's tacit agreement, which presumably reflects in part his concern to keep channels of communication open as he continued to pursue a strategy for rapprochement. At the same time, this arrangement had a further, more immediate and practical advantage:

---

33. F. Millar, 'Rome, Constantinople and the Near Eastern Church under Justinian: two synods of CE 536', *JRS* 98 (2008), 62–82; Menze, *Justinian*, 196–208.
34. Cf. Price, *Council of Constantinople*, 14 n.23.
35. For Theodora's efforts, and the figure of 500, see John of Ephesus, *Lives of the Eastern Saints* 47 (PO 18.676–84).

'Holding the dissidents in Constantinople permitted the authorities to keep them supervised and to take them out of circulation, depriving their congregations of pastoral care.'[36]

Agapetus' adventitious intervention in 536 put paid to Justinian's immediate hopes of reaching an accommodation with anti-Chalcedonians, but did not end them definitively. In the early 540s he initiated another attempt at achieving his objective, an attempt whose underlying impetus may well have derived from the dramatic setbacks of recent years, above all the pandemic of 542 (pp. 289–91 below); if Justinian saw these events as the judgement of God – and one of his laws in the aftermath of the pandemic refers to it as 'the chastisement which God visited upon men' (*Nov.* 122 [544]) – then it is quite plausible that he should have seen renewed efforts to ameliorate church disagreements as an appropriate response.[37] Justinian's attempt drew on what he had learned from the discussions of 532 concerning anti-Chalcedonian objections to the rehabilitation of Theodoret and Ibas in 451, and focused on trying to assuage those objections by condemning the writings of these two men from the 430s which had been critical of Cyril, together with the person and writings of their teacher, Theodore of Mopsuestia, who was widely regarded by anti-Chalcedonians as the ultimate source of Nestorian ideas. This was initially done in an edict of 'Three Chapters' issued by Justinian in late 544 or early 545 (whose text is no longer extant), where the term 'chapters' referred to the three anathemas it contained; however, somewhat confusingly, the phrase 'the Three Chapters' soon came to be used with reference to the object of those anathemas – the condemned writings of the three theologians.[38]

It must have become apparent to Justinian fairly quickly that this was not going to be the elegant solution for which he had hoped. Not only did it fail to win support even from moderate anti-

---

36. C. Pazdernik, '"Our most pious consort given us by God": dissident reaction to the partnership of Justinian and Theodora, AD 525–548', *Classical Antiquity* 13 (1994), 256–81, at 275.
37. As argued by M. Meier, *Das andere Zeitalter Justinians: Kontingenzerfahrung und Kontingenzbewältigung im 6 Jahrhundert n. Chr.*, Göttingen: Vandenhoeck & Ruprecht, 2003, ch. 3, and by Price, *Council of Constantinople*, 16, who also suggests that Justinian's own recovery from the illness could have convinced him that he still had an important mission to fulfil in relation to the church.
38. A. Grillmeier, *Christ in the Christian Tradition* II.2 (tr. J. Cawte and P. Allen), London: Mowbray, 1995, 412 n.375.

Chalcedonians, for whom the absence of any criticism of the Council of Chalcedon was now a more fundamental flaw than had been the case a decade or so ago, but it also provoked a strongly antagonistic reaction from church leaders in the west – an unfortunate consequence in the context of Justinian's military difficulties in Italy and north Africa in the mid-540s (pp. 286–9 below). Justinian had no doubt assumed that since Chalcedon had confirmed the condemnation of Nestorius himself in 451, his contemporary Chalcedonians would have no objection to an edict condemning the writings of three long-deceased individuals who had been closely associated with Nestorius. However, that was not how Chalcedonian leaders saw the matter.

The first inkling of a problem came when Justinian found he even had to pressure leading Chalcedonian bishops in the east to give their formal support to the edict, which, worryingly, Menas of Constantinople only agreed to do on the understanding that he could withdraw it if the bishop of Rome did not give the edict his approval. By this time, the bishop of Rome was Vigilius, a cleric who had accompanied Agapetus to Constantinople in 536 before being installed as bishop of Rome himself with the support of Belisarius and his troops in 537, and who might therefore have been confidently expected to endorse Justinian's strategy. As the months of 545 passed, however, without Vigilius issuing any such endorsement, Justinian arranged for the bishop to be 'collected' from Rome and escorted to Constantinople. En route, he was permitted to stop over in Sicily and consult with a gathering of bishops, eventually reaching the imperial capital in January 547.

Vigilius' consultations and communications with western bishops and clergy had left him in no doubt that Justinian's condemnation of the Three Chapters was unacceptable to them: Theodore, Theodoret and Ibas might have been closely associated with Nestorius, but Theodore had died in 428 before Nestorius' condemnation at Ephesus (431) and therefore in communion with the church, while the rehabilitation of Theodoret and Ibas at Chalcedon meant that any condemnation of them was seen as casting aspersions on the integrity of Chalcedon as a whole. Opposition from north African clergy proved to be particularly vociferous – a reaction about which Justinian might well have had cause to feel aggrieved, after his efforts had so recently freed north Africa from Arian Vandal rule. However, north Africa had a long tradition of independence in church affairs, most obviously in the Donatist schism of the fourth century, which a century without imperial control seems only to have intensified.[39]

Against this background, it is hardly surprising that on first arriving in Constantinople, Vigilius refused to take communion with Menas. However, Justinian maintained the pressure on him, while also allowing him to hold a gathering of seventy bishops who had not yet given their support to the edict. Eventually, in April 548, Vigilius succumbed and issued a formal judgement upholding the condemnation. Far from settling the issue, however, Vigilius' judgement provoked a barrage of criticism from the west. A north African bishop who had participated in the conference, Facundus of Hermiane, produced a lengthy tract *In Defence of the Three Chapters* which, among other things, warned Justinian against usurping the function of a priest by meddling in theological matters (12.3), while a synod in Carthage in 550 refused to recognise Vigilius as bishop of Rome.

Since it was clear that he could not rely on the authority of the bishop of Rome to secure the assent of the western churches, Justinian's next move was to begin preparations for an ecumenical council in Constantinople which would endorse the condemnation of the Three Chapters. In 551 he issued a further edict which, while reiterating the condemnation of the Three Chapters, was also explicit in its endorsement of the Council of Chalcedon. He also arranged for the removal of recalcitrant bishops from important sees and their replacement by incumbents who would be more amenable at the forthcoming council; fortunately, such a step proved unnecessary in the case of Constantinople itself where Menas died in the course of 552, allowing Justinian to appoint a compliant successor.

The council duly convened in May 553, but with an attendance of only 145 bishops, its credibility was compromised from the start – Chalcedon had involved more than double that number (about 370). Furthermore, Vigilius had once again changed tack and refused to attend, thereby depriving the council of the presence of the bishop of Rome, while only six bishops came from north Africa. Over the course of four weeks, the assembled bishops held eight sessions, culminating in the promulgation of a series of canons which

---

39. Y. Modéran, 'L'Afrique reconquise et les Trois Chapitres' in C. Chazelle and C. Cubitt (eds), *The Crisis of the* Oikumene: *The Three Chapters and the Failed Quest for Unity in the Sixth-Century Mediterranean*, Turnhout: Brepols, 2007, 39–84.

included, on the one hand, a reassertion and clarification of Chalcedon and, on the other, the condemnation of the Three Chapters.[40] Six months later, Vigilius finally agreed to endorse the condemnation of the Three Chapters. In 555 he was allowed to leave Constantinople for Rome, but died en route.

The council proved an empty victory for Justinian. Although Chalcedonians in the east generally accepted it, anti-Chalcedonians did not, which rather defeated its purpose. Indeed, the decade culminating in the council of 553 saw the consolidation of a separate anti-Chalcedonian church hierarchy in the east, as increasing numbers of bishops and clergy were secretly ordained, above all through the activities of Jacob Baradai, who, ironically, was commissioned in 542 to undertake this work by anti-Chalcedonian leaders living under Theodora's protection in the imperial palace.[41] In the west Vigilius' eventual endorsement did nothing to persuade those who saw the whole exercise as tampering unnecessarily with Chalcedon, and the installation of a new bishop of Rome, Pelagius, in 556 did little to improve the situation, since he was clearly an imperial appointee. Nonetheless, open opposition to the outcome of the council gradually crumbled. In north Africa, this was facilitated by the imperial authorities exiling leading opponents and forcing others into hiding, but elsewhere reluctant acquiescence eventually prevailed, with only the sees of Milan and Aquileia holding out for substantial lengths of time (the former until 573, the latter until the early seventh century). Nonetheless, the whole episode left a legacy of resentment and distrust.[42] Justinian's public career had begun in 518 with his involvement in negotiations to end the Acacian schism between Constantinople and Rome, so there was a bitter irony in his reign ending with acrimony between east and west which had developed directly out of his attempts to achieve reconciliation within the church.

40. For translation and discussion of the proceedings, see Price, *Council of Constantinople*.
41. W. H. C. Frend, *The Rise of the Monophysite Movement*, Cambridge: Cambridge University Press, 1972, 285–7; P. Wood, *'We have no king but Christ': Christian Political Thought in Greater Syria on the Eve of the Arab Conquest (c. 400–585)*, Oxford: Oxford University Press, 2010, ch. 6.
42. Modéran, 'L'Afrique reconquise'; C. Sotinel, 'The Three Chapters and the transformations of Italy' in Chazelle and Cubitt, *Crisis*, 85–120.

CHAPTER 14

Justinian and the end of antiquity

The limits of empire

Despite it appearing in 540 that the war in Italy was effectively over (p. 263 above), this soon proved not to be the case. There were sufficient Goths in northern Italy who were disenchanted with Vitigis' surrender and had not yet relinquished their arms to provide the basis for ongoing resistance. The first couple of leaders they chose were ineffective, but by the autumn of 541 they had found, in the person of Totila, a highly capable commander who quickly turned the tables on Justinian's generals. During the course of 542 he inflicted a series of defeats on Roman forces and by the end of the year had regained control of most of the Italian peninsula, leaving only Rome, Ravenna and a number of coastal towns in imperial hands. Totila's success was due in part to his strategic skills, but also to a lack of coordination between Roman commanders, with no single individual in overall charge following Belisarius' return to the east in 540. These problems were exacerbated by further developments outside of Italy, particularly the renewal of warfare with Persia in 540, the continuation of the unsettled conditions in north Africa already evident in the mid-530s, and the impact of a virulent pandemic which reached Constantinople in 542, all of which meant that imperial resources became severely stretched.[1]

By the late 530s the Persian king Khusro had consolidated power and implemented fiscal and military reforms which left him in a stronger position to pursue an aggressive foreign policy. Well aware of Justinian's western campaigns in north Africa and Italy, Khusro saw an opportunity to take advantage of the commitment of imperial troops in regions distant from the Persian frontier and invaded Syria in the spring of 540. There were now insufficient Roman units stationed in the region to resist Khusro's army, and

---

1. Justinian also suffered the personal loss of Theodora (probably to cancer) in 548.

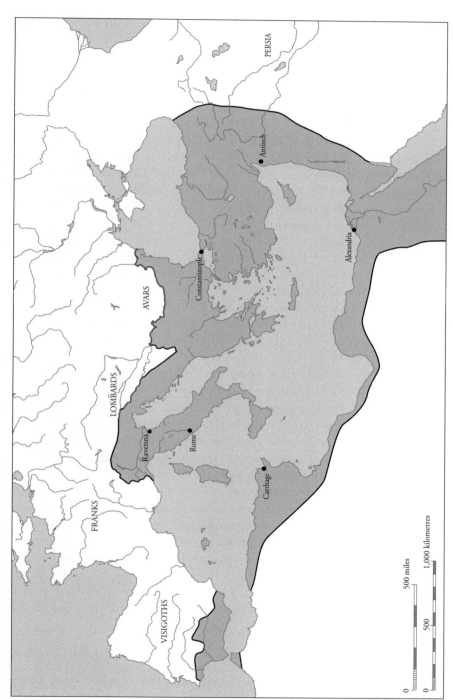

Map 8 The Roman empire at the death of Justinian (565)

Syria's cities were either sacked and their populations enslaved – as happened to Antioch – or agreed to hand over their gold and silver in return for being spared (Procop. *Wars* 2.5–13). To add insult to injury, Khusro made a point of bathing in the Mediterranean at Seleucia, where he also offered sacrifices to his gods, and, in the manner of an emperor, he presided over chariot races at Apamea (2.11.1, 31–5).

Justinian responded to this unwelcome turn of events by reassigning Belisarius to the Persian frontier with a view to preventing another Persian invasion of Syria in 541, but Khusro proceeded to widen the conflict by turning his attention to the Caucasian region of Lazica, which Persian forces occupied in 541, fuelling Roman fears of a Persian seaborne offensive across the Black Sea against Constantinople. After further inconclusive engagements in northern Mesopotamia during the next few years, a truce was agreed for that region in 545, and renewed in 551 and 557, but fighting continued in Lazica until 557.[2] Eventually, during the winter of 561/2, a definitive peace settlement was agreed, a detailed account of which is preserved among the surviving excerpts from one of Procopius' historical continuators, Menander (*fr.* 6.1–2). Most of the agreement was concerned with regulating various aspects of frontier interaction, but it included Justinian's conceding Persian demands that they receive 30,000 *solidi* per annum for its duration (fifty years). Although the total amount involved was a substantial sum, it was manageable on an annual basis. More serious was the loss of prestige involved,[3] but Justinian evidently considered this a necessary price to pay to avoid a recurrence of fighting simultaneous conflicts on multiple fronts.

The problems arising from renewed warfare with Persia in the 540s were not lessened by events in north Africa, where the elation of rapid victory in 533–4 had soon been replaced by frustration. Belisarius' successor as commander in north Africa, Solomon, quickly found himself having to deal with attacks by the indigenous Moorish tribesmen, and then, in 536, with a mutiny by some of his own troops. The disaffection of these soldiers was fuelled partly by delays in the dispatch of their pay from Constantinople, partly by

---

2. Further detail (with sources) in G. Greatrex and S. Lieu, *The Roman Eastern Frontier and the Persian Wars, AD 363–630*, London: Routledge, 2002, 102–34.
3. Cf. H. Börm, 'Anlässe und Funktion der persischen Geldforderungen an die Römer (3. bis 6. Jh.)', *Historia* 57 (2008), 327–46.

anger at the new administration's measures against Arianism. Many troops (being of barbarian origin) sympathised with Arianism, while others had taken up with Vandal women, who resented being required by the imperial authorities to surrender land to the descendants of those from whom it had been expropriated in the previous century.[4] Solomon only just escaped a plot to murder him and was forced to flee to Sicily, leaving Justinian to send his cousin, Germanus, a respected commander, to restore order in the army. Solomon eventually returned in 539 to take over from Germanus and resumed trying to tackle the ongoing Moorish problem. Although he gained some successes, he was eventually defeated and killed at the battle of Cillium (Kasserine) in 544, and it was only through the energetic efforts of a new general, John Troglita, between 546 and 548 that the Moorish problem was for the time being contained and a measure of peace at last achieved.[5]

In addition to all these military setbacks, Justinian's ambitions had to contend with the impact of a phenomenon which could not reasonably have been anticipated – the advent of a devastating pandemic in the early 540s.[6] Probably originating in central Africa, it first reached the Mediterranean through Egypt in 541, from where it diffused along routes of trade and communication, first in the eastern Mediterranean, and then on to the west; it reached Constantinople in the spring of 542 (Justinian himself is reported to have fallen ill before recovering)[7] and Rome in late 543 or early 544. Identification of the disease has relied primarily on the three most detailed contemporary descriptions (those by Procopius, John of Ephesus and Evagrius), which, with their references to swellings,

4. Further discussion in W. E. Kaegi, *Byzantine Military Unrest, 471–843*, Amsterdam: Hakkert, 1981, 41–63.
5. The main sources for these events in Africa are Procop. *Wars* 4.10–28 and Corippus' panegyrical epic poem in honour of John Troglita, the *Iohannis*, with discussion and further references in J. A. S. Evans, *The Age of Justinian*, London: Routledge, 1996, 133–6, 151–3, 169–71; Y. Modéran, *Les Maures et l'Afrique romaine*, Rome: École française de Rome, 2003.
6. The best discussion of the pandemic is P. Hordern, 'Mediterranean plague in the age of Justinian' in M. Maas (ed.), *The Cambridge Companion to the Age of Justinian*, Cambridge: Cambridge University Press, 2005, 134–60; see also L. K. Little (ed.), *Plague and the End of Antiquity: The Pandemic of 541–750*, Cambridge: Cambridge University Press, 2007.
7. A recent study has suggested that coinage from these years reflects this through its depiction of Justinian's face as deformed, while also advertising his identification with his people in their hardship: H. Pottier, 'L'empereur Justinien survivant à la peste bubonique (542)', *Mélanges Cécile Morrisson = T&M* 16 (2010), 685–92.

black pustules, fever, diarrhoea and vomiting, usually culminating
in death, point to bubonic plague, and although some scholars are
sceptical about this diagnosis, it remains the most plausible option.[8]
As for what triggered its outbreak at this particular point in time,
there have been attempts to link this pandemic causally back to the
effects of a mysterious dust cloud (perhaps fallout from a major
volcanic eruption or other cataclysmic event) which appears to have
obscured the sun for lengthy periods during the mid-530s. However,
a recent careful assessment of the data and arguments has concluded
that the impact of the cloud must have been extremely limited,[9]
although it remains possible that significant climatic dislocation
played a role through extending the habitat range of disease-bearing
central African rodents to the point where they came into contact
with Mediterranean rodents on ships involved in trade from the Red
Sea down the coast of east Africa.[10]

There are also those who are sceptical about the impact of the
pandemic, drawing attention to Procopius' apparent reliance on
Thucydides' description of the Athenian plague and the very limited
indications of its impact in non-literary evidence (inscriptions,
papyri, archaeology).[11] However, while there can be no doubt about
Procopius, in true classicising style, deliberately evoking Thucydides
in many features of his account of the plague, there are also important divergences which reflect his eye-witness status, while the
absence of epigraphic evidence is only to be expected since it is
the poor, lacking the wherewithal to afford inscribed tombstones,

8. R. Sallares, 'Ecology, evolution, and epidemiology of plague' in Little, *Plague*,
231–89.
9. A. Arjava, 'The mystery cloud of 536 CE in the Mediterranean sources', *DOP* 59
(2005), 73–94, taking particular issue with D. Keys, *Catastrophe: An Investigation into
the Origins of the Modern World*, London: BCA, 1999. For the apocalyptic discourse in
contemporary literature to which the dust cloud, pandemic and other natural disasters
such as earthquakes gave rise, see M. Meier, *Das andere Zeitalter Justinians: Kontingenzerfahrung und Kontingenzbewältigung im 6 Jahrhundert n. Chr.*, Göttingen: Vandenhoeck & Ruprecht, 2003, 45–100.
10. Hordern, 'Mediterranean plague', 153.
11. J. Durliat, 'La peste du VIe siècle: pour un nouvel examen des sources byzantines' in
V. Kravari et al. (eds), *Hommes et richesses dans l'Empire byzantin*, Paris: Lethielleux,
1989–91, 1.107–19, endorsed by C. Wickham, *Framing the Early Middle Ages: Europe
and the Mediterranean, 400–800*, Oxford: Oxford University Press, 2005, 548. The only
explicit epigraphic reference to the plague in 542 appears to be an inscription recording
the building of a church at Zora in southern Syria in 542 when the local bishop Uaros
(Varus) died from 'swellings in the groin and armpits': J. Koder, 'Ein inschriftlicher Beleg
zur "justinianischen" Pest in Zora (Azra'a)', *Byzantinoslavica* 56 (1995), 13–18.

who will have been worst affected.[12] Furthermore, evidence for the impact of the plague has been identified in non-literary sources, with a decline in the weight of coinage in the years after the early 540s plausibly reflecting the effects of demographic decline on the government's tax revenues, and an increase in security of tenure for peasants' leases of farm land, attested in legal and papyrological documents, likewise consistent with a fall in population strengthening the bargaining position of survivors.[13] The periodic recurrence of the plague every ten to fifteen years over the next two centuries is another way in which its impact was felt. At the same time, however, it does not look as though military manpower was adversely affected in the longer term, perhaps reflecting the greater impact of the pandemic in major population centres, with rural areas, from where the bulk of soldiers were recruited, less severely affected.[14]

This is not, however, to deny the immediate short-term disruption which the pandemic caused in the context of the empire's military campaigns of the 540s. Certainly in Italy it took another decade to defeat Totila as successive imperial commanders (including a second stint by Belisarius from 544 to 548) struggled to contain him against a background of shortages of troops and pay, as well as uncooperative local communities disaffected by the renewed impositions of imperial tax collectors. Meanwhile, numerous cities and towns underwent siege by one or other side in the conflict, including Rome itself on two further occasions, while some regions of the peninsula experienced significant economic hardship. Totila was eventually defeated in 552 at the battle of Taginae in central Italy by Narses, a general with tactical skill, but perhaps more importantly, with a fresh infusion of manpower from the east, and after a further two years of campaigning against remaining pockets of Gothic

12. Cf. M. Meier, 'Beobachtungen zu den sogennanten Pestschilderungen bei Thukydides II 47–54 und bei Prokop, *Bell. Pers.* II 22–23', *Tyche* 14 (1999), 177–205; W. Brandes, 'Byzantine cities in the seventh and eighth centuries: different sources, different histories?' in G. P. Brogiolo and B. Ward-Perkins (eds), *The Idea and Ideal of the Town between Late Antiquity and the Early Middle Ages*, Leiden: Brill, 1999, 25–58, at 32–6.
13. P. Sarris, 'The Justinianic plague: origins and effects', *Continuity and Change* 17 (2002), 169–82 (reprinted in Little, *Plague*, 119–32). For cautionary comments about the limitations of the lease evidence, however, see Arjava, 'Mystery cloud', 89–90.
14. M. Whitby, 'Recruitment in Roman armies from Justinian to Heraclius (ca. 565–615)' in Averil Cameron (ed.), *The Byzantine and Early Islamic Near East* III: *States, Resources and Armies*, Princeton: Darwin Press, 1995, 61–124, at 93–9. Note also the *Life of Nicholas of Sion* 52, which refers to farmers avoiding towns in order to escape the disease.

resistance, Italy was once more under imperial control, albeit considerably the worse for wear.[15]

The reassertion of imperial authority in Italy during the 540s was hampered not only by the renewed conflict with Persia and ongoing problems with the Moors in north Africa, but also by the intensification of raiding across the lower Danube by various tribal groups referred to in the sources by names such as Bulgars, Antes, Gepids, Heruls and Sclavenes (Slavs). Justinian's primary response was to strengthen and extend frontier fortifications in the northern Balkans and Thrace – a strategy which appears to have achieved considerable success by the early 550s, in so far as references to raids decline significantly thereafter.[16] There was nonetheless one major scare in the winter of 558/9 when a tribal group referred to as Cutrigur Huns crossed a frozen Danube and penetrated almost to the walls of Constantinople itself, where they were induced to turn back only through the wily tactics of the now elderly Belisarius working with very limited numbers of troops (Agathias 5.11). More significant and ominous for the future, however, was the first appearance on the Danube at around this time of the powerful nomadic confederation of the Avars. For the time being, nonetheless, Justinian was able to neutralise any threat they might have posed through financial incentives; his successors would have to deal with the full ramifications of this new development.

One might have thought that the difficulties which the Italian campaign had presented would discourage Justinian from any more foreign ventures. However, at about the same time that Narses defeated Totila, the emperor initiated further imperial intervention in the western Mediterranean by dispatching a force to Spain, where civil war between the Gothic ruler, Agila, and a member of the aristocracy, Athanagild, presented an opportunity to promote Constantinople's interests. Responding to an appeal for help from Athanagild, an imperial army (size unknown, but presumably modest) assisted him to gain the upper hand against Agila while also

15. For further detail on the events of the war in Italy from 540 to 554, see Evans, *Justinian*, 171–81, and J. Moorhead, 'The Byzantines in the west in the sixth century' in *CMH* 1.118–39, at 127–9. For a good discussion of the decisive battle and the effectiveness of the army, see P. Rance, 'Narses and the battle of Taginae (Busta Gallorum) 552: Procopius and sixth-century warfare', *Historia* 54 (2005), 424–772.

16. F. Curta, *The Making of the Slavs: History and Archaeology of the Lower Danube Region, c. 500–700*, Cambridge: Cambridge University Press, 2001, 75–89; A. Sarantis, 'War and diplomacy in Pannonia and the north-west Balkans during the reign of Justinian', *DOP* 63 (2009), 15–40.

consolidating an imperial presence in south-eastern Spain (no doubt with the security of the northern African provinces partly in mind). Agila's eventual murder by his own supporters in 555 ensured that Athanagild could assume the rulership of Gothic Spain without the need for further fighting, but, unsurprisingly, he found his erstwhile imperial allies unwilling to evacuate the region they occupied, which included the major centre at Cartagena. If, however, Justinian hoped that this enclave would provide the base for the future conquest of the whole of the Iberian peninsula at some point in the near future, he was to be disappointed.[17]

Procopius' detailed narrative of imperial history concluded in the early 550s, with his continuator Agathias providing coverage only until the late 550s. Since the history of Agathias' continuator, Menander, has survived only in the form of excerpts preserved by later writers, the final half decade or so of Justinian's reign is known in much less detail. As the emperor moved into his late seventies and early eighties, briefer chronicle entries indicate a series of unfortunate events, including food shortages and protests in Constantinople, the apprehension of suspected plotters against the emperor, and a succession of earthquakes, some of which resulted in major damage to the dome of Hagia Sophia in the late 550s. The dome was repaired and the church rededicated at the end of 562 – the occasion for much ceremonial fanfare in the capital – but that same year also saw the improbable implication of the elderly Belisarius in one of the plots, as a result of which his property was confiscated.[18]

The sense of an aged emperor increasingly out of touch is reinforced by the marked decline in the number of laws he issued[19] and by the final twist in the theological saga of his reign. During his last year, Justinian appears, surprisingly, to have abandoned his lifelong adherence to Chalcedonian doctrines in favour of a minority strand of anti-Chalcedonian theology known as Aphthartodocetism which emphasised the incorruptible nature of Christ's earthly body. The consequences of this puzzling shift of stance for the empire's ecclesiastical politics were limited by Justinian's death in November

17. For imperial involvement in Gothic Spain, see E. A. Thompson, *The Goths in Spain*, Oxford: Clarendon Press, 1969, 320–34. Imperial forces eventually had to withdraw from Spain during the 620s, when Constantinople itself was under dire threat from Persians and Avars.
18. Details and references in Evans, *Justinian*, 253–7.
19. Noted by J. Moorhead, *Justinian*, London: Longman, 1994, 172 (36 surviving laws from the 540s, 13 from the 550s, 3 from 560–5).

565 and the position's reversal by his successor, but it did play a part in determining who that successor would be. For in early 565 Justinian deposed Eutychius, bishop of Constantinople, when he refused to endorse the emperor's new theological position, and his replacement, John Scholasticus, an Antiochene lawyer and clergy-man, was to play an influential role in the accession of Justinian's successor.

Justinian and Theodora had had no son, and Justinian had apparently refrained from designating a successor in his final years, perhaps so as not to weaken his own position prematurely.[20] He did, however, have two male relatives with potential claims, both named Justin. One of these, the son of Justinian's cousin Germanus, was, like his father, a capable military commander but for that reason was absent from Constantinople at the time of Justinian's death. The other Justin, the son of Justinian's sister, was a middle-ranking palace bureaucrat, but by virtue of being on hand at the crucial juncture was able to seize the initiative as soon as news of Justinian's death became known. John Scholasticus had previously encouraged Justin to think in these terms by reporting that an eminent Syrian holy man had foretold his succession to the throne, while as bishop of Constantinople John was in a position speedily to formalise Justin's accession before news of Justinian's death was widely known in the capital, let alone had reached the other Justin on the lower Danube frontier. The inhabitants of Constantinople and the empire were therefore presented with a smoothly orchestrated *fait accompli*, as well as a further interesting insight into the dynamics of political power in late antiquity (cf. pp. 101–9, 159–61, 174–5 above).

Justinian's legacy

Justinian presented himself as a tireless and energetic ruler through public pronouncements such as the following: 'Long hours of work and careful planning have, with God's help, given us success in both these fields [namely law- and war-making]' (*Institutes* preface [533]), and 'It is our habit constantly to spend our days and nights in wakefulness and thought so that we may provide for our subjects that which is useful and pleasing to God' (*Nov.* 8 preface [535]). Although it was conventional to present emperors in this way, this is a theme echoed by a number of contemporary authors, not only

20. The suggestion of Moorhead, *Justinian*, 174.

those broadly supportive of the regime ('the most sleepless of all emperors': Lydus, *Mag.* 3.55), but also those who were critical ('he had little need of sleep as a rule': Procop. *Anecdota* 13.28),[21] and is consistent with the sheer array of projects he initiated from early in his reign. He certainly cannot be faulted with regard to his work ethic or willingness to be proactive. The crucial question, however, is whether his initiatives and efforts ultimately benefited the empire or not.

Since the first decade or so of his reign was mostly characterised by remarkable successes, whereas the years from 540 onwards saw a preponderance of setbacks, it is understandable that some contemporaries might have become disillusioned with his rule and seen it in negative terms overall. This seems to have been the case with Procopius. According to his unpublished *Secret History* (*Anecdota*), quite different in tone (and genre) from the *Wars*, Justinian devoted his waking hours to formulating policies which ruined the empire – a view which, with due adjustments, continues to find modern exponents.[22] With the benefit of hindsight, it is difficult to dispute the long-term significance of his legal projects for the development of European law, or the influence of the Hagia Sophia and its dome on the architecture of a number of different cultures. These, however, were outcomes which Justinian can hardly have anticipated and which had no real bearing on the immediate condition of the empire, and it is primarily his foreign policy and its ramifications which have been the focus of contention.

Justinian certainly achieved far more in terms of extending a Roman presence back into the western Mediterranean than could have been predicted at the start of his reign. While he was happy to claim much of the credit for this and capitalise on the kudos it brought, he was undoubtedly aided by circumstances beyond his control – the change of ruler in Persia which facilitated the peace settlement of 532 and the release of troops from the eastern frontier, the various internal problems of the Vandal kingdom in the early 530s, and the succession of ineffective Gothic rulers in Italy after the death of Theoderic in 526. At the same time, further circumstances also beyond his control – Khusro's decision to violate the peace, the

21. Cf. Margaret Thatcher's reputation for being able to manage on only four hours of sleep a night.
22. Most recently, J. J. O'Donnell, *The Ruin of the Roman Empire*, London: Profile, 2009.

emergence of Totila in Italy, and the impact of the pandemic – meant that early successes were soon offset by reverses and failures. The situations in Italy, north Africa and the east were eventually stabilised, so that he could with some justification be described towards the end of his reign as 'Emperor of the Romans in fact as well as in name' (Agathias 5.14.1). Nonetheless, the question remains whether Justinian was too ambitious and thereby did long-term damage to the empire. In particular, did his reliance on monetary payments to ensure peace on some fronts and his commitment of imperial forces to multiple theatres of war impose burdens on the empire's resources which handicapped it in the longer term?

The 11,000 lbs of gold which were paid to Persia in 532 was undoubtedly a vast sum of money, equivalent to nearly 800,000 *solidi* – the largest individual payment of its kind on record from late antiquity by some distance. It could, however, easily be covered out of the 320,000 lbs of gold which Anastasius had bequeathed to Justin and Justinian, while the Vandal expedition which its payment made possible could be expected to recoup much more in the event of success. Subsequent payments to Persia in the 540s and 550s were more modest; as already noted, the annual payments of 30,000 *solidi* agreed in 562 would gradually have mounted up if they had been paid for the full fifty years of the agreement, but were not a heavy burden on an annual basis and were terminated within ten years anyway. The cost of diplomatic subsidies is therefore unlikely to have proved a long-term handicap.[23]

As for Justinian's military campaigns, it is evident from complaints in the sources about delays in the payment of troops and troop shortages, particularly in Italy, that the problem of multiple theatres of war created severe difficulties in the 540s. This in turn contributed to the failure to bring the war in Italy to a speedy conclusion, with resulting damage to the economy of the peninsula and to its fiscal contribution to the empire after the end of the war. An argument can certainly be made that Justinian's policies had a negative impact on Italy, compounded soon after his death by the Lombard invasion of the peninsula (568). However, Italy was only one small part of the empire. Although there were, as previously noted, also difficulties in north Africa, it did eventually contribute to the empire's finances,[24]

23. Details and discussion in A. D. Lee, *War in Late Antiquity: A Social History*, Oxford: Blackwell, 2007, 120–2.
24. Wickham, *Framing*, 124.

while the continuing economic prosperity of the eastern Mediterranean (pp. 229–31 above) was obviously beneficial for imperial revenues.

The long-term consequences of Justinian's policies can also be assessed against developments over the following half century or so. Early in his reign, Justin II (565–78) certainly complained about having inherited an exhausted treasury, but this can only have been a short-term problem, since by the end of his reign, a substantial surplus appears to have accumulated, despite renewed warfare with Persia and on the lower Danube. That warfare included some significant setbacks, notably the loss of the frontier fortress of Dara to the Persians in 573 and of Sirmium to the Avars in 582, but under his successors, Tiberius II (578–82) and Maurice (582–602), the empire's eastern and northern frontiers were gradually stabilised and strengthened, aided by civil war in Persia in 590, which forced the new king Khusro II to flee to Roman territory. The Emperor Maurice intervened to restore Khusro to the throne in 591, thereby gaining various territorial concessions, including the restoration of Dara, and peace in the east. This unexpected development freed forces to focus on the lower Danube frontier during the 590s. Although Italy remained a problematic region, as reflected in the correspondence of the energetic bishop of Rome, Gregory I (590–604), the empire was otherwise in a strong position at the end of the sixth century. Justinian may not have succeeded in restoring the empire to all its former glory, but it is difficult to see him as having left the empire a toxic inheritance.[25]

It was events in the decades after 600 which altered the empire's position dramatically and irrevocably for the worse. In 602 military units on the lower Danube mutinied, marched on Constantinople and proclaimed one of their officers, Phocas, as emperor in place of Maurice, who was executed along with most of his family. This in turn prompted Persia to invade imperial territory, taking advantage of the internal turmoil to make major inroads. Phocas was overthrown in 610 by Heraclius, son of the imperial governor of north Africa, who eventually proved himself a capable general – but not before Persian forces exploited this further upheaval to extend their control into Egypt and across Anatolia. By 626 Constantinople itself

---

25. For further detail, discussion and references, see M. Whitby, 'The successors of Justinian', *CAH*[2] 14.86–111; M. Whittow, *The Making of Orthodox Byzantium, 600–1025*, London: Macmillan, 1996, 38–53.

was threatened by a combination of Persian and Avar forces, but managed to hold out while the absent Heraclius finally initiated a successful drive from the Caucasus into the Persian heartlands, which resulted in the overthrow of Khusro in 628 and the end of the 'last great war of antiquity'.[26] This success was, however, to be short-lived, for less than a decade later, Heraclius found himself facing the unexpected phenomenon of Arab forces from the south, energized by Islam, advancing into Syria and inflicting a major defeat on imperial forces at the River Yarmuk (636). This signalled the permanent loss of the most economically productive regions of the empire – above all, Egypt – and a fundamental reconfiguration of the empire's strategic priorities and organisation.[27] It was these developments, which had little if anything to do with Justinian's actions and policies, which have the strongest claim to signal the end of antiquity.

From Rome to Byzantium

As a result of Justinian's actions, the city of Rome was once again a part of the empire, after more than half a century under barbarian rule. Even before that phase of its history, however, it had, of course, long ceased to play the central role in the political life of the empire to which it had been accustomed for many centuries in the more distant past, and its return to imperial control in the sixth century did not alter that. Constantinople – ancient Byzantium – was now firmly established as the centre of power in the empire, while Italy had effectively become what has, in a striking inversion, been described as 'a frontier province'.[28] Moreover, despite Justinian's efforts, the political unity of the Mediterranean world which had been one of Rome's singular achievements had fractured irreversibly by the sixth century, even if elements of its associated economic unity persisted into the seventh century.

The clearest thread of continuity with Rome's past during the sixth century remained the traditional senatorial aristocracy, but

26. J. Howard-Johnston, 'Heraclius' Persian campaigns and the revival of the east Roman empire, 622–630', *War in History* 6 (1999), 1–44 (whose phrase this is); W. E. Kaegi, *Heraclius, Emperor of Byzantium*, Cambridge: Cambridge University Press, 2003.
27. Whittow, *Making*, 69–89; J. Howard-Johnston, *Witnesses to a World Crisis: Historians and Histories of the Middle East in the Seventh Century*, Oxford: Oxford University Press, 2010, chs 14–16.
28. M. Humphries, 'Italy, AD 425–605' in *CAH*² 14.525–51, at 542.

although Theoderic had sought to uphold their status for most of his reign, the material basis of their position had contracted during the fifth century as they lost their extra-Italian land-holdings amidst the turmoil created by barbarian incomers, while the viability of their estates in Italy suffered further blows during the Gothic war and then with the establishment of the Lombard presence in the peninsula soon after.[29] The senate as a body in Rome persisted into the early seventh century, but not for much longer, since soon after 625 the senate house was turned into a church. While the emperor's vicarious presence in the city should not be underestimated even at this stage,[30] the bishop of Rome was becoming the pre-eminent figure in the life of the city, as epitomized in the description of Gregory I on his epitaph as 'God's consul' (Bede, *Hist. eccl.* 2.1), and it was the bishop of Rome who maintained elements of imperial traditions and practices into the medieval period of the city's history, above all through the papal chancery.[31]

As for the eastern Mediterranean, now the empire's heartland, the inhabitants continued to refer to themselves as Romans – 'Byzantines' is an invention of early modern scholarship. The continued use of the term 'Roman' in a world where it could encompass individuals of Greek, Thracian, Isaurian, Armenian or even Gothic origin might be regarded as analogous to late Republican and early imperial traditions of extending citizenship to encompass non-Romans, which had played such an important role in the growth of Roman power. Of course, citizenship itself had long ceased to have the caché which it had carried in the distant past,[32] and 'Romanity' was now defined with reference to other criteria, above all loyalty to the emperor, but also allegiance to Christianity, especially orthodox Christianity.[33] And it is this latter criterion which is one of the

29. T. S. Brown, *Gentlemen and Officers: Imperial Administration and Aristocratic Power in Byzantine Italy, AD 554–800*, Rome: British School at Rome, 1984, ch. 2.
30. As emphasised by M. Humphries, 'From emperor to pope? Ceremonial, space and authority at Rome from Constantine to Gregory the Great' in K. Cooper and J. Hillner (eds), *Religion, Dynasty and Patronage in Early Christian Rome, 300–900*, Oxford: Oxford University Press, 2007, 21–58.
31. See T. F. X. Noble, 'Morbidity and vitality in the history of the early medieval papacy', *Catholic Historical Review* 81 (1995), 505–40, esp. 514–17.
32. For citizenship in late antiquity, see R. W. Mathisen, '*Peregrini, barbari* and *cives Romani*: concepts of citizenship and the legal identity of barbarians in the later Roman empire', *American Historical Review* 111 (2006), 1011–40.
33. G. Greatrex, 'Roman identity in the sixth century' in S. Mitchell and G. Greatrex (eds), *Ethnicity and Culture in Late Antiquity*, London: Duckworth, 2000, 267–92.

strongest indicators that, despite the continuity of 'Roman' terminology, there had nonetheless been a fundamental shift in the
character of the empire. For it was now a strongly Christianised
society, as well as being a society in which another archetypal feature
of the Roman past – the centrality of the Latin language – was dis-
appearing. To be sure, Latin maintained its position in Italy and
north Africa, but Justinian was probably the last emperor for whom
Latin was his first language, and it has already been noted how there
was a shift away from Latin as the language of administration
during his reign (p. 256 above). Greek was the prevalent means of
communication for a majority of inhabitants. This did not prevent
them from describing themselves as 'Romans', but they did so in
Greek, as *Romaioi*, rather than *Romani*. The predominance of
Greek language and of Christianity, together with the centrality
of Constantinople, are the features most closely associated with
medieval Byzantium, and their growing prominence during the sixth
century is symptomatic of the transformation of the Roman empire
into an entity which, while the recognisable descendant of ancient
Rome, was nonetheless increasingly different in fundamental ways.[34]

---

34. For Byzantine identity and culture, see Averil Cameron, *The Byzantines*, Oxford:
Blackwell, 2006.

Chronology

For the regnal dates of Roman emperors and other rulers in this period and the dates of bishops of Rome, see the lists which follow this table.

Political/Military	Religious/Cultural	Events elsewhere
363 Nisibis surrendered to Persia	363 Jovian proclaims religious toleration	
365 Usurpation of Procopius		
		376 Goths are permitted to cross lower Danube into imperial territory
378 Gothic victory at Adrianople		
		379 Death of Shapur II of Persia, after seventy-year reign
	381 Council of Constantinople c. 382 Gratian ends funding for state cults	
383 Usurpation of Magnus Maximus		
	384 Valentinian II declines to reinstate Altar of Victory in Roman senate	
392 Revolt of Arbogast and Eugenius		
394 Battle of the River Frigidus and defeat of Arbogast and Eugenius		
400 Revolt of Gainas in east		
	403 Synod of the Oak deposes John Chrysostom	

Political/Military	Religious/Cultural	Events elsewhere
		406 Vandals, Sueves and Alans cross Rhine
408 Overthrow of Stilicho in west		
410 Goths sack Rome		
	412 Cyril becomes bishop of Alexandria (until 444)	
	431 Council of Ephesus (1)	
	438 *Codex Theodosianus* issued	
439 Vandals capture Carthage		
	440 Leo becomes bishop of Rome (until 461)	
	449 Council of Ephesus (2)	
451 Stalemate between Aetius and Attila at the Catalaunian Plains	451 Council of Chalcedon	
453 Death of Attila		
454 Murder of Aetius in west		
455 Vandals sack Rome		
468 Leo's failed expedition against the Vandals		
471 Murder of Aspar in east		
475 Zeno temporarily overthrown by Basiliscus		
476 Last western emperor (Romulus) deposed; Odoacer rules as king in Italy		
	482 Zeno issues the *Henotikon*, provoking the Acacian schism with Rome and the west	
		488 Kavad becomes king of Persia

Political/Military	Religious/Cultural	Events elsewhere
493 Theoderic rules as king in Italy		
		496 Kavad temporarily overthrown
502–5 War with Persia		
513–15 Revolt of Vitalian against Anastasius		
	519 Justin I ends the Acacian schism	
	529 First edition of *Codex Iustinianus* issued	
		531 Kavad dies and is succeeded by Khusro I in Persia
532 Nika riot in Constantinople; 'endless peace' with Persia		
533 Belisarius captures Carthage from Vandals	533 Promulgation of the *Digest*	
	537 Dedication of Hagia Sophia in Constantinople	
540 Belisarius captures Ravenna from Goths; Persians sack Antioch		
542 Pandemic reaches Constantinople		
		550 End of Gupta dynasty in India
552 Victory over Goths at Taginae		
	553 Council of Constantinople	
562 Fifty-year peace treaty with Persia		
565 Death of Justinian and accession of Justin II		

Lists of rulers

Roman emperors during late antiquity

This list presents the names and dates of emperors from the early fourth to the early seventh century. The frequent overlapping of dates is due to the common late Roman practice of having co-emperors. Those whose rule was exercised primarily or solely in the west are italicised.

Constantine I	306–37
Constantine II	337–40
Constans	337–50
Constantius II	337–61
Julian	361–3
Jovian	363–364
Valentinian I	364–75
Valens	364–78
Gratian	375–83
Valentinian II	375–92
Theodosius I	379–95
Arcadius	395–408
Honorius	395–423
Theodosius II	408–50
Constantius III	421
Valentinian III	425–55
Marcian	450–7
Petronius Maximus	455
Avitus	455–6
Majorian	457–61
Leo I	457–74
Libius Severus	461–5
Anthemius	467–72
Anicius Olybrius	472
Glycerius	473–4
Leo II	473–4
Zeno	474–91
Julius Nepos	474–5

Romulus Augustus	475–6
Anastasius	491–518
Justin I	518–27
Justinian	527–65
Justin II	565–78
Tiberius II	578–82
Maurice	582–602
Phocas	602–10
Heraclius	610–41

Other rulers during late antiquity

Persian kings

Shapur II	309–79
Ardashir II	379–83
Shapur III	383–8
Vahram IV	388–99
Yazdgerd I	399–420
Vahram V	420–39
Yazdgerd II	439–57
Hormizd III	457–9
Peroz	459–84
Valash	484–8
Kavad	488–531
Zamasp	496–8
Khusro I	531–79
Hormizd IV	579–90
Khusro II	590–628

Visigothic rulers

Alaric	391–410
Athaulf	410–15
Vallia	415–18
Theoderic I	418–51
Thorismodus	451–3
Theoderic II	453–66
Euric	466–84
Alaric II	484–507
Gesalicus	507–11
Amalaricus	511–31
Theudis	531–48
Theudigisel	548–9

Agila   549–55
Athanagild   555–68

Vandal rulers

Geiseric   428–77
Huneric   477–84
Gunthamund   484–96
Thrasamund   496–523
Hilderic   523–30
Gelimer   530–4

Ostrogothic rulers

Theoderic   493–526
Athalaric   526–34
Theodahad   534–6
Vitigis   536–40
Totila   541–52

Burgundian rulers

Gundobad   474–516
Sigismund   516–23

Frankish rulers

Note that Clovis divided his kingdom between his four sons.

Childeric   456–82
Clovis   482–511
Childebert   511–58
Theoderic   511–33
Chlodomer   511–24
Chlothacar   511–61
Theudebert   533–47

List of bishops of Rome

Liberius	352–66
Damasus	366–84
Siricius	384–99
Anastasius	399–401
Innocentius	401–17
Zosimus	417–18
Bonifatius	418–22
Celestinus	422–32
Sixtus III	432–40
Leo	440–61
Hilarius	461–8
Simplicius	468–83
Felix II	483–92
Gelasius	492–6
Anastasius II	496–8
Symmachus	498–514
Hormisdas	514–23
Iohannes	523–6
Felix III	526–30
Bonifatius II	530–2
Iohannes II	533–5
Agapetus	535–6
Silverius	536–7
Vigilius	537–55
Pelagius	556–61
Iohannes III	561–74
Benedictus	574–9
Pelagius II	579–90
Gregory	590–604

Guide to further reading

Ancient sources and modern translations

There is a vast range of diverse sources for the period 363 to 565, so the following brief comments focus on only the more important. Understanding of the political and military history of the period relies above all on a number of 'classicising' histories, so called because of their being modelled on the great classical histories of Herodotus, Thucydides, Tacitus and the like. Pre-eminent among these are the Latin history of Ammianus Marcellinus and the Greek history of Procopius of Caesarea. Probably from a well-off family in Antioch, Ammianus served as a middle-ranking officer in the army during the 350s and early 360s. His history began where Tacitus' *Histories* had ended, in 96, but only the second half has survived, covering the years 354 to 378, with the period from Jovian's accession to the battle of Adrianople being dealt with from the second half of Book 25 to Book 31. Ammianus was a pagan and an admirer of the Emperor Julian, and his treatment of Julian's successors is intended to enhance Julian's reputation by comparison. Despite this, and the fact that, surprisingly for an ex-army officer, his accounts of military actions often leave the reader with more questions than answers, his history contains a wealth of circumstantial detail about contemporary events and people, of which he was shrewd observer. He is generally regarded as the last great Roman historian writing in Latin. There is a good Penguin translation (by W. Hamilton, 1986) which does, however, omit some chapters, chiefly digressions. A full, though older, translation is available in the Loeb series (by J. C. Rolfe).

Procopius came from Caesarea in Palestine and was probably a lawyer by training. He became secretary to Belisarius, one of the Emperor Justinian's leading generals, and as such witnessed many of the dramatic events of the 530s and 540s. During the 550s he produced his history of the *Wars* in eight books – the first two focusing on conflict with Persia, the next two on the campaign against the Vandals, the next three on the Gothic war in Italy, and the final book a composite narrative updating developments in all three theatres in the early 550s. His account does not neglect major domestic crises, notably the Nika riot of 532 and the pandemic of the the early 540s. His history aspires to comparison with Thucydides, but its interpretation is complicated by a second, unpublished work (hence

Anecdota), popularly known as the *Secret History* – a vitriolic critique of the Emperor Justinian and his wife Theodora, and also of Belisarius. Scholars have long struggled to reconcile this intemperate and bitter work with the detached approach of the *Wars*, with the most plausible explanation being that it was a product of disillusionment with prolonged warfare during the 540s, and the impact of the pandemic. To complicate matters even further, Procopius also produced a panegyrical work in praise of Justinian's buildings. All these works are translated in the Loeb series (by H. B. Dewing), with the *Secret History* also being available from Penguin (rev. edn G. A. Williamson and P. Sarris, 2007) and Hackett (tr. A. Kaldellis, 2010).

Other classicising historians were active during the fifth century, but none of their histories has survived complete. Substantial excerpts are, however, preserved in later writers and compilations. Eunapius of Sardis wrote an account of the period from 270 to 404, with the primary aim of defending paganism and preserving the memory of the Emperor Julian. Olympiodorus of Thebes continued the narrative from 404 to 425, and was in turn continued by Priscus of Panium from 425 to 472, including a celebrated account of his participation in an embassy to Attila the Hun in 449, while Malchus of Philadelphia covered at least the 470s. All wrote in Greek and are available in a translation by R. C. Blockley (*The Fragmentary Classicising Historians of the Later Roman Empire* II, Liverpool: Francis Cairns, 1983). Procopius' prestige was such that he too had continuators, in the persons of Agathias (550s) (tr. J. D. Frendo, *CFHB*, 1975) and Menander (late 550s to 582) (tr. R. C. Blockley, 1985). The history of Zosimus also warrants mention, not because of any merits as a historian on his part, but rather because his uncritical use of Eunapius and Olympiodorus has preserved important portions of their histories (tr. R. T. Ridley, *ByzAus*, 1981). The historical fragments associated with John of Antioch are important for aspects of the fifth and sixth centuries (tr. S. Mariev, *CFHB*, 2008).

Late antiquity also witnessed the emergence of new historical genres in the form of, on the one hand, chronicles, and on the other, church histories. Chronicles were characterised by briefer, year-by-year recording of significant public events, often with a focus on a particular city. So the *Chronicle* of John Malalas, written in the mid-sixth century and covering the history of the world from creation to his own day, shows a particular interest in events in Antioch (trs. E. Jeffreys et al., *ByzAus*, 1986), while the anonymous *Chronicon Paschale* (*Easter Chronicle*), written in the early seventh century, focuses on events in Constantinople (trs. M. and M. Whitby, TTH, 1989). The Latin *Chronicle* of Marcellinus covers the more restricted period of 378 to 548 (tr. B. Croke, *ByzAus*, 1995), while the ninth-century work of Theophanes preserves much important material from earlier texts (trs. C. Mango and R. Scott, 1997). Joshua the Stylite wrote an invaluable

account (in Syriac) of events in northern Mesopotamia during the late fifth
and early sixth century, especially the Emperor Anastasius' war with Persia
(tr. F. Trombley and J. Watt, TTH, 2000). The important sixth-century
Syriac *Chronicle* attributed to Zachariah Rhetor is also available in translation with commentary by G. Greatrex, R. Phenix and C. Horn (TTH,
2011).

Eusebius of Caesarea wrote the first church history in the early fourth
century, inspiring a number of continuators. Socrates Scholasticus covered
the period from 305 to 439, while his fifth-century contemporary Sozomen
took his from 324 to 439. Evagrius in turn dealt with the years from 428
to 592. Although Eusebius' original template maintained a firm focus on
church affairs, except when persecution impinged, his successors found
themselves having to devote increasing amounts of space to secular affairs
as well, as church and state became ever more closely intertwined. However, they did maintain a distinctive feature of Eusebius' history, namely his
extended quotation of original sources, primarily those relating to church
councils and synods. Despite their importance, only Evagrius has been
translated in recent times (M. Whitby, TTH, 2000); for Socrates and
Sozomen, one must resort to nineteenth-century translations (e.g., in the
Nicene and Post-Nicene Fathers series), which are based on out-of-date
editions. Another important category of Christian source is saints' lives.
They are too numerous and diverse to single out specific examples, but
despite their tendentious character, they contain much invaluable circumstantial detail about provincial society in late antiquity.

Rhetoric continued to play an important part in Roman public life, and
from the later fourth century, there are a number of important orators
whose works have survived, particularly Libanius, an eminent teacher of
rhetoric in Antioch, and Themistius, a philosopher-cum-rhetorician, who
established a position of trust with successive eastern emperors. Many of
Libanius' speeches (and letters) are available in translations by A. F.
Norman and S. Bradbury (Loeb, 1969–92, and TTH, 2000, 2004), while a
selection of Themistius' speeches has been translated with commentary by
P. Heather and D. Moncur (TTH, 2003).

Letters also remained an important medium of communication, at both
the public and private levels. As prefect of the city of Rome in 384, the
senatorial aristocrat Symmachus wrote a series of letters to the emperor
about public matters (his *Relationes*, tr. R. H. Barrow, 1973), while another
senator, Cassiodorus, produced official correspondence for the Gothic
regime in Italy, which he subsequently gathered together as his *Variae*
(*Miscellany*), a selection of which have been translated by S. Barnish (TTH,
1992). Bishops were also prolific letter-writers, with Ambrose of Milan
and Augustine of Hippo producing some particularly important letters in
the later fourth and early fifth century; W. Liebeschuetz has translated a
good selection of the former (TTH, 2005), while the Fathers of the Church
series covers all of Augustine's. In this context, mention should also be

made of the *Collectio Avellana* (ed. O. Günther, 1895), an important compilation of correspondence between emperors and the bishop of Rome from
the fourth to the sixth centuries, although no translation currently exists.

Legal sources include the two great codes, which range across many
subjects from administration and the army to society and religion. Their
edited form has deprived them of valuable contextual detail, but they
remain extremely important evidence. The *Theodosian Code* is available in
a translation edited by C. Pharr (1952), while one of the *Justinianic Code*
will soon appear from Cambridge University Press. Pharr's translation also
includes the so-called novels ('new laws') issued by Theodosius II and other
fifth-century emperors; a translation of Justinian's novels is also in progress
from Cambridge University Press, but will not appear for some time.

The important administrative document the *Notitia Dignitatum* is available in the edition by O. Seeck (1876), with a new edition and translation
by P. Brennan imminent. There are a number of translations of John Lydus'
treatise on the Roman state (T. F. Carney, 1971, A. C. Bandy, 1983).

Church councils also generated a large volume of paperwork, much of
which has been preserved from this period; they shed light on the major
theological controversies of the period, as well as ecclesiastical politics and
much else. Invaluable translations of the Council of Chalcedon in 451 (by
R. Price and M. Gaddis, TTH, 2005) and the Council of Constantinople in
553 (by R. Price, TTH, 2009) are now available.

As in earlier periods of Roman imperial history, inscriptions and papyri
have an important contribution to make on a variety of fronts; for their
value for the economic history of late antiquity, e.g., see p. 225 above.

Collections of sources in translation include M. Maas, *Readings in Late
Antiquity* (London: Routledge, 2000), A. D. Lee, *Pagans and Christians in
Late Antiquity* (London: Routledge, 2000), R. Valantasis, *Religions of Late
Antiquity in Practice* (Princeton: Princeton University Press, 2000),
B. Ehrman and A. Jacobs, *Christianity in Late Antiquity, 300–450* CE
(New York and Oxford: Oxford University Press, 2004), and G. Greatrex
and S. Lieu, *The Roman Eastern Frontier and the Persian Wars, AD 363–
630* (London: Routledge, 2002).

For those who read French, there are good recent translations of many
late antique sources in the Budé series and in *Sources chrétiennes*.

For archaeological evidence, the best entrée is the Late Antique
Archaeology series (2003–) overseen by L. Lavan, with successive volumes
devoted to the countryside, social and political life, housing, technology
and religion.

Modern works

Late antiquity is a period of interest to historians of the Roman empire, of
early Byzantium, of the early medieval west, and of early Christianity, so
relevant modern literature is vast and can come in a variety of guises. The

following comments aim only to highlight a number of starting points and reference works. For a succinct introduction to the period, see G. Clark, *Late Antiquity: A Very Short Introduction* (Oxford: Oxford University Press, 2011). An excellent one-volume overview is S. Mitchell, *A History of the Later Roman Empire, AD 284–641* (Malden, MA and Oxford: Wiley-Blackwell, 2007), while Averil Cameron covers similar ground, albeit even more thematically, in two related surveys – *The Later Roman Empire, AD 284–430* (London: Fontana, 1993) and *The Mediterranean World in Late Antiquity, AD 395–700* (2nd edn London: Routledge, 2011). The early chapters of C. Wickham, *The Inheritance of Rome: A History of Europe from 400 to 1000* (Oxford: Oxford University Press, 2009) offer valuable, and very readable, discussion of many aspects of late antiquity, especially socio-economic matters. Volumes 13 (337–425) and 14 (425–602) of the new edition of the *Cambridge Ancient History* (1998 and 2000) provide detailed coverage of late antiquity, combining narrative chapters with thematic studies of institutions, society, economy, religion and, in the case of vol. 14, regions. Volume 1 of *The New Cambridge Medieval History* (c. 500–700) (2005) also includes a number of relevant and helpful chapters.

Useful and accessible reference works include G. Bowersock et al., *Late Antiquity: A Guide to the Postclassical World* (Cambridge, MA: Harvard University Press, 1999), which includes both encyclopedia-style articles and extended essays on important themes, and the *Oxford Handbook of Early Christian Studies*, eds S. A. Harvey and D. G. Hunter (Oxford: Oxford University Press, 2008), comprising short essays for orientation on a large range of relevant subjects. The three-volume *Prospopography of the Late Roman Empire* (Cambridge: Cambridge University Press, 1970–92) makes few concessions to the non-specialist, but is nonetheless a vital resource, providing as it does full details about every individual of any importance, with the important exception of churchmen (for whom there is a separate, ongoing French project); it should also be noted that, quite reasonably, it provides details of emperors only up to their accession, so as not to become a general history of the period. Also fundamental is A. H. M. Jones, *The Later Roman Empire, 284–602* (Oxford: Blackwell, 1964), which includes narrative chapters, but whose strength is its thematic chapters on institutions, society and the economy; with its excellent index, it functions like a reference work. An *Oxford Dictionary of Late Antiquity* is currently in preparation. P. Rousseau (ed.), *A Companion to Late Antiquity* (Malden, MA, and Oxford: Wiley-Blackwell, 2009) is a recent valuable collection of essays on important aspects of the period.

Select bibliography of modern works

This bibliography does not include every item cited in the footnotes, but only those cited more than once, for ease of identifying an item via its 'short title' format.

Amory, P., *People and Identity in Ostrogothic Italy, 489–554*, Cambridge: Cambridge University Press, 1997

Ando, C., *Imperial Ideology and Provincial Loyalty in the Roman Empire*, Berkeley: University of California Press, 2000

Arjava, A., 'The mystery cloud of 536 CE in the Mediterranean sources', *DOP* 59 (2005), 73–94

Bagnall, R. S., 'Evidence and models for the economy in Roman Egypt' in J. G. Manning and I. Morris (eds), *The Ancient Economy: Evidence and Models*, Stanford: Stanford University Press, 2005, 187–204

Banaji, J., *Agrarian Change in Late Antiquity: Gold, Labour and Aristocratic Dominance*, rev. edn, Oxford: Oxford University Press, 2007

Barnes, T. D., 'Religion and society in the age of Theodosius' in H. A. Meynell (ed.), *Grace, Politics and Desire: Essays on Augustine*, Calgary: University of Calgary Press, 1990, 157–75

Barnes, T. D., *Athanasius and Constantius*, Cambridge, MA: Harvard University Press, 1993

Blackburn, M., 'Money and coinage' in *CMH* 1.660–74

Blockley, R. C., *East Roman Foreign Policy: Formation and Conduct from Diocletian to Anastasius*, Leeds: Francis Cairns, 1992

Bowes, K., *Private Worship, Public Values, and Religious Change in Late Antiquity*, Cambridge: Cambridge University Press, 2008

Brown, P., *Augustine of Hippo*, London: Faber, 1967

Brown, P., 'The rise and function of the holy man in late antiquity', *JRS* 61 (1971), 80–101

Brown, P., *Power and Persuasion in Late Antiquity*, Madison: University of Wisconsin Press, 1992

Brown, T. S., *Gentlemen and Officers: Imperial Administration and Aristocratic Power in Byzantine Italy, AD 554–800*, Rome: British School at Rome, 1984

Bury, J. B., *History of the Later Roman Empire from the Death of*

Theodosius I to the Death of Justinian, London: Macmillan, 1923

Cameron, Alan, 'Theodosius the Great and the regency of Stilicho', *Harv. Stud.* 73 (1969), 247–80

Cameron, Alan, *Claudian: Poetry and Propaganda at the Court of Honorius*, Oxford: Clarendon Press, 1970

Cameron, Alan, *Circus Factions: Blues and Greens at Rome and Byzantium*, Oxford: Clarendon Press, 1976

Cameron, Alan, 'The last pagans of Rome' in W. V. Harris (ed.), *The Transformations of Vrbs Roma in Late Antiquity*, Portsmouth, RI: *JRA* Supp. 33, 1999, 109–22

Cameron, Alan, 'The antiquity of the Symmachi', *Historia* 48 (1999), 477–505

Cameron, Alan, *The Last Pagans of Rome*, Oxford: Oxford University Press, 2011

Cameron, Alan and Long, J., *Barbarians and Politics at the Court of Arcadius*, Berkeley: University of California Press, 1993

Cameron, Averil, *Procopius and the Sixth Century*, London: Duckworth, 1985

Caner, D., *Wandering, Begging Monks: Spiritual Authority and the Promotion of Monasticism in Late Antiquity*, Berkeley: University of California Press, 2002

Chavarría, A., and Lewit, T., 'Archaeological research on the late antique countryside: a bibliographic essay' in W. Bowden et al. (eds), *Recent Research on the Late Antique Countryside*, Leiden: Brill, 2004, 3–51

Chazelle, C., and Cubitt, C. (eds), *The Crisis of the Oikumene: The Three Chapters and the Failed Quest for Unity in the Sixth-Century Mediterranean*, Turnhout: Brepols, 2007

Christie, N., *From Constantine to Charlemagne: An Archaeology of Italy, AD 300–800*, Aldershot: Ashgate, 2006

Christie, N., and Loseby, S. (eds), *Towns in Transition: Urban Evolution in Late Antiquity and the Early Middle Ages*, Aldershot: Scolar Press, 1996

Cribiore, R., *The School of Libanius in Late Antique Antioch*, Princeton: Princeton University Press, 2007

Croke, B., 'Dynasty and ethnicity: Emperor Leo I and the eclipse of Aspar', *Chiron* 35 (2005), 147–203

Croke, B., 'Justinian under Justin: reconfiguring a reign', *Byz. Zeitschr.* 100 (2007), 13–56

Curran, J. R., *Pagan City and Christian Capital: Rome in the Fourth Century*, Oxford: Clarendon Press, 2000

Dagron, G., *Naissance d'une capitale: Constantinople et ses institutions de 330 à 451*, Paris: Presses Universitaires de France, 1974

Decker, M., *Tilling the Hateful Earth: Agricultural Production and Trade in the Late Antique East*, Oxford: Oxford University Press, 2009

de Ste. Croix, G. E. M. (with M. Whitby), 'The Council of Chalcedon' in his *Christian Persecution, Martyrdom and Orthodoxy*, eds M. Whitby and J. Streeter, Oxford: Oxford University Press, 2006, 259–319

Deliyannis, D. M., *Ravenna in Late Antiquity*, Cambridge: Cambridge University Press, 2010

Drinkwater, J. F., *The Alamanni and Rome, 213–496*, Oxford: Oxford University Press, 2007

Errington, R. M., 'Church and state in the first years of Theodosius I', *Chiron* 27 (1997), 21–70

Errington, R. M., *Roman Imperial Policy from Julian to Theodosius*, Chapel Hill: University of North Carolina Press, 2006

Evans, J. A. S., *The Age of Justinian*, London: Routledge, 1996

Feissel, D., 'Les édifices de Justinien au témoignage de Procope et de l'épigraphie', *AnTard* 8 (2000), 81–104

Festugière, A. J., *Éphèse et Chalcédoine: Actes des conciles*, Paris: Beauchesne, 1982

Frankfurter, D., *Religion in Roman Egypt: Assimilation and Resistance*, Princeton: Princeton University Press, 1998

Frend, W. H. C., *The Rise of the Monophysite Movement*, Cambridge: Cambridge University Press, 1972

Garnsey, P. and Humfress, C., *The Evolution of the Late Antique World*, Cambridge: Orchard Press, 2001

Garnsey, P. and Whittaker, C. R., 'Trade, industry and the urban economy' in *CAH*² 13.312–37

Gillett, A., 'Rome, Ravenna and the last western emperors', *PBSR* 69 (2001), 131–67

Goffart, W. A., *Barbarians and Romans, AD 418–584: The Techniques of Accommodation*, Princeton: Princeton University Press, 1980

Goffart, W. A., *Barbarian Tides: The Migration Age and the Later Roman Empire*, Philadelphia: University of Pennsylvania Press, 2006

Goffart, W. A., 'The techniques of barbarian settlement in the fifth century: a personal, streamlined account with ten additional comments', *JLA* 3 (2010), 65–98

Greatrex, G., 'Flavius Hypatius, *quem vidit validum Parthus sensitque timendum*: an investigation of his career', *Byzantion* 66 (1996), 120–42

Greatrex, G., 'The Nika riot: a reappraisal', *JHS* 117 (1997), 60–86

Greatrex, G., *Rome and Persia at War, 502–532*, Leeds: Francis Cairns, 1998

Greatrex, G., 'Roman identity in the sixth century' in S. Mitchell and G. Greatrex (eds), *Ethnicity and Culture in Late Antiquity*, London: Duckworth, 2000, 267–92

Greatrex, G., 'Byzantium and the east in the sixth century' in M. Maas (ed.), *The Cambridge Companion to the Age of Justinian*, Cambridge: Cambridge University Press, 2005, 477–509

Greatrex, G., and Lieu, S., *The Roman Eastern Frontier and the Persian*

Wars, AD 363–630, London: Routledge, 2002

Gregory, T. E., Vox Populi: *Popular Opinion in the Religious Controversies of the Fifth Century* AD, Columbus: Ohio State University Press, 1979

Grey, C., 'Revisiting the "problem" of *agri deserti* in the late Roman empire', *JRA* 20 (2007), 362–76

Gwynn, D. (ed.), *A. H. M. Jones and the Later Roman Empire*, Leiden: Brill, 2008

Haarer, F., *Anastasius I: Politics and Empire in the Late Roman World*, Cambridge: Francis Cairns, 2006

Halsall, G., *Barbarian Migrations and the Roman West, 376–568*, Cambridge: Cambridge University Press, 2007

Halsall, G., 'The technique of barbarian settlement in the fifth century: a reply to Walter Goffart', *JLA* 3 (2010), 99–112

Harries, J., *Sidonius Apollinaris and the Fall of Rome, AD 407–485*, Oxford: Clarendon Press, 1994

Harris, W. V. (ed.), *The Transformations of* Vrbs Roma *in Late Antiquity*, Portsmouth, RI: *JRA* Supp. 33, 1999

Heather, P., *Goths and Romans 332–489*, Oxford: Clarendon Press, 1991

Heather, P., 'New men for new Constantines? Creating an imperial elite in the eastern Mediterranean' in P. Magdalino (ed.), *New Constantines: The Rhythm of Imperial Renewal in Byzantium, 4th–13th Centuries*, Aldershot: Ashgate, 1994, 11–30

Heather, P., *The Goths*, Oxford: Blackwell, 1996

Heather, P., 'Christianity and the Vandals in the reign of Geiseric' in J. Drinkwater and B. Salway (eds), *Wolf Liebeschuetz Reflected*, London: Institute of Classical Studies, 2007, 137–46

Heather, P. and Moncur, D., *Politics, Philosophy and Empire in the Fourth Century: Select Orations of Themistius*, Liverpool: Liverpool University Press, 2001

Hen, Y., *Roman Barbarians: The Royal Court and Culture in the Early Medieval West*, London: Palgrave Macmillan, 2007

Hendy, M. F., *Studies in the Byzantine Monetary Economy, c. 300–1450*, Cambridge: Cambridge University Press, 1985

Honoré, T., *Tribonian*, London: Duckworth, 1978

Hordern, P., 'Mediterranean plague in the age of Justinian' in M. Maas (ed.), *The Cambridge Companion to the Age of Justinian*, Cambridge: Cambridge University Press, 2005, 134–60

Howard-Johnston, J., 'The two great powers in late antiquity: a comparison' in Averil Cameron (ed.), *The Byzantine and Early Islamic Near East* III: *States, Resources and Armies*, Princeton: Darwin Press, 1995, 157–222

Humphries, M., 'From emperor to pope? Ceremonial, space and authority at Rome from Constantine to Gregory the Great' in K. Cooper and J. Hillner (eds), *Religion, Dynasty and Patronage in Early Christian*

Rome, 300–900, Oxford: Oxford University Press, 2007, 21–58

Hunt, E. D., 'Imperial law or councils of the church? Theodosius I and the imposition of doctrinal uniformity' in K. Cooper and J. Gregory (eds), *Discipline and Diversity*, Woodbridge: Boydell, 2007 (= SCH 43), 57–68

James, E., *The Franks*, Oxford: Blackwell, 1988

Jones, A. H. M., *The Later Roman Empire 284–602*, Oxford: Blackwell, 1964

Kaster, R. A., *Guardians of Language: The Grammarian and Society in Late Antiquity*, Berkeley: University of California Press, 1988

Kelly, G., *Ammianus Marcellinus, the Allusive Historian*, Cambridge: Cambridge University Press, 2008

Krause, J.-U. and Witschel, C. (eds), *Die Stadt in der Spätantike: Niedergang oder Wandel?*, Stuttgart: Franz Steiner, 2006

Kulikowski, M., *Late Roman Spain and its Cities*, Baltimore: Johns Hopkins University Press, 2004

Kulikowski, M., *Rome's Gothic Wars from the Third Century to Alaric*, Cambridge: Cambridge University Press, 2007

Lançon, B., *Rome in Late Antiquity* (tr. A. Nevill), Edinburgh: Edinburgh University Press, 2000

Lane Fox, R., 'The *Life of Daniel*' in M. J. Edwards and S. Swain (eds), *Portraits: Biographical Representation in the Greek and Latin Literature of the Roman Empire*, Oxford: Clarendon Press, 1997, 175–225

Laniado, A., *Recherches sur les notables municipaux dans l'empire protobyzantin*, Paris: Collège de France, 2002

Lee, A. D., *War in Late Antiquity: A Social History*, Oxford: Blackwell, 2007

Lenski, N., *Failure of Empire: Valens and the Roman State in the Fourth Century A.D.*, Berkeley: University of California Press, 2002

Leone, A., *Changing Townscapes in North Africa from Late Antiquity to the Arab Conquest*, Bari: Edipuglia, 2007

Liebeschuetz, J. H. W. G., *Antioch: City and Imperial Administration in the Later Roman Empire*, Oxford: Clarendon Press, 1972

Liebeschuetz, J. H. W. G., *Barbarians and Bishops: Army, Church and State in the Age of Arcadius and Chrysostom*, Oxford: Clarendon Press, 1990

Liebeschuetz, J. H. W. G., *The Decline and Fall of the Roman City*, Oxford: Oxford University Press, 2001

Little, L. K. (ed.), *Plague and the End of Antiquity: The Pandemic of 541–750*, Cambridge: Cambridge University Press, 2007

Loseby, S. T., 'Decline and change in the cities of late antique Gaul' in J.-U. Krause and C. Witschel (eds), *Die Stadt in der Spätantike: Niedergang oder Wandel?*, Stuttgart: Franz Steiner, 2006, 67–104

Loseby, S. T., 'The ceramic data and the transformation of the Roman world' in M. Bonifay et al. (eds), *LRCW2: Late Roman Coarse Wares, Cooking Wares and Amphorae in the Mediterranean*, Oxford: British

Archaeological Reports, 2007, 1–14

Loseby, S. T., 'Post-Roman economies' in W. Scheidel (ed.), *The Cambridge Companion to the Roman Economy*, Cambridge: Cambridge University Press (forthcoming)

Maas, M. (ed.), *The Cambridge Companion to the Age of Justinian*, Cambridge: Cambridge University Press, 2005

MacGeorge, P., *Late Roman Warlords*, Oxford: Oxford University Press, 2002

Mango, C., *Le Développement urbain de Constantinople (IVe–VIIe siècles)*, Paris: Boccard, 1985

Matthews, J., *Western Aristocracies and Imperial Court*, AD 364–425, Oxford: Clarendon Press, 1975

Matthews, J., *The Roman Empire of Ammianus*, London: Duckworth, 1989

Matthews, J., *Laying Down the Law: A Study of the Theodosian Code*, New Haven: Yale University Press, 2000

Mattingly, D. J. and Hitchner, R. B., 'Roman Africa: an archaeological review', *JRS* 85 (1995), 165–213

McCormick, M., *Eternal Victory: Triumphal Rulership in Late Antiquity, Byzantium and the Early Medieval West*, Cambridge: Cambridge University Press, 1985

McCormick, M., 'Emperor and court', CAH^2 14.135–63

McLynn, N. B., *Ambrose of Milan: Church and Court in a Christian Capital*, Berkeley: University of California Press, 1994

McLynn, N. B., '*Genere Hispanus*: Theodosius, Spain and Nicene orthodoxy' in K. Bowes and M. Kulikowski (eds), *Hispania in Late Antiquity*, Leiden: Brill, 2005, 77–120

Meier, M., *Das andere Zeitalter Justinians: Kontingenzerfahrung und Kontingenzbewältigung im 6 Jahrhundert n. Chr.*, Göttingen: Vandenhoeck & Ruprecht, 2003

Meier, M., *Anastasios I: Die Entstehung des byzantinischen Reich*, Stuttgart: Klett-Cotta, 2009

Menze, V., *Justinian and the Making of the Syrian Orthodox Church*, Oxford: Oxford University Press, 2008

Merrills, A. and Miles, R., *The Vandals*, Oxford: Wiley-Blackwell, 2010

Meyendorff, J., *Imperial Unity and Christian Divisions: The Church, 450–680 AD*, Crestwood, NY: St Vladimir's Seminary Press, 1989

Millar, F., 'The Jews of the Graeco-Roman diaspora between paganism and Christianity, AD 312–438' in J. Lieu et al. (eds), *The Jews among Pagans and Christians*, London: Routledge, 1992, 97–123

Millar, F., *A Greek Roman Empire: Power and Belief under Theodosius II (408–450)*, Berkeley: University of California Press, 2006

Mitchell, S., and Greatrex, G. (eds), *Ethnicity and Culture in Late Antiquity*, London: Duckworth, 2000

Modéran, Y., 'L'Afrique reconquise et les Trois Chapitres' in C. Chazelle and C. Cubitt (eds), *The Crisis of the* Oikumene: *The Three Chapters and the Failed Quest for Unity in the Sixth-Century Mediterranean*, Turnhout: Brepols, 2007, 39–84

Moorhead, J., *Theoderic in Italy*, Oxford: Clarendon Press, 1992

Moorhead, J., *Justinian*, London: Longman, 1994

Moorhead, J., *Ambrose: Church and Society in the Late Roman World*, London: Longman, 1999

Moorhead, J., 'The Byzantines in the west in the sixth century' in *CMH* 1.118–39

Müller-Wiener, W., *Bildlexikon zur Topographie Istanbuls*, Tübingen: Wasmuth, 1977

Noy, D., 'Immigrants in late imperial Rome' in S. Mitchell and G. Greatrex (eds), *Ethnicity and Culture in Late Antiquity*, London: Duckworth, 2000, 15–30

O'Donnell, J. J., *Cassiodorus*, Berkeley: University of California Press, 1979 (www9.georgetown.edu/faculty/jod/texts/cassbook/toc.html).

Pietri, C., *Roma christiana: Recherches sur l'église de Rome, son organisation, sa politique, son idéologie de Miltiade à Sixte III (311–440)*, Rome: École française de Rome, 1976

Price, R., *The Acts of the Council of Constantinople of 533*, Liverpool: Liverpool University Press, 2009

Price, R. and Gaddis, M., *The Acts of the Council of Chalcedon*, Liverpool: Liverpool University Press, 2005

Rapp, C., *Holy Bishops in Late Antiquity*, Berkeley: University of California Press, 2005

Ripoll, G., and Gurt, J. M. (eds), *Sedes Regiae (ann. 400–800)*, Barcelona: Reial Acadèmia de Bonas Lletres, 2000

Roueché, C., *Performers and Partisans at Aphrodisias in the Roman and Late Roman Periods*, London: JRS Monographs 6, 1993

Roueché, C., 'Provincial governors and their titulature in the sixth century', *AnTard* 6 (1998), 83–9

Roueché, C., *Aphrodisias in Late Antiquity: The Late Roman and Byzantine Inscriptions*, 2nd edn (http://insaph.kcl.ac.uk/ala2004)

Rousseau, P., 'Inheriting the fifth century: who bequeathed what?' in P. Allen and E. M. Jeffreys (eds), *The Sixth Century: End or Beginning?*, Brisbane: Byzantina Australiensia 10, 1996, 1–19

Salzman, M. R., *The Making of a Christian Aristocracy: Social and Religious Change in the Western Roman Empire*, Cambridge, MA: Harvard University Press, 2002

Saradi, H. G., *The Byzantine City in the Sixth Century*, Athens: Society of Messenian Archaeological Studies, 2006

Sarris, P., *Economy and Society in the Age of Justinian*, Cambridge: Cambridge University Press, 2006

Sarris, P., 'The early Byzantine economy in context: aristocratic property and economic growth reconsidered', *Early Medieval Europe* 19 (2011), 255–84

Seager, R., 'Roman policy on the Rhine and Danube in Ammianus', *CQ* 49 (1999), 579–605

Shanzer, D. and Wood, I., *Avitus of Vienne: Letters and Selected Prose*, Liverpool: Liverpool University Press, 2002

Shaw, B. D., *Sacred Violence: African Christians and Sectarian Hatred in the Age of Augustine*, Cambridge: Cambridge University Press, 2011

Stein, E., *Histoire du Bas-Empire* (tr. R. Palanque), Paris: de Brouwer, 1949–59

Stickler, T., *Aëtius: Gestaltungsspielräume eines Heermeisters im ausgehenden Weströmischen Reich*, Munich: Beck, 2002

Swanson, R. N. (ed.), *The Church and Mary* (= SCH 39), Woodbridge: Boydell, 2004

Trombley, F. R., *Hellenic Religion and Christianization, c. 379–527*, 2nd edn, Leiden: Brill, 2001

Waelkens, M. et al., 'The late antique to early Byzantine city in southwest Anatolia – Sagalassos and its territory: a case study' in J.-U. Krause and C. Witschel (eds), *Die Stadt in der Spätantike: Niedergang oder Wandel?*, Stuttgart: Franz Steiner, 2006, 199–255

Ward-Perkins, B., *From Classical Antiquity to the Middle Ages: Urban Public Building in Northern and Central Italy, AD 300–850*, Oxford: Oxford University Press, 1984

Ward-Perkins, B., 'Constantinople: a city and its ideological territory' in G. P. Brogiolo, N. Gauthier and N. Christie (eds), *Towns and their Territories between Late Antiquity and the Early Middle Ages*, Leiden: Brill, 2000, 325–45

Ward-Perkins, B., *The Fall of Rome and the End of Civilization*, Oxford: Oxford University Press, 2005

Watts, E., *City and School in Late Antique Athens and Alexandria*, Berkeley: University of California Press, 2006

Wessel, S., *Cyril of Alexandria and the Nestorian Controversy*, Oxford: Oxford University Press, 2004

Whitby, M., 'John of Ephesus and the pagans: pagan survivals in the sixth century' in M. Salamon (ed.), *Paganism in the Later Roman Empire and in Byzantium*, Cracow: Byzantina et Slavica Cracoviensia 1, 1991, 111–31

Whitby, M., 'The violence of the circus factions' in K. Hopwood (ed.), *Organised Crime in Antiquity*, London: Duckworth, 1999, 229–53

Whitby, M., 'Factions, bishops, violence and urban decline' in J.-U. Krause and C. Witschel (eds), *Die Stadt in der Spätantike: Niedergang oder Wandel?*, Stuttgart: Franz Steiner, 2006, 441–61

Whittow, M., *The Making of Orthodox Byzantium, 600–1025*, London:

Macmillan, 1996

Wickham, C., *Framing the Early Middle Ages: Europe and the Mediterranean, 400–800*, Oxford: Oxford University Press, 2005

Wilken, R. L., *John Chrysostom and the Jews: Rhetoric and Reality in the Late 4th Century*, Berkeley: University of California Press, 1983

Wood, I. N., *The Merovingian Kingdoms, 450–751*, Harlow: Longman, 1994

Zuckerman, C., 'L'Empire d'Orient et les Huns: notes sur Priscus', *T&M* 12 (1994), 160–82

Index

Abasgi, 279
Abundantius, general, 91
Acacian schism, 150, 177, 189, 193, 265, 285
Acacius, bishop of Constantinople, 149–50, 177
Academy, Athenian, 276
accession ceremonial, imperial, 161, 175, 294
acclamations see chanting
Achaemenids, 15
Acholius, bishop of Thessalonica, 45
actors, 191, 245; see also theatres
Ad Salices, battle of, 34
adaeratio, 166, 234; see also taxation
administration, imperial see bureaucracy
Adrianople, battle of, 25, 35–8, 44
Adriatic Sea, 112
Aegean region, 237, 254
Aegidius, general, 95, 125–6
Aemilius Paullus, general, 162
Aetius, general, 85–9, 94, 95, 101, 102, 103, 116, 120, 178
African Red Slip ware, 226, 237–8
Agapetus, bishop of Rome, 281–2, 283
Agathias, historian, 293
Agila, Visigothic ruler, 292–3
Agri Decumates, 1, 2
agri deserti, 223, 224, 235
Alamanni, 2, 30–1, 189
Alans, 93, 112
Alaric, Gothic leader, 86, 110–14, 178, 206
Alavivus, Gothic leader, 33, 34n
Albenga, 85
Albinus, senator, 193–4
Alexander the Great, 15, 19, 199
Alexandria, 5, 52, 74, 220
    food supply, 215
    grain fleet, 237–8

religious violence in, 53–4, 148–9, 216
rivalry with Antioch and Constantinople, 46, 134, 147
theological orientation, 134–5, 141, 146, 148–9, 280
Altar of Victory, 49, 68
Amalasuintha, Ostrogothic princess, 194–5, 262
Amantius, eunuch (early 5th c.), 102
Amantius, eunuch (early 6th c.), 174
Ambrose, bishop of Milan, 49, 73, 142
    and Altar of Victory, 50–1, 68
    Callinicum episode, 54–5
    crisis of 386, 48
Amida, 169
Ammianus Marcellinus, historian, 37, 57, 142, 168, 199, 224, 233
    critique of senatorial aristocracy, 65, 67
    favourable attitude to Julian, 12, 19–20
    negative portrayal of Jovian, 19–20
amphitheatres, 106, 208, 209, 244
amphorae, 226–7, 237, 238
Anastasius, emperor, 104, 177, 192–3, 204, 217, 234, 243, 244, 251, 256, 257, 272
    background and accession, 159–61
    distribution of offices and honours, 162–3
    financial policies, 163–8, 203, 296
    relations with Persia, 168–71
    relations with Theoderic, 192–3
    religious stance and policies, 160–1, 171–3, 266
Anatolia, 15, 29, 94
    Christianisation of, 152, 274
    cities, 206
    economy, 231
    war in, 24, 91, 111, 161–2, 297

Anazarbus, 225
Ancyra, 39
Anicia Juliana, aristocrat, 271–3
Anicii, senatorial family, 65, 182, 194
annona, 4, 236–9
Anomoian Christians, 8, 42
Antes, 292
Anthemius, emperor, 95, 121, 188
Anthemius, praetorian prefect, 93
Anthimus, bishop of Constantinople, 281
anti-Chalcedonians, 147–50, 172–3,
    279–85
Antioch, 12, 13, 43, 52, 72, 74, 99, 136,
    174, 212, 220, 229, 234, 258
    as imperial base, 5
    loss of *curiales*, 202–3
    magic trials, 42
    Riot of the Statues, 108, 215
    rivalry with Alexandria, 134
    sacked by Persians, 288
    theological orientation, 134–5, 141,
    146
Antiochus, eunuch, 93, 102
Antony, ascetic, 11
Aphrodisias, 206
Aphrodito, 225
Aphthartodocetism, 293
Apion, aristocrat, 163, 176
Apiones, aristocratic family, 228, 235
apologetic works, 12–13, 114, 139
apostasy from Christianity
    to Judaism, 56
    to paganism, 6, 51–2
Apulia, 192
Aquileia, 285
Aquitania, 95, 115, 116, 126, 178, 232
Arab invasions, 232, 298
Arabs, 170
Aramaic language, 14, 168
Arbogast, general, 26–7, 31, 82, 83, 89,
    111, 125
Arcadius, emperor, 23, 26, 81, 83, 90–3,
    106, 110, 135, 151
archaeological evidence
    for cities, 205–10
    for the economy, 224, 226–7
Ardabur, father of Aspar, 93
Ardabur, son of Aspar, 98–9
Areobindus, general, 173, 272
Ariadne, empress, 98–9, 104, 105, 159–
    61, 174, 244

Arianism, 99, 132, 137, 152, 184,
    259–60, 283, 288
    adoption by barbarians, 33n, 48–9,
    187–9, 278
    as obstacle to imperial throne, 98
    divisions, 8
    origins, 7–8
Aristotle, philosopher, 194
Arius, clergyman, 7
Arles, 208–9
Armenia, 23, 29–30, 32, 247, 258, 299
army
    donatives, 161
    field, 4–5, 35, 92–3, 98–9, 110, 169
    in barbarian kingdoms, 180
    manpower and recruitment, 34, 94,
    112, 291
    mistreatment of civilians, 169–70
    organisation in west and east, 83, 92–3
    pay shortages, 288, 291, 296
    praesental, 92, 98
    size, 3, 202
    supply, 236, 254
    see also billeting; *comitatenses*;
    federates; generals; *limitanei*; logistics
Arsaces (Arshak), Armenian ruler, 29–30
Arsacids, Parthian dynasty, 1
asceticism, 11, 47,135, 154–8, 203, 228
Ashkelon, 148
Aspar, general, 93–4, 97–9, 102, 116,
    122
assassination, as political and diplomatic
    tool, 30–1, 34, 87, 88, 99, 102, 115,
    118, 120, 122, 125, 177
Athalaric, Ostrogothic ruler, 194, 262
Athanagild, Visigothic usurper, 292–3
Athanaric, Gothic leader, 32, 33, 34
Athanasius, bishop of Alexandria, 11,
    42–3, 44, 108
Athaulf, Gothic leader, 115, 132
Athens, 220, 221, 276, 290
Attila, Hunnic ruler, 87, 96, 98, 110,
    119–20, 122, 127, 191, 199–200
Augustine, bishop of Hippo, 153, 233
    and Manichaeism, 9
    City of God, 114
    criticism of public entertainments,
    211–12
    education, 220, 221–2
Augustus, first emperor, 2, 49, 60, 245
Aurelian, emperor, 24

Aurelianic Walls, Rome, 73
Ausonius, teacher of rhetoric, 57–9, 128
Auxentius, bishop of Milan, 48
Avars, 292, 297, 298
Avitus, emperor, 94
Axum, 278

Balearics, 121, 154
Balkans, 175, 253
    barbarian settlement in, 33–4, 37,122
    Chalcedonian allegiance, 177
    cities, 206–7
    Latin language in, 160, 256
    war in, 34–8, 110–12, 119–20, 192,
        292
baptism, 9, 189, 245, 274, 279
barbarian kingdoms, 178–95
    administration, 180–3
    building activities, 184–6
    collaboration of local elites, 181–3
    maintenance of power, 183–7
    relations with empire, 191–5
    religious policies, 187–90
barbarian settlement in Roman empire,
    33, 37, 128–32
barbarians see Alamanni; Alans;
    Burgundians; Franks; Goths; Huns;
    Sueves; Vandals
Basil, bishop of Caesarea, 44, 221
Basiliscus, usurper, 98, 100, 104, 121,
    123, 149, 157
bath houses and bathing, 61, 67, 74, 76,
    94, 176, 183, 185, 200, 206, 215,
    219, 231, 299
Bauto, general, 90, 125
Bay of Naples, 66, 96
Beirut, 13, 220
Belalis Maior, 207
Belgica, 180
Belisarius, general, 224, 247, 283, 286,
    292
    as possible threat to Justinian, 262–3,
        293
    consulship, 261–2
    defeat at Callinicum and dismissal, 258
    defence of Dara, 257–8
    Gothic war, 261–2, 291
    Nika riot, 260
    triumph, 261
    Vandal expedition, 260–1
billeting of soldiers, 128, 130, 170–1

bishop of Rome
    contested elections, 63, 102
    growing influence and status, 46–7,
        62–3, 135, 141–3, 299
bishops
    as judges, 10
    concerns about ascetics, 158
    prominence in urban society, 203–5,
        211
    ransoming prisoners, 127
    theological disagreements, 7–9,
        134–41, 143–50, 279–85
Black Sea, 33, 136, 279, 288
Bleda, Hunnic ruler, 119–20
Blues, circus faction, 217–18, 247–8
Boethius, praetorian prefect (5th c.), 87
Boethius, senator (6th c.), 184, 189,
    194–5
Boniface, general, 85–6, 103
booty, 121, 127, 261, 263
Bordeaux, 59, 128, 208, 220n
Bosporus, 73, 104
Bostra, 230
bouleutai see curiales
bribery, 103, 140, 175, 250
Brigetio, 24, 25, 31
Britain, 26, 112, 113n, 228, 232, 238
Bulgars, 292
bureaucracy, imperial, 3–4, 13, 104, 201,
    220; see also comes sacrarum
    largitionum; count of the res private;
    master of the offices; praetorian
    prefect; quaestor
Burgundian kingdom, 96, 180
Burgundian language, 182
Burgundians, 31, 87, 95, 125, 128
burning of books and records, 148, 151,
    165
Buzes, general, 247
Byzantium, 5, 70, 298, 300
Byzas and Strombos, 70

Caelian Hill, 66
Caesaraugusta, 208
Caesarea Maritima, 205–6
Calabria, 222
Calama, 216n
Calendion, bishop of Antioch, 149
Callinicum, 54–5
    battle of, 258, 260
Campus Martius, 63

Candidianus, imperial official, 140
Cannae, battle of, 36
Caria, 254
Cartagena, 292
Carthage, 102, 119, 188, 191, 207, 259, 261, 284
    captured by imperial forces, 224, 260
    captured by Vandals, 116–17, 121, 178
    Vandal building projects, 185–6
Cassiodorus, senator, 182, 184, 222
Castra Maurorum, 28
Catalaunian Plains, battle of, 120
Caucasus, 111, 157, 257, 278–9, 288, 298
Celer, master of the offices, 163, 169, 176
Central Asia, 117
cereal cultivation, 84, 227, 230–1, 233–4
ceremonial, 3, 5, 104, 106–7, 161, 293
Chalcedon, 135
Chalcedon, council of, 102, 104, 144–7, 156, 158, 264, 279–80, 284–5
Chalcis, 203
Chalke (Bronze Gate), Constantinople, 162, 217, 263
chanting and acclamations, 159, 213–14, 248
chariot-racing, 66, 186, 209, 211–13, 244, 288
charitable activities, 6, 54, 211, 228, 246, 273
Childeric, Frankish ruler, 126
China, 9
Chlothild, wife of Clovis, 189
Christianisation, 6, 52, 150–4, 300
    in 5th century, 150–4
    in 6th century, 273–7
    limits, 153
    of cities, 211
Christianity
    apostasy from, 6, 51–2
    divisions, 7–9, 42–9
    Nicene, 7–8, 11
    persecution of, 8, 51, 121, 122, 132, 187–8
    in Persia, 279
    see also anti-Chalcedonians; asceticism; bishops; Christological controversies; church councils
Christodorus, poet, 162
Christological controversies, 103, 137–41, 143–50, 157, 218, 279–85

Chrysaphius, eunuch, 93, 98, 102, 143
chrysargyron, 164
Chrysopolis, 72
church buildings
    attacked by pagans and Jews, 51, 56
    construction, 6, 63, 106, 183–4, 211, 266–73
church councils, 264, 279–80, 284–5; see also Chalcedon; Constantinople; Ephesus; Nicaea
church–state relations, 42–9, 50–2, 54–5, 134–41, 143–50, 158, 172–3, 177, 187–90, 279–85
church, wealth, 6, 62, 132, 141, 228
Cilicia, 204
Cillium, battle of, 289
circumcelliones, 9, 216n
circus factions, 215, 217–18, 247–50; see also Blues; Greens
circuses see hippodromes
cisterns, 74, 102
cities
    absence of among barbarians, 199–200
    administration, 201–5
    and rural hinterland, 200
    councils, 201–4
    cultural life, 219–22
    fabric and amenities, 205–14
    heavier concentrations in east, north Africa and Italy, 200
    imperial (re)foundations, 200
    'notables', 203–5
    Persian, 199
    revenues, 201–2, 227
    unrest and riots, 214–18
    walls, 183, 206–10
    see also curiales
citizenship, Roman, 299
city councillors see curiales
civil war, 23–4, 26, 27, 84, 85, 96, 100–1, 161–2, 173, 292–3, 297
Claudian, poet, 67, 83, 91
clothing, 115, 142, 174, 279
Clovis, Frankish ruler, 126, 178, 180, 186, 192
    conversion of, 189–90
coinage, 23, 107, 166, 235, 291
    Anastasius' reform of bronze coinage, 167
    in barbarian kingdoms, 184–5
    solidus, 167, 234

collatio lustralis, 164
Cologne, 126
coloni, 224, 232–3
Colosseum, Rome, 60, 182
comes civitatis, 204
comes rei privatae see count of the *res privata*
comes sacrarum largitionum, 4
comitatenses, 4–5; *see also* army: field
confiscated property *see* land
consistory, 160
Constans, emperor, 8
Constantine, usurper (5th c.), 84, 112
Constantine, emperor, 12, 14, 16, 22, 23, 42, 62, 73, 74, 76, 77, 125, 164, 167, 183–4, 200, 202, 227
  foundation of Constantinople, 3, 5–6, 70–2
  impact on empire, 5–8, 16
  intervention in church disputes, 7–9
  introduction of *solidus*, 234
  military reforms, 5
  other emperors as 'new Constantines', 145–6, 175, 177, 190
  policies towards Jews, 56
  support for Christianity, 6–7, 39, 228
Constantinople, 16, 20, 22, 24, 26, 29, 35, 116, 157, 200, 215, 218, 222, 238–9, 288
  as educational centre, 13, 220
  as imperial residence, 5–6, 46, 72, 82, 298
  as new or second Rome, 46, 70–2, 78, 147
  attacks on, 36, 92, 124, 173, 297–8
  bishop of and status, 46–7, 134–41, 147, 149, 150, 172, 280–4
  churches, 74, 106, 266–73
  food supply, 3, 60–1, 71–2, 76–7, 214, 234, 237, 239
  foundation, 70–2
  granaries, 74, 107
  hippodrome, 104, 107, 248–9
  pandemic in, 289
  population, 76
  public buildings, 74–6, 104, 106
  senate, 64, 72, 77
  walls, 73, 106
  water supply, 74–6, 102, 120
Constantinople
  council of (381), 46, 73, 134, 147, 264

  council of (553), 284–5
Constantius II, emperor, 8, 19, 20, 42, 59, 72, 73, 74, 77, 100n, 227
Constantius III, emperor, 81, 82, 84–5, 87, 102, 103, 115, 116, 131
consulship
  as honour or reward, 162, 163, 261–2
  Justinian's restrictions on, 262
  used for self-advertisement, 244, 262
conversion
  from Nicene to Arian Christianity, 187
  to Christianity, 52n, 68–9, 152–3, 189–90, 257, 278–9
  see also apostasy; Christianisation
Coptic, 14
Corinth, 206–7
corruption, 128, 253; *see also* bribery
Corsica, 121
Corycus, 204
Cotyaeum, battle of, 162
count of the *res privata*, 4, 164, 227
Crete, 154n
Crispus, son of Constantine, 12
Cuicul, 203
cultural life, 11–14, 219–22; *see also* dancing; education; entertainments; literature; panegyric; poetry; rhetoric; theatres
curiales, 166, 201–4, 215
  obligations and avoidance of, 201–2, 204, 237
customs tolls, 225, 235, 237
Cutzes, general, 247
Cyclades, 254
Cyprus, 148, 254
Cyril, bishop of Alexandria, 103, 136–41, 144, 146–8, 156, 280, 282

Dacia, 1
Dakhleh Oasis, 226, 234
Dalmatius, monk, 157–8
Damascius, philosopher, 276
Damasus, bishop of Rome, 44, 63, 141
dancing, 13, 211–12
Daniel the Stylite, ascetic, 156–7
Dara, 164, 169–71, 297
  battle of, 257–8
De Caerimoniis, 159, 174
decretals, 141
decuriones see curiales

defensor civitatis, 204
Demophilus, bishop of Constantinople, 46
Demotic language, 14
Digest, 251–2, 257, 259
Diocletian, emperor, 15, 28, 51, 109, 166, 202, 232, 234
Diogenianus, general, 163, 176
Dioscorus, bishop of Alexandria, 144, 146–8
diplomacy, 4, 27–8, 30–1, 125, 192, 258, 278–9; *see also* embassies; gift-giving; hostages; subsidies
divine judgement, 169, 282
domestici, 99
Domnica, wife of Valens, 36
Donatist Christians, 8–9, 187, 283
Donatus, Donatist bishop, 9, 118
dust cloud (530s), 290
dux, 5
Dyrrhachium, 160

earthquakes, 200, 206, 210, 293
economy in late antiquity
    ancient evidence for, 224–7
    historiography of, 223–7
Edeco, 96
Edessa, 42, 164–5, 170
education, 11–13, 123, 168, 262, 275, 276
    Christian attitudes to, 221–2
Egypt, 152, 219, 225, 228, 289
    anti-Chalcedonian allegiance, 177, 259
    as place of exile, 140, 161, 280
    conversion to Christianity, 152, 274
    economic productivity and wealth, 2–3, 76, 126, 234, 235, 236, 298
    monasticism in, 11, 135, 152
embassies, 97, 102, 113, 118, 119, 177, 192, 255, 278, 281
Emerita, 186, 208
emperors,
    and military affairs, 15, 21, 25, 26, 27, 82, 91, 101, 155, 256–7
    as law-makers, 108–9, 256–7
    as 'new Constantines', 145–6, 175, 177, 190
    dynastic intentions, 20–1, 26, 98–9
    legitimation of power, 20, 24, 26, 32, 97, 161, 244

    portraits and statues of, 107–8, 173, 215
    tombs of, 73
    see also church–state relations
empresses, political influence, 36, 46, 103–4, 246, 250
Ennodius, aristocrat, 184
entertainments, popular, 11, 211–14, 244, 246
    Christian criticisms of, 13–14, 211–13
    see also dancing; games, public; hippodromes; theatres
Ephesus, council of (431), 139–40, 148, 156, 157, 264
    council of (449), 144, 148, 157, 280, 283
Ethiopia, 278
Eucherius, son of Stilicho, 84
Eudaemon, prefect of Constantinople, 248–9
Eudocia, wife of Theodosius II, 121, 139
Eudoxia, wife of Arcadius, 90, 102, 136
Eudoxia, wife of Valentinian III, 107, 109, 144
euergetism, 183, 201
Eugenius, usurper, 27, 37–8, 68, 73, 83, 89, 111
Eugubium, 142
eunuchs, 90–1, 90n, 93, 102–3
    political influence of, 159–60, 174–5
Euphemia, wife of Justin I, 246
Euphemius, bishop of Constantinople, 159, 161, 172
Euric, Visigothic ruler, 178, 182, 186, 188
Eutropius, eunuch, 90–2, 102, 111, 135
Eutyches, monk, 143–4, 148, 150, 157–8
Eutychius, bishop of Constantinople, 294
Evagrius, historian, 289
excubitores, 174–5
exile, 42, 44, 92, 136, 140, 148, 149, 161, 177, 187, 217, 280

Facundus of Hermiane, 284
fasting, 155
federates, Gothic, 37, 91, 110
Felix, martyr, 153
field survey, 226, 228–32
fire, in cities, 62, 102, 248
flamen perpetuus, 190
Flavian, bishop of Antioch, 172

Flavian, bishop of Constantinople, 143–4, 157
Florence, 112
foederati see federates
follis, 167
food shortages, 113, 115, 120, 125, 214–15, 293
fortifications, 30, 118–19, 169–71, 207–8, 292
Frankish kingdom, 178, 209
Franks, 2, 30, 31, 87, 121, 125–6
Fravitta, general, 92–3
Frigidus River, battle of, 27, 38, 110
Fritigern, Gothic leader, 33, 34n, 35

Gainas, general, 91–2, 106, 111, 118, 233
Galatia, 233
Galla Placidia, empress, 81, 82, 85,103, 115, 132, 144
gambling, 211–12
games, public, 77, 201, 244
Gaudentius, father of Aetius, 85
Gaudentius, son of Aetius, 87
Gaul, 25, 26, 30, 143, 219, 232, 238
    barbarian kingdoms in, 95, 178, 180
    cities, 208–9
    war in, 112, 115, 120, 126
    see also Aquitania; Bordeaux; Trier
Gaza, 102, 151
Geiseric, Vandal ruler, 110, 116–17, 120–2, 178, 187–8
Gelasius, bishop of Rome, 191
Gelimer, Vandal ruler, 259–61
generals, barbarian *see* Arbogast; Aspar; Bauto; Gainas; Plintha; Richomer; Ricimer; Silvanus; Stilicho
generals, political influence of, 25, 82–9, 91–101, 101–2, 103, 261–2
Geneva, 186
Genoa, 189
Gepids, 192, 292
Germanic language, 128
Germanus, cousin of Justinian, 176, 243, 289
Greuthungian Goths, 33–4
gift-giving, 70, 93, 103, 140, 164, 180, 244, 246; *see also* subsidies
Gildo, African prince, 84, 111
Glycerius, emperor, 96
Goffart, Walter, on barbarian settlement, 128–32
Goths, 2, 16, 22, 93
    conversion to (Arian) Christianity, 33n, 48, 132
    entry to empire, 33
    in mid 4th century, 16, 23, 32
    in later 4th century, 26, 30, 33–8, 74
    in early 5th century, 84, 110–14
    in mid 5th century, 87, 120
    in later 5th century, 122–5
    kingdom in Gaul, 95, 115, 126
    provision of troops to empire, 32, 34, 38
    sack Rome, 104, 113–14
    settlement in Aquitania, 115, 131
    support usurper Procopius, 29
    victory at Adrianople, 24, 25
    see also Alaric, Ostrogothic kingdom, Roman–Gothic relations, Theoderic, Visigothic kingdom
governors, 180, 253
grain *see* cereal cultivation; Constantinople: food supply; Rome: food supply
grammarians, 219
Gratian, 21, 47, 57n, 73, 142, 219
    accession, 24–5
    death, 26, 50
    military activities, 31, 35
    relations with Valens, 35
    religious policies, 49–50
Greece, 110, 206–7
Greek language, 11, 14, 22, 67, 123, 219, 256, 300
Greens, circus faction, 217–18, 248
Gregori(an)us, lawyer, 109
Gregory of Nazianzus, bishop of Constantinople, 46
Gregory of Tours, historian, 188–9
Gregory, bishop of Rome, 297, 299
Grepes, Herul ruler, 279
Grod, Hun ruler, 279
Gundobad, Burgundian ruler, 96
Gunthamund, Vandal ruler, 187

Hadrian, emperor, 251
Hadrumetum, 186
Hagia Eirene, church of, Constantinople, 106
Hagia Sophia, church of, Constantinople, 74, 267–71, 273, 293, 295

Hannibal, 36
Hauran, 230, 232
Hebdomon, 106
Helion, master of the offices, 93, 103
Hellespont, 237
Henotikon, 149–50, 172, 177
Heraclius, emperor, 297–8
Heraclius, eunuch, 102
Hercules, 216
Hermogenianus, lawyer, 109
Hermopolite nome, 225
Heruls, 279, 292
Hilderic, Vandal ruler, 121, 185, 187, 259–60
Himyarites, 278
hippodromes, 211, 215, 217–18
Holy Apostles, church of, Constantinople, 74
Holy Land, as focus for pilgrimage, 10
holy men, 154–8, 275, 294
Homer, 12, 94
Homoian Christians, 8, 42, 43, 48
Homoiousian Christians, 8, 43, 46
Homoousian Christians, 8, 42
honorati, 203
Honorius, emperor, 23, 26, 81, 82, 83–4, 86, 90, 111, 113, 116, 187, 191
Hormisdas, bishop of Rome, 177
Hormizd, Persian prince,15
hospices, 211, 273
hospitalitas see billeting
hostages, 86, 123
Huneric, Vandal ruler,121, 182, 186, 187–8
Hunericopolis, 186
Huns, 33, 86–7, 92, 93, 110, 111, 127, 144, 207, 292
Huns, Crimean, 279
hymns, 48, 165
Hypatia, philosopher, 137
Hypatius, aristocrat and usurper, 162–3, 173, 174, 176, 248–50
Hypatius, monk, 152

Ibas, bishop of Edessa, 143–4, 146–7, 280, 282, 283
Illus, general, 100–1, 124, 165
Illyricum, 93, 143, 254
immigration
   to Constantinople, 249, 253
   to Rome, 60

imperial cult, 7, 190
imperial estates, 227; *see also* land, confiscation of
imperial residences *see* Antioch; Constantinople; Milan; Ravenna; Rome; Sirmium; Trier
incense, 49, 53
inflation, 166, 167
influencing public opinion, 27–8, 40, 83, 87
Innocent, bishop of Rome, 142
irrigation, 231, 235
Isaac, monk, 135, 157–8
Isauria, 94, 99, 100–1, 136, 159–62, 164, 175
Isis, 7, 216, 274
Islam, 298
Italy, 26, 110, 116, 143, 228, 232,
   cities, 57–63, 209
   impact of Gothic war, 292, 296, 299
   Ostrogothic kingdom in, 97, 124–5, 178
   senatorial landholdings, 66, 299
   war in, 85, 113, 120, 121, 259
ivory diptychs, 53, 88–9, 107, 244

Jacob Baradai, bishop, 285
Jerome, monk, 221
Jerusalem, 121, 148, 261
Jews, 10, 11, 54–6, 137, 153–4, 189, 277
John Chrysostom, bishop of Constantinople, 56, 134–6, 157, 212, 215, 216
John Lydus, bureaucrat, 256
John, bishop of Ephesus, 274, 289
John Scholasticus, bishop of Constantinople, 294
John the Cappadocian, praetorian prefect, 247, 248–9, 250, 250–1, 253, 256, 260
John the Hunchback, general, 162
John the Paphlagonian, financial official, 168
John the Scythian, general, 162
John Troglita, general, 289
John, usurper, 103
Jovian, emperor, 19–20, 23, 72, 73
   peace settlement with Persia, 20, 23, 28–9, 42
   policies towards Christians, 40, 42–3
   policies towards pagans, 39–41

Judaism *see* Jews
Julian Alps, 111
Julian, emperor, 12, 14–16, 23, 72, 73–4,
 73n, 82, 125, 139, 227
 Gothic policy, 16
 law against Christian teachers, 15, 41,
  51
 Persian expedition, 15, 19, 21, 24, 34,
  40, 234
 polarisation of religious attitudes, 216,
  221
 religious policies, 6, 14–15, 39, 55
Julius Nepos, emperor, 95, 96, 97
Jupiter, 7
jurists, 109, 251–2
Justin I, emperor, 174–7, 193, 194, 243,
 251, 256, 272, 278–9
Justin II, emperor, 294, 297
Justin, son of Germanus, 294
Justina, mother of Valentinian II, 48
Justinian, emperor, 150, 174, 256
 accession and background, 243–4
 administrative and military
  appointments, 246–7
 administrative reforms, 253–6
 and Christological controversies,
  279–85
 and circus factions, 218, 247–50
 and Gothic war, 262–3, 281
 and Nika riot, 247–50
 and Spain, 292–3
 and Theodora, 244–5, 250, 281
 as sleepless, 267, 294–5
 attitude to education, 221
 building projects, 266–73, 274, 292
 final years, 293–4
 illness from pandemic, 282, 289
 interest in theological debate, 265,
  280
 legacy, 294–8
 legal projects, 251–2, 295
 policies towards Jews, 277
 policies towards pagans, 274, 276
 prejudice against, 243–6, 254
 relations with Persia, 257–8, 286–8,
  296
 religion and foreign relations, 277–9
 religious commitment, 246, 259, 264–6
 revival of triumph, 261
 role during Justin I's reign, 175–7,
  243–4

 self-promotion, 200n, 244, 246, 252,
  253–4
 theological writings, 265
 Vandal expedition, 121, 207, 239,
  258–61
 see also Justinianic Code
Justiniana Prima, 253–4
Justinianic Code, 224, 251–3, 257, 259,
 264
Juvenal, bishop of Jerusalem, 148
Juvenal, satirist, 67

Kasserine, 231, 289
Kavad, Persian king, 165, 169–70, 257–8
Kellis, 226, 234
Khusro I, Persian king, 255, 257–8, 276,
 286–8, 295
Khusro II, Persian king, 297–8
ktētores see possessores

Lactantius, teacher of rhetoric, 12–13
Lakhmids, Arab tribe, 170
land
 confiscation of, 164, 194–5, 227, 248,
  276, 293
 distribution to barbarians, 130–2
 large estates, 227–8, 234
 ownership, 201–5, 227–33
languages, 14; *see also* Aramaic;
  Burgundian; Coptic; Demotic;
  Germanic; Greek; Latin; Punic;
  Syriac
Latin Anthology, 185
Latin language, 11, 14, 22, 67, 123, 160,
 194, 219, 256, 300
law codes
 barbarian, 130, 184–5, 204
 Roman, 108–9, 224–5, 232, 236, 264
 *see also Justinianic Code; Theodosian
  Code*
Lazica, 157, 257, 258, 278–9, 288
legal education, 13, 220–1, 252
legislation
 against pagans, 52–3, 151, 276
 codification of, 108–9
 dissemination of, 108
 papal, 141, 299
Leo, bishop of Rome, 143, 144–7, 149
Leo I, emperor, 98–9, 102, 104, 149, 156,
 157, 160, 175, 251
 accession, 98, 106–7

relations with Aspar, 98–9
relations with Goths, 122–3
Vandal expedition, 121–2, 163, 191, 260
Leo II, emperor, 99–100
Leo, senator, 182
Leontia, daughter of Leo I, 99, 100
Leontius, usurper, 100–1
Leovigild, Visigothic ruler, 186
Libanius, teacher of rhetoric, 13, 72, 134, 202–3, 215, 220
defence of pagan cults, 52
libations, 49, 53
Liberius, senator, 182
Libius Severus, emperor, 94–5
libraries, 206, 222
Licinius, emperor, 72
Liguria, 85
Limestone Massif, Syria, 229–30, 232, 234
limitanei, 5
literacy, 108, 177, 219, 275
literature, classical, 12, 221–2
logistics, 166, 173, 234, 236, 254, 262; *see also* army: supply
Lombards, 209, 296, 299
Long Walls, Thrace, 120
Longinus of Cardala, 161
Longinus of Selinus, 161
Longinus, brother of Zeno, 161
Lupercalia, 190–1
Lusitania, 208
Luxorius, poet, 185
Lycaonia, 255
Lycia, 231, 232
lynchings of prominent figures, 84, 90, 148, 215, 216–17; *see also* urban rioting

Macedonia, 122
Macedonius, bishop of Constantinople, 172
Madauros, 220
Maeander River, 225
magic, 42, 47
magister, 4; *see also* generals
magister officiorum see master of the offices
Magnus Maximus, usurper, 26, 31, 48, 51n, 57, 73, 74
religious policies, 45, 47

Majorian, emperor, 94, 121
Mani, religious leader, 9
Manichaeism, 9, 47
Marcellinus, general, 95
Marcian, emperor, 97–8, 103, 104, 106, 145–8, 159, 244
Marcian, usurper, 100, 104, 124
Marcianople, 34, 174
Maria, wife of Honorius, 83
Marinus of Apamea, praetorian prefect, 163, 168, 176
Marius Maximus, biographer, 67
Marius Victorinus, philosopher, 68–9
marriage
as a political tool, 83, 87, 90, 97, 103–4, 107, 109, 121, 132–3, 144, 161, 244
between Romans and barbarians, 115, 121, 132–3
Mars, 7
Marseille, 209
martyrdom, 188
Mary, cult of, 137–9, 146, 157
Mascezel, African prince, 84
master of the offices, 4, 104, 180, 182
Maternus Cynegius, praetorian prefect, 52
Mauretania, 66, 84
Maurice, emperor, 297
Maximus of Ephesus, philosopher, 40, 42n
Melania the Younger, ascetic, 228, 233
Menander, historian, 288, 293
Menas, bishop of Constantinople, 281, 283–4
merchants *see* traders
Merobaudes, poet, 87
Miaphysites *see* anti-Chalcedonians
Milan, 27, 73, 125, 209, 220, 285
as imperial base, 5, 26, 30, 48, 49, 50, 53, 111–12
Miletus, 225
mime, 13, 211, 213, 217
Minorca, 154
Mithras, 7
Moesia, 254
monasteries, 11, 246, 273
as focus of education, 222
see also asceticism; monks
monetisation, 234
monks, 56, 154, 156–7, 157–8

as intermediaries, 215
destruction of pagan shrines, 52
in Constantinople, 135, 140, 157–8
in Egypt, 11, 135
in Palestine 148
Monophysites *see* anti-Chalcedonians
monotheism, pagan, 7
Moors, 122, 207–8, 260, 288–9, 292
music, 13, 48, 165; *see also* hymns
Myra, 231
mythology, pagan, 13, 211

Naples, 262
Narses, general, 291, 292
navicularii see shipmasters
Nedao River, battle of, 122
Negev, 230, 232, 235
Neoplatonism, 7, 40, 276
Nero, emperor, 267
Nerva, emperor, 12
Nessana, 230
Nestorius, bishop of Constantinople,
    136–41, 150, 151, 157, 283
'new Constantines', 145–6, 175, 177, 190
Nicaea, 21, 144, 146
    council of, 7–8, 46, 134, 149, 264
Nicopolis ad Istrum, 207
Nika riot, 247–50, 253, 255, 258–9, 260,
    267
Nisibis, 15, 28–9, 169
Nola, 153
north Africa, 84, 207–8, 228, 231, 233,
    238
    ecclesiastical independence, 8–9,
        142–3, 283–5
    economic productivity, 3, 117, 234
    see also Vandals
northern Mesopotamia, 15, 28–9,
    168–70, 234, 257, 288
'notables', emergence as urban elite,
    203–5, 218
Notitia Dignitatum, 109n, 311
Notitia urbis Constantinopolitanae, 75–6
Nu'man, Arab leader, 170
Nubians, 279
Numidia, 116, 203
nummi, 167

Odoacer, general, 96–7, 124–5, 180, 182,
    191
oil presses, 207, 231, 235

olive oil, 3, 226, 229–30, 231, 233, 234,
    237, 238
Olybrius, emperor, 95, 96, 272
Olybrius, son of Juliana, 272
Olympias, aristocrat, 136
oracles, 153
Orestes, general, 96, 97
Orestes, prefect of Egypt, 137
Oribasius, philosopher, 42n
Origen, theologian, 221
Orleans, 120
Osrhoene, 52
Ostia, 66, 237
Ostrogothic kingdom
    administration, 180–2
    establishment, 124–5, 178
    maintenance, 183–7
    relations with Anastasius, 191–3
    relations with senate, 182, 193–5
    religious policies, 187–91
    war with Justinian, 209, 222, 262–3,
        286, 291–2
Ostrogoths, history of name, 178n
Oxyrhynchus, 225, 228

Pachomius, monk, 11
paganism
    diversity of cults, 7
    legislation against, 52–4, 151
    persistence, 153, 273–6
    restrictions on, 49–52
paideia see education
palace guards, 174–5, 243
Palace of Hormisdas, 266, 281
Palatine Hill, 63, 104
Palestine, 148, 205–6, 228, 234
Pamphylia, 247
pandemic of 542, 282, 289–91, 296
    cyclical nature, 291
panegyric, 23, 31, 37, 123, 162, 184–5
Panium, 119
Pannonia, 22, 24,122
pantomime, 13, 217
Pap, Armenian ruler, 30
papa, term for bishop of Rome, 142
papyri, 225–6, 230, 290–1
Paris, 26, 95, 186
Parthians, 1
Patara, 231
Patricius, aristocrat, 163, 174, 176
Patricius, son of Aspar, 98–9

patronage, 13, 64, 83, 155–6, 164, 209, 213, 218, 228
Paulina, wife of Zeno, 94
Paulinus of Pella, aristocrat, 128
Pavia, 209
Pelagius, ascetic, 142
Pelagius, bishop of Rome, 285
Périgueux, 208
Perinthus, 36
persecution of Christians, 8, 51
  of Nicene Christians by Arians, 121, 122, 132, 187–8
Persia, 1, 22, 99, 126
  as challenge to Roman power, 1–2, 27
  cities, 199
  see also Roman–Persian relations
Peter the Iberian, bishop, 148n
Peter, bishop of Alexandria, 44
Petronius Maximus, emperor, 94
Petronius Probus, senator, 67, 68
Philae, 274
philosophers, 137, 276–7
philosophy, 12, 194, 221
Philoxenus of Hierapolis, bishop, 172
Philoxenus, official, 176, 177
Phocas, usurper, 297
Phoenice Libanensis, 247
Phrygia, 162
Pincian Hill, 104
Placidia, daughter of Valentinian III, 87
plague see pandemic
Plato, philosopher, 194, 276
Plintha, general, 103
Poetovio, battle of, 26
poetry, 67–8, 83, 87, 92, 94, 162, 219
Poitiers, 178
political power, dynamics of, 101–9, 159–61, 174–5, 213–14, 294
Pollentia, battle of, 111
Polycarp, financial official, 168
Pompeius, aristocrat, 162–3, 174, 176, 248, 250
pontifex maximus, 7, 49n
Porphyry, bishop of Gaza, 102–3
Porphyry, philosopher, 151
possessores, 204
pottery, as evidence for trade, 226, 236–7
praepositus sacri cubiculi, 91
Praetextatus, senator, 67
praetorian prefect, 4, 62, 180, 182, 253, 260

prefect
  of Constantinople, 72, 163, 217, 248
  of Rome, 50, 61–2, 102
priests, pagan, 41, 49, 190
Priscillian, ascetic, 47
Priscus Attalus, usurper, 113
Priscus, historian, 119, 127–8
Priscus, philosopher, 40, 42n
prisoners of war, 114, 170, 233, 261, 288
Probus, nephew of Anastasius, 248
Procopius, historian, 169, 177, 185, 208, 224, 244, 247, 289, 290, 293, 295
  on Justin I, 244
  on Justinian, 254–5
  on Theodora, 245–6
Procopius, usurper, 23–4, 29, 32, 44, 72
Proculus, quaestor, 243
prostitution, 245–6
protectores domestici, 19
Proterius, bishop of Alexandria, 148
Pulcheria, empress, 97–8, 103–4, 139, 144–5, 244
Punic motifs, used by Vandals, 185
Punic language, 14

Quadi, 24, 31
quaesitor, 253
quaestor exercitus, 254
quaestor sacri palatii see quaestor
quaestor, 4, 180, 182

Rabbula, ascetic, 203
Radagaisus, Gothic leader, 112, 233
rape, 127, 171
Ravenna, 104, 106, 107, 183–4, 189, 191, 209, 286
  as imperial residence, 82, 111–12
  captured by Belisarius, 263
  water supply, 111, 183
rebellions, 100–1, 110, 122, 124, 277
  military, 83–4, 91–2, 95, 111, 112, 173, 288–9, 297
Reccopolis, 186
Recitach, Gothic leader, 124
Red Sea, 290
religious violence, 54, 63, 215–16, 221
rhetoric, 13, 51, 219
Richomer, general, 125
Ricimer, general, 94–6, 97, 99, 121
Riot of the Statues, Antioch, 108, 215
riots see urban rioting

Roman–barbarian relations, 110–33
Roman empire, east–west relations, 22–3,
    85, 109, 113, 116–17, 121–2, 127,
    191
Roman–Gothic relations, 32–8, 84,
    110–15, 122–5, 191–5, 262–3, 286,
    291–2
Roman identity, 159–60, 299–300
Roman–Persian relations
    Julian's invasion, 15, 19, 21
    peace settlement of 299, 15, 28
    peace settlement of 363, 15, 20, 28–9
    later 4th century, 27–30, 34
    in 5th century, 118
    early 6th century, 164, 165, 168–71,
        175, 192, 234, 272
    in 6th century, 257–8
    'endless peace' (532), 258, 276–7, 295
    war in 540s, 286–8
    peace of 561/2, 279, 288
    post-565, 297
    war in early 7th century, 232, 297–8
Rome, city of, 52, 57–63, 209, 283, 286,
    298
    absence of emperors from, 5, 27, 57,
        61
    as imperial residence, 5, 82, 95
    fabric, 59–60, 182
    food supply, 2–3, 60–1, 84, 102, 183,
        214, 234, 236, 237
    magic trials, 42
    pandemic in, 289
    population, 3, 60, 114
    prestige, 57–9, 78, 114, 184
    sack of (410), 84, 104, 113–14
    sack of (455), 121, 261
    sieges of, 113, 263, 291
    water supply, 61
    see also bishop of Rome; senate,
        Rome
Romulus and Remus, 70, 190
Romulus, emperor, 191
Rua, Hunnic ruler, 118
Rufinus, praetorian prefect, 90, 110
Rutilius Namatianus, poet, 85

Sabinianus, general, 163
Sabratha, 207
sacrifice, 40–1, 53, 288
    Christianised, 153, 275
    prohibition of, 6, 52–3, 151, 191

    see also Altar of Victory; incense;
        libation
Sagalassos, 206
St Anastasia, church of, Rome, 63
St Laurence, church of, Rome), 63
St Nicholas, holy man, 275
St Paul, church of, Rome, 60, 63
St Peter, church of, Rome, 60
St Polyeuctus, church of, Constantinople,
    271–3
Sts Sergius and Bacchus, church of,
    Constantinople, 266–7
Sallust, historian, 12
Salutius, praetorian prefect, 19
Samaritans, 277
Sardinia, 121, 260
Sardis, 206
Sarmatians, 31
Sarus, Gothic officer, 113
Sasanians, 1; see also Persia; Roman–
    Persian relations
Saxons, 30
Sclavenes, 292
scholae palatinae, 174
scriptorium, 222
Scythia, 85, 254
Scythopolis, 148, 205
Secundinus, prefect of Constantinople,
    163
Segermes Valley, 231
senate, Constantinople, 64, 77, 83, 202,
    243, 263
senate, Rome, 64–70, 87, 299; see also
    senatorial aristocracy
senatorial aristocracy, 3, 42, 49–50,
    64–70, 84, 97, 191, 298–9
    Christianisation of, 68–9
    redefinition, 64, 77–8
    under barbarian rule, 131, 125, 182,
        193–5
    wealth, 66, 96, 112, 228
Septimius Severus, emperor, 65
Serapeum, 54, 135, 216
Serena, wife of Stilicho, 83
Severus, bishop of Antioch, 172, 177,
    220, 280–1
Shapur II, Persian king, 15, 30
Shapur III, Persian king, 30
Shenute, monk, 152
shipmasters, 236–8
Sicily, 66, 114, 116, 117, 119, 121, 228,

262, 283, 289
Sidonius Apollinaris, aristocrat, 128, 182,
    188, 222
Sigismund, Burgundian ruler, 193
silentiaries, 160
Silvanus, general, 27n, 125
Simeon 'the mountaineer', monk, 275
Simeon the Stylite, 155–6
Singara, 28
Siricius, bishop of Rome, 47, 141
Sirmium, 5, 22, 30, 192, 254, 297
Siscia, battle of, 26
Sittas, general, 247
slavery, 10, 34, 112, 127, 220, 224, 233;
    see also eunuchs
Slavs, 292
Soissons, 126, 186
soldiers see army
solidus, 167, 234
Solomon, general, 288–9
sortes, Biblicae and sortes sanctorum,
    153
Spain, 25, 143, 224, 232, 234, 238, 259,
    292–3
    cities, 208
    war in, 115, 116, 121,
    see also Visigothic kingdom
spolia, 200, 206, 210
Stephen, bishop of Antioch, 149
Stilicho, general, 82–4, 86, 87, 90, 91,
    92, 110–13, 115, 136, 233
subsidies to barbarians, 32, 118–20, 165,
    292, 296
Sueves, 112
Sufes, 216
Syagrius, aristocrat, 182–3
Syagrius, general, 95, 125–6, 180
Symmachus, senator (4th c.), 39, 50–1,
    62, 66, 67, 68
Symmachus, senator (6th c.), 194
synagogues, 55, 153–4
    destruction of, 54, 137, 277
Synod of the Oak, 135
Syria, 13, 14, 15, 24, 29, 140, 155, 237,
    286–7, 298
Syriac language, 14, 168

Tablettes Albertini, 226
Tacitus, historian, 12
Taginae, battle of, 291
Tarraco, 208

taxation, 117, 215
    assigned to barbarians, 130–2
    burden, 24, 128, 291
    collection, 166–7, 180
    commutation, 166
    exploitation by curiales, 166–7
    in barbarian kingdoms, 180–1
    in gold and silver, 4, 164
    in kind, 4, 234
    remission, 102, 164
technological change, 235
temples, 40–1, 55 102, 151, 211, 227
    conversion to churches, 153, 274
    destruction of, 52, 54, 151, 211, 274
Tenedos, 237
Tertullian, theologian, 221–2
Tervingian Goths, 33–4
Thagaste, 220
Thannuris, 257
theatres, 13, 201, 211, 215, 217, 245
Themistius, philosopher, 37
    and Jovian, 39–41
    and Theodosius I, 37
Theodahad, Ostrogothic ruler, 262–3
Theodemer, Gothic leader, 123
Theodericopolis, 184
Theoderic, Ostrogothic ruler, 121, 262,
    295, 299
    as hostage in Constantinople, 123, 222
    character of rule in Italy, 180, 182,
        183
    move to Italy, 124–5, 165, 178
    relations with senate, 131, 182, 193–5
    relations with Zeno, 123–4
    relations with Anastasius, 191–3
Theoderic Strabo, Gothic leader, 122–4
Theoderic, Visigothic ruler, 115, 120
Theodora, empress, 246, 294
    background, 245–6
    charitable activities, 246, 267
    dissuades Justinian from flight?, 248,
        249–50
    influence on Justinian, 250
    marriage to Justinian, 244–6
    protection of anti-Chalcedonians, 250,
        281, 285
    religious views, 246
Theodore, bishop of Mopsuestia, 136–7,
    282, 283
Theodoret, bishop of Cyrrhus, 143–4,
    146–7, 280, 282, 283

Theodosian Code, 108–9, 184, 224, 237, 251, 264
Theodosian Walls, 106, 118–19
Theodosius I, emperor, 22, 57, 72–3, 78, 81, 83, 89, 106, 108–9, 110, 111, 132, 134, 142, 159, 191, 267
    and Antioch, 215
    and Eugenius, 27
    and Goths, 25–6, 36–7, 38
    and Magnus Maximus, 26
    background and accession, 25, 45
    policies towards church, 44–7
    policies towards Jews, 54–6
    policies towards pagans, 52–4, 151
    residence in Constantinople, 72–3, 82
Theodosius II, 81, 93, 94n, 97, 101, 103,139–41, 144, 157–8, 160, 220, 251–2
    and circus factions, 218
    piety, 155, 264
    see also Theodosian Code
Theophilus, bishop of Alexandria, 135
Theotokos, 137–9, 146
Thessalonica, 36, 45, 217, 254
Theudebert, Frankish ruler, 185, 278
Thrace, 24, 26, 33, 93, 98–9, 118, 157, 173, 174, 292, 299
    cities, 207
    war in, 34–8, 120, 122, 124
Thrasamund, Vandal ruler, 185, 187
'Three Chapters' controversy, 282–5
Thuburbo Maius, 207
Thucydides, historian, 290
Tiberius II, emperor, 297
Ticinum, 84, 90, 183
Timasius, general, 91
Timothy Aelurus, bishop of Alexandria, 102, 148–9
Titus, emperor, 55, 261
toleration, religious, 6, 39–41, 50–1, 43, 216
torture, 42
Totila, Ostrogothic ruler, 286, 291, 292, 296
Toulouse, 185, 186
Tournai, 126
Tours, 192
trade, 224, 226, 229, 231, 235–9
    as vector for disease, 289, 290
    cross-frontier, 32
traders, 127–8, 164, 224, 236–9

traditores, 8
Trajan, emperor, 55, 74, 183
translations from Greek to Latin, 194, 222
Tribonian, lawyer, 247, 248–9, 250, 250–3
Trier, 126
    as imperial base, 5, 23, 25, 30, 47, 49
Tripolitania, 207
triumph, 162, 192–3
Trojans, 125
Tzani, 279
Tzath, ruler of Lazi, 278–9

Uldin, Hunnic ruler, 118
unity of empire *see* Roman empire, east–west relations
urban cohorts, 62
urban rioting, 61, 108, 136, 173, 214–18, 247–50, 253; *see also* Nika riot; Riot of the Statues
Urbicius, eunuch, 159
Ursinus, clergyman, 63
usurpers, 23–4, 25n, 26, 27, 29, 32, 84, 100, 113, 249

Valens, 72, 74, 78, 82, 118, 227
    background and accession, 21–2
    and Goths, 29–30, 32–6, 132
    and Persia, 23, 27–30, 34
    death, 24, 25, 35, 44, 82
    policies towards Christians, 44
    policies towards pagans, 41–2
    relations with Gratian, 35
    relations with Valentinian I, 22, 23, 24, 32
    tax policy, 24
    usurpation of Procopius, 23–4
Valentinian I, emperor, 73, 78, 183, 227
    background and accession, 21
    death, 24, 31
    military activities, 23, 30–1
    policies towards Christians, 43
    policies towards pagans, 41–2
    relations with Valens, 22, 23, 24, 32
Valentinian II, emperor, 25, 26, 57, 50–2, 2, 73, 82
Valentinian III, emperor, 81, 85, 87–8, 93, 94n, 97, 102, 103, 107, 109, 121, 144, 178, 191, 272

Vallia, Gothic leader, 94, 115, 116
Vandals, 82, 94, 110, 112, 120–2, 132,
    157, 207, 296
  conquest of north Africa, 115–17
  economic impact on north Africa, 231,
    238
  Justinian's Vandal expedition, 258–61
  kingdom, 178–87
  new Punic empire?, 185
  religious allegiance and policies, 48,
    187–8
  settlement, 131
  treasures, 261–2
Verina, empress, 100–1, 104
Verona, 125, 183, 209
Vestal Virgins, 49
Victor of Vita, chronicler, 187
Victorinianus, official, 182
victory celebrations, 107, 162, 261, 263
victory monuments, 74, 92, 106, 162
Vigilius, bishop of Rome, 283–5
villages, 199–200, 229–32
Viminacium, 127
vindices, 166, 168, 203
Virgil, poet, 12
Visigothic kingdom in southern Gaul and
    Spain, 178, 180, 182, 184–5, 186,
    188, 189, 192, 292–3

Visigoths, history of name, 178n
Vitalian, general, 173, 174, 175, 176,
    177, 243, 266
Vithicabius, Alamannic ruler, 31
Vitigis, Ostrogothic ruler, 263, 286
Vivarium 222
Vouillé, battle of, 178

Walls, Theodosian, 106, 118–19
wine, 226, 231, 233, 234, 237, 239
women see Anicia Juliana; empresses;
    Melania; Olympias
wooden tablets, 226

Xanthos, 231

Yarmuk River, battle of, 298
Yemen, 278

Zachariah, biographer, 220
Zeno, emperor, 104, 122, 159, 160, 165,
    244, 251
  background and accession, 99–100
  political instability, 100–1, 163, 191
  relations with Goths, 123–5
  religious policy, 149–50, 172, 174, 177
Zeno, general, 94, 97–8
Zoroastrianism, 278, 279